BLACKBURN
BEVERLEY

Bill Overton

BLACKBURN
BEVERLEY

Bill Overton

This book is dedicated to the work-force of the Blackburn and General Aircraft Company who designed, built and developed the Beverley; the RAF aircrews who flew the Beverley; the RAF and civilian ground technicians who kept the Beverley flying; and the many people who flew in the Beverley, some to their delight, some to their disgust, and the many thousands of parachutists who jumped from the Beverley.

Copyright © 1990
W. J. A. Overton

First published in 1990 by
Midland Counties Publications
24 The Hollow, Earl Shilton
Leicester, LE9 7NA, England.

ISBN 0 904597 62 8

All rights reserved. No part of this
publication may be reproduced, stored
in a retrieval system, transmitted in any
form or by any means, electronic,
mechanical or photo-copied,
recorded or otherwise, without the written
permission of the copyright owners.

Printed in the United Kingdom by:
BL&U Printing, Wellingborough, Northants.

Contents

Foreword 6
Acknowledgements 6
Preface 7
Chapter 1: The Beginning 9
Chapter 2: The Abingdon Wing - 47 and 53 Squadrons 17
Chapter 3: 30 Squadron 51
Chapter 4: 84 Squadron 71
Chapter 5: The Far East Beverley Force 99
Chapter 6: 242 Operational Conversion Unit 121
Chapter 7: The Army and the Beverley 123
Chapter 8: The Brough 'planemakers' and RAF Ground Staff . 133
Chapter 9: The Bristol Centaurus Engine 143
Chapter 10: Where did all the Beverleys Go? 145
Appendix 1: Beverley C Mk.1 General Specification 154
Appendix 2: Colour Schemes and Squadron Markings 155
Bibliography 156
List of Abbreviations 156
Index 157

List of Maps

Map 1: The Fahoud Oil-drilling equipment airlift 14
Map 2: The Arabian Peninsula 20
Map 3: The Northabout Route to Aden 28
Map 4: The El-Adem - Khartoum Route to Aden 28
Map 5: East Africa 54
Map 6: East Africa and Arabia 58
Map 7: Oman and the Persian Gulf 65
Map 8: The El-Adem - Cairo Route 66
Map 9: The Belvedere Ferry Route 78
Map 10: The UK and/or Bust Route 97
Map 11: The Far East 102
Map 12: North Borneo 103

Front cover from a specially commissioned painting by Keith Woodcock GAvA.

Foreword

'It's a fine machine, but it'll never replace the aeroplane'. This was the verdict of a US Air Force Captain seconded to the Royal Air Force as first pilot of a Beverley. It was uttered while he was still in shock from his introduction to an aircraft produced during the era which saw aeronautics move into supersonic flight, but which itself looked more like an exercise in marine engineering, or bridge-building, than something off an aircraft designer's drawing board.

But he too grew to love the clumsy old monster, as did all its crews, ground and air. In the air it was complaisant and forgiving; to the ground crews it was an aeroplane whose engineering they could comprehend, and whose adventures they could understand and share. This was probably the greatest attraction of service in a Beverley squadron. Most military flying was then, and still more is now, constant practice for the future unthinkable; which makes continual training and continual enthusiasm a difficult mental exercise. Not so with the Beverleys.

Certainly Beverley squadrons carried out 'continuation training', but most of their flying was practical work, closely tied to practical worldly problems, understandable problems, solvable problems. The RAF Beverleys were not above carrying bricks and coal, reinforcements and refugees, parachutists and pilgrims, vehicles and animals, helicopters and hay, guns and butter, beer and skittles; in fact anything which would go into their yawning holds.

I remember when Beverleys were used to fly up and down the Berlin air corridor, solely because the Russians had suddenly and illegally forbidden air access to Tempelhof airport. I recall with mixed feelings how the aircrew, my Coldstream Guards ADC and I had marked our quick-exit route from the aircraft, in case we were 'done' by Russian fighters, so that we could scamper down the various ladders and corridors until we could fling ourselves out of the side door, like rats leaving the proverbial sinking ship; and I remember very vividly the sight of a MiG 17 staggering along close beside us, trying to match the snail's pace of the Beverley, or perhaps trying in vain to drop astern for purposes best not thought about. It seemed a very long corridor.

I remember their remarkable performance in *Starlight*, the last big three-service overseas deployment exercise from UK into North Africa, and how the General Commanding 3 Division and I rode back to El Adem in an empty Beverley, when the exercise was over, and realised that we could have played badminton in the hold if we had brought rackets and a shuttlecock.

I remember standing on an airfield and being sprayed with a cold shower of tinned milk, when the first, less than brilliantly successful attempts were made to land a freight sled by pulling it out of a low-flying Beverley by a drag parachute. Back to the old drawing-board, and never a dull moment with the Beverley fleet.

Why did no other customer but the RAF buy the Beverley? Perhaps it was too simple for new countries looking for something impressive to fly past on the President's birthday. Perhaps the customers took fright at the indifferent airframe and engine reliability. Perhaps, like many good British products, it just cost too much. Whatever the reasons, the Beverley remained a Royal Air Force speciality, and for more than ten years it served faithfully, all over the world, a rough, clumsy, ugly but good-hearted maid-of-all-work to the Fighting Services.

In this book it is remembered with the affection it deserves.

December 1983

Air Marshal Sir Peter Wykeham, KCB, DSO and bar, OBE, DFC and bar, AFC, former AOC No.38 Group and AOC, FEAF.

Acknowledgements

The author gratefully acknowledges the assistance given by the following persons and organizations; without this assistance, this book could never have been written:

Air Marshal Sir Peter Wykeham, KCB, DSO, OBE, DFC, AFC for his kindness in writing the Foreword; Air Commodore H. A. Probert, MBE, MA, RAF (Ret'd), Head of the Air Historical Branch (RAF) and his staff who allowed me access to official records and who gave me every assistance in my researches; The RAF Museum, Hendon; The Officer Commanding No.30 Squadron (January 1980); The Officer Commanding No.84 Squadron (April 1980); British Aerospace, M. Byrne and E. Barker; Rolls-Royce Limited, Aero Division, W. Royce; Joint Air Transport Establishment, RAF Brize Norton; Hull Flying Club, David Carsberg; Jean Hudswell who prepared the maps; Jill Buckingham, Frank Bradford and Ann Moncrieff who typed most of the manuscript; my wife Grace who helped with the dreaded proof-reading and general tidying-up, and who gave me much support and encouragement; Peter Symcox whose photographic wizardry created photographs suitable for reproduction from well-thumbed, dog-eared and faded prints contributed by so many people; Brian Haynes and Neville Underwood for retouching photographs as necessary; *The Hull Daily Mail; The Sarawak Tribune;* the *Pretoria News: The Rotorua Post; The Lyneham Globe; Air Clues;* Group Captain F. C. Griffiths, DFC, AFC, RAF (Ret'd), who apart from contributing numerous anecdotes, also assisted with research; and Lieutenant Simmonds, Air Adviser Malaysia.

Acknowledgements are also due to the many persons who contributed anecdotes: it would be repetitive to name them here since they are all acknowledged in the text.

Preface

This is the story of the Blackburn and General Aircraft Beverley and of the units which operated it. The story is complemented by accounts of the Army's involvement with the Beverley in the parachuting and supply-dropping roles.

The Beverley was a bizarre, ugly, ungainly and massive aeroplane: so massive in fact that when it entered squadron service, it was the largest landplane ever to be acquired by the Royal Air Force. However, despite its ungainly and ugly appearance, the Beverley showed surprising agility, and throughout its entire career, always impressed spectators at air shows when it demonstrated its incredible STOL capabilities. The typical air show Beverley party-piece was for it to execute an amazingly short landing, disgorge troops and artillery which proceeded to demolish a set-piece, and then for the Beverley to reverse back to its touchdown point from where it took to the air again in an impressive short field take-off. The Beverley's STOL performance certainly belied its ungainly appearance.

In other respects though, the Beverley was a disappointment, especially to crews about to convert to the type. They regarded it as a monstrosity whose fixed undercarriage, antiquated piston engines and appallingly low cruising speed condemned it as a retrograde step in aviation history.

Many aircrew though, regarded the Beverley with typical sardonic humour and a 'we're stuck with the beast, let's get on with it' attitude. One such crewman was flight engineer Gerry Hatt who was motivated to compose the following poem:

Near the factory owned by Blackburns
By the waters of the Humber,
Was a small decrepit airfield
Filled with junk and strewn with lumber.

'Waste not, want not'. Said the boss man
'Nobody will ever buy it,
'Let us put it all together
'Then perhaps the RAF will fly it'.

So they started work in earnest
All with hacksaws madly cutting
Bits of lorries, bits of fencing,
Bits of barn and Nissen hutting.

Thus a structure was created
Roughly nailed and tied together,
Covered o'er by Nissen hutting
To keep out the winter weather.

Antique wheels from ancient tractor
All were fastened by a clamper
Underneath the metal mountain
Just before the Bogie Damper.

In each engine cowling snugly
Firmly held by special fixer
Was a shining power unit
Special 'modded' concrete mixer.

When they ran the mighty motors
All the airframe madly quaking
Some were pulling, some were pushing,
They'd discovered airscrew braking.

So beware you budding birdmen,
Lest you drop an awful clanger,
Don't fly Blackburn's pet abortion
Better try to fly the hangar.

Not satisfied by his poetic prowess, Gerry then tried his hand at sardonic prose, producing the following send-up:

The Beverley - Another Thoroughbred:
'A famous aircraft designer saw a dutch barn blow past in a gale. The basic concept of the Beverley was born at that moment.

'The original design of the machine was intended to fulfil single-seater specifications, but as full power was required to taxi the aircraft forward at a slow walking pace, another engine was added. The resulting increase in all-up-weight necessitated the addition of two further engines to enable it to move at all.

'By this time, the general dimensions had increased somewhat, and work was often delayed for several days at a time while the aircraft was utilized by the airport manager as a spare hangar for visiting aircraft. This state of affairs continued for such a long time, that by the time the prototype was ready for flight, other types of aircraft were jet powered.

'The rather embarrassed designer, fearing to appear behind the times, had the propellers placed much higher than he had originally intended, in the hopes that they would not be noticed. This entailed the raising of the mainplane and the fuselage sides (the production manager raised the roof) and accounts for the immense height of the machine.

'As no adequate runway was available, the undercarriage was adapted to take locomotive wheels, and the first take-off was from both tracks of the Brough-Hull railway. It was in fact airborne by the time it had reached the passenger station at Beverley; hence its name.

'A conversion kit for this purpose is still in existence. While the aircraft is in use in this role, the flight deck should at all times be referred to as the driver's cab, and the VHF should be re-crystallized to include the frequencies of Crewe signal box, and the head office of the National Union of Railwaymen.

'Spinning of this aircraft is not recommended, as the torque reaction involved causes the Earth to rotate in the opposite direction to the spin, to the accompaniment of terse notes from Greenwich Observatory.

'The aircraft is extremely versatile, and may be employed in many roles, particularly those which do not include flying or movement of any kind. It is also highly amenable to modification. For example, wind tunnel tests have shown that the wings could be placed at the bottom, and the wheels at the top, without any appreciable drop in performance.

'Taken in all, the Beverley is an ideal aircraft for a civilian enthusiast with a million pounds, a private oil well, and a total abhorrence of flying.'

Gerry's poem and prose typifies the cynical reaction of many aircrew, and indeed, ground crew, when they found themselves posted on to Beverleys. At first, the sheer size was impressive: with a wing span of 162 ft, a length of 99 ft 5 in, and a height to the top of the twin fins of 38 ft 5 in, this enormous aeroplane dwarfed all other British military landplanes.

The slab-sided rectangular freight compartment, measuring 10 x 10 x 40 ft was definitely unaerodynamic looking, and the non-retractable undercarriage was immediately ridiculed and thought of in terms of how much ice it would carry when flying in adverse weather conditions. But the designers had not been stupid: the cavernous box-section freight bay could accommodate virtually any piece of mobile military equipment and the fixed undercarriage, although crude and ungainly to the eye, had been deliberately specified for simplicity, robustness and reliability.

As crew soon found out, the Beverley had been designed as a rugged, bulk-load carrying, short-haul aeroplane, and as such was absolutely ideal for that purpose. Its power-assisted flying controls gave it good handling characteristics, and flying the Beverley was quite pleasant once one became accustomed to the hideous din and intense vibration which was always a feature of a Beverley flight.

The engines however, were a let-down. With every other aircraft manufacturer producing pure jet or turbo prop-powered aeroplanes, here was the Beverley with antiquated piston engines. Despite the fact that the Bristol Centaurus was the ultimate in sleeve valve engine design, by contemporary standards it was archaic and a disappointment to crews who were hoping to convert on to jets or turbo props. Again, the designers had not been stupid: in the '50s, only piston engines could drive the reverse-pitch propellers which gave the Beverley its ability to make short landings and to propel itself backwards. The Beverley was incredibly slow, cruising at a mere 135 knots, slower than the ageing Dakotas, Valettas, Yorks and Hastings of Transport Command and indeed, slower than the wartime Lancasters, Halifaxes and Stirlings. The crews could hardly be blamed for thinking: 'We've got a right one here'.

However, these crews were now stuck with the Beverleys with characteristic stoicism, applied themselves to the task of operating these aircraft efficiently. Their stoicism soon turned to enthusiasm when the tremendous capabilities of the Beverley were revealed, and in due course, their enthusiasm was tempered by affection and pride in flying an aeroplane, that in the turbulent years of the '50s and '60s, by transporting troops and equipment to various trouble spots, made such a splendid contribution to the maintenance of law and order in the 'brush fire' emergencies frequently occurring in the many troubled outposts of the declining British Empire.

RAF personnel were not alone in developing a special affection for the Beverley: men of the Parachute Regiment found the Beverley to be a very stable jumping platform, especially from the tail boom where engine slipstream was almost negligible. In addition, men of the Air Despatch units of the Royal Corps of Transport, and the Royal Army Service Corps who rigged the air-dropped platforms with just about every conceivable piece of military equipment, also developed an affection for the immense bulk load-carrying capacity of this enormous aircraft.

The infantrymen of many Army units, plus gunners and sappers, cooks and butchers, clerks and medics, in fact, all those who made up the Strategic Reserve, seldom spoke ill of the Beverley, despite long flights sometimes in the freight compartment with its horrendous clamour and vibration.

Those who travelled in the tail boom were somewhat more fortunate: it was much quieter in the boom, somehow it seemed almost isolated from the remainder of the aircraft, particularly from 'up front', where the noise and vibration were worst. Smoking was permitted in the boom - a welcome concession to most soldiers. The view from the rearward facing seats was also good, being completely unobstructed by wings, as was the case on many other aircraft. In addition, the Bev was no 'high flier', so unless flying over the sea or in cloud, there was always something down below to look at.

Ex-corporal Colin Secker, who served in the Royal Army Dental Corps in the Arabian Peninsula, wrote of his many trips in the Beverleys, recalling that 'the RAF looked after us 'Pongos' well. We were invariably provided with a decent meal and a constant supply of orange juice.' (An essential in the heat of Arabia).

The roles in which they operated their aircraft imbued Beverley crews with a rough and ready, 'let's muck in' type of attitude, which was completely compatible with that of the Army, thus strengthening the links between these two arms of the Services.

The experience of taking off in this bizarre, enormous aeroplane and then to be gently set down, in an immense cloud of dust, to the roar of four Centaurus engines in full-power reverse thrust, on some tiny desert airstrip, was a never-to-be-forgotten experience to be indelibly stamped on the minds of all those who were privileged to fly in the Blackburn Beverley.

Chapter One

The Beginning

In the closing months of the Second World War, the embryo Beverley appeared, in the form of rough design sketches, on the drawing board of Mr F.F. Crocombe, chief designer of the General Aircraft Company, based at Hanworth Air Park, Feltham, Middlesex. General Aircraft's design team were carrying out a series of studies for a large, ruggedly constructed, four-engined bulk-carrying transport, which, with commendable foresight, they anticipated would be a requirement for the post-war Royal Air Force. This move, by a company which in pre-war years had mainly specialised in building light aircraft, notably the well-known Monospars, was prompted by the company's wartime experience of constructing the tank-carrying Hamilcar glider.

General Aircraft entered the glider-building business in 1940 with the Hotspur, a light glider with seating for seven fully equipped troops. The Hotspur never saw operational service but was used extensively as the standard trainer for pilots of the Glider Pilot Regiment. More than a thousand Hotspurs were produced, giving their manufacturers much useful experience in glider design and development.

Due undoubtedly to their success with the Hotspur, General Aircraft were awarded a contract for a glider capable of carrying a tank, and after the successful construction and test programme of a half-scale prototype, the GAL50, the full-scale GAL49 Hamilcar glider went into production and entered service in 1942.

With its 110 foot wing span, the Hamilcar, by 1942 standards, was an extremely big aeroplane and was the largest wooden aircraft ever to be constructed during the Second World War. At an all-up-weight of nearly sixteen and a half tonnes, half of which was payload, the Hamilcar could carry a Tetrarch or a Locust light tank plus crews. Alternative loads comprised a pair of armoured cars, various pieces of artillery or forty fully equipped troops. The Hamilcar saw service in the Normandy landings, at Arnhem and at Wesel in the Rhine crossing assault. Hamilcars were also used to deliver supplies to units of the French resistance in isolated parts of France.

A powered version of the Hamilcar, the Hamilcar Mark 10, fitted with two Bristol Mercury engines, was developed for operations in the Far East but the war in that theatre ended before this aircraft could see service there. According to James E. Mrazek in *Fighting Gliders of World War Two*, over 400 Hamilcars were built and although it lacked grace and beauty, the type did its job well and enjoyed the distinction of being the only tank-carrying aircraft available to the Allies throughout the Second World War.

The GAL60 Universal Freighter Mark 1
In late 1945 therefore, General Aircraft Ltd., backed by their Hamilcar experience, carried out a number of feasibility studies for a large, all-metal-construction, cargo-carrying aircraft powered by four Rolls-Royce Merlin engines. Other designs aimed at increasing the load-carrying ability called for the Bristol Hercules and the newly developed Centaurus engine. Consequently, when in 1946 the Air Ministry issued Specification C3/46, the firm were well ahead of their competitors and succeeded in winning a contract for one prototype, designated the GAL60.

The Beverley's predecessors - a pair of Hotspur gliders in free flight formation, and the tank carrying Hamilcar Mark 1 glider. *both RAF Museum*

Above: **The powered version of the Hamilcar, the Mark 10.** *RAF Museum*

Below: **The GAL60 overhead Beverley Minster, October 1952.** *Hull Daily Mail*

Specification C3/46 demanded an aircraft suitable for troop-carrying, parachuting, casualty evacuation and heavy load supply-dropping. Further requirements were for a still air range of 500 miles, with a payload of 25,000 pounds, a service ceiling of 18,000 feet, plus the ability to operate from short unprepared airstrips.

To meet this specification, the GAL60 was powered by four specially designed Bristol Hercules engines driving fourteen foot Rotol constant speed, feathering, reversible-pitch propellers. Large-area, electrically-operated slotted flaps together with the reversible pitch propellers ensured a STOL performance which adequately met the requirements of the specification. For simplicity and strength, the tricycle undercarriage was non-retractable. Each main undercarriage, which distinctly resembled that of the Hamilcar, consisted of a Lockheed oleo-pneumatic strut attached by a spherical joint to the wing main spar. The strut was braced to the fuselage by an aerofoil-section sponson, reputed to have an area equivalent to that of a Meteor wing. The immense low tyre pressure single main wheels, six and a half feet in diameter, gave a wheel loading suitable for soft grass fields. During subsequent development, the single main wheels were replaced by a four-wheel bogie unit. A turning circle of thirty three feet was achieved by the Lockheed twin-wheel steerable nosewheel assembly.

The Hamilcar-type high-wing configuration was retained to afford easy loading of cargo and to give maximum headroom in the freight bay. The wings, which again bore a resemblance to those of the Hamilcar, were simple, two-spar construction with a heavy-gauge Alclad skin supported by span-wise stringers. The two-part centre section was bolted to the fuselage and carried the four Hercules power plants, slightly underslung for minimum drag. The leading edge of the wings incorporated crawlways, for access in flight if required, to components and controls and to the engine accessory bays.

The vast fuselage comprised a deep rectangular section freight bay terminating in an enormous tail boom. Access to the freight bay for cargo loading was via two downward-opening doors and a ramp which was hydraulically operated by hand pump. Stressed for a distributed loading of 325 lb/ft^2, the freight bay fuselage floor consisted of detachable panels, each panel being fabricated from corrugated light alloy covered by flat, flush-riveted sheeting.

The GAL60 Universal Freighter Mark 1 en route to the 1950 SBAC show at Farnborough. *RAF Museum*

Loading a single-decker bus into the GAL60 Universal Freighter Mark 1.
British Aerospace

BLACKBURN BEVERLEY

Flush-mounted sockets recessed into the floor structure at a pitch of twenty inches could either accept five and a half tonne lashing rings or seat-fixing attachments. Additional lashing rings stressed to one tonne were fixed to the side frames at eighteen inch intervals.

The all-metal empennage comprised a forty two foot cantilever two-spar tail plane with a dihedral of 7 degrees 47 minutes. Twin fin and rudder assemblies, rectangular in shape, were mounted at the tail plane tips. Flying controls were power-assisted by Fairey hydraulic boosters with manual reversion. The two pilots were accommodated side by side in the nose. In a compartment behind the pilots, the navigator and signaller sat back to back on a bench-type seat with the signaller facing rearwards. To accentuate its suitability for civil as well as military use, the GAL60 was named the Universal Freighter Mark 1.

In January 1949, General Aircraft merged with Blackburns to become Blackburn and General Aircraft Ltd. Erection of the Universal Freighter was completed at Feltham in the following October, but by that time, Hanworth Aerodrome, which was adjacent to the Feltham works, was considered inadequate for the first flight of the GAL60. The aircraft was accordingly dismantled and taken by road to Blackburn's factory at Brough for re-erection, where it was allocated Constructor's number 1000.

The Blackburn workers were somewhat daunted by the size of the this vast aeroplane. The company, who hitherto had built in the main, comparatively small aircraft - mostly Fleet Air Arm types - had never tackled a project of this size. However, despite headroom difficulties in Blackburn's North Sea erection hall, the GAL60 was rolled out in the spring of 1950.

Painted in RAF livery and bearing the serial WF320, the GAL60, now known as the Blackburn and General Aircraft Universal Freighter Mark 1, made its first flight on 20th June 1950. Chief test pilot the late H. 'Tim' Wood was at the controls with D.G. Brade as co-pilot. In deference to the GAL60's vast size, Tim Wood is reported to have said to his co-pilot at lift-off: 'My side's airborne, how about yours?'

The 48-tonne Universal was Britain's second largest landplane: the Bristol Brabazon had beaten it into the air by a mere nine months. However the GAL60's descendant, the Beverley, survived the Brabazon for almost two decades. In twenty one flights completed in about twenty eight days, sufficient flying hours had been logged to qualify the GAL60 for participation at the SBAC show at Farnborough.

A view of the Beverley production line at Brough. The final erection of the Beverley was carried out in the nose-up attitude shown, so that the tail fins would not come into conflict with the roof; there was a distinct lack of headroom in Blackburn's North Sea Erection Hall. *British Aerospace*

The GAL65 Universal Freighter Mark 2

In September 1950, the Ministry of Supply placed an order for a second prototype. Suggestions made to the Ministry by the manufacturers led to a number of changes including a redesigned fuselage with clamshell doors which were removable for supply-dropping, and a 36-passenger tail boom roughly the size of a Dakota fuselage. The Universal Freighter Mark 2 was powered by four 2850 hp Bristol Centaurus 171 engines driving sixteen and a half foot diameter de Havilland Hydromatic hollow steel, four-bladed, constant speed, fully-feathering, reverse pitch propellers. An auto-coarsening facility was also provided so that in the event of engine failure on take-off, the propeller of the failed engine was immediately driven towards the feathered position, thus giving minimum drag.

Propeller de-icing was by electrically heated elements moulded into rubber sheaths and fitted to the leading edge of each propeller blade. The propeller braking facility afforded by the reverse-pitch propellers always attracted interest. With Dunlop Maxaret anti-skid braking units on the eight main wheels acting in unison with reverse thrust, incredibly short landings could be made. In fact, both the Universal Mark 1 and Mark 2, inevitably stole the show at the Farnborough SBAC displays in the early '50s by making spectacular short landings and then taxying backwards up to the runway threshold for a short-field take-off. This demonstration became the

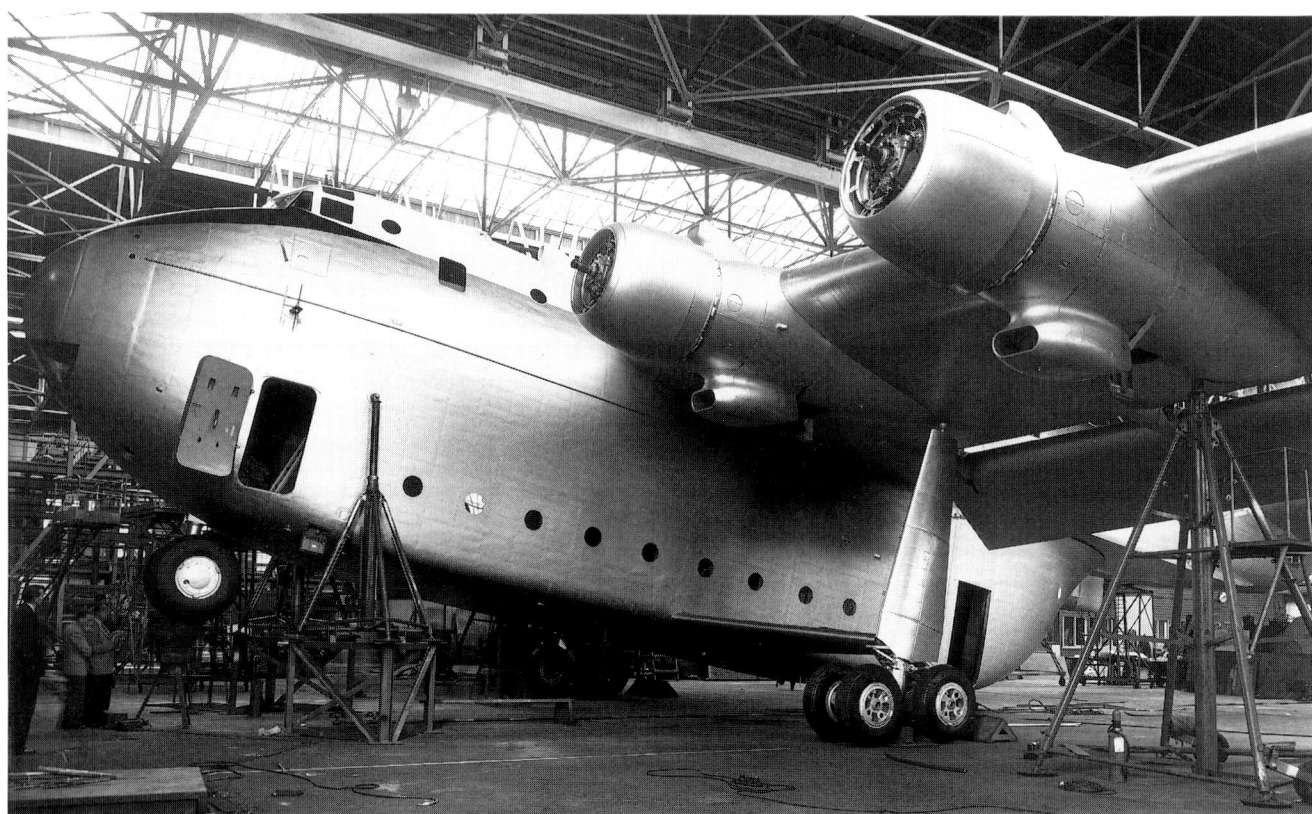

The GAL65 Universal Freighter Mark 2 WZ889 seen on an early test flight. *BAe*

standard Beverley 'party piece' at many air displays in later years and was always much appreciated, not only by the spectators, but by other air show participants also. After all, no other contemporary transport aircraft possessed the attribute of propelling itself backwards. Many other technical changes were incorporated in the Universal Freighter Mark 2, which whilst retaining General Aircrafts' designation GAL65, also carried the Blackburn type number B-100. Work commenced on building the Universal Mark 2 in 1952, and in June 1953, bearing serial WZ889, the first flight was made uneventfully.

During design and construction of the Universal Mark 2, a considerable amount of additional flight test development, particularly with regard to heavy supply dropping, was carried out using the Mark 1. Most of the heavy-dropping trials were done at Blackburn's satellite airfield, Holme-on-Spalding Moor. For most of these trials, the rear loading doors and ramp were removed thus giving completely unobstructed egress for supplies leaving the cargo compartment.

The Universal Mark 2 was exhibited in model form at the 1952 Farnborough SBAC show. The model depicted the aircraft equipped for cross-channel car ferrying, with seating for passengers provided in the tail boom.

The Beverley

No interest was shown by civil operators but in late 1952 the Ministry of Supply placed an order for twenty aircraft for Royal Air Force Transport Command and the aircraft was named the Beverley C.1. The choice of this name was most appropriate - not only because 'Blackburn Beverley' was suitably alliterative, but also because it was the county town of the East Riding of Yorkshire, where Brough, the site of Blackburn and General Aircraft's factory was located.

Whether by accident or design, the name Beverley was even more appropriate since 47 Squadron, the first unit to receive the aircraft, had been formed at Beverley in 1916. The initial Ministry of Supply order for twenty aircraft was subsequently increased to forty seven - again by coincidence - the same number as that of the first squadron to operate the aircraft.

The production aircraft was designated the B-101 and incorporated minor changes, full technical details being given in Appendix 1. The first two Beverleys, XB259 and XB260, came off the Brough production line in late 1954 and early 1955 respectively and flew shortly after their roll-out dates, their first flights being on 29th January and 30th March 1955. Both aircraft were retained by the manufacturers for further flight test development. They were also allocated civil registrations, XB259 as G-AOAI and XB260 as G-AOEK. Later on, after conducting RATOG (Rocket Assisted Take-off

Gear) trials at Brough, using Napier Scarab rockets, XB259 was issued to the RAE Farnborough with whom it spent its entire service career. RATOG was never used 'in anger' in the Beverley's service career, but mounting points for the Scarab rockets, located just forward of the clamshell doors, were retained.

In September 1955, XB260 was issued a four-month C of A and under its civil registration G-AOEK, carried out an airlift of oil-drilling equipment in Arabia. The operation was a joint Blackburn and General Aircraft/Hunting Clan venture and was undertaken at the urgent request of the Iraq Petroleum Co.Ltd., who wished to transport 131 tonnes of bulky oil-drilling equipment from the Persian Gulf port of Umm Said to a rough desert airstrip at the oil exploration site of Jebel Fahoud in Oman. The direct 'as-the-Universal-flies' distance between these points is 365 miles. There were two alternative routes available: The first, an overland trip across the northern desert, was immediately rejected since it passed close to the Buraimi Oasis which was, at that time, the subject of political disagreement between Britain and Saudi Arabia; the second route was a sea/land circular route of 1,250 miles as shown by *Map 1*. A further disadvantage of the sea/land route was that, at Ras Duqm, there were practically no harbour facilities; this meant that the heavy bulky equipment would have to be lightered ashore with much manhandling.

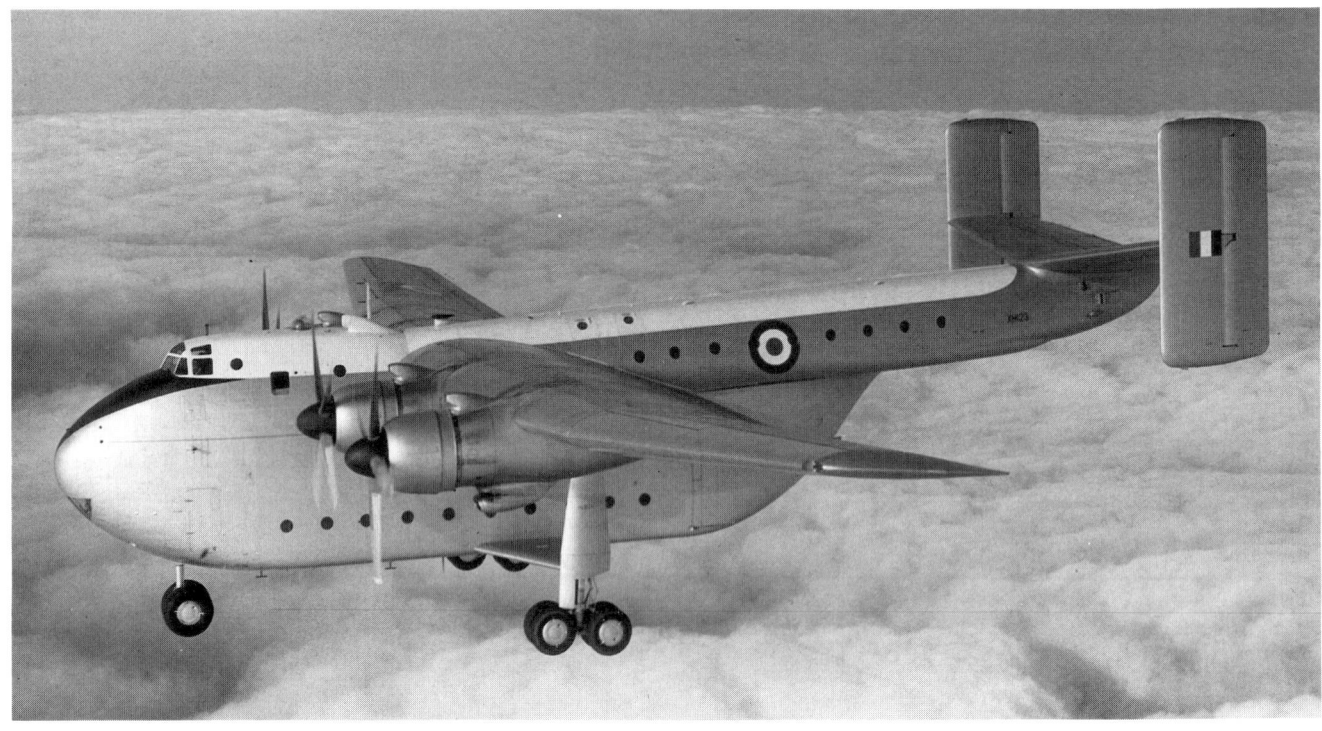

Beverley on manufacturer's test flight prior to delivery. *British Aerospace*

RATOG take-off at dusk. *British Aerospace*

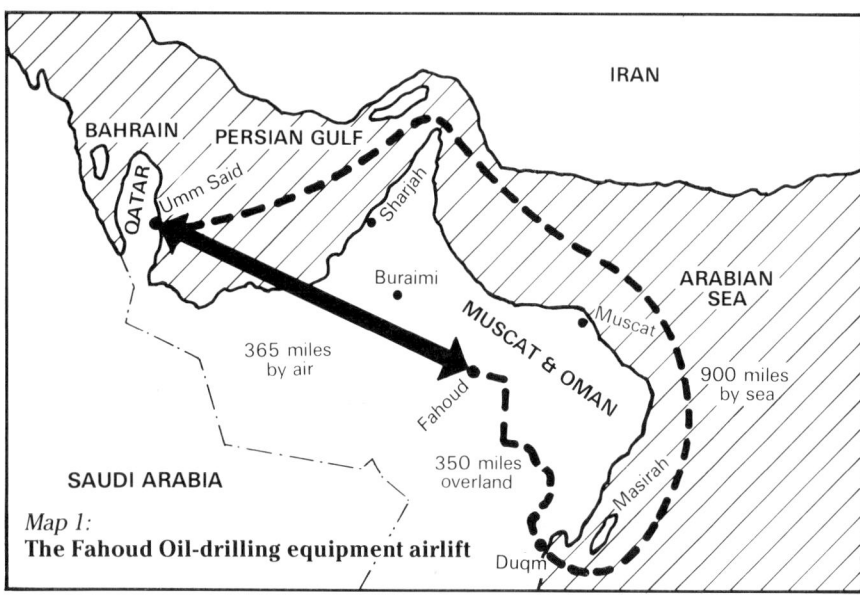

Map 1:
The Fahoud Oil-drilling equipment airlift

Clearly, this was an excellent opportunity to demonstrate the Universal's short-haul, bulk load-carrying ability and the massive aircraft acquitted itself beyond all expectations, airlifting the 131 tonnes of equipment in a mere nine flights, totalling approximately twenty flying hours, spread over a week. The heaviest lift consisted of a draw-works transmitter unit weighing approximately seventeen tonnes and measuring 21½ft by 9ft by 8½ft.

Despite this impressive demonstration of its freighting potential which was extensively reported by *Flight* and *The Aeroplane*, no customers for the freighter were forthcoming. *The Aeroplane* reported that 'no aircraft hitherto available has been able to carry the bulky loads that have had to be moved'. This and other similar phrases such as 'No other aircraft....' were to characterize the Beverley in the coming years.

On its return from its Arabian 'muscle-flexing' exercise G-AOEK reverted to XB260 and was used by Blackburn and General Aircraft Ltd. for intensive flying trials, including flights of long duration.

The next two production Beverleys, XB261 and XB262 were delivered to the A & AEE Boscombe Down for acceptance testing. These tests included paratrooping and heavy supply dropping. XB262 undertook tropical trials at Idris, the Second World War Castel Benito airfield in Tripoli, Libya. Later on, in December 1955, the same aircraft flew the Atlantic for winterization trials at Edmonton, Canada, the crossing being made via Prestwick, Keflavik, Goose Bay and Montreal. During its stay in Canada, the aircraft transported a 20-tonne load of equipment for a Canadian mining company.

Blackburn and General Aircraft's Canadian agents made several proposals to potential civil operators, including a plan for Universals to be used as tankers to transport fuel to remote Arctic airstrips. These schemes failed to materialize.

On its return flight to the UK in June 1956, XB262 'gave a lift' to an Auster AOP.9 aircraft which had also been on winterization trials. A spare Bristol Centaurus engine and a Rolls-Royce Avon gas turbine engine helped to fill up some of the space remaining in the freight bay.

Early in 1957, XB260 was sent to Canada for a second series of winterization trials. These were completed uneventfully. In the meantime, further aircraft had rolled off the line and had been test-flown. In December 1955, XB263 was delivered for trials to the RAF Handling Squadron at Boscombe Down.

Deliveries to Transport Command commenced on 12th March 1955 when XB265 was flown to Abingdon to join 47 Squadron, commanded by Squadron Leader D.P. Boulnois. By the end of March, XB264, XB267 and XB268 had also been delivered to 47 Squadron and crew conversion from the ageing Hastings was well under way. Three weeks from the first delivery, 47 Squadron took time out from crew training

The rear half of the 'draw works' loaded and ready for lashing down.
British Aerospace

G-AOEK on arrival at Heathrow on return from the oil-drilling equipment airlift.
British Aerospace

to provide a formation of four Beverleys led by Group Captain Griffiths, Abingdon's Commanding Officer, to fly over the factory at Brough to greet H.R.H. the Duke of Edinburgh who was visiting the Blackburn and General Aircraft works. During his stay at Brough, Prince Philip flew the Beverley and is reported to have said that it behaved 'like an amiable elephant'.

The reaction of aircrews posted for conversion on to Beverleys varied enormously. The 'jet set' thought it was a retrograde step to be flying a lumbering, noisy, piston-engined aircraft, apparently so primitive that its wheels did not even 'tuck up'. The crews converting from Valettas and Hastings however, found the Beverley to have the most pleasant flying characteristics and were surprised to find that such an archaic-looking aeroplane contained some of the most modern and sophisticated equipment, especially in navigation aids and avionics.

The Beverley introduced a new concept to Transport Command by being declared a Class A aeroplane by civil airworthiness standards. No longer were pilots to unstick at say, 100 knots and then wait those agonizing seconds until the airspeed had built up to the safety speed of say 115 knots. An engine failure in those few seconds often resulted in disaster. The Beverley's unstick speed was its safety speed. This was known as V2. A few knots before V2 came V1, the decision speed, before which a take-off could be safely abandoned and after which could be safely continued. Many other Vs were introduced such as *Vno* and *Vne* 'normal operating speed' and 'never exceed' speed.

Although V-speeds had already been used for some time in civil aviation, Transport Command crews had hitherto only read about them in the aeronautical press; but suddenly, V-speeds had arrived with the Beverley and its ODM. The ODM (Operating Data Manual) revealed every possible capability of the Beverley. Masses of complex charts and graphs gave take-off data, climb data, cruise data and landing data.

Three-engined performance was covered in detail and one section even gave three-engined take-off data with due allowance for failure of a further engine. Another invaluable feature of the ODM was the acceleration time check where the time, in seconds, for the aircraft to reach eighty knots could be calculated. As with the take-off section of the ODM, every possible variation could be allowed for such as: aircraft weight; runway slope; runway surface, e.g. wet, dry, grass, concrete etc.; wind direction; engine power corrected for temperature and humidity; and of course, airfield height.

The acceleration time check proved an invaluable aid to enable take-off performance to be monitored, especially on marginal airstrips. If eighty knots was not attained within the calculated time, take-off could be abandoned with complete safety.

The Beverley had arrived.

XB263 en route to the 1955 SBAC show. *BAe*

Chapter Two

The Abingdon Wing - 47 and 53 Squadrons

47 Squadron - brief history
Formed at Beverley in March 1916, the squadron saw service in the First World War in Greece. Between the wars, the squadron spent most of its time at Khartoum operating such aircraft as the Fairey Gordon, Vickers Vincent and Vickers Wellesley. In the Second World War, the squadron saw service in both the Middle East and Far East theatres.

In September 1946, 47 Squadron began its long association with transport aircraft when it acquired Halifaxes, these bombers being used in the transport role. In 1948, the squadron became the first unit to equip with Hastings aircraft, using these on the Berlin airlift. In 1953, the squadron moved to Abingdon where, in 1956, it became the first unit to equip with Beverleys, receiving its first Beverley on 12th March.

53 Squadron - brief history
Formed in May 1916 at Catterick, 53 Squadron saw service in the First World War in France. In 1919, the unit disbanded. Reformed in June 1937, the squadron moved to France on the outbreak of the Second World War, operating Blenheims. After withdrawal from France in July 1941, 53 re-equipped with Hudsons and flew anti-submarine patrols, later converting to Liberators. In June 1946, the squadron took up the transport role when it acquired Dakotas, flying these on the Berlin airlift before disbanding once again.

In August 1953, the squadron reformed at Topcliffe with Hastings, retaining these until February 1957 when it moved to Abingdon to equip with Beverleys.

First Beverleys go to 47 Squadron
As soon as the squadron received its first Beverleys in March 1956, an intense working-up period began, not only converting aircrew to flying the massive aeroplane but also familiarizing the ground staff with its various technicalities. One of the biggest problems was the sheer bulk and size of the aircraft: it was too large for any of the hangars then at Abingdon and the side-tracking equipment that enabled the Beverley to be hangared sideways was not yet available. All servicing therefore had to be done outside in all weathers. Access to the engines was a constant problem and until the 'Giraffe' hydraulic platforms became freely available, access equipment had to be improvised with much resourcefulness and ingenuity.

The biggest headaches were caused in general by the propeller braking electrical circuits and the space heating and aerofoil anti-icing combustion heaters. These were new concepts in aircraft engineering and until the various tradesmen had mastered their idiosyncrasies, much time was taken 'learning the hard way.' The propeller braking system also caused embarrassment to aircrew when propellers inadvertently went into reverse pitch (never in the air thankfully) and when in reverse pitch, failed to come out. On one occasion, a Beverley landed at an en-route airfield, and after using reverse thrust for braking - standard practice to avoid wear and tear on the wheel brakes - tower requested: 'Expedite your clearance please, we have an aircraft on finals'. The captain selected forward thrust and opened up the engines in order to taxi off the runway quickly, but alas, a malfunction had kept the propellers in reverse pitch and the Beverley moved gracefully astern, back towards its touchdown point. Needless to say, the aircraft on finals went round again.

The combustion heaters which supplied hot air for cabin heating and wing and tail surfaces thermal de-icing, burnt Avgas from the aircraft's fuel tanks. Because of the potential fire hazard with this type of heater, a great many safety devices were provided to ensure safe and satisfactory operation. These safety features resulted in complex electrical circuits which were prone to malfunction often due to spurious signals, and until these circuits and their peculiarities were fully understood, a lot of heater unserviceability was experienced. By sheer hard work however, these problems were overcome and quite soon, 47 Squadron was making the Beverley work.

After a two-month conversion and working-up period the squadron commenced route flying in May with a flight to Malta. A week later special flights started to Cyprus and at the end of May, a bi-weekly schedule to Wildenrath was inaugurated. Soon after this, an aircraft returning from Wildenrath force-landed at Coxyde in Belgium with engine failure.

Due to the lack of repair facilities at Coxyde, the aircraft was later flown back to base on three engines by the squadron commander - the first Beverley three-engined ferry flight undertaken by a squadron.

A 30 Squadron technician investigates a fault on an 84 Squadron aircraft from a Giraffe access platform. *via 30 Squadron*

Above: **Loading a radar scanner 47 ft long, 8 ft wide and 7 ft high into XB267 of 47 Squadron for delivery to Cyprus.**
British Aerospace

Below: **Line-up of Beverleys at Nicosia, Cyprus during the Suez campaign.**
British Aerospace

In addition to route flying, air portability training with the army had commenced and in early June, 94 troops were landed on the grass airfield at Watchfield where they deplaned in less than two minutes - a remarkably short time for troops with no previous experience of the aeroplane.

At about this time, with the Army's co-operation, trials were carried out to see how many persons could be crammed into a Beverley should the need for any Dunkirk-type evacuation ever arise in the future. The trials showed that 480 soldiers without weapons could comfortably stand inside the Beverley. All-up-weight limitations however, necessitated a reduction in numbers to 300 in order that an hour's fuel could be carried. Group Captain F.C. Griffiths RAF (ret'd), Abingdon's Commanding Officer at the time, recalls: 'This was not a serious experiment, but from the York evacuations from India and Pakistan on our withdrawal from the Indian continent, it was felt that we should find out just how many persons could get into the Beverley in an emergency'.

Group Captain Griffiths also recalls the occasion when he showed a local farmer around a Beverley. The Group Captain writes: 'As you know, the Beverley hold (freight compartment) was big and damned impressive to strangers. I took him up some steps and in by the port paradoor into the hold, flinging the door back and saying: 'What do you think of this for size?'

'He was chewing a piece of grass and said nothing at first; just looked around then stopped chewing and said: 'It would hold a hell of a lot of hay wouldn't it?'

'I felt quite humble. Just shows how your thoughts are governed by your profession'.

The Beverley's First Mercy Mission
In the small hours of 30th October, Flight Sergeant Frank Bradford, co-pilot to Flight Lieutenant Ken Webster, was sleeping off the effects of a particularly nasty tooth extraction. Not for long though; at about four am, Frank was awakened by a service policeman who told him to report to the squadron immediately. On arrival at dispersal he found preparations afoot to dispatch Beverley XB285 to Vienna with a load of medical supplies for refugees from the Hungarian uprising. In due course XB285 got airborne, captained by Flight Lieutenant Webster, with Frank in the right hand seat. Chief Technician Bill Binfield was also aboard as a 'flying spanner'. During the climb, Frank suffered intense pain from his jaw, caused probably by the change in pressure. He carried on gamely however, and the load was safely delivered to its destination. The aircraft became unserviceable at Vienna, necessitating a twenty-four hour delay which fortuitously enabled Frank to get teatment for his infected jaw. A few days later, the same crew took another load of medical supplies to Vienna. Both trips were reported in the national press and pictures were published in the *Illustrated London News*. In the two trips, about eighteen tonnes of supplies were delivered, demonstrating dramatically the Beverley's suitability for such tasks.

Further Army support work was carried out in the closing months of 1956 with crews training and qualifying for paratrooping and heavy supply dropping.

However, the Suez crisis interrupted these training activities, and before the Beverleys had seen six months service, they were called upon to show their mettle in the Suez operations. One Beverley, detached to Nicosia in Cyprus, flew over twenty sorties into Gamil airport at Port Said, delivering over 270 tonnes of fuel in drums for the Army. Other notable Suez 'weight-lifting' operations included the airlift from Abingdon to Nicosia of an outsize radar scanner measuring 47 feet long, 8 feet wide and 7 feet high; a signals vehicle weighing over eight tonnes; and in a

Loading a Folland Gnat for shipment to the Middle East. *British Aerospace*

single lift by one Beverley, three power unit trailers weighing over four tonnes each.

By March 1957 over 2,000 paratroops had been dropped and according to Jackson's *Blackburn Aircraft since 1909*, the squadron had moved approximately 4,700 tonnes of freight and carried 27,000 passengers. By modern airline standards this does not seem very impressive but it must be remembered that in 1957, flight simulators were almost unheard of and indeed, little provision was made for any form of synthetic flying training apart from the well-worn Link trainer. Consequently, all forms of flying, ranging from the time-honoured 'circuits and bumps' to instrument flying and precision Army support work, had to be done 'in anger' with aeroplanes that were frequently unavailable due to teething-trouble unserviceabililty. Training therefore, accounted for a large proportion of aircraft utilization.

Cont. (continuation training) consisted, in the days before flight simulators, of circuits and landings, simulated emergencies such as engine failures, and although necessary to enable aircrew to maintain peak efficiency, was regarded as a 'bit of a bore'. Cont. was hard work for the poor aeroplanes, however, hence this cartoon, from an original believed to be by Flight Lieutenant Chris Dyson, a 30 Squadron captain. *via J. Ward*

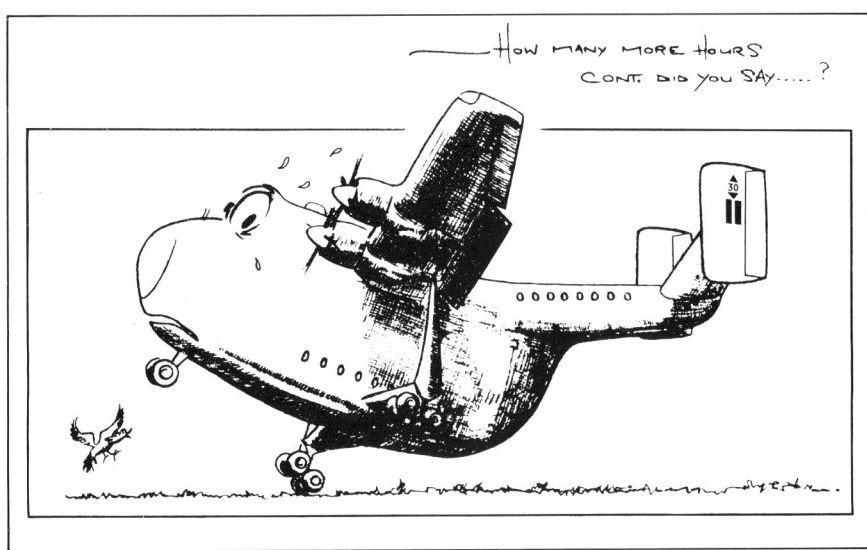

The Aden Detachments

In January 1957, two Beverleys were detached to Aden to assist 84 Squadron's Valettas in Army support duties in the Aden hinterland, then known as the Aden Protectorate and later as the Federation of South Arabia. After the British withdrawal from Aden in 1967, this territory became the South Yemen Republic. Each Beverley carried two crews, XB268 being captained by Flight Lieutenants Webster and Ogilvie, XB284 by Squadron Leader Sleaman and Flying Officer 'Dad' Owen.

In 1957, dissident tribes in the then Aden Protectorate, responding to incessant anti-British propaganda broadcasts from Cairo, were pursuing suitable terrorist activities. Such activities included mining the Dhala road, see *Map 2* (virtually the only vehicular road in the territory) and shooting up anything that moved on it. Some tribes, loyal to the British, resisted the Egyptian and Yemeni incitements to engage in anti-British terrorism and this led to inter-tribal conflicts with the loyal tribes requesting and receiving all the support the British could give.

In terms of air support requirements, this meant that there was a constant demand for troops, arms and supplies to be airlifted from Aden into airstrips which served the many outposts of the Protectorate. For the Beverley aircrews, it meant landing on and taking off from rough airstrips involving the most precise flying through mountainous country. Some airstrips were so 'hairy' that due to high ground close to their perimeters, overshooting was impossible and once on finals, a pilot was irrevocably committed to land. Apart from the hostile terrain, many strips were at high altitude and the Beverley as yet had done practically no 'hot and high' trials. At a 'hot and high' airfield, engine power is considerably reduced and much thumbing through the Operating Data Manual was needed to see what the book said: the predictions of the ODM were then put to the test, invariably proving that flying by the book worked. In addition to moving troops and their supplies and equipment, an airlift of cement to Ataq was undertaken to improve the surface of Ataq's airstrip. By May 1958, when the Aden detachments of UK-based Beverleys ceased, the Beverleys had airlifted over 700 tonnes of cement into Ataq.

The 'Battle of Dhala'

In the early days of the Aden detachment, one of the 'hairiest' strips that the Beverley was ever called upon to land on and take off from was Dhala. The Valettas of 84 Squadron could just get in and out of Dhala but the payload they carried out was pitifully small. Thus, when the Beverley detachments began, the inevitable question was: 'Can you land at Dhala?' The answer was of course 'Try us'. To the delight of the Army, the Beverley could and did operate in and out of Dhala, taking payloads far in excess of what was thought possible. Dhala, and the only road leading to it, often came under fire from dissident tribesmen in the surrounding hills and frequently, due to this murderous cross-fire, the garrison at Dhala was completely isolated. At one time the state of siege became extremely serious; Group Captain Griffiths, in his inimitable style, takes up the story of the first Beverley to land at Dhala:

'Dhala is a sheikdom up in the mountains to the north of Aden. It can only be approached by a road on one side of a valley and Dhala itself sits high up at the top of the valley and has a very small airstrip 'suitable for biplanes'. The airstrip was somewhat akin to Bluie West One in Greenland in that one had to land up-hill with cliffs facing the pilot and no possibility of overshooting. The landing had to be right first time. Take-off was easier, being downhill in the opposite direction but could be difficult in the heat of the day. Aircraft are always reluctant to leave the ground in high temperature conditions and Dhala was no exception, its high altitude making matters even worse.

'In 1957 trouble was brewing in the Aden Protectorate. This was not unusual for

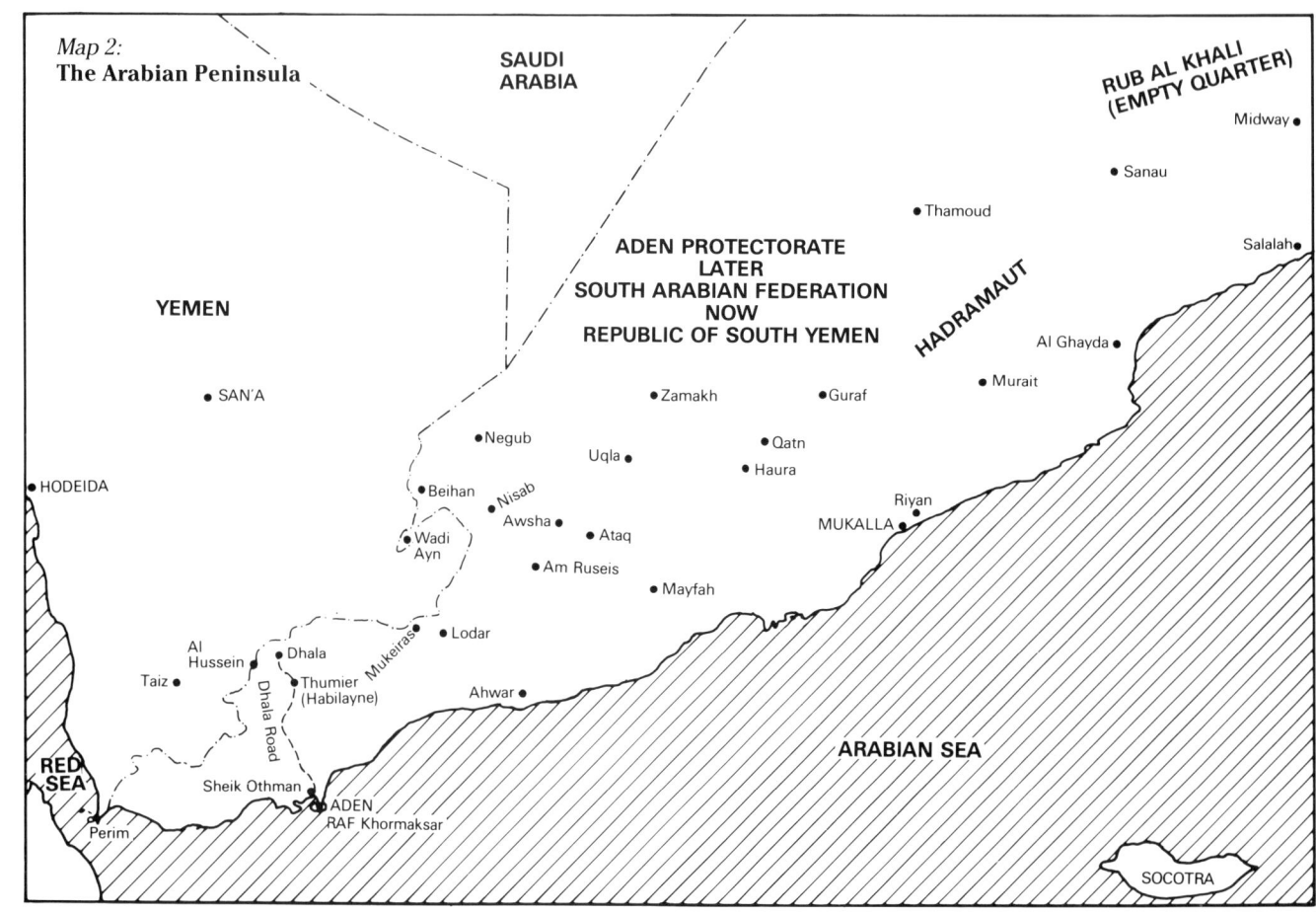

Map 2: The Arabian Peninsula

that area. Whether the trouble was caused by a local warring sheikdom or insurgents from North Yemen I am not sure but whoever the enemy were, they enfiladed the pass up to Dhala, and from the hills around they were successful in stopping all supplies and reinforcements reaching Dhala.

'Fighter aircraft were sent in from Khormaksar at Aden to shoot up the enemy and encourage them to depart but the modern jet fighters proved quite unequal to the task. They could not fly slow enough to see their targets and when they could see them, seemed unable to hit them. What was required was a slow-flying biplane but alas, such was aviation progress that they had been phased out many years previously.

'When supplies at Dhala were getting low and the siege, for siege it was, showed no sign of being raised, Headquarters Land Forces Aden approached the RAF with the suggestion that a gun of some considerable calibre should be flown into Dhala by a Beverley aircraft, two of which were on detachment to Aden at the time. No four-engined aircraft had ever landed at Dhala before and even twin-engined aircraft such as the Valetta treated Dhala with the utmost respect. Nevertheless, the powers that be requested that the Beverley should have a go. But it wasn't the sort of operation that could be 'tried'. It had to work first time or there would, at best, be a broken aeroplane of some considerable dimensions high up in the mountains.

XB265 landing at Ibri, Oman during the uprising, July 1957. *Author*

'So the task was undertaken and the Beverley flew into Dhala without any difficulty. The clamshell doors were opened, the ramp dropped and the gun rolled out to the edge of the escarpment where it proceeded to pump shells with considerable accuracy into the enemy behind the rocks. In half an hour the enemy withdrew and the battle of Dhala was over.

'Verily the motto of Transport Command *Ferio Ferendo* (I fight by carrying), had been adequately demonstrated'.

The Aden detachments were not all confined to flying within the Aden Protectorate. In March 1957 trouble flared up in Oman with an attempt, reportedly backed by Saudi Arabia, to depose the Sultan of

Unloading stores at Dhala. The mountain in the background is at the end of the airstrip; it made overshooting impossible. *W. Binfield*

Muscat and Oman. The Aden detachment of Beverleys was promptly ordered up to the Persian Gulf, where, from Sharjah and Bahrain, troops and supplies were flown into remote Omani airstrips, such as Ibri, Firq and Fahoud - the latter being somewhat more civilized than the others due to the amenities provided for the oil men who were prospecting there, successfully as later events have shown. Unserviceability dogged the Bev's Oman campaign: XB268, due to an undetected slit in the

aerodynamic elevator/tailplane rubber seal, failed to get airborne from Ibri, and the captain, Flying Officer John Nimmo, aborted the take-off. A stunted tree, alleged to be the only one in that part of the Omani desert, obstructed the overrun area and the aircraft hit it, damaging a propeller.

A new prop was flown out, the various components of it being carefully tucked away in robust packing cases that bore notices with dire warnings of what would happen if the prop was not assembled in absolutely clean and dust-free conditions. These warnings could not of course be complied with; one thing Arabia does not lack is sand and dust. Nevertheless, the long-suffering ground crew, who fortuitously, were carried on that sortie, set to and assembled the prop in spite of the intense heat, sand, dust and flies. After fitting to the engine concerned, the prop functioned perfectly and XB268, still with its undetected elevator fault, got airborne after another series of aborted take-offs. After more difficulties on getting airborne on take-off from Bahrain, 268 was flown back to Khormaksar, where at first, some freight bay floor panels were lifted to see if the aircraft was carrying an excessive amount of sand and/or cement in the underfloor area. This check revealed nothing untoward, so attention was turned to the elevators where the fault was soon found and rectified.

XB269, the 'other half' of the detachment, had suffered quite a lot of petty unserviceability during the detachment, but otherwise had performed reasonably well, some faults being of such a minor nature that they could be tolerated until the aircraft returned to the UK. On the homeward-bound trip however, having been replaced by a 53 Squadron aircraft, XB269, captained by Flight Lieutenant Ashe Goodhew, suffered an engine failure at Masirah Island. Masirah enjoys a pleasant, almost temperate climate, and whilst waiting for the replacement engine to be 'Bevved' out, both aircrew and ground crew enjoyed pleasant outings on the island. Such activities included swimming, watching turtles coming ashore to lay their eggs at night, and a shark-fishing trip on an Arab dhow.

The engine change was accomplished using the invaluable Zip Up collapsible staging which was always carried when Beverleys ventured into remote airstrips. Masirah's Coles crane was suitable for propeller removal but the jib could not be raised high enough for attachment to the engine change sling. The dreaded wing gantry had to be used therefore. This contrivance bolted on to the wing overhead the engine to be changed and served the purpose of a crane, lifting and lowering being effected by means of a block and tackle and muscle power. The wing gantry was a large and heavy contraption and in order to get it on to the aircraft's wing, it had to be dismantled and hauled up, by rope and muscle power, on to the wing where it was reassembled and bolted into position. The whole tedious procedure was then repeated in reverse after completion of the engine change.

This then was the theme of the Aden detachments until 84 Squadron at Khormaksar received its first Beverleys in May 1958. The detachments had been carried out on a rota basis by 47 and 53 Squadrons and later by 30 Squadron from Dishforth, after their crews had converted on to Beverleys in April/May 1957.

The Aden detachments were not popular; Aden was never a plum posting and up-country flights demanded precise flying in hot, turbulent conditions, with the prospect of the entire crew assisting with the unloading at the destination in the event of there being no available manpower. For the ground crews, it was worse: billeted in inferior accommodation due to overcrowding of the Khormaksar base; working around the clock sometimes to get an aircraft serviceable to meet its scheduled take-off time; working in one of the hottest, most humid parts of the world demanded stamina that was maintained purely by *esprit de corps* and pride in being part of a team that kept the Beverleys in the air. Nevertheless, the Aden detachments provided invaluable experience both for air and ground crews that was to stand them in good stead during the Beverley's service.

Two photographs illustrating the engine change on XB269 at Masirah. The Coles crane at Masirah was high enough for removing and replacing the propeller, but the wing gantry had to be used for the engine. *Author*

53 Squadron Receives its Beverleys

By January 1957, the squadron had been allocated four aircraft and under the watchful eyes of fully trained crews from 47 Squadron, training began. More aircraft were delivered in February and March, and despite a tragic setback in early March when the squadron lost XH117 in a fatal crash at Drayton near Abingdon, by the end of March, 53 Squadron was fully equipped and operational. From then on, 47 and 53 Squadrons operated jointly from Abingdon as a Wing. At one side of the airfield, 47 Squadron was quartered at Shippon dispersal, so named due to its proximity to the village of that name; 53 Squadron resided at the other side of the airfield at Sleepy Hollow dispersal, so named, according to 47 Squadron, 'because nothing much ever happened there'. 53 Squadron's quarters were next to the bomb dump, wherein Abingdon's station mascot, an ill-tempered goat with an insatiable appetite for cycle saddles and rubber handle-grips lurked, as many cyclists found to their cost after leaving their mounts leaning against the bomb dump fence.

Members of 53 Squadron; this taken around 1958. *D. Lawson*

Due to the operations in the Oman uprising having been dogged with unserviceability, it was decided to conduct further tropical trials. Accordingly in October 1957, three 57 Squadron Beverleys were detached to Sharjah. Full ground crew and spares back-up, together with technical representatives from Blackburns and Bristols were provided.

All aircraft performed remarkably well and unserviceability was negligible: this was attributed to the know-how and experience gained by both ground crew and aircrew. In addition, the ground technicians now knew what faults to look for on after-flight inspections and such faults, when found, were rectified usually at night. Rectification of these faults which were invariably of a minor nature prevented development of more serious and potentially dangerous problems. The conclusions drawn from the Sharjah trials were that experienced technicians must always be on hand for servicing the aircraft and that adequate spares back-up should always be provided.

Beverley visits South Africa

In October 1957 rumours reached RAF Abingdon that a Beverley would be required to visit Rhodesia. It is thought that the original requirement was to demonstrate to the Rhodesian Forces the suitability of the Beverley for transporting large numbers of troops and vehicles into small remote airfields, in the event of civil unrest. This rumour then gave rise to a snowball effect in that No.1 Parachute Training School suggested that they send six Parachute Jump Instructors with the aircraft to study the problems of jumping at high altitude: subsequently this requirement was changed to studying the problems of parachutists 'landing' at high altitudes, Rhodesia being ideal for this purpose.

Group Captain Griffiths, station commander of RAF Abingdon at the time, takes up the story:

'Not all that far from RAF Abingdon at Reading was the Headquarters of Flying Training Command whose Air Officer Commanding was Air Marshal Sir Richard Ll.R. Atcherley known throughout the Air Force as 'Batchy' Atcherley, the survivor of the Atcherley brothers whose exploits in their younger days and in the early days of the Royal Air Force were legendary. Yet despite the brothers' sense of fun which resulted in many a wild escapade, such were their personalities, drive, enthusiasm and leadership tempered with extraordinary kindness and understanding that they reached the highest ranks of the Royal Air Force.

'One morning a phone call came in from Air Marshal Sir Richard:"That you Griff? I hear you've got a Beverley going to South Africa. Would there be a seat for me on it?

I've been on to your C-in-C and he's happy if there's room. I'm to visit the South African Air Force Headquarters in Pretoria to discuss training matters!"

"Well, we're only going to Rhodesia" I replied "and it will be a rather long trip."

'Somehow the request seemed rather out of context. Surely I thought, an Air Officer Commanding should be flown out by a 24 Squadron crew in a VIP Hastings aircraft or he should travel in the luxury offered by BOAC.

"The Beverley has a fixed undercarriage, Sir. It will take an awful long time to get there." It just didn't seem right putting an Air Marshal in a slow freighter aircraft and carrying him half-way across the world.

"The fixed undercart won't worry me. I was brought up on them" he replied.

'He seemed very determined to go. I was also hoping to go myself as captain of the aircraft but my category wouldn't allow me to carry a VIP such as an Air Marshal and that would mean finding a VIP-qualified crew. But it would be great fun travelling with him for it was a delight to be in his company.

"Well Sir, if you don't mind a slow trip we'd be very glad to have you aboard. The aircraft is due to depart on the 18th of November".

"Splendid. I'll be there. I hear you are being sent on to South Africa as the South African Air Force might be interested in the Beverley. You should be able to take me right through".

'It was the first I had heard of the trip going beyond Salisbury (now Harare) but it seemed a logical course of action; while we were demonstrating to the Rhodesians why not take in the South Africans as well?

'He went on. "I've got a few bits and pieces I'd like to take with me Griff, will there be any restrictions on baggage?"

"Not at all", I replied, feeling full of pride in the load-carrying capability of the Beverley and being in a somewhat euphoric mood. Rather injudiciously I added "This aircraft's a great weightlifter. We'll have 20,000 lb of payload to spare."

'Two days later he rang me again: "Were you serious about that spare payload you mentioned? I've got some chairs and a dining room table I'd like to take to my sister in South Africa and if you can carry them indulgence freight I'd like to take them".

'There was no problem about this so I suggested he send them along. Indulgence freight, provided that it could be carried at no cost to public funds has been a perquisite of the Services ever since the time of Samuel Pepys. The chairs and table were duly delivered and then another unusual item of freight arrived with the compliments of the Blackburn and General Aircraft Company. Three dozen bottles of champagne 'which might be of assistance in any entertaining which might be necessary and appropriate.'

'Came the day of departure, 18th November 1957. A rather hectic day, for the Mayor of Abingdon was to unveil the town's Coat of Arms which had been painted on the port bow of Beverley XB291. RAF Abingdon had recently been granted the Freedom of the Borough of Abingdon and now the town's Coat of Arms was to be carried to wherever the Abingdon Beverleys should fly and this Beverley, the first to carry the Coat of Arms, would carry it to Capetown.

'The Air Marshal was smuggled aboard early on because he didn't want to get mixed up with the ceremonies. Speeches were made, the Mayor unveiled the Coat of Arms, gave me a letter for the Mayor of Capetown then we all clambered aboard with Flight Lieutenant 'Piano' Adams as captain of the aircraft and another VIP pilot, Flight Lieutenant Baker as co-pilot. It goes without saying that 'Piano' Adams was so-called because of his musical ability. With the Air Marshal and myself it meant that we had four pilots all told and you certainly needed four pilots to drive a Beverley from Abingdon to Capetown without an autopilot. The trip to Luqa (Malta) was routine. We landed two hours after dark and set off again early next morning for El Adem to top up tanks for the long desert crossing to Khartoum. The Mediterranean can produce some wicked weather in late autumn and this autumn was to be no exception. Thunderstorms were forecast and the cloud build-up soon after take-off looked sinister. There was no question of going over the top. So we flew straight into it and despite its appearance it was completely calm inside but gradually grew darker and darker until we had to have all the instrument lights on. The Beverley mushed along seeming to become quieter as time passed. It was eerie. Then Saint Elmo's Fire appeared on No.3 engine, grew larger and danced away along the leading edge of the wing on No.4 engine. It seemed to be attracted by the engines. This fireball was shortly accompanied by two more on the port engines and finally we had four fireballs - quite the largest I have ever seen. Perhaps Saint Elmo sent large ones to complement the size of the aircraft. Then the four fireballs cavorted along the wings and back to the engines in a graceful ballet. In many years of maritime and aeronautical activity I have never experienced such a graceful ballet by Saint Elmo nor over such a long period.

'Finally, the dancing was concluded by a Wagnerian thunderclap as we flew, carrying our static, into a cloud of opposite polarity. Even then there was no turbulence; just great sheets of lightning flashing miles ahead of us. The smell of sulphur was so strong I felt sure we had had a serious lightning strike and that the devil had come aboard, yet 291 flew on serenely, compasses continued working and when we examined the aircraft on the ground, much to our surprise, there was no sign of a lightning strike.

'On landing at El Adem, we executed a plan that we had previously devised to impress those who watched the Beverley's arrival by taxying in, opening the clamshell doors, lowering the ramps and with the six parachutists dressed in their white overalls, lining the ramps, three on each side, I drove the Air Marshal out of the aircraft in his Land Rover. This was the sort of thing which 'Batchy' loved. However, when we left Abingdon, the MT Section had almost drained the Land Rover's fuel tank and when we drove out at El Adem, the fuel gauge was reading zero, The Air Marshal and I drove round to El Adem's MT section for fuel. The airman issuing the fuel was astounded to learn that we had come from RAF Abingdon. He remarked on the Land Rover's dark paint (UK paint scheme) as opposed to the khaki paint scheme of MEAF and asked where we were going. I said 'Khartoum' to which he replied: 'Don't you want a spare can of fuel Sir, Khartoum's a hell of a long way from here'. He didn't realize that we were 'Bevving' the Land Rover.

'We made similar spectacular arrivals at Khartoum, Nairobi and Salisbury, each time driving the Air Marshal out in his Land Rover, the Parachute Jump Instructors standing three on each side of the ramp in their white overalls to pay compliments to the Air Marshal as we emerged. It suited him to drive out in the Land Rover for he was quite lame on one leg and had difficulty negotiating steps and ladders.

'During our three days at Salisbury, the aircraft was loaded and unloaded with a variety of Army, police vehicles and mining equipment to demonstrate its versatility. These demonstrations were concluded by our six Parachute Jump Instructors doing a drop: despite the high altitude and consequent high rate of descent they managed to land on their feet. Then on to Waterkloof at Pretoria where a very different atmosphere prevailed.

'The South Africans were correct and polite but they weren't interested in the Beverley . . . . . officially. Proposals to demonstrate the load-carrying capacity of this 'Giant of the Air' were not taken up. Whether the purpose of our visit had been misunderstood or whether the ground had been ill-prepared, there was undoubtedly a very obvious lack of interest. We had, of course, requested permission to use our Land Rover for camp running but even this was refused.

'It was the Air Marshal who thought up the solution to break the ice. The day after our arrival, the South Africans had asked us to a formal party in the Officers Mess at which some politicians were present. It was a pleasant friendly occasion but it was still difficult to introduce the Beverley into any conversation. The Air Marshal, however, dreamed up the idea of throwing a return party in the Beverley itself but how to lure the guests into the Beverley was the problem.

'We issued invitations for the guests to come to our party at the Waterkloof Officers Mess. In the early evening, Piano Adams demonstrated the Beverley's ability to taxi backwards, using reverse pitch, by 'backing' her across the veldt and along a narrow track which crossed the veldt to the Officers Mess Gardens. A most fortunate feature of the Beverley design is the height of the sill of the freight compartment, for as we discovered on two occasions, it was possible to back up to a fence, open the clamshell doors and drop the ramps over the fence without interfering with the fencing in any way.

'So the guests arrived, and floodlit alongside the gardens was the Beverley with its welcoming ramp down over the fence. On one clamshell door was the flag of the Union of South Africa and on the other a Union Jack. The white-overalled Parachute Jump Instructors entered into the spirit of the party, ushered the guests into the aircraft and plied them with the champagne which had been kindly contributed by Messrs. Blackburn and General Aircraft. The party certainly went with a swing. One person present, a lady reporter from the *Pretoria News* had that afternoon witnessed a parachute display we had been able to lay on during a quiet period at Johannesburg International Airport. After the display, the Air Marshal invited her to come to the party in Pretoria and offered to give her a lift back to Pretoria in the Beverley (we were cleared to offer flying experience flights to citizens of note). She demurred. 'But I would have to leave my car here in Johannesburg and it would be difficult to get back' she said. 'No problem' said the Air Marshal: 'Drive your car into the aircraft now and we'll take you and the car to Pretoria.' And so it came to pass.

'Two days later there was a slightly embarrassing article in a Jo'burg newspaper headed 'Volkswagen gains Johannesburg-Pretoria speed record in an elapsed time of 14 minutes'. This was followed by a photograph of a Volkswagen and a description of the flight in the Beverley. We just hoped that the article didn't appear in European papers.

'It was a great party. Music had been laid on and the hold proved ideal for intimate dancing while the upper deck was an excellent spot for young couples to sit out. Dancing was not entirely confined to the freight compartment for to my horror I saw a couple dancing on the wing. Appropriate action was taken on this (they had climbed out there via the flight deck).

'When the guests were finally departing I noticed a young South African girl walking barefoot across the lawn carrying her shoes. I didn't think much of it at the time but next morning as I was about to sign the

THE PRETORIA NEWS, FRIDAY, NOVEMBER 29, 1957

One Of Most Original Parties Ever Given In City

THE BACK of the Beverley opened, the ramp came down, and instead of military vehicles and soldiers going in, women in smart cocktail dresses and their escorts mounted the steps to be guests at one of the most original cocktail parties ever given in Pretoria. This was the first occasion that such a party had been given in one of the R.A.F. Transport Command aeroplanes, and those lucky enough to have been invited were shown all over the plane. Some even walked about on top of it.

The Beverley was in Pretoria and Johannesburg for two days, and the idea for Tuesday's party was born when the United Kingdom Air Liaison Officer and Mrs. Philip Haynes drove Air Marshal Sir Richard Atcherley home from a party the previous evening. Sir Richard is on a liaison visit to the S.A.A.F. to exchange ideas on flying training. Commander-in-Chief R.A.F Flying Training Command, this distinguished looking man is a former Commandant of Cranwell, as well as a former Commandant of the Central Fighter Establishment. He was no stranger to Group Captain Haynes, for when the latter was British Air Liaison Officer in Washington, Sir Richard was head of the R.A.F. Mission to the States.

'Pioneers'

The Beverley was drawn up on the road at Waterkloof Air Station, and Sir Richard greeted the "Cock'ail party pioneers" just inside the aircraft, under the flag. Earlier at Jan Smuts Airport, he had invited a newspaper woman to come to the party, but when she said that it was impossible as she had to have her car to drive back from Pretoria to Johannesburg, she was told to drive it in. She did. It must qualify as the quickest drive she has ever made.

Cocktails in a transport aircraft seems to have caused a great deal of mirth, or it may have been Group-Captain F. C. Griffiths's "snake charmer reed pipe" which brought the laughs. In any case everyone was obviously enjoying his story in the Beverley. (Left to right): Air-Marshal Sir Richard Atcherley, Mrs. C. Gey van Pittius, Commandant B. Boyle, Mrs. Boyle, the Senior United Kingdom Air Liaison Officer, Group-Captain Philip Haynes, Mrs. Haynes, and Group-Captain Griffiths.

The aircraft was capable of transporting 180 men with full kit, or 450 in retreat, so there was no lack of space to entertain people, who made the most of their opportunities, climbing up steep ladders to the upper deck and sitting in the pilot's seat. Some of the women, however, forgot that full skirts were not the best clothes in which to come down ladders, and there was much laughter as they tried to descend gracefully. Later in the evening Group Captain F. C. Griffiths provided a set of overalls for any woman who wished to be venturesome and climb out on top.

Stoop

This visit to Pretoria was an especially pleasant one for him, for he and Wing Commander Eustace Slade, Chief Air Traffic Control Officer at the Air Ministry, met old friends in Commandant C. Gey van Pittius, who served with them in Cyprus, and Mrs. Gey van Pittius.

Round-shouldered Group Captain Griffiths has quite a history, and towards the end of the party, he was persuaded to tell the story of how he acquired his stoop.

form 700, the flight engineer produced the heel of a lady's shoe from his pocket. In the top of the Beverley wing were some sockets into which eyebolts could be fitted. Any technician working on top of the wing could then hook the monkey chain from his safety harness into an eyebolt as a safety measure, for it was an awful long way from a Beverley wing to the ground if you once started sliding. In one of these socket holes the flight engineer had found the lady's heel. It obviously belonged to the Cinderella tripping across the grass to her pumpkin coach.

'The party certainly broke the ice with the South Africans and next day, with our furniture, baggage and Land Rover reloaded, we set off for Capetown. Here the Air Marshal had meetings at Ysterplaat (Capetown) and at the South African Training Base Lambangweg, half an hour's flying to the east. Again we were able to give parachute displays. It was a change for those taking part to be landing at sea level.

'The flight back north was to be via Kimberley, Salisbury, Leopoldville (now Kinshasa), Kano and Luqa. As there was no military base at Kimberley, the Air Marshal, in collaboration with his sister who lived alongside the airfield, fixed up accommodation for the whole crew with local inhabitants. It was a marvellous opportunity to stay with a South African family in their home and experience how they lived. The hospitality was quite overwhelming and while Kimberley from the air looked like a bunch of tin shacks in a desert with a big hole alongside the town (the largest man-made hole in the world where they dug out the diamonds in the last century), once you were on your feet in the town you really felt that you were in the Middle West of the USA. The wide streets, the planked sidewalks and hitching rails gave you the feeling that the sheriff was going to ride into town with a posse at any moment. It was a perfect setting for the film *High Noon*.

'But before we started sightseeing we taxied the Beverley across the veldt to a pleasant house on the far side of the airport. We backed her up to the fence, opened the clamshell doors, dropped the ramps and delivered the chairs and table straight into the house from the aircraft. Surely this use of the aeroplane was what the Wright Brothers must have envisaged? No other aeroplane but the Beverley could have achieved this in 1957. Then we were whisked away by our hosts for a fabulous round of picnics, parties and sightseeing and for anyone wishing to study industrial archaeology with regard to diamond mining, then Kimberley is the place.

'On 1st December we departed for Salisbury but before doing so, we laid on a demonstration by our parachutists and also a short field landing demonstration by the Beverley; Kimberley, with its dusty dirt-covered airfield, was ideal for this. It was 'now you see an aeroplane, now you don't' as the propellers were slammed into reverse pitch and enveloped the aircraft in a massive cloud of dust. After leaving Kimberley, we flew high to avoid turbulence and as we were now about to land on British territory and could use the Land Rover again, we desired to make our usual spectacular arrival by driving the Air Marshal out of the aircraft. In the haste of departure, some freight and baggage had been loaded between the Land Rover and the ramps and a rather delicate airborne operation was required to bring the freight forward and move the Land Rover aft without unduly changing the centre of gravity. I decided to supervise the job myself.

'We must have been at about 11,000 feet in fairly rarified air. Whether the rarified atmosphere was the cause of my problem or whether it was straining to lift a box in an unusual position I don't know, but the fact remains that something happened inside me. I felt discomfort and then quite intense pain but managed to drive the Air Marshal out on arrival at Salisbury, then off to sick quarters. I came to at midnight with a tube up my nose, a drip feed in my arm and the laughing faces of the Air Marshal and Piano Adams swimming into focus. I had been admitted to Salisbury Hospital for an operation to untwist a *volvulus* (twisted bowel). This resulted in a six-inch gash in my stomach and Beverley XB291 going on without me. Onward to what almost became her demise.

'My visitors, who had been to what was obviously a most enjoyable party, assured me that I wasn't going to die and left me for a month's stay in Rhodesia. At Leopoldville the Beverley was parked on a dispersal adjacent to some tall palm trees· During the night a great storm arose with whirlwind characteristics, the centre of which passed over the airfield. When dawn came there was no sign of Beverley 291. Lying on the dispersal where she had been parked, were half a dozen enormous palm trees and away across the airfield in some swamplike ground at a rather unusual angle was the Beverley. She had blown away from her dispersal, luckily before the trees had blown down and although she was bogged she was quite undamaged. To the uninitiated, to get her back on to dry land looked a problem but not to Piano Adams who was used to extracting Beverleys from sticky places. Luckily she was light and with all four engines at full throttle she drew herself out of the mire when Piano used the fore-and-aft rocking technique. And so 291 returned to the United Kingdom leaving some Africans with memories of a most unusual aircraft.'

Glad to say, the Group Captain made a complete recovery, later returning by civil airline to resume command of RAF Abingdon.

47 Squadron Wins Lord Trophy - Beverley goes to Far East

In January 1958, 47 Squadron won the coveted Lord Trophy, with Flight Lieutenant Webster and crew scoring top marks. Flight Lieutenant Clarke captained the second competing crew. In the same month, XB263 left Abingdon on a proving flight to the Far East. Commanded by the OC Squadron, Squadron Leader B.W. Taylor, and flown on alternate legs by two crews, skippered respectively by Flight Lieutenants Peter Dudley and Don Hugget, the aircraft also carried a full servicing team.

The trip got off to a bad start when the nose oleo strut deposited its charge of hydraulic fluid on to the dispersal at Istres in France during a refuelling stop. A replacement strut and the necessary jacks were flown out next day and despite attempts by the *Mistral* to blow 263 off the jacks, the strut was successfully changed, a taxying test carried out and the flight was able to be resumed on the following day.

The rest of the trip was uneventful, the aircraft staging through Luqa, Nicosia, Habbaniyah, Bahrain, Karachi, Palam (Delhi), Dum Dum (Calcutta), Mingaladon (Rangoon), Butterworth (Malaya) and Changi (Singapore), the outbound trip taking about forty-five hours flying time. Two legs were flown each day. After a brief rest at Changi, the aircraft was flown up-country to Kuala Lumpur from where it visited various airfields in the then Federation, including Ipoh, Kluang and Butterworth.

Various demonstrations and trials were carried out including heavy drops and an operational drop of SAS troops into the Malayan jungle for anti-terrorist duties in the Malayan Emergency. The tour was highly successful and undubtedly led to the decision being made to form a Far East Beverley squadron.

The flight back to Abingdon was via Butterworth, Katunayake (Ceylon) and Karachi, from where the outbound route was retraced. An interesting sortie was flown from Katunayake in which a large number of Indian labourers were flown out to Gan in the Maldive Islands, these men comprising the main work-force which developed Gan into the major staging post that it later became.

The Far East proving flight carried two long-awaited pieces of equipment, the Mark 10 autopilot and the ignition system analyser. The former malfunctioned on the first leg and the trouble was diagnosed as a faulty amplifier. Although a new amplifier was despatched by priority air freight, it never caught up with 263 until Karachi was reached on the homeward flight. After changing the amplifier, the autopilot performed impeccably for the rest of the flight, despite the suspicions of the pilots who had become so used to hand-flying the aircraft.

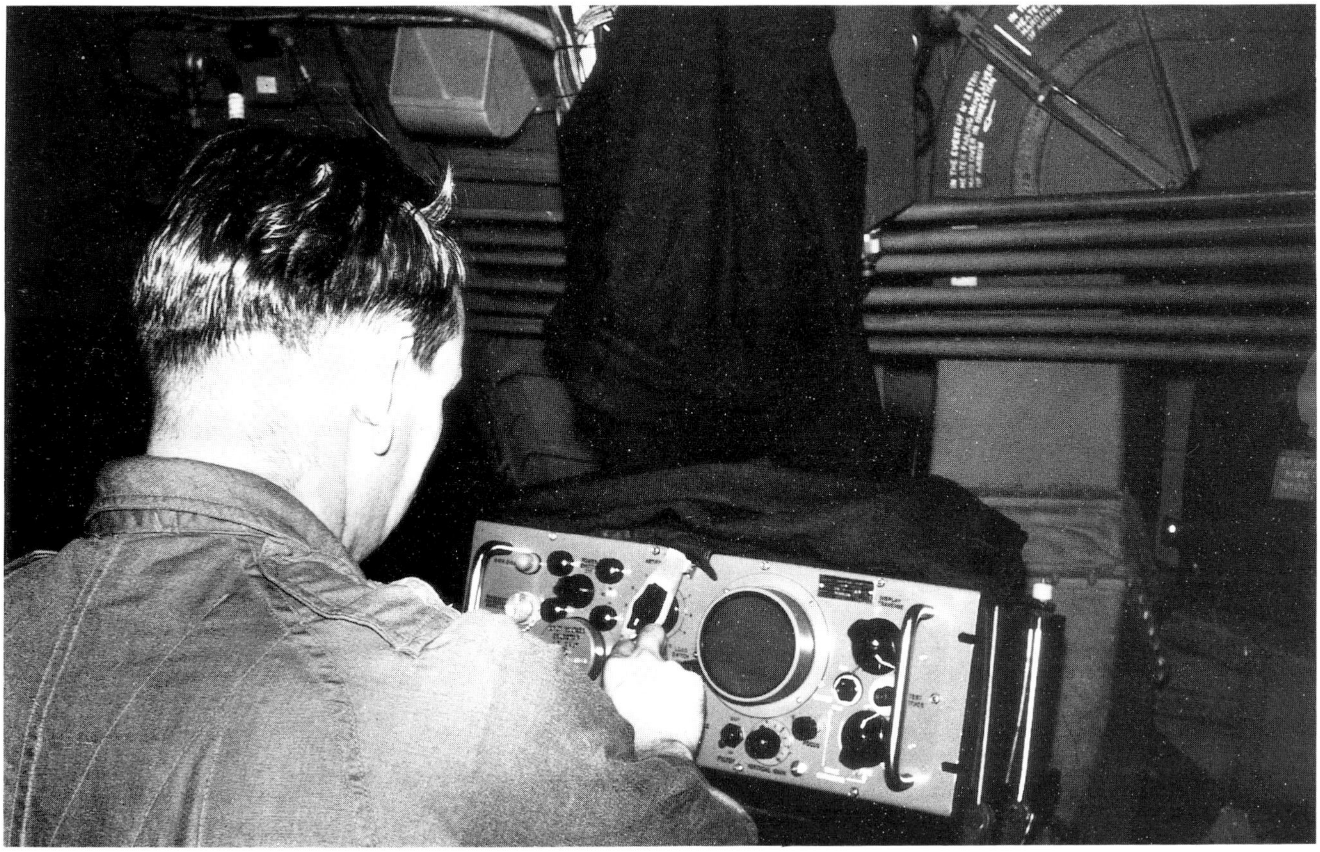

The ignition analyser was a device which showed, on an oscilloscope, a pattern depicting the performance of the ignition system of any selected engine. Faulty sparking plugs, defective contact breaker points, incorrect timing and any other ignition faults could be diagnosed using this valuable device. Little training was required in its operation and a useful manual showing the displays relating to various faults was provided. The most important thing the operator had to know was the firing order of the engine cylinders so that a faulty sparking plug could be easily located. The principle of the ignition analyser is used today in the Crypton electronic car engine tuning equipment found in most garages. The analyser proved its worth at Bahrain on the return journey, a 'mag drop' on an engine being traced to a single faulty sparking plug which was changed in approximately fifteen minutes. Without the analyser, a full plug change (thirty-six plugs) would have been necessary taking anything up to three hours.

The Far East trip, occupying about 100 flying hours, had demonstrated the tremendous potential of the Beverley for Army support work in that theatre, this work at that time being done mainly by the popular but ageing Valetta.

March 1958 saw two Beverleys, one from each squadron, showing the flag again on a goodwill tour of Nigeria, visiting Lagos, Kano, Enugu and Kaduna and carrying out various demonstrations and exercises with the Nigerian Army. The 47 Squadron Beverley was captained by Flight Lieutenant Clarke: the 53 Squadron Beverley by Flight Lieutenant Stan Alden.

During the previous month, a massive air portablility exercise, code-named *Quickstep*, was mounted. Four Beverleys from Abingdon Wing plus one from 30 Squadron at Dishforth, this squadron having been recently re-equipped with Beverleys, airlifted some 500 men, 10 tonnes of equipment, plus 11 Land Rovers and trailers, from Abingdon to Idris in Libya and back. This exercise conclusively proved the Beverley's worth in moving men and materials to potential trouble spots overseas.

May '58 saw the end of the Aden detachment, 84 Squadron at Khormaksar having been re-equipped with Beverleys. Manned by experienced crews drawn mainly from 47 and 53 Squadrons, 84 was able to undertake the MEAF commitments without further ado.

The author 'trying to get a picture' on the ignition analyser (located at the rear of the flight deck). *C. Pearson*

The first Beverley in Malaya. XB263 at Kuala Lumpur being prepared for heavy drop, January 1958. *G. Murray*

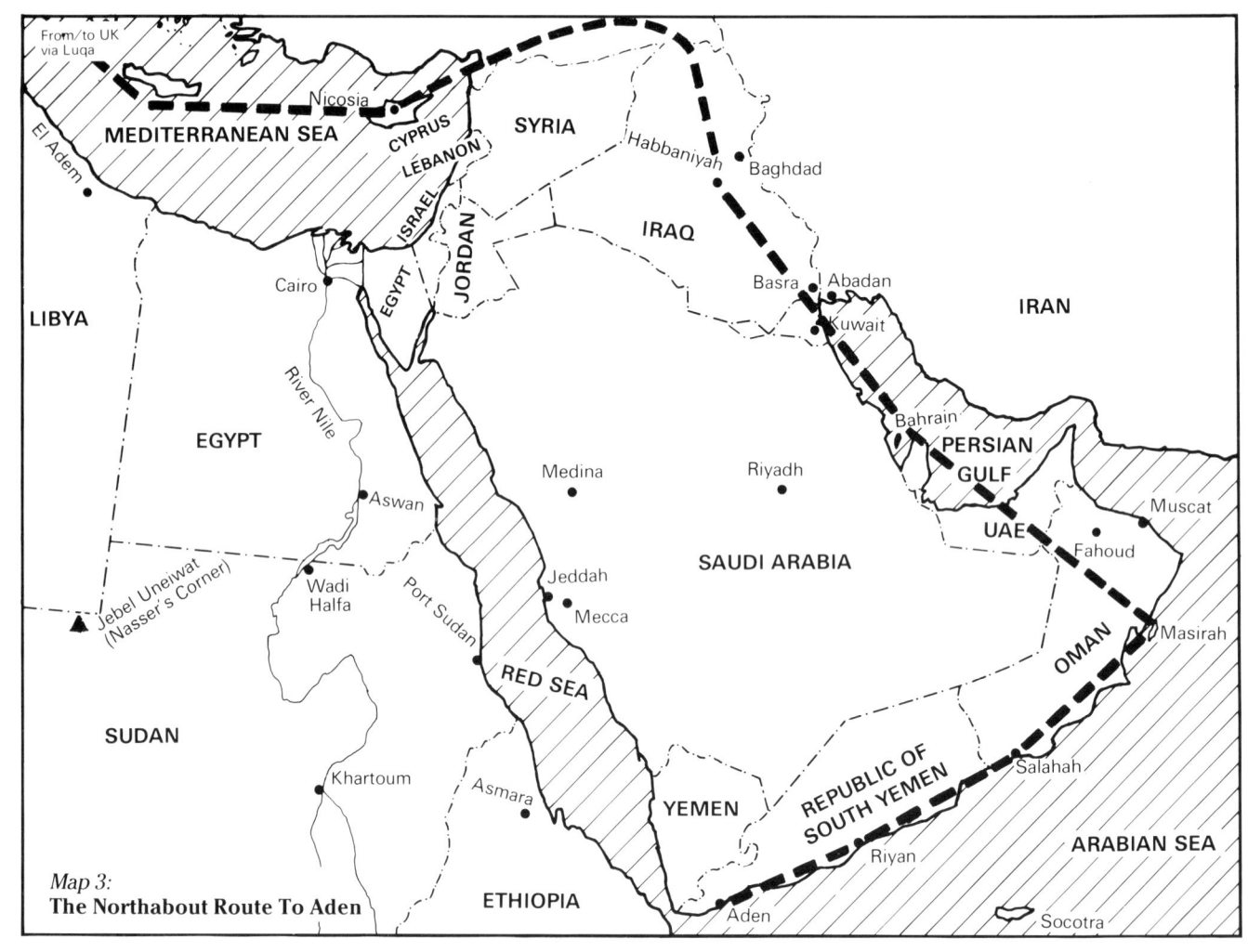

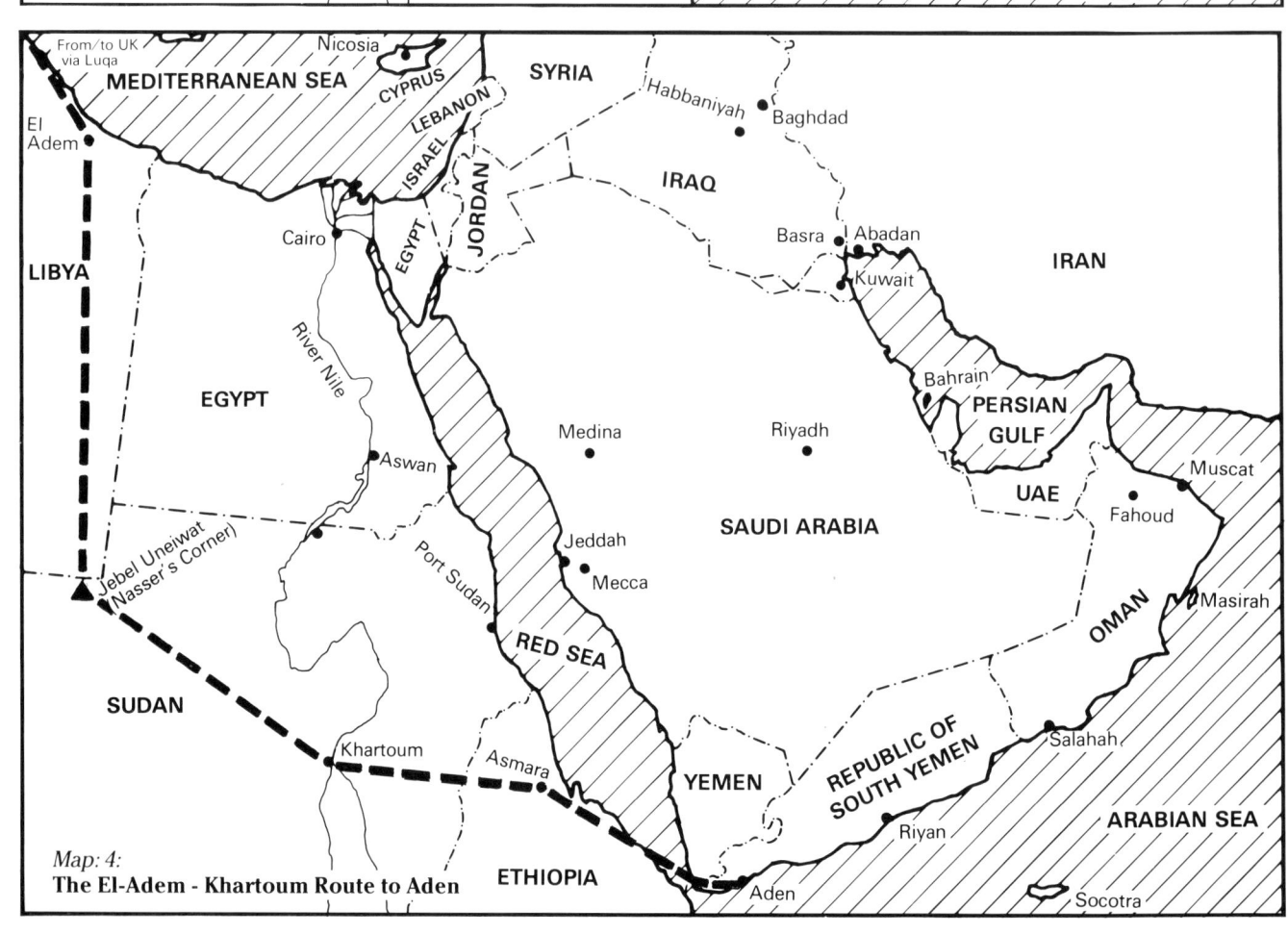

Map 3:
The Northabout Route To Aden

Map: 4:
The El-Adem – Khartoum Route to Aden

The Aden Routes

When Beverleys commenced flights to Aden, the route was via Malta, Cyprus, Habbaniyah, Bahrain and Masirah as shown in *Map 3*. This route was known as the 'Northabout' route and it can be seen from the map that this route was about three times the direct distance between Cyprus and Aden. Total mileage from the UK was about 5,000. Due to political differences with Syria and Saudi Arabia, overflying these countries was prohibited, hence the long hauls around Syria and the Trucial Oman Coast. Worsening political relations between the UK and Iraqi governments led to Habbaniyah being denied to Transport Command as a staging post. A new route was accordingly required and after some experimental trips via Kano and Entebbe, the El Adem-Khartoum route as shown in *Map 4* became standard. The route via Kano and Entebbe was occasionally used when flying out troops to Arabia, since the Sudanese government objected to planeloads of troops staging through Khartoum.

Soldiers packed into the freight bay. *BAe*

The El Adem-Khartoum route became known as the 'Southabout' route.

On this particular route political differences between the UK and Egypt resulting from the Suez campaign, prohibited overflying Egypt and in fact it was decidedly unhealthy to do so since the appearance of any British aircraft anywhere near the Egyptian border invited the attention of the Egyptian Air Force MiGs. Accordingly, the route from El Adem near Tobruk, as shown in *Map 4*, ran almost due south to Jebel Uneiwat in Sudan - a 6,500 foot high mountain and a prominent landmark situated almost on the borders of Egypt, Libya and Sudan. In deference to the then Egyptian president, Jebel Uneiwat became known as 'Nasser's corner' to Transport Command aircrew, since the Jebel (mountain) was the turning point for the Khartoum leg of the flight.

Sudanese ex-47 Squadron member

The first 47 Squadron Beverley to stage through Khartoum was met by an energetic Sudanese employee of BOAC who undertook to supply all the needs of the aircraft. He introduced himself as Ahmed Osman who had served with 47 Squadron, as a civilian tradesman from 1928 onwards until the squadron left its Khartoum base during the Second World War. Ahmed personally undertook to meet every Beverley staging through Khartoum and he became a familiar figure to Beverley crews as he rushed around organizing fuel, oil, oxygen and drinking water - all the requirements of a large transport aircraft during a refuelling stop. In appreciation of his loyalty, a 47 Squadron brooch was presented to Mr Osman, and later on, at the inviation of 47 Squadron, he came to Abingdon for four days where he was suitably entertained by the squadron personnel. How refreshing in those days, when practically every African and Arab was anti-British, to meet such a charming, pro-British Sudanese who did everything possible to assist the men of his old squadron and their associates.

When the rule of King Idris of Liyba came to an end, the new Libyan government gave the British their marching orders from Idris and El Adem and yet another route to Aden was sought. This is described in Chapter 4.

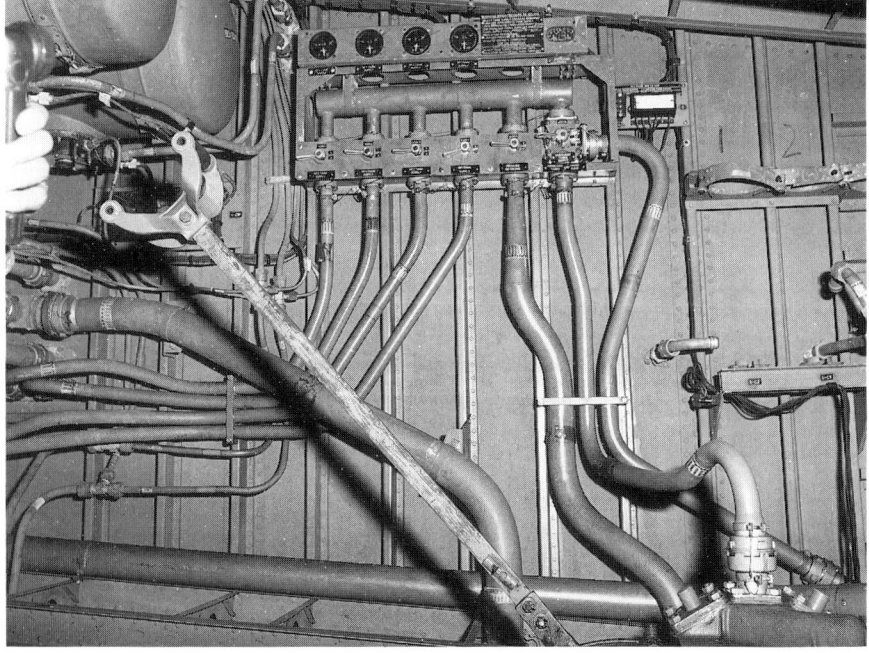

Jordan Emergency

Much of 1959 was occupied with Army support training, particularly developing supply dropping techniques. However, in June, the small kingdom of Jordan was threatened by Iraq and at King Hussein's request, a massive airlift of about 5,000 troops and their equipment from the UK to Cyprus was carried out with Comets, Shackletons and Hastings aircraft assisting the Beverley force from Abingdon Wing and 30 Squadron. Typical loads for each of the aircraft were quoted as follows: *Beverley* — 30 troops plus 9½ tonnes of freight, or 80 troops plus their equipment. *Comet* — 44 troops. *Hastings* — 45 troops. *Shackleton* — 31 troops.

From Cyprus, the troops and equipment were airlifted into Amman, Jordan, by seventeen Beverleys assisted by a number of Hastings. In 24 hours, 80 sorties were flown to transport 2,000 troops and their equipment; 114 tonnes of frieght; 6,000 gallons of fuel; and 120 vehicles and trailers. The Beverleys were mainly used for bulk freight carrying, but some aircraft also carried passengers in their 36-seat tail booms.

This impressive show of force stabilized the political situation in Jordan, but for good measure, the troops remained there for three months and were then brought out again in similar manner to that adopted by the inbound airlift. One 47 Squadron Beverley, skippered by Flight Lieutenant Ron Wing, arrived back at Abingdon with an unusual cargo comprising two Arab horses, a present from King Hussein to Her Majesty the Queen. The aircraft was met by a batttery of TV and film cameras.

Engineers Arrive

Also in June 1959, flight engineers were officially established as Beverley crew members. The original Beverley concept for a short-haul aircraft had with hindsight, wrongly made no provision for engineer crew members since it was thought that short-haul work could easily be handled by two pilots plus navigator, signaller and air quartermaster. However for their first two years of service, the Beverleys had to get by without autopilots and it was not until early '58 that the first Smith Mark 10 autopilot was fitted and proven. This meant that the aircraft had to be flown manually - an irksome chore on long route flights. It also meant that excessive demands were made on the co-pilots, who were responsible for engine handling, systems management, and pumping oil, by hand from the oil overload tanks in the 'dog kennel' to the ever oil-thirsty Centaurus engines, each of which consumed, on average, three gallons of oil per hour.

Early in 1957, 53 Squadron lost XH117 in a fatal crash near Abingdon. This accident was attributed to fuel starvation caused by

Opposite page, top: **Desert scene - XB267/B of 47 Squadron seen at Sebha Oasis in the Sahara; note the French Foreign Legion Fort in the background, and the Abingdon crest on the nose beneath 'Transport Command' titling.** *J. Knight*

Opposite page, centre: **Entering the 'dog kennel' of XH124 of the Royal Air Force Museum.** *Author*

Opposite page, bottom: **Inside the 'dog kennel' showing the oil transfer pump, oil contents gauges and selector cocks.** *Author*

First pilot's position and instrument panels. *Author*

a fuel system non-return valve having been fitted the wrong way round. In February 1958, 30 Squadron lost XH118 in a crash at Beihan, South Arabia, which caused one fatality. It was rumoured that this accident was also due to fuel starvation. Further incidents, happily of a minor nature, involving fuel system management, occurred from time to time until it was decided to put 'another pair of hands and eyes' on the flight deck of each Beverley in the form of a flight engineer. Accordingly, Modification 513 made provision for a folding jump seat, located behind and between the two pilots, together with safety harness, intercom point and oxygen supply for the engineer.

The engineers took over systems management and the often Herculean task of oil pumping (no joke at 12,000 feet with no oxygen), leaving the co-pilots free to perform duties more appropriate to their trade and to gain suitable flying experience to fit them for future captaincy. The establishment of flight engineers proved highly successful since as skilled tradesmen, they were able to undertake repairs, not only in flight, but also on the ground thus greatly contributing to the efficient operation of the aircraft.

Berlin Flights Commence

By mid-'59, Berlin flights were a regular feature of the Wing's activites. In March, Russia and East Germany adopted an obdurate policy concerning the entry of persons and consumer goods into Berlin, and vehicles were subjected to long delays at the infamous 'Checkpoint Charlie'. HM Government decided that should this obduracy develop into another Berlin blockade, then Transport Command must prepare itself for yet another Berlin airlift. Berlin flights were accordingly inaugurated to give crews practice in corridor flying and also to demonstrate to the oppositon that the UK was determined to preserve her right to fly the corridors to Berlin.

Exercise Bar Frost

The Beverley had by now been well blooded in tropical conditions but had not yet operated to any degree at squadron level in Arctic conditions. Exercise *Bar Frost*, a NATO exercise mounted at Vaernes airfield near Trondheim, Norway, provided the opportunity for the Beverley force to prove its worth in low-temperature conditions. But with typical meteorological awkwardness, conditions at Vaernes were mild, muddy and humid. However, the Beverley force, backed up by eleven Hastings, dropped many hundreds of troops at Bardufoss within the Arctic Circle.

Supplies were air-landed by Beverleys due to adverse weather preventing aerial delivery, and the recovery phase was carried out without incident. *Bar Frost* was stated at the time to have been the largest NATO exercise since the organisation was formed.

The Royal Navy's participation in *Bar Frost* was highlighted by the ubiquitous Russian trawler 'happening to be in the area'. This was fortuitous since this trawler rescued the crew of a Naval Skyraider which had been forced to ditch, reportedly due to engine failure.

Most of the Vaernes detachment, by way of light relief, took the opportunity to 'go to Hell'. This was a delightful and typical Norwegian village situated just outside the airfield perimeter.

Grandfather Pilot

In October 1959, Flight Lieutenant 'Taff' Richards distinguished himself by becoming the first recorded grandfather in Transport Command. Taff was well known throughout the Command and was characterized by his cheerfulness and his 'rough diamond' type of humour. He was known to most of the NCOs and other ranks as 'Effendi' (Turkish for 'Lord' or 'Master', a word used widely throughout the Near and Middle East), due to the fact that during the Omani uprising, he had acquired a colourful Arabian headdress from an officer of the Trucial Oman Scouts, this head-gear being part of the Scouts' official uniform. Taff occasionally wore this attire, and his rotund figure plus his beaming countenance was said to make him resemble an opulent Arab. He was not only a first-class pilot and captain, but also an excellent engineer with first-rate practical skills, which he often demonstrated when tasks, such as loading and off-loading items of freight, and rectification of snags were being carried out by his crew at

The flight engineer's seat, located behind and between the two pilot's seats, folded to give access to the rear flight deck. The row of six dials are fuel flow meters. *Author*

remote airstrips. Before leaving 47 Squadron, Taff made the headlines in the local press by driving, during a week's leave, an old steam traction engine, from the Midlands to his home in Wales.

The closing months of 1959 were uneventful apart from Exercise *Dry Martini* which was mounted at Nicosia and involved dropping troops and vehicles at Derna. This was a prelude to Exercise *Starlight* which was being planned for 1960.

38 Group Forms - Exercise Starlight
In January 1960, 38 Group formed up and incorporated the Beverley force and other tactical medium-range units. The build-up for Exercise *Starlight* also commenced with the Wing flying out all the paraphernalia for a major 'war game', plus helicopters of 215 Squadron, to El Adem. *Starlight* was a massive airborne assault exercise, specially designed to test the Beverleys in constant operation from a rough, virtually unprepared airstrip. The strip selected was Tmimi, a Second World War airfield, which was resurrected by HQ MEAF (Cyprus).

Squadron Leader Reeder (Ret'd), a flight lieutenant at the time of *Starlight*, writes: 'I, as Signals Officer at HQ MEAF, was 'chosen' to take the advance ground party via El Adem, along the coast road towards Derna in a convoy of twenty eight vehicles and fifty six men in January 1960. These vehicles and men were installed at Tmimi to provide communications, airfield control, CRDF, medical, domestic, security and administrative facilities for the exercise.

'The main party and aircraft arrived two weeks later when all facilities were working. The main party was commanded by Wing Commander G. Sproates from HQ MEAF. He became CO of RAF Tmimi during the ensuing two months.

'Beverley aircraft operated continuously during the exercise between Cyprus, El Adem and Tmimi, moving heavy loads of supplies, personnel and vehicles. Pioneers (Single and Twin) operated forward of Tmimi to support troops logistically and to carry out casevac by day and night, but the main task at Tmimi was to handle Beverleys. On the desert surface, these heavy aircraft gouged deep furrows and

Flight Lieutenant Reeder's convoy en route for Tmimi for Exercise *Starlight*, February 1960. *F. Reeder*

Airfield control caravan at Tmimi for Exercise *Starlight*. *F. Reeder*

Beverleys taking off from Tmimi. The engines seemed to keep going with the minimum of service - a tribute to the system of air intake filtering. *F. Reeder*

moved masses of sand with their slipstream, so much so that during each day's opertions the Beverleys were axle deep in sand during take-offs and landings. Ground parties were deployed each evening to move the airstrip bodily sideways for the next day's operations. The accompanying photographs give some idea of these conditions in which all ground-handling crews had to wear breathing masks and eye-shields in the perpetual sand clouds made by the aircraft. Nevertheless, the engines seemed to keep going with the mimimum of service - a tribute to the system of air intake filtering.

'Since this was the first exercise of its kind, many high-ranking officers were interested in its conduct. The photograph below taken in our mess tent, shows a fair amount of double gold braid on VIP visitors' caps! Among the vistors were Air Vice Marshal Peter Wykeham, Air Vice Marshal Weir (SASO MEAF) Air Commodore MacDonald (C-in-C MEAF), the Director of Signals, Air Ministry, General Harrington and many others whom I cannot now remember.'

There is little to add to the Squadron Leader's letter except that the Tmimi airstrip was 800 yards long and that the Beverley force comprised twelve aircraft. Their maximum utilization was twenty eight sorties into and out of Tmimi in one day. The Air Officer Commanding 38 Group at the time of *Starlight*, Air Vice Marshal P.G. Wykeham, also wrote of Tmimi: 'The surface, restricted because the landing ground was bordered by wadis, soon broke up and became quite appalling. It was a horrid mixture of loose dust and rocks, which would bog a normal car, deeply rutted and far worse than a ploughed field. This unattractive surface received over 200 fully loaded Beverley landings and, I am glad to say, a similar number of take-offs. Most people who saw the performance compared it to a flying boat landing, and it was our opinion that no other aeroplane in the world could have done it.

'The Beverleys were magnificent, and in spite of this treatment, their serviceability remained between 85 and 95 percent for the whole exercise. They certainly stole the show'.

After the 'land battle', the troops were airlifted to Derna. Many VIPs flew on Exercise *Starlight* including the late Lord Louis Mountbatten and the Chief of the Air Staff. Airlift statistics for the Beverley force are as follows: *Passengers* 3,987, *Vehicles* 672, *Guns (25 pounders)* 40, *General freight (tonnes)* 1,150.

53 Squadron's Guinness Connections
How the association between the Guinness brewery and 53 Squadron came about is not quite clear, but it is known that Flight Lieutenant Peter Lewis was deeply involved. The association blossomed, with Messrs. Guinness 'adopting' 53 Squadron and entertaining the squadron personnel at visits to the Park Royal brewery in London where 47 Squadron's assertion that 53 'couldn't organize a 'booze-up' in a brewery' was invariably disproved.

A large papier-mache toucan was presented by Guinness to the squadron and was adopted as the squadron mascot enjoying a prominent position in the crew room. Sometimes it would be taken on prestigious route trips. A squadron tie with a motif combining a Beverley and the toucan was also produced, a photograph of which appears opposite.

Cameroons Interlude
The early months of 1960 passed without any noteworthy incident; however, both squadrons were kept busy on routine flights to Aden and other places in the Middle East. These flights were a boon to personnel stationed at Middle East bases, particularly Khormaksar as there was invariably space available on UK-bound Beverleys for private cars. Thus, tour-expired personnel were able, due to an indulgence passage scheme, to get their cars shipped home for a nominal fee.

In May, a 53 Squadron aircraft, XB284, flew out to Bangui in French Equatorial Africa, returning via Mamfe in the Cameroons and Kano, Nigeria. Due to Nigeria's forthcoming independence, the British armed forces undertook patrol duties in the Cameroons. A base was established at Mamfe and a squadron of Twin Pioneer aircraft operated from there, airlifting troops and their supplies to any trouble spots. Mamfe was supplied almost completely by the UK-based Beverley force, and personnel, food, arms, ammunition and vehicles were flown to Mamfe via Idris and Kano.

Casevac Duties
Although the Beverley was occasionally used in the casevac (air ambulance) role on exercises, it seldom performed in this role with 'real' casualties. The freight bay could be rigged with a total of forty eight stretchers and the boom provided seating accommodation for thirty four walking wounded. But the horrendous noise in the freight bay, together with intense vibration from the engines, precluded the use of the Beverley for any large-scale casevac operations.

However, with remote outposts like Mamfe, possessing only a rough grass airstrip, few aircraft but the Beverley could be used to airlift casualties to airports like Kano, where the casualties could be transferred to the carpeted and pressurized comfort of the 'shiny fleet' - the Comets, Britannias, and later, the VC-10s. Thus some casevac work was done on the Mamfe to Kano legs, with just the required amount of stretchers rigged, in what was considered to be the least noisy, draught-free and vibration-free areas of the freight bay. A drawing of the freight bay rigged for casevac duties is shown opposite.

Operation Full Cock
In July 1960, trouble in the Belgian Congo, now named Zaire, flared up with the Congolese population revolting against the Belgian colonists. Because of the atrocities committed by the Congolese forces, it became imperative to evacuate the Belgian civilians.

Accordingly, the Beverley force was called in on one of its many mercy missions, this one being code-named Operation *Half Cock*. A detachment from each of the Abingdon squadrons quickly flew out to Accra in Ghana, and from there, operated a shuttle service between Leopoldville and Ghana, flying out European civilians,

Officers Mess tent at Tmimi showing headgear of visiting brass. Visitors included Lord Louis Mountbatten, the Chief of the Air Staff, C-in-C Transport Command, AOC 38 Group and C-in-C MEAF. *F. Reeder*

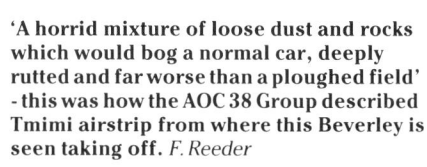

'A horrid mixture of loose dust and rocks which would bog a normal car, deeply rutted and far worse than a ploughed field' - this was how the AOC 38 Group described Tmimi airstrip from where this Beverley is seen taking off. *F. Reeder*

53 Squadron tie with Guinness toucan/ Beverley motif. *Author*

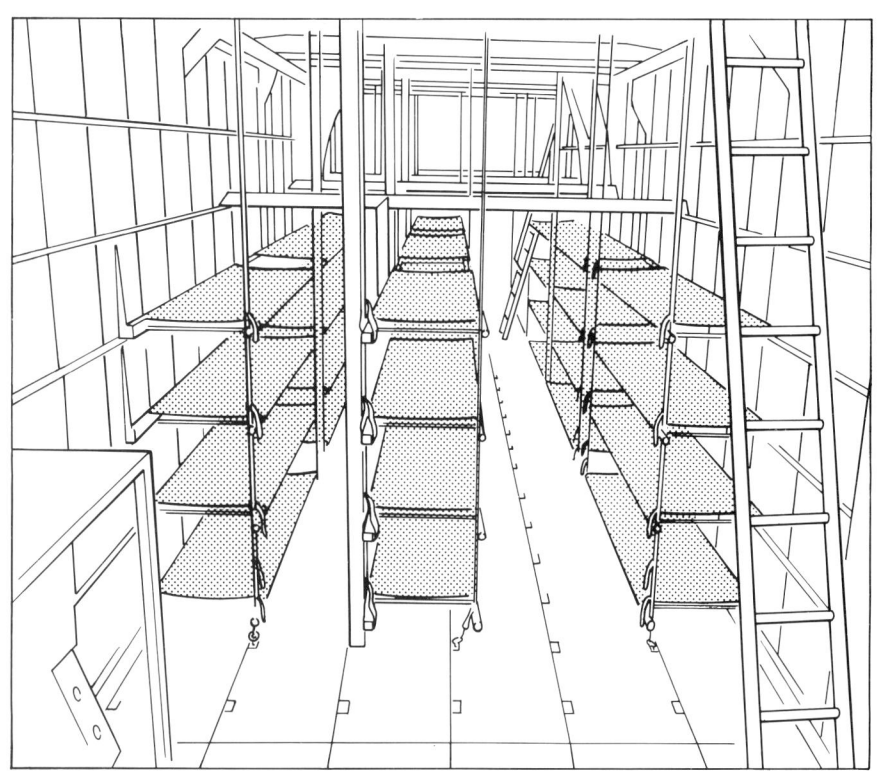

Artist's impression of freight bay rigged in the air ambulance (casevac) role. *W. Wright*

mainly women and children. On the inbound flights to Leopoldville, UNO troops, who were instrumental in stabilizing the situation eventually, were carried together with food, medical supplies and vehicles. Aircraft from 30 Squadron, based at Eastleigh near Nairobi, were also involved in evacuating Belgian refugees and John Ward, ex-air quartermaster (AQM) recalls an amusing incident:

He writes: 'We went to Entebbe to pick up a load of Belgian refugees. I got all these refugees up into the boom but none could speak English. However, this superb air stewardess came on board (she was with an airline somehow involved in the operation) and she said that she would brief my passengers. She stood just above the entry hatch from the freight bay to the boom, and looking up, the view was very interesting (AQM's perks).

'So I called the captain to come and have a look. He thought the view was fantastic and said to me: 'Aren't I the lucky fellow I'm getting married to her shortly.' I thought he was joking but it was true!'

Exercise Holdfast

September 1960, saw the Wing participating in Exercise *Holdfast*. Mounted from Sylt, with troops of the 16th Parachute Brigade, aircrew and ground crew living under canvas, the exercise was an airborne assault on the Kiel Canal. This exercise was reported at that time to have been the heaviest concentration of air-dropped troops and equipment this side of the Iron Curtain since the Second World War. In two lifts, 47 Squadron dropped 580 troops and sixteen supply platforms; in the third lift the squadron dropped 540 troops and twelve platforms. A similar number of troops and supplies were dropped by 53 Squadron, the total weight of supplies dropped by the squadron being sixty three tonnes.

The CARP aiming sight

To date, paratroops and supplies had been dropped mainly by the 'eyeballs Mark 1' of many navigators. When dropping troops, an experienced para would often drop as a 'drifter', allowing himself to reach the ground without any attempt to steer himself, to enable the navigator establish conditions and plan his sighting technique accordingly. A 'bean bag', a sack of similar size and weight to that of a paratrooper, was also used for this purpose on occasions. But experienced paratroops could, by manipulation of their rigging lines, often make good a navigator's error and put themselves down on the DZ successfully. This did not apply to heavy drop platforms however, and there were many irate farmers in Berkshire and Oxfordshire whose crops had been damaged by mis-dropped platforms.

Wing Commander A.A.J. Sanders, 53 Squadron's CO, recognized this shortcoming and being a bombing specialist, produced, in October 1960, with the aid of Flight Lieutenant Weir, a workable drop-sight. The CARP (Calculated Air Release Point) technique was used in conjunction with the instrument and proved successful, allowing a much greater accuracy to be achieved with supply dropping than hitherto. The drop-sight was further developed and later was used throughout the Beverley Force, being known officially as the 'CARP aiming sight'.

'Clipkey' Bomber Command Standby

This was introduced in December 1960 when it was decided that under certain states of alert, Bomber Command's V-bombers and ground crews would be dispersed to a large number of airfields away from their home bases, thus making the V-force much less vulnerable to surprise attack. No other aircraft but the Beverley could lift the ground crew together with all the equipment for V-bomber servicing to the dispersal airfields.

A standby system was accordingly implemented, ranging from crews being on immediate readiness, and standing by in their quarters or messes; to a six-hour standby, where crews had to remain on camp, with ears tuned to the Tannoy; up to a 12-hour standby where crewmen could leave camp so long as they were on the end of a telephone. This was something of a chore but there were many practice scrambles with crews, and indeed squadrons, competing with each other to see who could get airborne the quickest. This put some interest into what could otherwise have become a very boring exercise. However, to keep the Wing on its toes, there were many alerts. Sometimes, aircraft were recalled to base shortly after getting airborne, but sometimes they 'went the whole hog' and completed the airlift to the dispersal airfields - places such as St Mawgan and Kinloss.

Flight Lieutenant Hugh Crawley of 53 Squadron claimed the scramble record, getting airborne in thirty five minutes on a practice alert. A long time, one may think, but the Beverley was a very large aircraft in those days, with a multitude of pre-flight checks to be carried out, and in view of the fact that passengers were to be carried, flight safety was never jeopardized. The 'Clipkey' routine became almost a way of life, but after two or three years it seemed to peter out much to relief of the Beverley force in general.

Operation Private Eye

This operation, although of great value, had a somewhat ludicrous twist. Elections were taking place in Nigeria and a referendum in the Cameroons, so two 53 Squadron Beverleys, XB290 and XB287 captained by Flight Lieutenants Lewis and Herbert respectively, were detached to Nigeria. All personnel were detailed to wear civilian clothes although no attempt was made to conceal the military markings on the aircraft. The supposedly cloak and dagger nature of this detachment therefore, seemed to fall completely flat. However, the participants agreed that those in high places knew best.

The detachment, which flew out a Single Pioneer complete with pilots and ground crew, to a small Northern Nigerian airstrip named Mubi, was based at Kano. The Pioneer flew around the Mubi district, on air observation duties. From Kano, the two Beverleys made frequent trips to Mamfe, flying in food and supplies to the garrison there. Flights were also made to potential trouble spots carrying vehicles in the Beverleys' freight compartments and Nigerian police in the tail booms. The police supervised the elections, and having ensured that they were properly conducted, were flown back to their bases. Places visited included Kaduna, Iola, Mubi and Maiduguri.

A highlight of the detachment was flying the Land Rover, belonging to the District Commissioner of Mubi, back to Kano for repair. After the vehicle had been overhauled, it was flown back to Mubi again where it arrived as new, having been spared the 400 mile drive over the appalling roads and tracks in that area. To fill up the freight bay, food and other supplies, plus the DC's yearly beer ration, were airlifted to Mubi together with the Land Rover. After off-loading, the aircraft was prepared for return to Kano, but a radio message stated that Kano was 'out' due to poor visibility caused by dust in suspension - in other words, a sand storm. The decision was therefore made to night-stop at Mubi, and crew members were farmed out as one-night lodgers to the European community.

The DC must have thought that this occasion called for a party, as he summoned, presumably by radio, all his neighbours who were scattered around the bush. These included missionaries, doctors, nurses, schoolteachers and forestry officials, who all arrived in remarkably quick time. A goat was barbecued, there was dancing on the DC's verandah, and a very convivial time was had by all. Next morning saw the DC ruefully surveying his newly replenished beer stocks, now sadly depleted by the binge of the previous night. After saying their farewells to their host and hostesses, the crew climbed aboard XB290 and flew back to Kano after one or two low-level beat-ups of Mubi. During a subsequent slack period, a 'training flight' was laid on to Mubi and a fresh supply of beer was delivered to a much relieved DC.

So ended Operation *Private Eye*, another demonstration of the Beverley's ability to move personnel and supplies into and out of remote outposts at short notice.

Operation Oliver

This operation was planned in March 1961 to airlift food into the Turkhana region of Northern Kenya. The annual rains had failed to arrive for the third year in succession and a serious famine situation existed. At about the same time, political disturbances in East Africa led to a request for assistance being made to HM Government. This resulted in a force of seven Beverleys, commanded by the OC 53 Squadron, being detached to Eastleigh, to provide air mobility for the military forces in East Africa. In the event, the political situation stabilized and because of this, the opportunity was taken to implement Operation *Oliver*, and 57 tonnes of supplies were either air-landed or dropped to help alleviate the famine.

Exercise Flat Earth

This exercise was another demonstration of the Beverley's extraordinary versatility and of the Royal Engineers' skills and capacity for sheer hard work. On 24th June, 200 Royal Engineers were parachuted, together with earthmoving equipment, on to a rough piece of scrubland in Norfolk, called Robins Lodge, near Stanford. After thirty three hours continuous work, a 750 x 50 yard strip had been levelled, cleared and re-turfed. Beverley XH116, captained by Flight Lieutenant Andruskeiwicz, then landed without difficulty on 'Flat Earth Airstrip', delivering welcome supplies to the weary sappers. XH116 then returned to Abingdon leaving the Army to pack up their equipment and return to base by road. There were many subsequent *Flat Earth* exercises but the first as described above, demonstrated dramatically the Army's and the RAF's capabilities when using that rugged maid-of-all-work, the Beverley.

Operation Vantage

On 19th June 1961, the treaty of 1899 between HM Government and the ruler of Kuwait was abrogated. A week later, Kuwait was threatened by Iraqi forces and the ruler of Kuwait requested the UK's assistance. All 53 Squadron crews were called to immediate readiness and flights to Aden, to position troops and equipment, were begun. Take-offs for these flights were permitted at the emergency all-up weight of 65 tonnes instead of the normal all-up weight of 62 tonnes. The flights were flown in two legs each of approximately twelve hours duration, with a welcome night stop at El Adem.

The author standing behind the first pilot on the flight deck. *C. Pearson*

Refuelling the hard way at Maiduguri in Northern Nigeria. The airport staff, fasting for Ramadan were lethargic so the crew had to hand pump 800 gallons into XB290. *Author*

Some aircraft however, merely 'flag-stopped' for refuelling at El Adem, where fresh crews, previously positioned there, took the aircraft over for the leg to Khormaksar. In July the operation, now codenamed *Vantage*, assumed a much greater urgency and ten Beverleys from the Abingdon Wing were detached to Khormaksar under the command of Wing Commander A. A. J. Sanders, OC 53 Squadron. This force backed up the Middle East Beverley force consisting of 30 and 84 Squadrons.

The Operation *Vantage* Beverley force flew sorties between Khormaksar and Kuwait, usually staging through Bahrain, and carrying troops, weapons and vehicles. The vehicles included Saracen armoured cars and Ferret light tanks. The bulk of the Strategic Reserve, about 7,000 men and their equipment, was flown by Beverley into Kuwait. In addition, RAF personnel and equipment for six Hunter/Canberra squadrons were airlifted, by Beverley, into Kuwait airport, then in only a partially completed condition. Again the Beverleys were operating at emergency all-up weights and many hair-raising take-offs were reported due to the hot and humid conditions of Aden and the Persian Gulf. One aircraft suffered engine failure immediately after take-off from Khormaksar and despite using full take-off power could only maintain a height of about fifty feet by using the ground cushion air effect. After an incredibly low, and slow circuit, a successful three-engined landing was made.

But this was against regulations. The maximum permissible landing weight was sixty-two tonnes. However with no fuel jettison system or any other means of reducing weight quickly, the captain had no alternative but to land his aircraft, especially as the temperatures of his three remaining engines were rapidly going 'off the clocks'. The aircraft was checked over thoroughly to see if any damage had been sustained by this overweight landing, but no damage was found - another tribute to the robust construction of the Beverley.

Another case was reported of a Beverley making repeated unsuccessful attempts to get airborne but each time aborted the take-off after failing the acceleration time check. The crew taxied the aircraft back to dispersal where the captain demanded a re-count of the weights of the varied items of cargo. It was then discovered that a lorry, loaded with about eight tonnes of ammunition, had been inadvertently manifested as an empty vehicle. An emergency all-up weight of 65 tonnes the Beverley could handle, but she drew the line at an all-up weight of 73 tonnes, an increase of 11 tonnes over the normal all-up weight. A cartoon, produced in contemporary edition of *Air Clues*, depicts the weary aircraft limping back to dispersal.

The work done in Operation *Vantage* recalled the words of Marshal of the Royal Air Force Sir John Slessor, quoted in *Flight* in November 1955: 'We have got to have a highly mobile reserve of land forces ready to move from A to B with their bulky equipment, which in my belief is another way of saying 'Beverley'. But *Vantage* took its toll of the Beverley force. Terrorists' time bombs damaged a 30 Squadron aircraft and wrote off an 84 Squadron aircraft: these incidents are described in Chapter 4. The weather was appalling too, the Inter Tropical Front prevailed from Khartoum through Asmara, Aden and Karachi, producing thunderstorms and other extreme meteorological conditions that even the Beverley was hard pressed to withstand. XB269, for example, sustained 36-inch long splits in the skin plating after flying through severe turbulence. It was tiring work for crews as well: in July 1961, the UK Beverley force flew over 1,700 hours instead of its normal monthly quota of 800.

However, *Vantage* did what the planners had intended and the enormous military force airlifted into Kuwait resulted in the Iraqi threat subsiding. Astute diplomatic moves then secured a guarantee of Kuwaiti independence by the Arab League, and the Strategic Reserve and RAF Hunter and Canberra squadrons were withdrawn.

Squadrons Rest

After the strenuous efforts of Operation *Vantage*, 47 and 53 Squadrons were officially resting during August. But even during a squadron's rest period, paratroops need practice, the Territorial Army, that famous 'mob of week-enders', need training and there was always some enormous piece of equipment that required airlifting to some remote outpost. So, in parallel with resting, 47 Squadron managed to log 233 hours and carry 25 tonnes of freight; 53 Squadron logged 277 hours and flew 136 sorties.

Beverleys Participate at Farnborough

This privilege fell to 53 Squadron; in September, four aircraft participated in the SBAC show, flying in troops, guns and vehicles to attack and demolish a set-piece fort in front of the public enclosure. The Beverleys did a stream landing, opening up their clamshell doors and lowering ramps as they rolled to a halt, whereupon the troops and vehicles deplaned in the record time of 150 seconds. The Beverleys then reversed back up the runway while raising ramps and closing doors, and finally roared off in a spectacular short-field stream take-off, leaving their erstwhile occupants to carry on with the show. Squadron Leader E. Strangeway led the formation and the whole exercise received an excellent press. This was a typical Beverley air-show demonstration which always characterized the performance of the Beverley in such events.

Kenya Flood Relief

In October 1961, the Tana river in Kenya burst its banks and in the worst flooding for many years, large districts and towns including Nairobi were completely cut off by the destruction of roads and railways. This led to a food shortage and another request to the UK for Beverley assistance. A detachment of four Beverleys, commanded by Squadron Leader Strangeway, was dispatched to Kenya, conveniently delivering four Sycamore helicopters. The laterite airstrip at Eastleigh was waterlogged and unfit for use, so 30 Squadron's aircraft and the Abingdon Wing detachment operated from Embakasi, Nairobi's airport

Resting during the 14-hour leg from Abingdon to El Adem. This pilot, believed to be Squadron Leader 'Paddy' King, takes a nap in the co-pilot's seat. *J. Knight*

47 AND 53 SQUADRONS

During the 1961 emergency, Beverleys were obliged to use the unfinished Kuwait Airport as this photo clearly shows.
B. Thatcher

It was: the truck in this Beverley carried a 10-tonne payload which had not been included in the loading calculations.
Crown Copyright (via Air Clues)

They suspected that the aircraft was overloaded . . . .

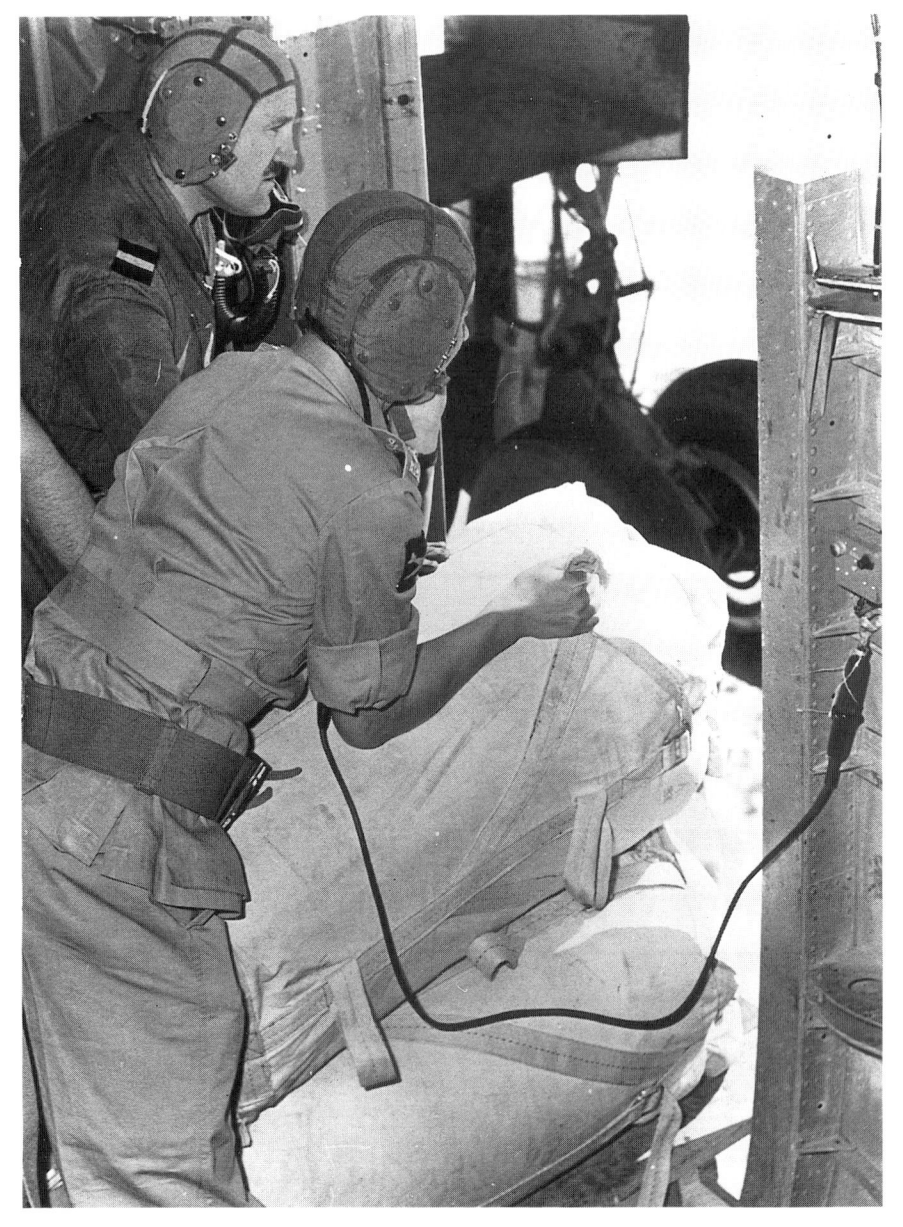

which had concrete runways. Operations started immediately and food was free-dropped by soldiers of No.16 Air Despatch Company, RASC.

The food, consisting mainly of maize, rice and flour, was dropped in 90 kilo 'Derby' sacks made of closely woven jute. These sacks were specially designed for free-dropping by the Army, and worked on the double-sack principle. The food was first sewn into an inner sack measuring about 33 x 33 inches. This sack was then placed in an outer sack measuring about 36 x 36 inches. The outer sack was then closed. The theory was that if the inner sack burst on impact with the ground, the outer sack would restrain the contents. It invariably did.

Drops were made at fifty feet, often on extremely difficult DZs. The average load dropped per sortie was ten tonnes but the DZs were so small that only approximately 1,300 kilos could be dropped at a time. This necessitated seven or eight, and sometimes more runs over the DZ, requiring a high degree of concentration from the pilot who, for the drop, had to maintain a precise altitude of fifty feet, using the radio altimeter.

The supplies were dropped from each para-door at the rear of the freight bay, the sacks being piled on a SEAC board, so named because it was designed for supply dropping in Burma during the Second World War. When the green 'drop' light came on, the despatchers simply lifted the end of the board, which was positioned at the para-door, and the sacks slid off the tilted board, out of the aircraft and hopefully, on to the DZ.

Supplies were dropped at numerous places, some too remote to be shown on any map; better known places such as Garissa, Marsabit and Malindi also received air-dropped supplies. In Northern Kenya supplies were dropped in the Turkhana region, in the vicinity of Lake

Above left: **Over Lodwar in the Turkana area, Air Commodore McDonald, Commander RAF East Africa, surveys terrain below while a soldier of No.16 Air Despatch Company stands by to release 100 lb food containers to the starving Kenyans below.** *Crown Copyright*

Left: **'Master switch on'. Flight Lieutenant Stan Hitchen arms the supply dropping signalling system during the run-in for a free drop from 50 feet during the Kenyan flood relief operations.** *S. Hitchen*

Page opposite, top: **Damage resulting from an engine fire (successfully extinguished and propeller feathered).** *C. Pearson*

Page opposite, bottom: **Kenyan countryside near Nairobi in the 1961 floods showing bridges (arrowed) washed away.** *S. Hitchen*

Rudolf at Lokitaung and Lodwar. A map of Kenya is shown on page 54. At one time, with road and rail links destroyed by the floods, Nairobi was completely cut off and shortages of consumer goods soon became evident. The Armed Forces ran short of MT fuel, and as a result, some Beverleys were deployed to Mombasa to airlift petrol, in drums, back to Nairobi for use by the RAF and the Army. On the flood relief operations, the UK Beverley force dropped 7,273 tonnes of supplies and the Governor of Kenya expressed his congratulations and appreciation of the efforts of the Abingdon Wing. So ended another Beverley mercy operation which was widely reported in the British and East African press. The operation was finished by mid-December, and all aircraft and personnel arrived home for Christmas.

More Middle East Standbys and Operation Dark Bottle

The festive season over, the Wing soon returned to business which started with a stand-by for Aden and a 47 Squadron detachment being sent out to Bahrain because of disturbances there. Despite these interruptions, 53 Squadron still managed to organize another outing to the Guinness Park Royal Brewery.

In February 1962, the Russians and East Germans stated that they needed the UK's air corridors to Berlin for tactical exercises. This was interpreted as an illegal move to take over the corridors. As a result, a Beverley force was detached, on Operation *Dark Bottle*, to Wildenrath from where probing sorties were flown into the corridors, in order to exercise the UK's legal right to use them. There were frequent interferences by Russian fighters, but the Beverleys stood their ground and eventually, won this round of the Cold War.

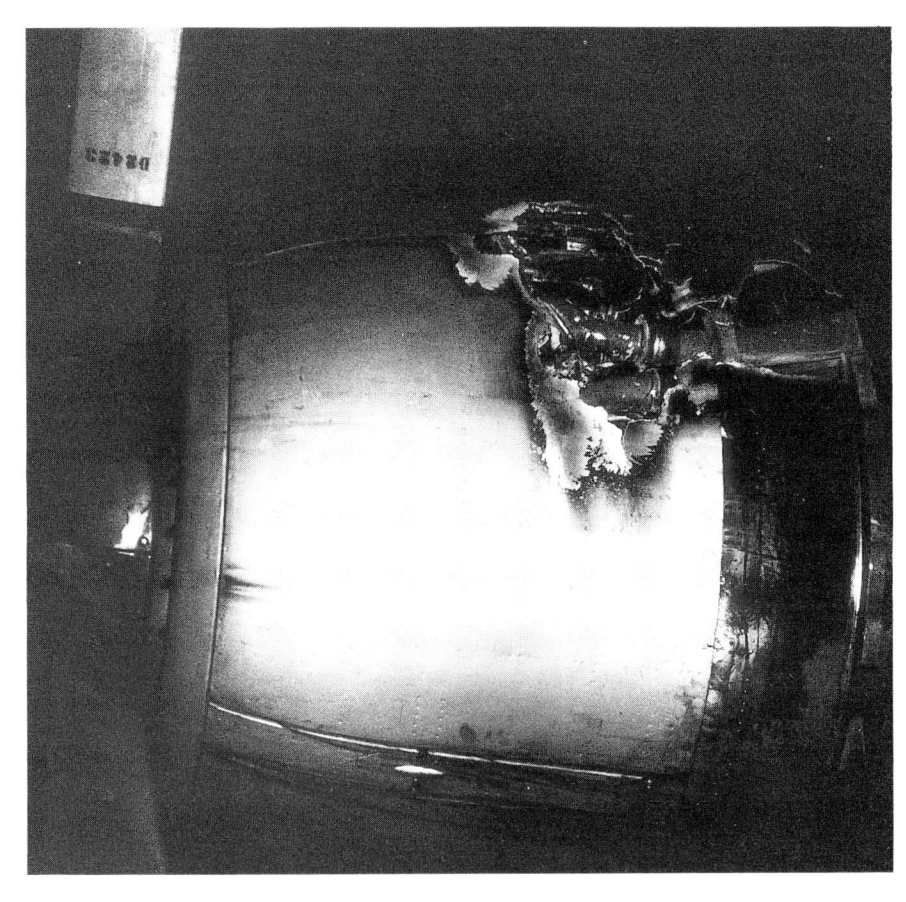

Beverley Force Grounded

May 1962 brought trouble in the form of a series of engine failures, and numerous crews experienced sudden engine failures accompanied by fire. Squadron Leader E. Strangeway, en route from Denmark to Abingdon, had an engine failure with uncontrollable fire over the North Sea. He managed to divert safely to Schiphol airport, Amsterdam. Shortly afterwards, 242 OCU at Thorney Island lost a Beverley with two fatalities as a result of an uncontrollable engine fire.

The trouble was traced to faulty cylinder holding down bolts which were shearing, causing the cylinders to blow off, sometimes with catastrophic results. The Beverley fleet was grounded while remedial action was taken. This action later resulted in the Centaurus 173 engines being replaced by the much improved Centaurus 175 series.

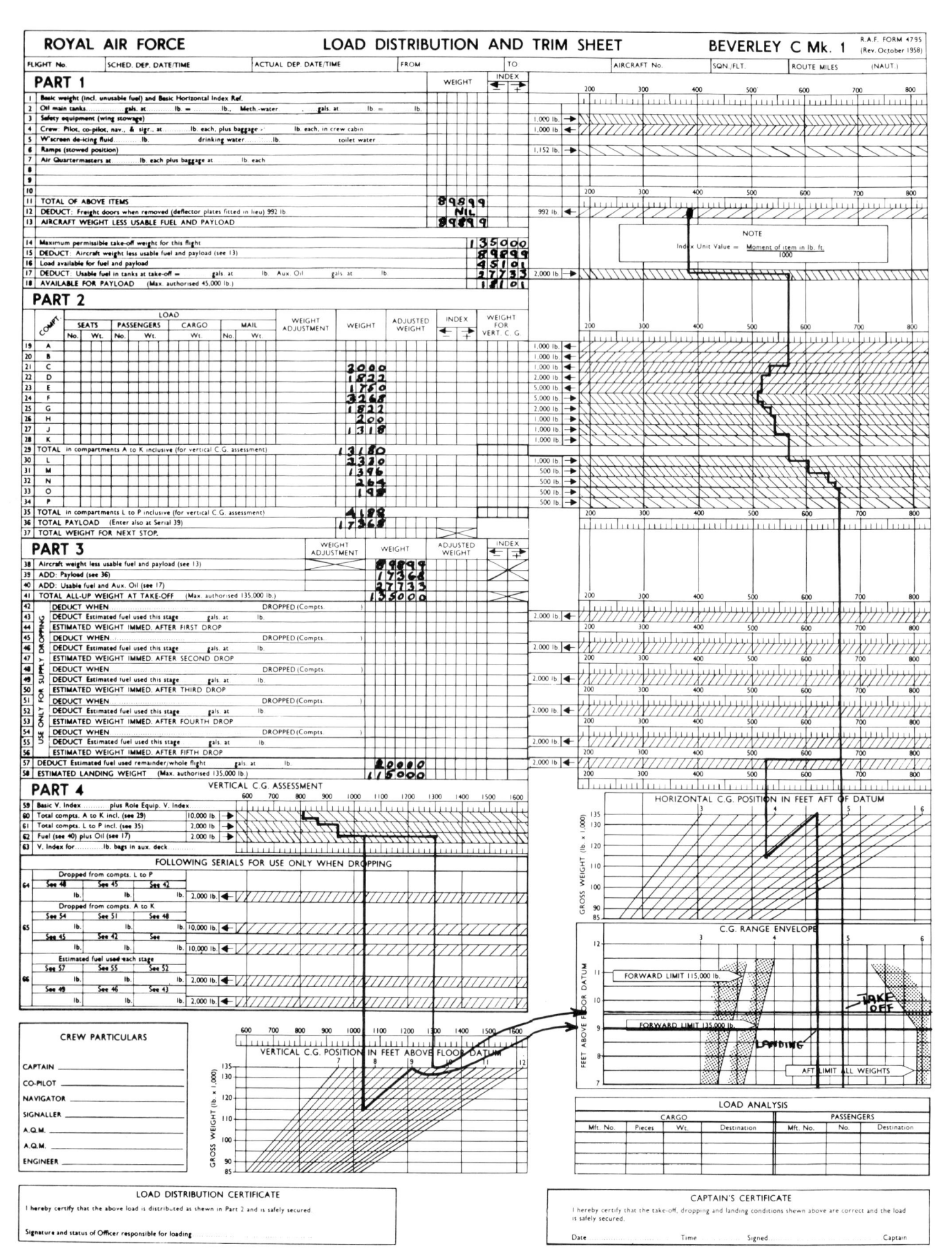

Specimen trim sheet as used for training AQMs. The Beverley trim sheet posed problems for newcomers: due to the height of the freight bay, a vertical CG (centre of gravity) had to be calculated in addition to the normal horizontal CG. *via JATE Brize Norton*

AQMs Become Full-time Aircrew

It is not generally known that up to 1962, air quartermasters were only part-time aircrew and wore no flying badges. These men, many of whom were ex-air gunners, an aircrew trade now extinct, had volunteered to become air quartermasters in order to continue flying, the only way of life known to most of these men. A small amount of flying pay went with the job but this was only a fraction of full-time aircrew flying pay. In addition, AQMs did not enjoy the same promotion prospects as their aircrew colleagues: thus there was little but a love of flying to attract personnel to the job.

On the 'shiny' long-range fleet, the AQMs performed the role of steward, attending to the needs of the passengers and crew and being responsible for the safe loading and security of baggage and sometimes, small amounts of freight. On the medium-range tactical force, however, which included the Beverleys, Hastings and Argosies, in addition to attending passengers and crew, the AQMs were also responsible for the cargo. This was often an enormous piece of equipment which in flight, had to be constantly checked to ensure that it was firmly secured.

The medium-range force AQMs were also responsible for loading and unloading at remote airfields which had no air movements staff. They also had to prepare the trim sheet, a document (see page 42) which gave precise details of the weight and disposition of the various items which made up the payload. In the days when pocket calculators were unknown, and only the more affluent AQMs could afford slide-rules, preparation of a Beverley trim sheet caused many mental gymnastics. Other tasks undertaken by AQMs of the medium range tactical force were dispatching paratroops and, in the early days of the Beverley, releasing heavy drop loads. Dispatching paratroops was fairly straightforward but occasionally a refusal had to be dealt with. Releasing a heavy drop load, in essence, merely involved pulling a lever, later moved by modification, to the supply aimer's position, but as the heavy drop platform was part of the aircraft's load, the AQM was responsible for the security of it. Consequently he was trained in all aspects of rigging and securing heavy drop loads and thus had to undertake the pre-flight checks associated with each load.

The Lord Mayor of London's coach being loaded at Abingdon en route for exhibition at a trade fair in Zurich. *via RAF Abingdon*

Pre-flight check (at night) of medium stressed platform extractor parachute. *J. Ward*

A rather hazardous responsibility of the Beverley AQM was dealing with heavy drop load hang-ups. Hang-ups occurred when the release mechanism which secured the platform to the aircraft, failed to open under the pull exerted by the extractor parachute. This was mounted on the rear sill of the freight bay and was released when the AQM pulled the release lever. The extractor parachute then fell into the slipstream and deployed, exerting a force which first released the platform from the aircraft and then, as the platform fell clear, opened the main parachutes. Photographs depicting a sequence of the above operations are shown in Chapter 7.

However, should the platform release mechanism fail to operate, the aircraft would then stream a large-size extractor parachute which of course, was guaranteed to cause a dramatic drop in airspeed. Full power then had to be applied in order to keep the aircraft flying, and in those few disconcerting moments, the pilot had to keep the aircraft away from built-up areas usually by orbiting the DZ, in case the platform release mechanism suddenly decided to operate. The AQM's first duty was to secure the platform by means of chains suitably pre-positioned for that purpose. With the load secure, he then armed himself with a pair of bolt croppers and made his way to the rear of the freight bay where he cut the extractor parachute cable, thus releasing the parachute. This was guaranteed to have an immediate beneficial effect on the morale of his crew, who would then thankfully throttle back to cruising power and set course for the return flight to base.

With regard to feeding his passengers and crew, a Beverley AQM was not exactly blessed with amenities. He had no galley and his only 'cooking' appliances were hot-water urns, one being provided in the freight bay and two in the boom. Despite this lack of 'mod cons', most Beverley AQMs looked after their charges splendidly. It gave great pleasure to most of Transport Command when the Air Ministry upgraded AQMs to full aircrew status and approved a flying badge, the standard half-wing with letters QM woven into the centre. When the RAF acquired the C-130K Hercules, after the demise of the Beverleys and other contemporary transport aircraft, AQMs became ALMs (air loadmasters) adopting the United States Air Force title. Ex-Beverley AQM John Ward related some hilarious events which highlighted his days on Beverleys. He writes of one amusing but expensive incident: 'One day passing through Muscat on a QTR (Quick Turn Round), several huge vulture-like birds landed on the Bev's wing. The captain, Flight Lieutenant Brian Clinch, told me to get rid of the birds. As soon as I threw the handful of stones, I knew that I had done the wrong thing! Half the stones went down the air intake of one of the engines and we were delayed for three days for the resultant engine change. No-one spoke to me for 72 hours'.

John also recalled another incident when he was AQM to a freight bay full of soldiers. A junior officer, obviously unaware of regulations appertaining to travel in military aircraft, asked John in all seriousness, when he would be round serving the gin and tonics. John replied: 'Just as soon as we get the undercart up Sir'. The officer spent the remainder of the flight with his eyes glued to the immovable main undercarriage.

Beverley AQMs were a splendid breed of men who did a strenuous, often dirty, sometimes hazardous and very responsible job which directly concerned the safety of their aircraft. Those who did the job before it was accorded full aircrew status, with its attendant benefits, must be commended for their dedication and their love of flying.

Exercise Soft Putty

Exercise *Soft Putty*, involving both squadrons, was mounted in August at Larissa in Greece, where all personnel were accommodated in tents and lived under field conditions. A freak storm turned the tented camp into a quagmire and indeed, literally flushed some of the occupants out of their tents. Undaunted, the Beverley boys made their way to their aircraft where at least, they managed to get a 'roof over their heads.' In August also, members of 53 Squadron visited the Belfast production line to see the aircraft on to which they would soon be converting. The Beverley days of 53 Squadron were numbered.

Unusual picture of an aircrew man with two flying badges: Flight Sergeant Morgan, ex-PJI (Parachute Jump Instructor) who remustered to AQM, declined to remove his PJI brevet until after the presentation of his AQM's brevet. Others left to right: Sergeant Crossan, Group Captain Sowery, Wing Commander Cropper, Sergeant Sale and Sergeant Ward. *via J. Ward*

Fuel Deposited in Desert
- Fodder to Farms

In December, a load of petrol was flown from El Adem to Kufra, an oasis in the Libyan desert which had been an outpost of the legendary Long Range Desert Group of the Second World War.

The load of fuel was positioned there for use by an overland expedition being planned by the Army.

The new year came in with heavy snowfalls and abnormally low temperatures and 1963 is still known as 'that bad winter'. As soon as the runways and taxi-ways were clear, the Wing undertook flights dropping fodder for farm animals on snowbound farms in Devon. The ground crew worked long, hard hours clearing snow from the wings of their Beverleys. A wing area of 2,916 square feet carried a lot of snow to be swept off, the men working on icy surfaces with a long way to fall if they lost their footholds. The efforts of the ground technicians are often overlooked when relating the successes of airborne operations.

Clipkey Stand-by Materializes
- Another 'Flat Earth'

In May, the appropriately named Exercise *Mayflight* took place, both squadrons participating in moving ground staff and V-bomber servicing equipment to dispersed airfields.

Thanks to Clipkey stand-bys together with the numerous alerts and practices carried out by the Wing, *Mayflight* was a complete success and demonstrated how quickly and efficiently the V-force could be dispersed should it ever be necessary.

In June, it was 47's turn to participate in a *Flat Earth* exercise. This was similar to the one described earlier in this chapter and involved two Beverleys dropping a detachment of 3 Division Royal Engineers, together with their earthmoving equipment and tools of their trade.

This exercise was also a complete success, the sappers preparing a reasonable airstrip from rough scrubland in about 24 hours.

The aircraft then landed and took off again without incident, proving that the first Exercise *Flat Earth* was no isolated fluke.

Squadrons Amalgamate

On 28th June 1963, the two squadrons merged. Wing Commander E. W. Cropper, OC 53 Squadron, handed over his squadron to Wing Commander J. J. Barr, OC 47 Squadron.

Wing Commander Cropper then assumed command of the much enlarged 47 Squadron, Wing Commander Barr taking command of two of the squadron's four flights. The whole occasion was marked by a ceremonial parade. The amalgamation over, 53 Squadron dispersed to prepare for its conversion at Fairford on to Belfasts. As one 53 Squadron crewman remarked: 'We're moving from one Dragmaster to another'.

This was a reference to a name with which, in the early days, the Beverley had been dubbed. However, it did not stick and was resurrected to apply to the Belfast which initially, did suffer severe drag problems. So ended 53's Beverley days, almost six years of hard work flying the slow, noisy, vibrating, oil-guzzling Bevs, which despite their infuriating idiosyncrasies, had found affection with the men now leaving them. During its Beverley era, 53 Squadron had flown over 6,500 sorties from Abingdon. This figure excludes sorties flown on detachments, which are estimated as over 2,000. The squadron also logged 26,424 hours, this figure again excluding hours flown on detachments, so an estimated total of 30,000 hours would not be unreasonable. This is equivalent to more than 3 years flying time and indicates 53's intensive activities whilst operating Beverleys.

Crews to Labuan

September also saw three crews being posted to Labuan, Borneo to assist the Far East Beverley force, 34 Squadron, which was based at Seletar in Singapore, in operations concerned with the Indonesian Confrontation.

The latter stemmed from the Indonesians' claim to the territories of North Borneo, previously Sarawak and Sabah, now part of Malaysia. The Indonesian confrontation was triggered in December 1962 by an armed revolt in Brunei, a British-protected Sultanate located between Sarawak and Sabah. The revolt was carried out by the so-called 'North Borneo Liberation Army' and was reportedly backed by the Philippines. Sarawak and Sabah had become part of the Federation of Malaysia on 16th September 1963, but Brunei did not join due to disagreements over oil revenues. Malaysia broke off diplomatic relations with Indonesia on 17th September after anti-British riots in Jakarta and a number of hit and run raids by guerillas from Indonesian Borneo into Sarawak and Sabah. The Brunei revolt was quelled in ten days by British and Gurkha troops flown in from Singapore. The British troops included the RAF Regiment.

'Don't Land Here It's a Minefield'

On 5th October 1963, XB284, skippered by Flight Lieutenant Galyer, was detached to El Adem to participate in an Army exercise. The Beverley's role was mainly ferrying troops and equipment from El Adem to Alpha and Bomba, two tiny desert airstrips about eighty miles north-west of El Adem. From these airstrips, the troops and their equipment were deployed, by Wessex and Belvedere helicopters to the battle zone.

Bob Wright, Flight Lieutenant Galyer's engineer, takes up the story: 'We had delivered our troops and freight to Bomba and taken off to return to El Adem. During the climb-out, we picked up a Mayday call from a Belvedere saying that an engine failure and fire had occurred and he was returning to Bomba. We immediately did a 180° turn and descended towards Bomba and as we turned we could see a column of black smoke. We headed towards it and saw that the Belvedere was lying on its side burning fiercely. About 100 yards away from the wreck stood a small group of survivors, who wisely had retired to a safe distance. Between this group of survivors and the burning helicopter, the ground seemed fairly level and after a discussion between the two pilots, the navigator and myself, the captain decided to attempt a landing and give what assistance we could. A low run was made first to take a closer look at the terrain and as we approached, one of the survivors detached himself from the group and ran into our flight path waving his arms furiously. Perplexed, we completed the low run, the captain decided the terrain was OK for a landing and we did a circuit. On finals for landing, the same survivor ran out, again waving furiously so we overshot. At about the same time, the signaller, who had been in touch with El Adem notifying our intentions to land in the desert, relayed instructions from El Adem that we were not to land but to orbit the crash and direct helicopters in to pick up the survivors.

'We did as instructed and when ordered, returned to El Adem, where at debriefing, it transpired that the Belvedere had crashed in a Second World War minefield and it wasn't until the survivors had ran a safe distance from the crash that they noticed the minefield warning signs. The survivor, a Sergeant in the REME had courageously ran out twice, through the minefield, to wave us off. Sadly, we never found out who this chap was: we all wanted to stand him a beer'.

Operation Desert Blenheim

The closing months of 1963 were highlighted by another *Mayflight* alert in which twenty sorties were flown, and by Operation *Desert Blenheim*. This was in support of the Libyan desert expedition carried out by the Army, for which fuel had been deposited at Kufra by Beverley in December 1962. The expedition had found near Kufra, three crashed Blenheims, victims of action in the Second World War. The bodies of the Blenheims' crews were with their aircraft. Two 47 Squadron Beverleys, under the command of Major 'Bonzo' Von Haven, USAF (on an 'exchange' posting to the RAF), flew to Kufra. The bodies were then flown out to El Adem, to be interred with full honours in the British Military Cemetery at Tobruk.

More Cyprus and Aden Troubles

January 1964 brought yet another Cyprus stand-by and an Aden detachment. Operation *Hogmanay* was mounted to fly helicopters, troops, vehicles and associated freight to Cyprus. It was a massive operation, outbound crews 'slipping' at Luqa, where a fresh crew took each aircraft on to Nicosia.

Due to the urgency of the situation, 242 OCU from Thorney Island was called in to assist, and the student aircrew under training at that time, were permitted to accompany the staff crews thus getting the bonus of additional route-flying experience. The operation carried on into February, when Whirlwind Helicopters of 230 Squadron were airlifted from Gutersloh in Germany, to Nicosia. The 1st Life Guards were also airlifted to Akrotiri.

Squadron Moves to Sleepy Hollow

In April, the squadron moved to 53 Squadron's old accommodation at Sleepy Hollow, on the other side of the airfield. This move brought some measure of quiet to the long-suffering inhabitants of Shippon village, who had for so long endured, largely without complaint, the noise of Centaurus engines being run up for testing at night time.

Radfan Troubles Start

Over the past years, terrorist activity in the South Arabian Federation had spread alarmingly, the guerillas inexorably moving south towards the Colony of Aden, in which anti-British feelings had long been running high. When the troubles began in the Radfan, the Abingdon Wing was called upon to assist Khormaksar-based 84 Squadron, and accordingly, XB284 and XB288 were dispatched, each carrying an Army helicopter. The flight was made in two legs via El Adem, the customary route for Aden 'panic stations'.

Another Cyprus Stand-by

The early months of summer 1964 passed comparatively uneventfully, the squadron being busy with routine work but not undertaking anything dramatic. In July, Exercise *Game Bird*, involving the 2nd Royal Tank Regiment, was mounted at Idris and more flights to Gatow in West Berlin were undertaken in order to assert the UK's right to use the corridors over East Germany.

However, in September, the volatile political situation in Cyprus flared up again and a Beverley with two crews was detached to Nicosia. Despite the Aden and Cyprus detachment plus other commitments, the squadron managed to find time to participate in the Lord Trophy competition but only managed 8th place. This was not surprising since 47 Squadron had had little time in which to practise for the competition which this year was mounted at El Adem.

Desert Rescue Team Airlift

In October, a Beverley flew the Desert Rescue Team, plus vehicles and equipment, from El Adem to Kufra from where the team drove off towards Cyrenaica on familiarization exercises. A week or two later, the Beverley was called in to search for the team, with whom radio contact had been lost. The search was successful, the team was found fit and well but with a defective radio.

Sudanese Government Prohibit Overflying

In October also, the Sudanese government prohibited the RAF overflying their territory. This move was not unexpected, as the Sudanese were also imbued with the wave of anti-British feeling sweeping Arabia and Africa. The diplomats did some smart work and a new route to Aden was established. This went by way of Luqa, Akrotiri, Muharraq (Bahrain), Salalah and Khormaksar.

Air Portability and Air Mobility
A few days into January 1965 saw the appropriately named Exercise *Twelfth Night* providing air portability training for the 1st Iniskillings with fourteen Beverley sorties. Another air portability exercise code-named *Jigsaw* took place in February. This exercise involved 32 Infantry Field Workshops, 34 Field Squadron and the Life Guards.

Spring and early summer of 1965 were uneventful in terms of noteworthy events, but the squadron was heavily engaged in paratroop and Army support training. Exercise *Parcel Post*, held in May, dropped 200 paratroops and 16 medium stressed platforms on to Fox Covert DZ on Salisbury Plain. In August, the squadron detached an aircraft to Khormaksar to make up for an 84 Squadron's aircraft detached to the Far East to back up 34 Squadron in its Indonesian Confrontation activities.

More Desert Work
In November, Exercise *Desert Grid* was mounted at El Adem and a Desert Rescue Team was airlifted to Kufra again. Due possibly to their radio problems experienced in their previous desert sortie, the team drove off into the desert to carry out long-range radio communication tests. This time a vehicle broke down, but good radio communication summoned a Beverley to drop the necessary spares and enable the team to complete their assignment.

Difficult Landing
On 2nd August 1966, XB269 shed a nose wheel on take-off. Since the twin nose wheels were mounted on a common 'live' axle, it was realized that the remaining nose wheel would probably become detached during landing. After orbiting for a considerable time to use up fuel, the pilot who preferred to remain anonymous at the time, and whose wish is respected here, brought the aircraft in for a perfect landing. The nose wheel was held off until the airspeed had dropped to a minimum and was then gently lowered on to the runway whereupon it came off and rolled ahead of the aircraft, the aircraft continuing its short landing run on the axle housing of the nose wheel oleo strut. Damage was remarkably slight a tribute to the brilliant airmanship of the pilot. Curiously, no carpet of foam was laid for this landing, a practice that has been standard for emergency landings for many years.

Back from the Desert
In November 1966, XB287 returned from detachment to 84 Squadron in Aden, complete with the 84 Squadron scorpion insignia painted on its fins. Obviously 84 Squadron must have thought that XB287 was theirs for keeps. In the same month, a flight was made, in XB285, to Brough in order to collect some much-needed spares. This visit aroused a great deal of nostalgia among the old Beverley planemakers now building Buccaneers.

Crack in Mainplane Attachment
In January 1967, XB263 was found to have a seven inch crack in the attachment bracket of one of the mainplanes. It had long been known that the Beverleys suffered from severe corrosion problems but this was the first known serious structural defect and was attributed to metal fatigue. The corrosion problems had been caused by the high humidity and salt-laden air typical of the many overseas theatres where the Beverleys operated. The decision was made to scrap XB263 as it was thought that there was little more work for the Beverley fleet to do, and whatever needed to be done, could be accomplished by the American C-13OK Hercules, shortly due to enter RAF service. Beverleys had done a magnificent job in East Africa, Arabia, the Persian Gulf and the Far East. But now, the UK was relinquishing its bases in those theatres, thus depriving the Beverley of much of its bulk-carrying, short-haul work at which it had excelled. Had the circumstances been different it is possible, that like their predecessors the Hastings, the Beverleys could have undergone major repairs by the manufacturers and given a new lease of life. This was not to be however and clearly the end of the Beverley fleet was now in sight. Sadly, XB263 was flown to Shawbury by Flight Lieutenant Hall, for disposal.

Left: **Whirlwind XK968 for attachment to 284 Squadron being unloaded at Nicosia.** *Crown Copyright*

Below: **XH116 of 53 Squadron being serviced at 'Sleepy Hollow' dispersal Abingdon 1958.** *C. Lowe*

These two photographs recall an incident when XB269 of 47 Squadron lost a nose-wheel in flight. The aircraft is shown on approach for landing with the remaining nose-wheel looking decidedly unsafe; and after a successful landing being made on the nose-wheel axle housing after the wheel (arrowed) had come off. *J. Litchfield*

Opposite page: Three Beverleys of 47 Squadron in formation over the Berkshire Downs; the leading aircraft is XB283/G. *RAF Museum*

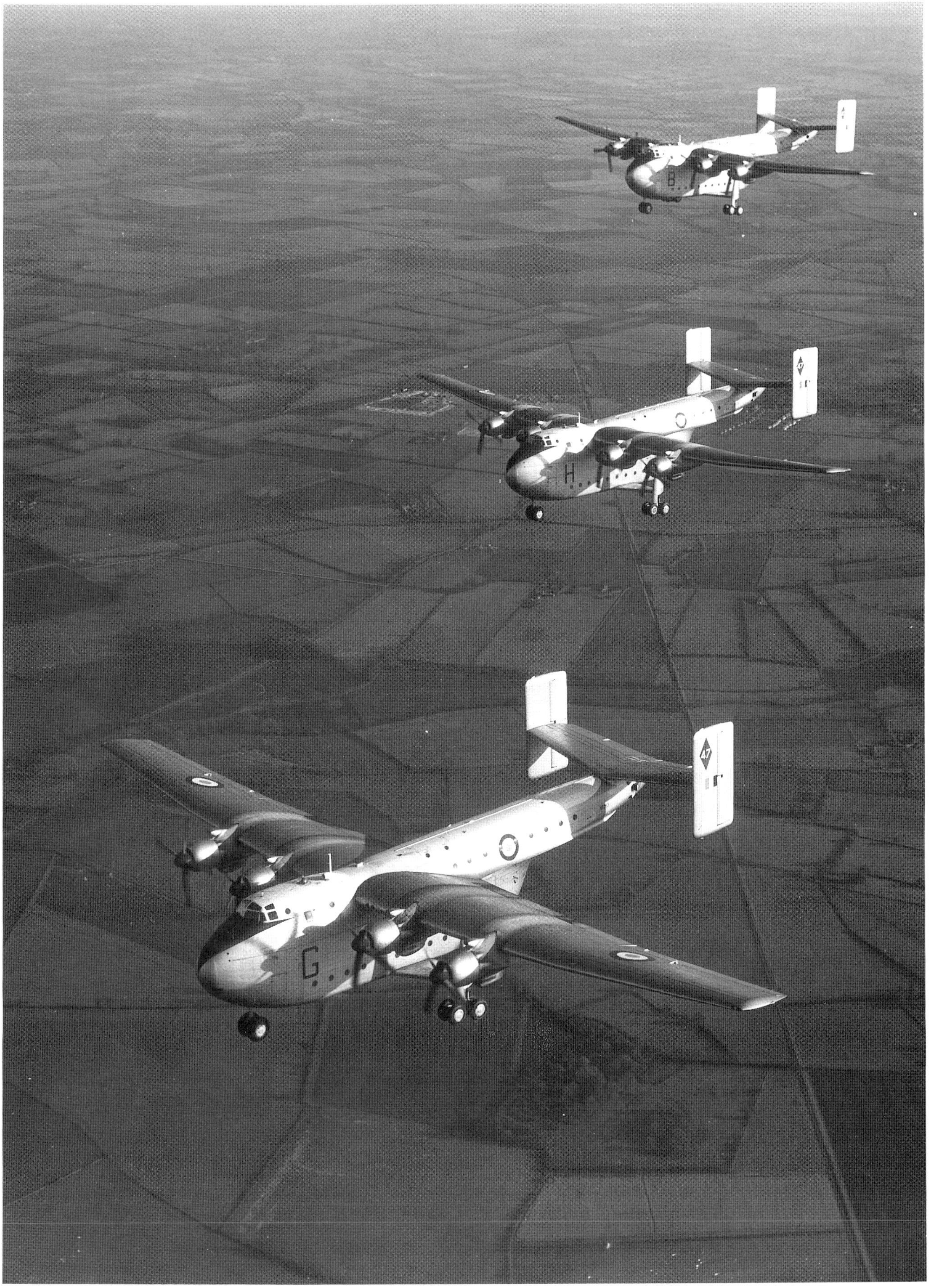

Detergent for Oil-polluted Beaches

In March, the supertanker *Torrey Canyon* ran aground on rocks off Lands End and thousands of tonnes of crude oil were released, later to be washed ashore to foul the beautiful Cornish beaches. There was an urgent requirement for large amounts of detergent to deal with the oil pollution, and a Beverley was used to airlift the required amount of detergent from Turnhouse, Edinburgh to Culdrose Naval Air Station in Cornwall, for collection by the local authority.

In March also, 47 Squadron competed for the last time with Beverleys in the Lord Trophy competition and gained fourth place.

Final Flight of the UK Beverley Force

Two noteworthy aerial deliveries were made in April. A Spitfire was flown from Kemble to Tours, France, for presentation to the Armee de l'Air. Some Concorde air intakes were also flown to Toulouse.

October 1967 saw 47's Beverleys participate in their final Army exercise. Exercise *Overdale*, mounted at Geilenkirchen Germany, involved eighteen Beverley sorties, all flown completely on schedule, with no unserviceability whatsoever - a fitting end to the squadron's Beverley era.

The remainder of the month was spent disposing of the remaining Beverleys, an impressive formation fly-past ending in a 'bomb-burst' break being performed before parting with these grand old aeroplanes. XH123 was flown to Bicester for breaking up, XL131, XB283 and XB288 were also flown to Bicester for disposal. Other Beverleys went to Shawbury for disposal. Mr Mike Keegan, a well-known entrepreneur, was reported to be interested in purchasing some Beverleys for use in the Middle East oilfields, but nothing materialized from this rumour.

Squadron Disbands

On 31st October 1967, 47 Squadron's Colour was paraded before being laid up at the RAF College Cranwell. The squadron then went into temporary disbandment until reforming at Fairford in March 1968 with Lockheed C-130K Hercules aircraft.

47 Squadron's Achievements with the Beverley

During its eleven and a half years of Beverley operation, 47 Squadron's Beverleys had flown almost nine million miles in a recorded total of 49,003 flying hours, equivalent to more than five and a half years flying time. Although this is a puny figure compared with those for commercial airlines, it should be noted that a great deal of Beverley time was spent on stand-bys with crews eargerly awaiting the chance to get airborne. Had the opportunity been given to utilize the aircraft more fully, it is certain that much more than half the life of each aircraft would have been spent in the air.

The squadron also carried 66,539 passengers and 26,878 tonnes of freight, these figures excluding paratroops and airdropped supplies. Indeed, the figures quoted are pessimistic since flights undertaken on the many detachments are not all documented in squadron records. Squadron records however, do reveal that in 1957, over 6,000 trained paratroops jumped from the unit's Beverleys on various exercises. This figure does not include paratroops under training. While training paratroops it was not unusual for a Beverley to drop 500 troops in a day, so in view of this, it is almost certain that 47 Squadron must have carried well over a million persons in the unit's Beverley era.

A 47 Squadron navigator interrupts his calculations for this picture. J. Knight

Chapter Three

30 Squadron

Brief history

Formed at Farnborough in 1914, the squadron moved to the Middle East and within a year became the first tactical support squadron of the RAF by air-dropping supplies on the beleagured town of Kut-el-Amara on the Tigris. This siege is described by Grant and Cole in *But not in Anger*.

In the 1920s, 30 Squadron flew DH9a aircraft on airmail routes in Egypt, thus establishing itself as one of the earliest transport squadrons.

In the Second World War, the squadron saw service in the Middle and Far East and in 1947 converted to Dakotas, flying these in the Berlin airlift. Valettas were acquired in 1953 and flown until April 1957.

Squadron Equips with Beverleys

The first Beverleys arrived in April 1957 and by the end of May the first phase of crew conversion had been completed. The squadron's Valettas were disposed of apart from the VIP flight which continued Valetta operations until the following January when this unit disbanded.

Scheduled flights to Wildenrath started in June followed by a Cyprus schedule. In August training was curtailed when some of 30 Squadron's aircraft were borrowed by the Abingdon Wing to help with the airlift of troops to Oman to deal with the uprising there. September saw the squadron fully operational for passenger and freight carrying duties but still engaged in training for Army support work which reached a high peak of activity in November.

Aden Detachments and Army Support Duties Begin

In December, 30 Squadron began its stint of Aden detachments, XH131 with two crews aboard captained by Flight Lieutenants Dye and Swales making 30 Squadron's first Beverley appearance at Khormaksar. Two more aircraft followed, XH118 and XH124 captained by Flight Lieutenants Garforth and Bell respectively. The squadron's participation in the Aden detachment gave a welcome respite to the Abingdon Wing who had performed this duty continuously for the past eleven months.

The squadron suffered its first Beverley accident on the Aden detachment, when a double engine failure occurred on XH118, reportedly due to fuel starvation. A forced landing was attempted at Beihan but the aircraft overturned with one fatality.

January 1958 saw the disbandment of the Valetta VIP flight at Dishforth whilst in February, the squadron participated in Exercise *Quickstep* which was mounted to test Transport Command's ability to move troops to the Middle East in the shortest possible time.

In March the squadron got down to Army support work in earnest, dropping 1,777 troops, 18 heavy drop platforms and flying numerous low level cross country exercises.

Exercise *Quickstep 2* was mounted in April and involved airlifting troops from Eastleigh to Khormaksar. All available aircraft and crews were used. Exercise *Sunspot* followed *Quickstep 2* and entailed postitioning aircraft and crews at strategic points in the Mediterranean area. This was believed to be in readiness for the evacuation of civilians from Lebanon where political unrest was brewing. The squadron then went on to participate in June in the massive airlift of troops and their equipment to Cyprus to stand by for moving into Jordan which was being threatened by Syria.

After a short stand-by period at Nicosia involving five 30 Squadron crews, the airlift of troops and equipment into Jordan's capital, Amman, commenced, 30 Squadron assisting the Abingdon Wing and the Hastings Force. The presence of the British force in Jordan relieved the political tension between that country and Syria and after three months, the force was withdrawn. Up to the withdrawal however, a Beverley force of five 30 Squadron crews remained on stand-by at Nicosia. The crews were rotated as often as possible by a 'slip crew' system on the UK-Cyprus-UK scheduled flights.

The Cyprus stand-by carried on into September 1958, when with political tension in both Jordan and Lebanon slackening, the crews returned to Dishforth. But their return was short-lived, the squadron being mobilized in October to assist with the withdrawal of the 16th Independent Parachute Brigade from Amman.

Due to the political situation, which although stable at that time was still delicate, the routes chosen for the withdrawal operation called for precise timing and impeccable navigation. Flight Lieutenant McCleod did a proving flight before the operation commenced in order to check out the flight planning. The withdrawal was carried out without incident, 30 Squadron providing four crews and three aircraft.

Aden Detachments Continue

The squadron continued with the Aden detachment, 30 Squadron taking turns with the Abingdon Wing squadrons. In November 1958, Flight Lieutenant Swales and crew had to extend their stint in order to help the newly formed 84 Squadron after a busy airlift of troops and equipment from Aden to Nairobi.

A tragedy occurred early in December, when a young flying officer, a 30 Squadron co-pilot, fell through the paratroop exit doors in the tail boom. The officer had been doing his pre-flight checks which involved passing through the toilets situated at the rear of the tail boom, into

Wreckage of XH118 which crashed and overturned at Beihan. *W. Brattan*

The parachutist exit doors in floor of tail boom; note also the doors to toilets at rear. Crown Copyright

the tail cone area to check various items of equipment located there. On completion of his checks in that area he made his way back into the passenger compartment. Unbeknown to him, however, someone had opened the para-doors which were located immediately in front of the toilet area and fell through the open para-doors to the tarmac some twenty feet below, sustaining fatal injuries. A similar accident had happened some months previously at Abingdon, but the airman involved escaped with only minor injuries.

A modification was immediately put in hand which incorporated locking pins which extended when the para-doors were opened and locked the toilet doors in the closed position thus preventing anyone from leaving the toilet compartment when the para-doors were open.

Squadron Becomes Proficient in Army Support

December also saw most of 30 Squadron detached to Abingdon for support training in paratrooping and supply dropping. Since No. 1 Parachute Training School was based at Abingdon together with the Air Despatch Units concerned with supply dropping, it was expedient for 30 Squadron to be detached to Abingdon for its month's stint on Army support work, rotating with 47 and 53 Squadrons. The squadron carried out its first Army exercise in January 1959, when it provided three aircraft for Exercise *White Christmas*, a parachute landing in the Thetford area of Norfolk.

Aden Detachments Finish (Temporarily)

In February 1959, Flying Officer Horrocks and crew completed the last routine Aden detachment, having logged sixty-four hours on up-country strip flying. The resident Khormaksar-based Beverley squadron No. 84 was now fully operational and despite heavy demands was managing to fulfil the many commitments in that troubled area.

More Army Support Work - Squadron Wins Lord Trophy

Spring and early summer of 1959 was spent in intensive Army support work at Abingdon. In June, the squadron dropped 1,926 paratroops and 22 heavy drop platforms, the parachute of one platform failing to open resulting in a sizeable hole and a tangle of wreckage on the DZ. In June, two aircraft were loaned to 84 Squadron at Khormaksar to deal with the heavy backlog of work. The aircraft were flown out by crews posted to 84 Squadron.

In June 1959 the coveted Lord Trophy was won for 30 Squadron by Flight Lieutenant Garforth and Flying Officer Douglas. This was a splendid achievement considering the short time the squadron had had to gain experience on their new aircraft.

In July rumours which had been circulating about a possible move to Kenya materialized, and there was an influx of new personnel to bring the squadron up to strength for the move planned for the coming November. In the meantime, the squadron worked up for and participated with Abingdon Wing in Exercise *Bar Frost* at Vaernes in Norway, supplying five aircraft and crews.

30 SQUADRON

Preparation for and Move to Kenya
In October 1959, the squadron prepared itself for the forthcoming move, the news of which had generally been greeted with delight. Between preparations however, the unit carried out Exercise *Sambar,* an airlift of fighter squadron personnel to North Africa.

The uneventful move to the squadron's new base at RAF Eastleigh, near Nairobi, took place between the 2nd and 12th of November. The bulk load-carrying capacity of the Beverley was adequate to lift practically the entire squadron and its equipment to its new base. Once installed at Eastleigh, the squadron crews lost no time in familiarizing themselves with their new territory and twelve days after completion of the move the squadron was able to carry out Exercise *Summer Flight 3*, an air mobility exercise for the 24th Infantry Brigade Group.

Scheduled flights were also started to Aden and Bahrain, with crews unfamiliar with the Aden airstrips being checked out on flights to various strips in the Protectorate.

Aden Detachments Resume
Now part of MEAF (Middle East Air Force), it was inevitable that 30 Squadron would be involved with the troubles in the Aden Protectorate. Consequently, detachments each comprising one aircraft and crew and of one week's duration were made to Khormaksar. At the same time, a weekly schedule to Bahrain was started via Khormaksar, Riyan, Salalah, Masirah and Sharjah.

In January 1960, an aircraft on the Bahrain schedule was commandeered at Sharjah and in eight trips, flew in 97 tonnes of supplies and equipment to Army units at Ibri in Oman, see *Map 7*. Meanwhile, XH122 the last aircraft required to bring the squadron up to strength, arrived from the UK with Flying Officer D. G. M. Wright in command.

'Signpost' at RAF Eastleigh Nairobi showing mileage to almost anywhere in the world. *S. Hitchen*

XH122 overhead its base at Eastleigh. *Crown Copyright*

Mauritius Cyclone

Preparations for the squadron to participate in the forthcoming Exercise *Starlight* in Libya were commenced in February but were interrupted by the squadron being placed on stand-by for flying relief supplies to the cyclone-stricken island of Mauritius.

One aircraft, however, with Flight Lieutenant George Dorricott in command, was released from the stand-by to proceed to El Adem to take part in Exercise *Starlight*. This was a major exercise in which the Beverley demonstrated its capabilities beyond all expectations and is described in detail in Chapter 2.

After a short stand-by period the Mauritius cyclone relief airlift commenced, all available aircraft being used. The route was by way of Dar Es Salaam in Tanganyika (now Tanzania) and Madagascar.

The airlift continued into March but heavy rains had damaged Eastleigh's laterite runway, curtailing flying for short periods during which the runway was repaired.

In April 1960, Exercise *Firebird* was mounted at Eastleigh and involved moving a large number of troops and their equipment to Embakasi, Nairobi's civil airport, now known as Jomo Kenyatta airport. Flights to Mauritius were still being undertaken and on one return flight, Squadron Leader Waugh flew the Rt Hon Iain McCleod MP into Embakasi.

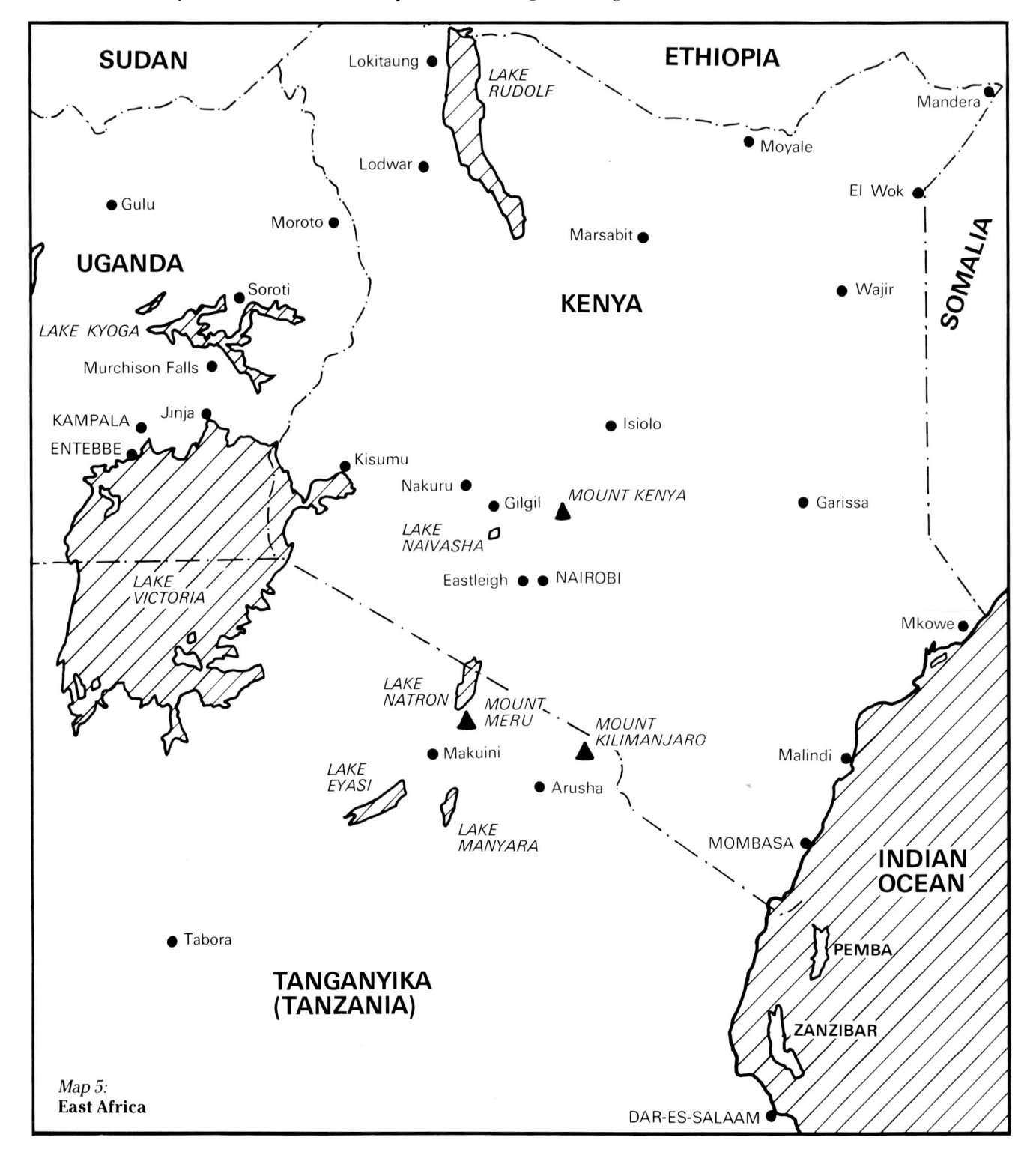

Map 5:
East Africa

Help for SASO

May 1960 was the squadron's busiest month since its arrival in Kenya. Exercise *Egress*, a major military exercise, was mounted for conveying troops and their logistic equipment to Aden and back. Initially, the plan was for Britannias to airlift the troops and 30 Squadron's Beverleys to airlift the equipment but many Britannias fell by the wayside with unserviceability and Beverleys were pressed into service to airlift the troops. Despite this extra demand on 30 Squadron, the exercise was completed on schedule, yet another demonstration of the Beverley's capabilities.

The month was highlighted by two noteworthy incidents: the first involved the SASO BFAP (Senior Air Staff Officer British Forces Arabian Peninsula) when he ran short of fuel in his Meteor aircraft and had to force-land at Garissa, see *Map 5*. A Beverley promptly flew in some Avtur kerosine fuel for the jet, enabling the SASO to take to the air once again.

The second incident involved Flight Lieutenant 'Tammy' Howell who experienced an engine fire which failed to go out when the automatic fire extinguishing system operated. Tammy was about to line up for a forced landing in the bush when fortuitously the fire extinguished itself: he then landed the aircraft safely at Embakasi.

Bandit Trouble

Flight Lieutenant Tammy Howell was busy again in June, spending three days evaluating up-country strips in Uganda. The reason for this reconnaissance was that bandits were terrorizing areas in North East Uganda and early in the month had ambushed and killed a European Police Inspector.

Strip recces involved first finding your strip, a difficult navigational exercise due to inaccurate maps and usually featureless terrain. Once located, a few approaches to the strip were made followed by a number of low runs in order to get a close look at the surface. If all appeared to be well, a 'touch and go' landing would be made. After a successful touch and go landing a 'full stop' landing was often made in order to check if the surface of the strip could bear the weight of a stationary Beverley. It usually did: Beverley boggings were rare due to the immense load-bearing area of the aircraft's ten wheels.

Due to the terrorism in Uganda, three Beverleys were promptly detached to Jinja on the northern shore of Lake Victoria, from where a company of the King's African Rifles plus two vehicles and their equipment, were flown into Moroto, a tiny airstrip north of Lake Kyoga. This was another demonstration of how the Beverley could be used to help deal with local 'brush fire' incidents.

Cyprus Exercise and Congo Evacuation

July was another busy month, a detachment participating in Exercise *Desert Hawk* in Cyprus. One of the squadron's aircraft dropped two Land Rovers which were written off when the parachutes failed.

The Congo, now named Zaire, rebellion took place in July and 30 Squadron supplied two aircraft for the evacuation of civilians from Stanleyville. Civilians who had been airlifted to Entebbe by civil airline were also flown to Kenya by the squadron.

Giraffes Impede Landing - Lord Louis Visits Squadron

In September 1960 Flight Lieutenant Scorey took XH124 to Wajir in Northern Kenya to deliver supplies to the garrison there. His landing at this small strip was made more difficult than usual by the presence of giraffes. Animals were a frequent hazard on the East African airstrips.

In September also, a Tasker trailer used for in-flight refuelling of Valiants was flown to Karachi via Khormaksar and Masirah. On the 23rd of September the squadron was honoured by a visit from Lord Louis Mountbatten who inspected three aircraft and crews at Eastleigh.

Medium stressed platform and load, one of whose 'chutes failed to open.
Crown Copyright

More Trouble in Uganda - Help for 84 Squadron

Terrorism in Uganda prompted reconnaissance flights of more potentially suitable airstrips at Murchison Falls, Gulu and Soroti, while further trouble in the Aden Protectorate called for a 30 Squadron aircraft to lift detachments of the King's African Rifles to Aden up-country strips.

In November 1960, 84 Squadron had the misfortune of total unserviceability of all its aircraft, no doubt caused by the tremendously punishing conditions in which they operated. 30 Squadron was called on to help out and Flight Lieutenant Dorricott flew to Khormaksar to uplift a replacement engine for a Shackleton grounded at Mauripur, Karachi. Unfortunately there was no freight-loading winch available on the aircraft, so the engine had to be manhandled down the ramps. Without the assistance of gravity however, on-loading the unserviceable engine was clearly beyond the capabilities of the muscle power available. Resourcefulness won the day when a Coles crane with jib lowered to Beverley freight bay height, pushed the engine up the ramps and into the aircraft.

Meanwhile, back in Kenya, a Boeing 707 crash-landed on Embakasi's main runway and the airport staff lacked the means to move it. Lifting gear in the form of air bags was located at Entebbe and a 30 Squadron Beverley was dispatched to collect them. This was done in record time (for a Beverley) and using the air bags, the crashed aircraft was lifted on to trolleys before being towed clear of the runway. The busy month of November culminated in Exercise *Fly March*, which consisted of shuttling troops between Dar Es Salaam and Zanzibar.

Operations Stunsail and Catechism

December 1960 brought a requirement for three aircraft and crews to position at Sharjah in readiness for the forthcoming Exercise *Placard*. The 30 Squadron Beverleys carried men and equipment of 208 Squadron which was also involved in the exercise. Due to the worsening Yemeni-inspired terrorism in the Aden Protectorate, Headquarters BFAP requested assistance for 84 Squadron from the UK-based Beverley force and 30 Squadron was also placed on stand-by. This operation was codenamed *Stunsail*.

At the same time, Kenya was suffering terrorism in the North East Province and the garrison strength of the King's African Rifles stationed at Wajir was increased. Just before Christmas, the rains having waterlogged the Wajir airstrip, Flight Lieutenant Calvert dropped 125 kilos of Christmas fare for the garrison - a much appreciated delivery.

Operation *Catechism* ended 1960 with the squadron airlifting a force of the KARs to Jinja where civil disturbances were worsening.

Exercises Placard and Rhino

The new year started with Exercise *Placard* which involved flying troops to the Persian Gulf. Whilst in the Gulf area, one of the squadron's Beverleys was used to fly a replacement engine for a Pembroke aircraft into Das Island, a newly opened airstrip, see *Map 7*.

Exercise *Rhino* involved airlifting troops and their equipment into Isiolo a small airstrip near Mount Kenya, for operations in the North Frontier district, where terrorism had again broken out.

In February, Flight Lieutenant Holloway and Flying Officer D. Wright and crews took two Beverleys to Tabora, Tanganyika, to fly a battalion of the King's African Rifles to Jinja to relieve the garrison there.

Casevac Duty and Operation Oliver

The squadron performed a casevac operation in early March, airlifting the casualties of a Twin Pioneer, which had crashed on Mount Neru, from Arusha in Tanganyika, to Nairobi.

March saw the beginnings of Operation *Oliver* which was mounted to supply food to the famine-stricken Turkhana tribe in Northern Kenya. Six famine relief sorties were flown, in which 49 tonnes of food were dropped. Further famine-relief sorties were flown in early April with 14 tonnes of maize being dropped at Kakuma, Ferguson Gulf and Lokitaung.

Zanzibar Disturbances

The civil unrest which had been fermenting in this pleasant island for many months came to a head in June with serious rioting. Seven aircraft were dispatched from Eastleigh, to fly in troops to quell the disturbances. One aircraft flown by Flight Lieutenant Brown, made three landings on the minute airstrip at Pemba, a small island between Zanzibar and Mombasa. As was the case with most other East African airstrips, the Beverley was the largest aircraft ever to land there.

Operation Vantage

As described in Chapter Two, this operation was mounted in July to protect Kuwait from the military threats being made by Iraq. The operation was top priority and involved the UK and Middle East Beverley forces comprising ten UK-based Beverleys and all the Beverleys that 30 and 84 Sqns could muster, 30 Squadron being detached to Bahrain. The aircraft were cleared to operate at emergency all-up weight and many 'hairy' take-offs were recorded due to inadvertent overloading.

The partially completed new civil airport at Kuwait possessed no landing aids and sandstorms were frequent, causing the most difficult flying conditions possible. Crews forced to night-stop at Kuwait had to 'doss down' wherever they could, as the airport hotel, restaurant and other such amenities were still in the process of construction.

The bulk of the Strategic Reserve was flown to Kuwait during Operation *Vantage* with the long-range fleet of Transport Command backing up the medium-range Hastings and Beverleys.

It was the Beverleys that moved the heavy gear though, field kitchens, and a complete field hospital, in addition to the Ferret light tanks, Saracen armoured cars and many other vehicles and equipment. Six squadrons of Hunters and Canberras also moved into Kuwait, their ground staff and equipment being lifted in by the Beverleys.

Vantage cost 30 Squadron an aircraft. XL131 was damaged by a terrorist's time bomb which went off during a flight from Kuwait to Bahrain. The aircraft was landed safely but the extent of the damage necessitated a quick patch-up job and a subsequent ferry flight to the UK for repairs by the manfacturers. As XL131 was being flown by an 84 Squadron crew when the time bomb went off, this incident is fully described in Chapter Four.

Vantage cost 84 Squadron a Beverley too, XM110 being written off by a time bomb that fortunately, exploded whilst the aircraft was on the ground and unoccupied. This incident is also described in more detail in Chapter Four.

Worse still, *Vantage* cost an airman his life: a corporal ground technician, no doubt fatigued by overwork, walked into the rotating propeller of a Britannia, sustaining fatal injuries.

The ground crews worked in appalling conditions during Operation *Vantage*, having to endure the incessant heat and flies, sandstorms and primitive living conditions.

The immense build-up of Army and RAF units in Kuwait, together with ships of the Royal Navy standing by in the Gulf, demonstrated to the Iraqis that the UK was determined to protect Kuwait at all costs. This massive show of military muscle prompted the Iraqi forces to withdraw from Kuwait's borders and a guarantee of peace was gained by the diplomats.

The task of pulling out of Kuwait then commenced. The immediate panic over, the UK-based Beverleys returned home, leaving 30 and 84 Squadrons to effect the withdrawal from Kuwait in a somewhat more leisurely manner than when the Strategic Reserve was moved in.

More Troops to Zanzibar

Although still engaged in the Kuwait withdrawal, part of 30 Squadron returned to base in September in order to move more troops from Dar Es Salaam to the trouble-stricken island of Zanzibar, to back up the hard-pressed garrison there whose troops were desperately trying to maintain law and order.

Flood relief

Late in October 1961, the 'short rains', which were overdue and had thus caused crop failures, started with a vengeance. The long-awaited rains were far in excess of normal, causing the Tana river to burst its banks and flood vast areas of farm-land and bush. Roads and railways were washed away and at one time the city of Nairobi was completely cut off. Remote towns and villages were also cut off and due to the previous poor harvest, stocks of food rapidly ran out.

Assisted by a detachment of four 38 Group, UK-based Beverleys, 30 Squadron immediately started an intensive flood relief supply dropping operation, mounted from Nairobi's civil airport Embakasi, due to rain damage on Eastleigh's laterite runway.

In the meantime, the King's Own Manchester and Liverpool Regiment, due to sail home to the UK from Mombasa, were stranded in Nairobi due to the wash-out of road and rail links. Not for long, though, they were soon 'Bevved' to Mombasa to catch their troopship.

Towards the end of the month, Flight Leiutenant Stalker was diverted after a supply drop, to search for a 38 Group helicopter which had forced landed with engine failure. The helicopter was found and it was established that there were no casualties. A ground party also found the helicopter at about the same time as the Beverley.

The squadron dropped 602 tonnes of food in November, all by the 'free fall' technique as described in Chapter Two. In addition to flood relief supply dropping, the squadron carried 948 passengers and nine tonnes of freight, this being mainly associated with the airlift of the UK-bound troops and their equipment to Mombasa.

December saw most of the squadron still at Bahrain moving men and 218 tonnes of equipment out of Kuwait. The detachment was also called on for para-troop work to keep the men of the Parachute Regiment at Bahrain in jumping practice.

In Kenya, flood relief work continued but on a reduced scale due to the Bahrain commitment. However, the squadron still managed to drop twenty one tonnes of food on some of the more difficult and inaccessible DZs.

Flood Relief in Tanganyika

The new year came in as the Kenyan floods subsided and with road and rail links re-established, stocks of food in towns and villages were built up and aerial delivery of food and supplies was no longer necessary. But the unusually heavy 'short rains' had affected Tanganyika too and as a result a famine situation existed in many remote parts of Kenya's neighbour. Accordingly 30 Squadron was called on to drop more food and the willing soldiers of No.16 Air Despatch Company, RASC, again did yeoman service making up the Derby sacks of food and then dispatching them from the Beverleys.

The Bahrain detachment participated in Exercise *Foamex 2*, a combined exercise between the Navy, RAF and the Second Battalion of the Parachute Regiment, The DZ for the para-drops was at Yas Island which lies to the east of the Qatar peninsula, see *Map 7*. During a heavy drop sortie from Manamah, a strip some forty miles east of Sharjah, Flight Lieutenant George Dorricott suffered the embarrassment of losing his load during take-off. This was due to equipment malfunction, but it did not save George and his crew from a few ribald remarks when they got back to the crew room and their messes.

February 1962 brought a requirement for two aircraft and crews to stand by at Bahrain, while back in East Africa the Tanganyika flood relief work continued, seventeen sorties being flown in which 200 tonnes of food were dropped. In March, Flying Officer Wright took His Excellency the Governor General of Tanganyika on a supply dropping trip impressing HE with the low-level approaches and runs over the DZ which were so essential for the intact delivery of a free-dropped load.

Flight Lieutenant George Dorricott and crew suffered another embarrassment later in the month when they flew a detachment of King's African Rifles into Wajir to relieve the garrison stationed there. As soon as the aircraft stopped, it broke through the crust of sun-baked sand that formed the airstrip surface and sank into the mud underneath. However, the crew and the KARs managed to extricate the aircraft. At this point, someone told George Dorricott that he should not have landed at Wajir but at Ngedis Nest, a strip some twenty miles to the south-east. The aircraft then took off, the crew glad to leave the mud of Wajir behind, found their destination and landed there, the first aircraft to do so for seventeen years.

Wajir acquired a reputation for bogging Beverleys, an aircraft which was thought to be pretty well 'unboggable'.

During trials in the UK before entering service, Beverleys had happily trundled through mud ten inches and deeper without any bother. But parts of East Africa and the Persian Gulf were endowed with mud of a consistency that not even the Beverley could cope with. Another Wajir bogging is described later in this chapter.

Mukeiras airstrip in South Arabia. Like many other airstrips near the Yemen border, Mukeiras often came under fire from tribesmen in the hills. *B. Thatcher*

Operation Vantage ends

In April all aircraft and crews returned from their long tour of duty in Bahrain in connection with the withdrawal from Kuwait, and Operation *Vantage* was officially declared to be ended. During April, while on stand-by, 30 Squadron had managed to fit in a great deal of supply-dropping, delivering eighteen tonnes to various places in the Gulf.

In May Squadron Leader Evans was diverted from circuit flying to search for a USAF C-130 aircraft reported missing whilst approaching Embakasi. The aircraft was found at the southern end of the Ngong hills: there were no survivors.

Oryx Preservation Flight

Flight Lieutenant Holloway undertook an interesting and unusual task whilst on a Bahrain schedule flying from Khormaksar into Sanau, an isolated strip in the Aden Protectorate, to pick up two male and one female white Arabian Oryx. This species was in danger of extinction due to relentless hunting by wealthy Arabs using modern high-powered rifles from motor vehicles, this method of hunting giving the unfortunate animals little chance of escape. On arrival at Khormaksar, the animals were transhipped to a Britannia which flew them to Nairobi, where it is hoped they survived and bred in the neighbouring game park.

Engines Modified

In May 1962 the squadron's aircraft were grounded for engine modifications, following the Thorney Island crash resulting from an uncontrollable engine fire. As soon as the squadron was mobile again, Squadron Leader Evans and crew took XB263 to the Central African Federation, i.e. Basutoland, Swaziland and Bechuanaland, to evaluate suitable airstrips.

Due to further terrorism in the Northern Frontier District of Kenya, Exercise *Air Wings* was mounted to test air traffic control and other general communications in that area, 71 sorties being flown, each of about one hour duration.

More Trouble in Aden Protectorate

Five special flights to Khormaksar were laid on in July to back up 84 Squadron which was carrying out an intensive airlift to various up-country strips. A large quantity of timber, cement and other building materials was airlifted into Mukeiras where building work to improve the living conditions of the garrison was in progress.

Squadron Back to Full Aircraft Strength

Ever since XL131 had been damaged by a terrorist's time bomb during Operation *Vantage* in September 1961, the squadron had been operating with one aircraft short. The arrival of XL131 back at Eastleigh, having been ferried from the UK by Flight Lieutenant Selway and crew was greeted by relief as intense demand for aircraft was being placed on the squadron. To indicate the squadron's work-load, in July 1962 116 tonnes of freight were carried and 27 tonnes of supplies and equipment were air-dropped.

Resumption of Bahrain Stand-by

The autumn of 1962 saw two aircraft and three crews on stand-by at Bahrain for Operation *Tantrum* which was planned in anticipation of another territorial threat on Kuwait by Iraq. During this Bahrain detachment, 30 Squadron carried out Exercise *Duffell 2* moving the 6th Parachute Brigade from Bahrain to Juweiza, a small airstrip some thirty miles inland from Sharjah. During this exercise an airborne assault in which 300 paras were dropped was carried out at Manamah followed by the usual series of resupply drops in which seven tonnes of supplies were delivered.

Meanwhile, back in East Africa, Uganda became independent and one Beverley was detached to Entebbe in support of 208 Squadron presumably in case the Independence celebrations became too boisterous.

Flight Lieutenant Field undertook a sad mission in October, flying via Khormaksar to Diredawa in Somalia (see *Map 6*) to collect a Beaver aircraft of the Desert Locust Survey. The Beaver had force-landed while spraying and the unfortunate pilot had been killed by hostile tribesmen. North East Africa and the Arabian Peninsula were fast becoming dangerous places for Europeans.

In November 1962, the squadron was called upon to provide yet another detachment, this time to Khormaksar to assist the hard-pressed 84 Squadron with their constant up-country airlifts in support of the Army desperately trying to repel attacks made by the dissident tribesmen supported by Egyptian-trained Yemeni troops.

Back in Kenya, Squadron Leader Evans air-dropped supplies to an RAF survey team in the Seychelles and air-snatched mail from the team by means of an improvised grappling hook and nylon rope arrangement. A Beverley 'first-off' was claimed for this operation as no records could be found of any similar operation having been done by a Beverley in the past.

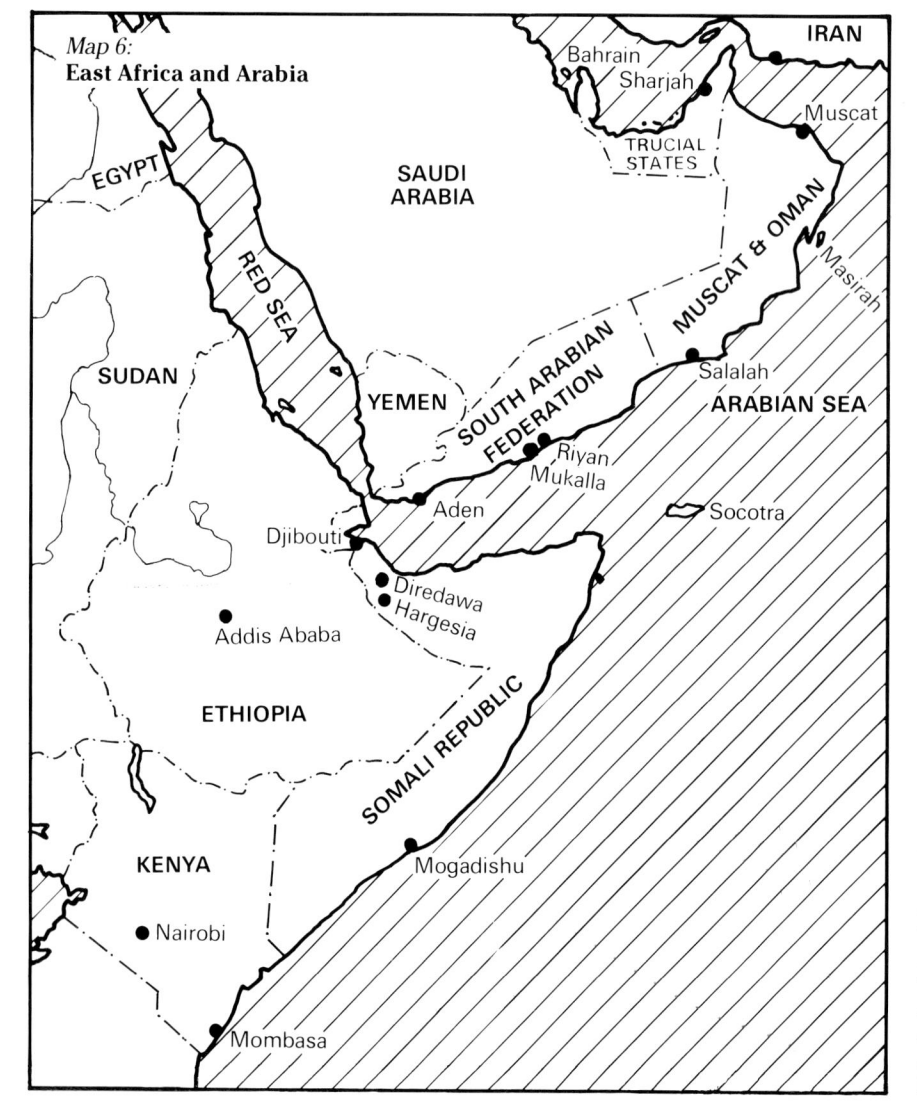

Map 6: East Africa and Arabia

XL152 of 30 Squadron photogenically placed over the imposing Mount Kenya.
Crown Copyright

Beverley Altitude Supply-drop Record Claimed

Squadron Leader Evans claimed another 'Beverley first' with a high altitude supply drop on Mount Kenya. Flying XB263, the Squadron Leader and crew dropped two prefabricated huts and building materials to the Mountain Club of Kenya. Two high-altitude drops were made: one at 13,500 feet at Clarwills Camp: the other at 14,700 feet at Kami Tarn. More drops were made on Mount Kenya later in the month.

In XH123, Flying Officer West and crew airlifted a nine-tonne grader from Eastleigh to Nakuru to improve the surface of the airstrip. This airlift added to the squadron's impressive 'weight lifting' figures for the month which worked out at 169 tonnes of freight carried plus thirty-three tonnes of supplies air-dropped. Over 400 passengers were also carried.

Fuel for Trucial Oman Scouts

With the stand-by for Operation *Tantrum* in Bahrain continuing, Exercise *Desert Nimble* was carried out of keep the RAF detachment and No.1 Battalion The Parachute Regiment in practice. Flight Lieutenant Butler in XH123 also dropped forty-eight drums of fuel to the Trucial Oman Scouts at Humer almost on the Saudi Arabian border. The DZ was a difficult one and twenty-four runs had to be made under the directions of a Twin Pioneer of 152 Squadron.

Exercise Seabird and Sharp Panga

The stand-by at Bahrain for Operation *Tantrum* continued into February 1963 with three aircraft and crews involved. Despite this depletion of its operational strength, the squadron carried out two major exercises in East Africa. The first, Exercise *Seabird*, involved a shuttle of troops from Mombasa to Zanzibar moving over 700 passengers in eight sorties. The next exercise mounted from Isiolo and code-named *Sharp Panga*, was in support of the King's African Rifles and was the biggest exercise ever to be held in East Africa. In addition to 30 Squadron's Beverleys assisted by two Beverleys from 84 Squadron, other units participating included 73 Squadron (Canberras), 21 Squadron (Twin Pioneers), and the Army Air Corps operating Beaver aircraft and Alouette helicopters. The Beverley force carried 959 troops and 287 tonnes of equipment in addition to dropping 125 paratroops and five tonnes of supplies.

In addition to Exercises *Seabird* and *Sharp Panga*, 30 Squadron managed other commitments too and achieved the following impressive set of statistics for February 1963:

Hours flown	309
Passengers carried	839
Troops carried	1688
Freight carried (tonnes)	452
Supplies dropped (tonnes)	36
Paratroops dropped	125

Bahrain Detachment Reduced - More 'Shifta' Trouble in Kenya

March 1963 saw some relaxation in the political tension in the Persian Gulf, permitting the Operation *Tantrum* stand-by to be reduced to two aircraft and crews. The Bahrain element was, however, kept busy by Exercise *Final Fling* for No.1 Battalion The Parachute Regiment prior to its return to the UK. The exercise involved para-drops at Jebel Ali and Juweiza.

In Kenya, outbreaks of terrorism by the Somali 'Shifta' in the Northern Frontier District worsened and Flight Lieutenant Aked and crew in XH123 flew supplies of fuel into Wajir and Mandera to increase the mobility of patrols from these garrisons. April and May were two comparatively slack months both in Kenya and in the Persian Gulf. In the latter theatre, paratrooping work was slack due to No.3 Battalion The Parachute Regiment taking up the duties relinquished by No.1 Battalion. However, the Trucial Oman Scouts were active and a number of supply sorties were flown in support of their operations.

Flight Lieutenant Don Selway and crew landed XH119 at Abu Dhabi and became bogged as described in the article reproduced from the Lyneham Globe. Although as the article states, 30 Squadron's history does not reveal the ultimate fate of the aircraft or its crew, they all get a mention shortly afterwards in the squadron records concerning a routine trip, so it can be safely assumed that XH119 was extricated safely from the tenacious sands of Abu Dhabi airstrip, now thanks to oil wealth, a major international airport.

As the new Parachute Regiment unit became acclimatized, Army support work intensified as the paras worked up to full efficiency.

Trouble in Swaziland

In June 1963, it was announced that Kenya would become independent in the following December. June also saw Operation *Alfred*, in which troops were airlifted into Matsapa in Swaziland where the country's economy was in danger of collapsing due to a general strike. In addition to the troops, the Bechuanaland Tribal Police were flown in as reinforcements and over 400 paratroops were dropped. The strike continued into July and the squadron was called upon to check out airstrips in the Matsapa area to assess their suitabiltiy for use by Beverleys. The squadron also dropped 128 paratroops of the Rhodesian SAS. Operation *Alfred* involved some very hard work and intensive flying, the squadron logging, in June and July, 796 flying hours, carrying 3,309 passengers, 542 tonnes of freight and air-dropping seventeen tonnes of supplies to remotely located units. These impressive statistics could never have been achieved without the hard work and dedication of the ground crews who worked incredibly long hours to keep their aircraft airborne. A large proportion of their work was done at night, particularly rectification of snags that had occurred during the previous day's flying.

Another Beverley bogged, this time at Abu Dhabi. Lyneham Globe

ONE OF THOSE DAYS

If you're reading the 'Globe' after a frustrating, depressing day, perhaps this look into 30 Sqn's history will cheer you up. April 25th 1963 certainly proved to be both depressing and frustrating for Flt Lt Don Selway, captain of XH119, a Beverley of 30 Sqn.

Flt Lt Selway and his crew landed at Abu Dhabi (a strip in those days) to collect No 2 Beach Survey Team. (Dosen't beach surveying sound an attractive job?). While taxying out for take off the port main undercarriage of the Beverley broke through the hard top crust of sand and sank.

A large number of the local Arabs surrounded the not-very-upright Beverley to offer 'advice'. All but two disappeared however when they were asked to help dig the aeroplane out! Eventually some more energetic, or perhaps more easily bribed locals were recruited. In temperatures of 110°F in the shade they dug for around 30 minutes before the labour force again diminished to two stalwarts.

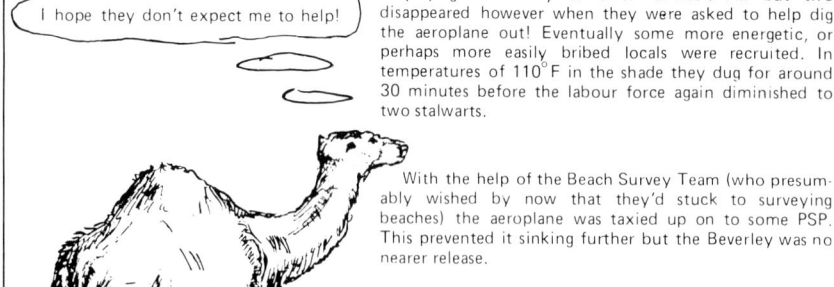

I hope they don't expect me to help!

With the help of the Beach Survey Team (who presumably wished by now that they'd stuck to surveying beaches) the aeroplane was taxied up on to some PSP. This prevented it sinking further but the Beverley was no nearer release.

An attempt to tow the machine out was abandoned when it became likely that the only outcome would be the sudden detachment of the noeswheel.

Although the Beach Survey Team were airlifted out next day by another Beverley, 30 Sqn history does not reveal the ultimate fate of the aircraft or its crew.

Perhaps they're still there today, tirelessly digging, though with all that experience of digging in sand the crew have probably formed No 1 Beach Survey Team.

Operation Tantrum Continues - Operation Instalment Commences

The political situation in the Persian Gulf was somewhat fluid in the closing months of 1963. The Bahrain detachment was reduced to one aircraft and crew in August but was increased again to two aircraft and crews in September and remained at that level for the remainder of the year. This period was highlighted by Exercise *Awex 10* in co-operation with the Royal Navy and the Sultan of Oman's Air Force. The exercise involved Beverley landings at Sohar, a small strip on the coast of the Gulf of Oman. The Beverleys cut up the strip so badly that they abandoned it and landed and took off from the adjoining desert. Apparently unaware of the dangerous Beverley wheel ruts in the airstrip, a Provost of the Sultan's Air Force landed on the strip and due to the rutted surface, tipped on its nose. The Omani pilot was last seen by the crew of a departing Beverley to be attacking the propeller of his Provost with a hammer. It is not known whether this attack was an outburst of rage or an attempt at repair!

In Kenya, the Shifta terrorists continued their attacks and Operation *Instalment* was mounted to change over the King's African Rifles detachments at the garrisons of Isiolo, Wajir, Garissa and Mandera. In addition, Operation *Instalment* called for a stand-by ready to fly troops to trouble spots in the Northern Frontier District and also to undertake supply deliveries and air-drops.

Beverley Stick-in-the-Mud

On one of the supply trips to Wajir, now renowned for its ability to ensnare unsuspecting Beverleys in its mud, yet another Beverley became bogged. Major I. A. D. Gordon, who at that time was in command of the Wajir garrison, was involved in the incident and wrote: 'As an officer in the Royal Highland Fusiliers, I flew on a number of occasions in Beverleys between 1957 and 1960. We (the Army) always looked on them as a flying monster! However, from 1960 to 1964 I was seconded to the 3rd Battalion, King's African Rifles in Kenya and came into close contact with these splendid machines and excellent crews. The aircraft based at RAF Eastleigh flew us to all the corners of Kenya. The expressions on the faces of many *askaris* were interesting when they got near enough to see the Beverley's actual size; many regarded it as something magical.

'Shortly before Kenya's Independence, trouble broke out in the North East Province where the Somali people wanted to break away to join Somalia. I was commanding D Company of 3 KAR at Wajir and had every reason to be thankful for the wonderful help given by the Beverleys and 21 Squadron's Twin Pioneers.

'When the Somali Shifta started 'hotting

Loading a 9-tonne earthmoving grader at Khormaksar. Note the Zip-up collapsible staging for engine servicing neatly stowed in the clamshell doors. *J. Knight*

up' the trouble, many other troops were flown in to other places by Beverley and supplied by us. Just before Christmas 1963, the main road into the North East (of the district) was broken by floods and soon all our supplies, and food for the civilian population were being flown in and air-dropped at Wajir airstrip which was too soft for Beverleys to land on - even Twin Pioneers took off from the taxi-way in preference to the waterlogged airstrip. The staff at Eastleigh was urging us to accept Beverleys to land despite my reports that in my opinion the sand of the strip was only dry to a depth of about one foot.

'Eventually, two Beverleys were tasked to land food and supplies: the first got in and out alright by not turning and instead, reversed back up the strip to its take-off point. What other aircraft could do that? The second Beverley stopped short in the marks left by the first and soon the port wheels began to sink through the hard crust of sand. Efforts were made to lay planks but as soon as the aircraft moved, it sank again.

'We were worried that the Shifta might attack such a good target so we got all the prisoners and tribal police from the base to help dig a huge channel in the sand down to bedrock; this was filled with stone to make a long sloping ramp so that the Beverley could taxi out. It took about twenty-eight hours of non-stop work and worry. I felt sorry for the pilot who was on a short detachment from Aden.

'When we had built a stone ramp and all surplus gear on board had been removed, the Beverley motored out on her own and flew back to Eastleigh.

'I was much relieved to see her go as we had to guard all round the area which was some way from our camp and my Company was stretched to its limits'.

In addition to the trip described above, which was part of Exercise *Late Gesture*, mounted to supply the North Frontier District outposts, a major air drop of supplies was carried out on Christmas Eve 1963. Garrisons supplied included Wajir, Moyale, El Wok, Mandera and Garissa, most of which were cut off due to flooding making the roads impassable. Special consignments of Christmas cheer were dropped together with the normal day-to-day requirements of rations, medical supplies and other commodities.

Zanzibar and Kenya Become Independent

The island of Zanzibar was granted independence on the 10th December: Kenya's independence was granted two days later. For Zanzibar's independence celebrations, Squadron Leader Harrison and crew took XH119 to Dar Es Salaam, carrying ground crew and equipment in support of 208 Squadron which was to participate in Zanzibar's Independence Day celebration flypast. Two other sorties, associated with the Zanzibar Independence celebrations, were flown to Dar Es Salaam later in the month, XH119 and XH120 being skippered by Flight Lieutenant Humphrey and Flying Officer West respectively.

Independence Troubles

January 1964 brought trouble in the armies of Kenya, Uganda and Tanganyika with troops mutinying against their white officers. Crews of 30 Squadron were called to immediate readiness and commenced an airlift of loyal troops to the various trouble spots where the mutinies were quelled. Troops were also flown to Mombasa to board HMS *Rhyl* and another destroyer which then stood to off the coast of Zanzibar in case of trouble there.

Four aircraft and crews were detached from 84 Squadron and were used in a night assault landing on Entebbe airport. Air Commodore J. C. McDonald, Commander of the RAF in East Africa, flew in the lead aircraft, a Shackleton of 37 Squadron, from where he directed the operation. The Shackleton crew had been briefed to drop flares to light the airfield in the event of it being in the hands of the mutineers. The landing however, was uneventful and the rebellion was put down with comparative ease.

Meanwhile in Tanganyika, President Nyere had left his country and was rumoured to be on board a ship in the Indian Ocean. In his absence, the Tanganyikan army mutinied and 30 Squadron, assisted by the 84 Squadron detachment, flew Royal Marines and troops from other units to Dar Es Salaam and Tabora, where they quelled the disturbance and disarmed the mutineers.

The next outbreak of 'independence fever' was in Nachinwea on the Tanganyika/Mozambique border. Two Beverleys of 30 Squadron, led by Squadron Leader Harrison, flew a detachment of Royal Marines into Nachinwea where again, the mutiny was quelled relatively easily. The ringleaders were identified, arrested and flown by the Beverleys back to Dar Es Salaam to be dealt with by the new government.

In parallel with all the activities concerned with the independence troubles, the squadron still had to fit in Operation *Late Gesture* in which men and supplies were flown to Wajir and other strips on the North Frontier District border which was still suffering terrorist attacks by the Somali Shifta.

Work in progress to dig out a Beverley bogged at Wajir in Northern Kenya. *I. Gordon*

Freed from Wajir's treacherous mud, the de-bogged Beverley taxies away - backwards, as indicated by the dust blown forwards by the propellers in reverse pitch. *I. Gordon*

Opposite page: **Detachment of King's African Rifles waiting to emplane at Wajir.** *I. Gordon*

The Bahrain detachment continued as well with two Beverleys and crews providing para and supply-dropping practise for the military force garrisoned there. At the end of January, 30 Squadron had exceeded its scheduled number of flying hours by 68 per cent, the result of prodigious efforts by the ground staff. Many aircraft however, were overdue for servicing, having run out of hours and been granted extensions permitting extra hours to be flown before servicing. This naturally created a large backlog of work for February but the ever-enthusiastic ground staff still continued to meet their commitments.

Stork Strike

In February 1964, XH123 suffered a major bird strike, the offending bird being a large Malibu stork which inflicted severe damage on the nose section in the area of the flight deck.

Indeed the crew were fortunate to have escaped injury. The aircraft was too badly damaged to be repaired by Eastleigh's Second Line Servicing Team and it took a working party from the Blackburn factory six weeks to repair the damage.

Wajir Airstrip Resurfaced

Two events highlighted March 1964. The first, carried out in anticipation of the 'long rains' involved delivering substantial amounts of supplies to all the North Frontier District garrisons.

The second, of immense importance, was the start of resurfacing work on the infamous Wajir airstrip, whose treacherous surface had disrupted the schedule of so many Beverleys. The work was undertaken by the Kenyan Ministry of Public Buildings and Works, the resurfacing equipment having been flown in by Beverley.

The earth-moving equipment used included a large power shovel which was one foot too high for the Beverley freight bay. Deflating the tyres however, did the trick and Flight Lieutenant Selway and crew flew the shovel into Wajir. Needless to say, the shovel was off-loaded with all possible haste for fear of its extra weight causing yet another Beverley to be ensnared by the Wajir mud.

Pilots Become Policemen

Another event highlighting March 1964 was the detachment of Flight Lieutenant Dickie Statham and Flying Officer M.P. Gale to the Kenya Police Air Wing for flying duties on Cessna 180 aircraft for reconnaissance work in the North Frontier District where renewed terrorist activities by the Shifta had overstretched the resources of the police. The two pilots worked extremely hard during their detachment and found the work interesting albeit very demanding and certainly vastly different from flying the huge Beverleys.

With Shifta raids increasing dramatically, troops of the General Service Unit were hurriedly airlifted to Marsabit but failed to engage the elusive terrorists. In an attempt to locate the Shifta raiding parties, a 21 Squadron Twin Pioneer was detailed to fly along a line from Marsabit to Garrissa at night dropping flares at intervals. This operation was backed up by XH124, captained by Flight Lieutenant M. Letton, acting as an aerial beacon and navaid for the Pioneer. This attempt at locating the Shifta was also unsuccessful.

Rumours of Move - SAR (Search and Rescue) Duties

In May and June 1964 rumours of a move to Muharraq, in Bahrain, pervaded the squadron. A move was inevitable since, on granting independence to Kenya, HM Government had undertaken to move all military units out of the country by December. Thus in view of the unstable situation in the Persian Gulf which demanded a permanent Beverley force detachment there, this rumour was considered to be more than an educated guess.

The Bahrain detachment was kept busy during this period by a succession of searches for missing aircraft. The first search was for a Middle East Airlines Caravelle reported to have ditched in the Gulf; nothing was found. The second was for a stolen civil aircraft reputed to be carrying smugglers en route from Karachi to Doha. The aircraft was eventually found crashed, 700 miles south of track. The smugglers seemingly were not good navigators.

The third search was for two 208 Squadron Hunters which crashed while on rocket firing practice near Jebel Dhana. 84 Squadron was involved in this search and located one survivor whose SARAH beacon was transmitting from the Arab dhow that had fortunately picked him up. He had presumably ejected safely. The pilot of the other Hunter was not so fortunate and was killed when his aircraft crashed on the coast near Yas Island. The body of this officer was taken by helicopter to Jebel Dhana South from where Flight Lieutenant G. H. Smyth and crew in a 30 Squadron Beverley, flew the body to Muhurraq.

Back in East Africa, another search took place in July, with Flight Lieutenant Humphrey and crew in XH120 searching for a Twin Pioneer in the North Frontier District. The missing aircraft was eventually found at Mkowe, a tiny airstrip on which it had force-landed due to fuel shortage. Flight Lieutenant Statham and crew, the former back from his detachment with the Kenya Police Air Wing, carried out a successful supply drop of fuel for the stranded aircraft which soon got airborne again and returned to base.

Rumours of Move Materialize

July 1964 also saw preparation for the move to Muharraq which, translated from the Arabic means 'place of the dead'. The squadron personnel however did not regard this as an ill omen but rather as a challenge to liven the place up on their arrival. There were many regrets about leaving Kenya: the pleasant climate, the superb amenities offered by the modern city of Nairobi, and the splendid social life. The wives and families regretted the move more than their menfolk, the barren island of Bahrain could never offer the same attractions as Eastleigh. However, on the premise that all good things must come to an end, the squadron took the preparations for the move in its stride and determined to make the best of things, the first two crews leaving for Muharraq in mid-July.

The ground staff were most affected by the move since all second line servicing facilities at Eastleigh were moved to Khormaksar. Muharraq was preferable to Khormaksar since Bahrain enjoys a cool 'winter' season during which personnel changed from khaki drill into blues. The cool season was similar to an English summer and was a welcome change after the torrid heat and exhausting humidity of the Bahrain hot season. But Aden had no cool season as such; in general, the climate was hot and humid, night and day all year round, the temperature seldom falling below 32°C (90°F) even at night. In addition to the intense heat, Aden was a depressing place: sand, sand and more sand, barren rocks and shark-infested sea was about all that Aden could offer. Compared with Eastleigh, Aden offered practically nothing in the way of interesting places to visit and certainly no social life outside the base unless one was befriended by a rich Arab.

Due to the incessant heat, working conditions were appalling particularly inside the aircraft and down the wing crawlways and in the accessory bays behind the engines. During the day, these places became so hot that it was impossible for a man to work in them for more than an hour or so at a time. He then had to emerge and drink copiously to avoid dehydration and heat exhaustion.

But despite the sweltering heat and humidity, the barren bleakness and the sheer inhospitality of Aden, the Eastleigh second line ground staff soon settled in with their Khormaksar colleagues and cheerfully resumed, with superb efficiency, their business of overhauling the Middle East Air Force Beverleys.

August brought official confirmation of the move which was scheduled to be complete by the end of the month. The squadron's move to Muharraq relieved 84 Squadron of their Bahrain detachment commitment and the 84 Squadron crews and aircraft returned to Khormaksar to continue their support of the Army in its operations against the Yemeni terrorists.

The principal event in Muharraq was Exercise *Sandstone* in which the 3rd Battalion The Parachute Regiment was dropped at Al Khatt, a DZ near the foothills of Jebel Ali, north-east of Sharjah. A number of troops were injured in this exercise, possibly by bad landings on the rocky terrain and sixteen casevac stretcher cases plus some walking casualties were Bevved out.

In Kenya, Squadron Leader Harrison and crew in XH119 did a successful night search for an Army Air Corps helicopter which had force-landed in the Northern Frontier District due to fuel shortage. Next day, XH124 skippered by Flight Lieutenant Brian Clinch, dropped fuel for the stranded chopper.

Members of 30 Squadron at Muharraq, Bahrain around 1964. *R. Honeybone*

Map 7:
Oman and the Persian Gulf

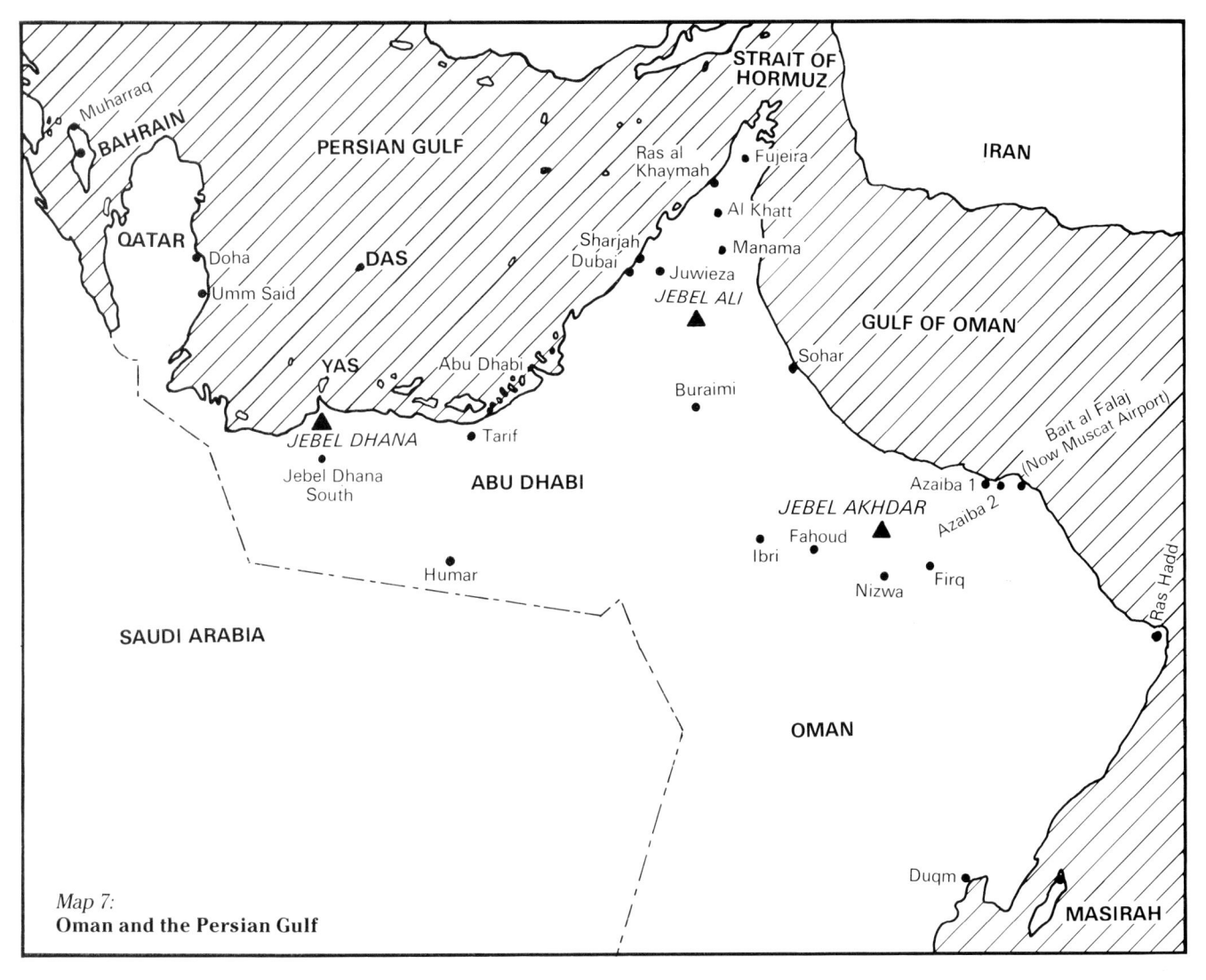

Trouble at Salalah
On 21st September, dissident tribesmen attacked the Sultan of Muscat and Oman's property near his palace at Salalah on the coast south of Masirah, see *Map 6*. This was the first major outbreak of terrorism in that area and was typical of the way in which terrorism was spreading from the Yemen border, not only southwards towards Aden, but to the east as well.

To deal with this outbreak, two aircraft, XH120 and XH122, skippered by Flying Officer C. W. Ellis and Flight Lieutenant Brian Clinch respectively, proceeded to Sharjah to fly a detachment of the 16/5 Hussars, together with their Land Rovers and Ferret armoured cars, to Salalah.

The 3rd Battalion, The Parachute Regiment, had by now made a permanent base camp at Jebel Ali and training drops were made in that area, the troops emplaning at Sharjah. The first series of drops resulted in twenty three casevacs, suggesting more heavy landings by the paras.

The squadron was still engaged on duties on Kenya and in the same month, Flight Lieutenant Statham and crew in XH124, took the AOC Air Forces Middle East, Air Vice Marshal 'Johnnie' Johnson, of Battle of Britain fame, on a tour of all the Northern Frontier District Beverley airstrips. Eastleigh's station commander, Group Captain I. S. Stockwell, accompanied the AVM. Despite some resurfacing, Wajir airstrip was still the *bête noir* of the Beverley force and XH124, captained by Flight Lieutenant Clark, became yet another victim of Wajir's treacherous mud. This time the aircraft sank so deeply that a propeller was damaged and had to be changed.

At Muharraq, November was highlighted by Exercise *November Handicap* - a combined Beverley and Argosy exercise dropping at Sohar, a tiny strip on the eastern Trucial coast. Sohar was chosen since it had a beach suitable for tank landing craft taking part in the exercise. The 'enemy' troops were positioned on the 11th, either being dropped or air landed, and the assault took place on the night of the 12th. Four 30 Squadron Beverleys, led by the CO, Squadron Leader R. A. W. Harrison, joined the formation of Argosies from 105 Squadron at Khormaksar. The TAP (Target Approach Point) was HMS *Mean*. The Beverleys dropped 152 paras and 68 tonnes of supplies. The exercise lasted until the 16th when the recovery phase was completed.

New UK-Aden route
December 1964 saw the inauguration of a new UK-Aden route due to the Sudanese government prohibiting British military aircraft from overflying their country. With Anglo-Egyptian relations now improved, a route via El Adem and Cairo to Khormaksar was begun; see *Map 8*. Aircraft for Bahrain had to fly the usual Khormaksar - Bahrain route, calling as necessary at Riyan, Salalah, Masirah and Sharjah.

One of the first aircraft to use the new route was XL152 flown by Flying Officer C. W. Ellis and crew, on a delivery flight from the UK after a major overhaul. On the Cairo-Khormaksar leg, the aircraft suffered a lightning strike over the Red Sea, and seeing the murderous banks of towering cumulo-nimbus ahead of him, the captain rightly decided to overfly Saudi Arabia and proceed direct to Muharraq. This was done without incident and all the crew were grateful that there was sufficient fuel on board to enable this diversion to be made.

Map 8:
The El-Adem - Cairo Route

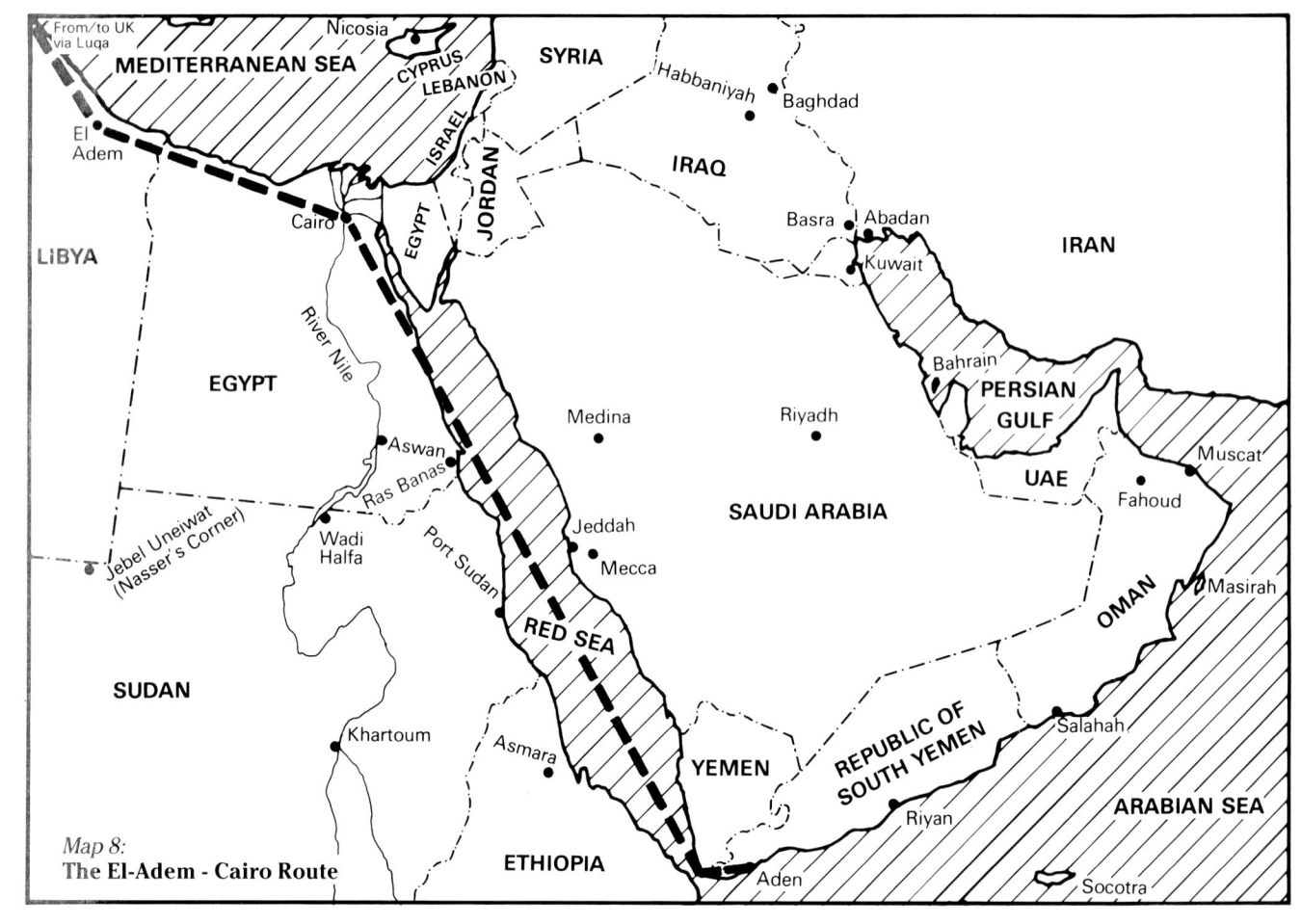

Mercy Flight to Masirah

December 1964 ended with XH123 being flown to Sharjah by Flight Lieutenant Lancaster and crew, to take a doctor to Masirah. A seaman, who was dangerously ill with acute peritonitis had earlier been landed at Masirah, from his ship the tanker *British Eagle*. On arrival at Masirah, the doctor gave the patient emergency treatment: the doctor and patient were then Bevved to Muharraq where the patient received surgery and recovered fully.

Another SAR Mission

On 23rd March, Flight Lieutenant Humphrey and crew were called out for a search and rescue detail and got airborne in XM105. Two fighters of the Saudi Arabian Air Force were reported to have ditched seventy-five miles north-east of Muharraq. Two ships of the Indian Navy were in the area - the *Brahmaputra* and the *Ramhov*. One pilot was picked up by the *Brahmaputra* but an intense search both by ship and Beverley, failed to locate his comrade.

April 1964 was marked by Squadron Leader R. P. J. 'Paddy' King taking command of the squadron from Squadron Leader Harrison. Shortly afterwards, the new CO captained a Beverley taking a team of Royal Navy divers to Masirah, to repair the undersea oil pipes that carried oil ashore from tankers.

More trouble with Arab Dissidents

Due to increasing troubles in the Radfan, more and more air support was requested by the Army and to meet their requests, 30 Squadron detached two aircraft and crews to Khormaksar to assist 84 Squadron. At about the same time, further attacks were made on the Sultan's property in the Salalah area, and reinforcements from the Sultan's Army at Firq were quickly Bevved to Salalah to deal with the trouble. Later in the month, Flight Lieutenant Brian Clinch and crew in XH119 flew a gang of prisoners, presumably captured dissidents, from Salalah to Azaiba 1. Ex-AQM John Ward, one of Brian's crew, wrote of this incident:

'I once took forty Arab prisoners from Salalah to Muscat: they were all manacled together ankle-to-ankle. I don't think many returned home from Muscat!'

John also recalled a night stop at Masirah which illustrates the primitive conditions under which Masirah's personnel lived:

'I awoke in my room in the 'new' Sergeants Mess to find a donkey standing by my bed!'

Ferrets to Saudi Arabia and Paras to Radfan

In June, Flight Lieutenant Clarke and crew flew XL152 to Riyadh with two Ferret scout cars and a detachment of the 10th Hussars. The Scout cars were for trials with the Saudi Arabian Army.

Later in the month, Flight Lieutenant Chris Dyson and crew in XH123 flew sixty-six men of C Company, First Battalion The Parachute Regiment to Khormaksar for duties in the Radfan to relieve the detachment from A Company.

In October, Flight Lieutenant J. Blount and crew in XH152 took another detachment from the First Para to Khormaksar to relieve their hard-pressed colleagues fighting in the Radfan.

Squadron's 50th Anniversary

The squadron's Golden Jubilee was celebrated on 20th November with formation fly-pasts and demonstration supply drops at Hafira DZ. The squadron's colour was paraded and a ceremonial tattoo was held during the evening. The proceedings were attended by His Excellency Sir William Luce, Political Resident in Bahrain. Air Chief Marshal Sir James Robb was due to attend the celebrations but was prevented from doing so by illness. The day ended with a series of parties in all the Messes.

Trouble at Das Island

The year ended with civil disturbances on Das Island and two crews were placed on stand-by to fly a contingent of the Trucial Oman Scouts there. Fortunately, the trouble fizzled out and the stand-by was cancelled in time for all squadron personnel to participate in the Christmas festivities.

LOX Deliveries to Sharjah

The new year started with regular deliveries to Sharjah of LOX (liquid oxygen), used for replenishing the oxygen systems in modern aircraft, especially fighters. LOX is a dangerous cargo and because of this the LOX package was invariably rigged on a heavy drop platform with an oxygen specialist in attendance. If the cargo became dangerous it could be jettisoned over an uninhabited area and would make a controlled parachute descent, thus enabling the cargo to be subsequently recovered intact.

Ferry Flights

The early months of 1966 were highlighted by Squadron Leader King and crew ferrying XB266 from St.Athan where it had undergone a major overhaul. The aircraft developed many snags en route causing incessant delays, but by the time Muharraq was reached most of the 'bugs' seemed to have been chased out of 266's system.

Another SAR Mission

Whilst en route to Kuwait with a cargo of rocket projectiles and general stores, Flying Officer Dave Jenkins was detailed to carry out a search and rescue mission. The task was to search for a European in a hired Arab dhow. After a half-hour search, the mission was called off when the dhow turned up safely at Bahrain, its crew completely unaware of the problems it had caused.

'Hairy' Fuel Leak

Flying Officer Dave Jenkins and crew suffered another problem later in the month, when ferrying a load of explosives from Khormaksar to Muharraq. A severe fuel leak developed causing fuel to run into the freight bay amongst the explosives. The captain wisely carried out an immediate return to Khormaksar. After four days, the tank that was losing fuel had been identified as No.1 port tank but the source of the leak was still eluding the technicians. The aircraft was accordingly flown to Muharraq with the offending tank drained and the Muharraq technicians found and rectified the fault.

Food Poisoning Panic

At about this time, Flying Officer Dave Jenkins and crew suffered the much-publicised aircrew dilemma - mass food poisoning. Chris Sierwald, ex-30 Squadron pilot, wrote of the incident:

'They departed Aden for Sharjah and en route, the whole crew, except co-pilot Flying Officer Eddie Webb, became violently ill and were incapacitated by stomach cramps. Of course, this caused panic back in Aden as several Britannias, Argosies and Shackletons which had received food from the same kitchens were now spread about the Indian Ocean.

'Eddie managed to find Sharjah and landed the aircraft by himself.

'Everyone was carted off to hospital and the food analysed: not a trace of food posoning was found. However, further investigations revealed that one of the bottles of orange squash was riddled with salmonella germs, and Eddie, for some unknown but fortuitous reason, had drunk water instead of his usual squash'.

Starter Motor Trouble

In May 1966 Flying Officer Chris Dyson in XH122 suffered starter motor trouble at Sharjah. Undaunted, Chris did a windmill start which involved charging down the runway fast enough for the airflow to turn the propeller of the defective engine which then hopefully burst into life. The aircraft was then hurriedly stopped so that the suspect engine could be test-run prior to take-off. Windmill start and run-up completed, Chris took off, but just after getting airborne, an engine failed which necessitated feathering it and landing. Definitely not Chris's day.

Flight line at night, Muharraq 1964. 30 Squadron's XM05/A is in the foreground. *R. Honeybone*

30 Squadron aircraft of 1915 and 1965 (cutting from programme of celebrations for the Golden Jubilee). *via J. Ward*

30 SQUADRON AIRCRAFT THEN AND NOW

FARMAN

BEVERLEY

First Beverely into Bait el Falaj

Another Beverley 'first' was claimed in May 1966 when Flying Officer Ellis extended the AFME (Air Force Middle East) schedule by landing at Bait el Falaj. This was the first Beverley to land at Bait - a difficult airstrip due to its approach being through narrow valleys. These problems have now been overcome, however, as Bait el Falaj is Muscat's main international airport.

War Game goes Wrong

The main event of June 1966 was Exercise *Junex* which involved an airborne assault on Yas Island. Somehow the logistics for the exercise had gone wrong and insufficient water was available for the troops who were operating in temperatures well over 38°C (100°F). As a result there were many casualties and the squadron flew numerous sorties to uplift them back to base. Twenty-seven stretcher-case casevacs were flown out from the island.

Coup in Abu Dhabi

In August Operation *Hazland* was mounted due to Sheikh Shakbut, Ruler of Abu Dhabi, being deposed by his brother Sheikh Zaid. Two Beverleys, XM105 and XH122, skippered by Squadron Leader King and Flight Lieutenant Blount respectively, flew a large detachment of the Trucial Oman Scouts into Abu Dhabi. Two other Beverleys captained by Flying Officer Jenkins and Flight Lieutenant Mulligan held off overhead Sharjah in case they were needed to take in reinforcements.

In the event, the coup was quite bloodless, Sheikh Shakbut's retainers deserting him and allowing Sheikh Zaid and his followers to take over. Members of the deposed Sheikh's family stated that he was incompetent to rule and was not using his country's increasing wealth for the benefit of his people. Accordingly, Sheikh Shakbut was flown into exile at Bahrain.

Another SAR Operation

A major search and rescue operation was mounted later in August when a Saudi Arabian Hunter T.7 carrying a British flying instructor and a Saudi student pilot disappeared in the Kuwait area.

Flight Lieutenant Philips was diverted from the AFME schedule and searched for four hours until fuel shortage forced him to return to base. Flight Lieutenant Mulligan then did a five-hour search but had to return to base due to the expiry of crew duty time.

The same crew searched for twelve hours next day and were then relieved by Flight Lieutenant Chris Dyson and crew who did another twelve-hour search. After a further nine-hour search carried out the following day by Flight Lieutenant Blount and crew, the airborne search was abandoned. An air cylinder was picked up by an Arab dhow and brought ashore - the only wreckage found. The two pilots were presumed dead.

Aircraft to Hong Kong

Due to the large number to Beverleys becoming due for major overhaul, the resources of the UK maintenance units were becoming stretched. It was decided therefore to send 30 Squadron aircraft to Hong Kong for major servicing by a civil organization known as HAECO (Hong Kong Aircraft Engineering Company), which had been overhauling 34 Squadron's Beverleys of the Far East Air Force for some time. The route to Hong Kong was via Bombay, Calcutta, Butterworth, Changi and Saigon and took five days, provided that the aircraft stayed serviceable.

More Work for Squadron

In November 1967, 84 Squadron and its Beverleys left Khormaksar as part of the planned pull-out of British forces in Aden. The squadron's Beverleys were ferried to the UK for disposal, squadron personnel then moved to Sharjah to reform the squadron with Andover aircraft.

LOX (liquid oxygen) is a dangerous cargo. This LOX replenishment trolley was rigged as a heavy drop load so that, in emergency it could be safely jettisoned.
via JATE Brize Norton

The loss of 84's Beverleys resulted in much more work for 30 Squadron, which now undertook duties which could have been carried out by 84 Squadron, especially commitments in the Arabian Peninsula, notably in Dhofar Province where the Yemeni terrorists were still active, particularly in the Salalah area. Troop movements to the island of Socotra, and the uplift of fuel from Salalah to alleviate the shortage of aviation fuel at Riyan (see later in this chapter) were tasks carried out by 30 Squadron, due to the absence of a Beverley squadron in the Arabian Peninsula.

Elevator Control Locks Engage

Most aircraft have a control locking system of some kind or another to prevent the control surfaces (ailerons, elevators and rudder(s)) from being buffeted and damaged by strong winds when the aircraft is parked. The Beverley control locking system consisted of retractable pins, operated from the first pilot's position, which engaged in reinforced holes in the leading edge of each control surface. An ingenious interlocking device ensured that only two symmetrical engines, i.e. the inners or outers, could be run up to full power with the control locks engaged, thus preventing any attempt to take off with the controls locked. The system was claimed to be failsafe due to the locking pins being spring loaded to the disengaged position.

However, on 13th January 1967, (was it a Friday?) 'Murphy's Law' prevailed during a continuation training detail at Muharraq with the Squadron Commander, Squadron Leader 'Paddy' King in command and with Flying Officer Chris Sierwald as co-pilot. Chris Sierwald wrote of the incident: 'Just after we got airborne, the elevators seemed to lock solid. A combined push from Paddy (height 6 feet 4 inches, weight 15 stone) and myself (6 feet 1 inch, 11½ stone) stopped the climb and we turned downwind for an emergency landing.

'The locks came in again several times round the circuit, but brute force seemed to free the control surfaces. Once the aircraft was lined up on finals, we managed to push the nose down but then had the problem of making sure that it didn't drop too low - it's much more difficult to pull the control column back than push it forward. Still, by pushing and pulling like mad things, and using the trimmers over the full range, we got reasonably close to the runway, chopped the throttles and 'arrived' on terra firma.

'Subsequently, I was on route with Squadron Leader King at Aden where we read the flight safety newsletter pertaining to the incident. His Irish temper was fired by the way the newsletter seemed to exonerate the engineers and imply that the aircrew were to blame, especially as no mention was made of the fact that the rubber bungee which was part of the control locks withdrawal mechanism had been found to be perished!'

So much for what could have been a very nasty incident had it not been for the muscle power and superb skill of the two pilots.

Main Spar Cracks

January 1967 saw XM111 being ferried from Akrotiri via Khormaksar by Flight Lieutenant P. F. H. Walker and crew. This aircraft had been sent to Akrotiri to replace XB266 which had been grounded there with suspected cracks in the wing main spar attachment brackets but when precision crack detection techniques were employed, the 'cracks' turned out to be no more than superficial scratches and blemishes. The ground technicians could not be blamed for over-enthusiastic crack searching though, since cracks had been discovered in various places in other Beverleys.

Rumours of Beverley Replacement

January 1967 also brought rumours that the Beverleys were to be withdrawn from service. These rumours were substantiated by the fact that it was now known that an order had been placed by MoD for C-130K Hercules and indeed crews were already undergoing conversion training in the USA. A further rumour did the rounds that 30 Squadron were to re-equip with 115 Squadron's Argosies after disposing of the Beverleys.

More SARs

In February, a 21-hour search and rescue operation was carried out by Flight Lieutenants Drew, Bentham, Walker and their crews looking for a missing Arab dhow between Sharjah and Qatar. Nothing was found and the vessel was officially presumed lost. A letter from the Ruler of Qatar expressed his thanks for the efforts of the squadron. In March, Flight Lieutenant Mulligan and crew did another SAR sortie lasting eight and a half hours looking for a Bahrain-bound Cessna aircraft. The search was fruitless and just as the Beverley was returning to base it became known that the Cessna had diverted to Karachi without informing anyone.

Trouble in Socotra

March 1967 was also highlighted by Operation *Snaffle* in which two Beverleys were detached to Riyan to uplift troops, vehicles and equipment of the Hadrami Bedouin Legion to Socotra Island to quell an outbreak of terrorism there. The disturbance was duly dealt with, the rebels taken prisoner and were then Bevved back to Al Ghaydah in the Hadramaut, see *Map 2*.

One More SAR

Ever since its arrival at Muharraq, 30 Squadron had participated in numerous SAR operations to the extent that such operations had almost become a way of life for the squadron. The squadron's penultimate Beverley SAR mission took place in April 1967 when a 208 Squadron Hunter was reported missing in the Qatar area. The search continued throughout April until the wreckage was found about eighteen miles from Masirah in line with the flight path of Masirah's runway.

Squadron's Final Stand-by

On 8th June, the squadron was brought to immediate readiness and all-out efforts by the ground staff ensured that all aircraft, including one borrowed from 84 Squadron at Khormaksar, were serviceable.

The stand-by was for the evacuation of British civilians in Jordan which was being threatened by the Israeli/Arab troubles. In the event, the airlift, which turned out to be much smaller than anticipated, was carried out by UK-based aircraft operating from the Mediterranean area and 30 Squadron was stood down.

Political instability, also caused by the Israeli/Arab war, caused the discontinuation of the AFME 9 schedule to Kuwait.

Fuel Shortage

A large-scale strike in Aden caused an acute aviation fuel shortage at Riyan. To meet this emergency, the squadron detached an aircraft to Salalah to ferry fuel to Riyan for use in helicopters being used against terrorists in the Mukalla area. A total of 1,575 gallons was uplifted in 45 gallon drums.

Gerry Hatt's Answer to the 'Glamour Boys'

The Beverley crews were somewhat disgruntled at the way in which the fighter pilots of 208 Squadron, with their supersonic Hunter aircraft impressed the civil population, especially the female European element. The Beverley assumed the status of a furniture van hack, driven by a bus driver and crewed by muscle men whose duties seemed merely to consist of moving furniture and other freight.

Gerry put the record straight by composing the following poem, naming it:

The Other Torch Bearers

Like merchant princes of an earlier day
The Transport crews go winging on their way. And though
the merchant ships were rather vaster
The Beverley is, very slightly, faster.

Off to the merchant ports of modern era
With magic names like Sharjah and Masirah
Returning to confront The Movements Man.
'It's all been changed, that load was meant for Gan!'

They battle now in peace time as in war.
Battles to get their spare parts from the store.
Battles for rations, transport for the crew.
They fight as many battles as the 'Few'.

They seek not fame, or treasures, or reward.
Or voices shouting praises in accord.
Nor mention in the Order of the Day.
(They know they wouldn't get it anyway).

And when all's past and to Valhalla's Hall,
They're welcomed by Saint Peter or Saint Paul
They'll probably be greeted by the yell
'You're on a month's detachment down in Hell!'

Gerry composed yet another poem in honour of Exercise *Billtong*, an army exercise which appears to have been something of a muddle.

There's inertia south of Persia.
At Azaibah something's wrong.
Whilst at Sharjah, bumf looms larger,
But the Bevs are pressing on.

In a freight bay; in dispersal
Figured out by swearing Sarge
There's a Trim Sheet, it's a grim sheet
With a payload much too large.

Force Commander takes a gander
Then remarks with British phlegm.
Don't shut the door yet, she'll take more yet.
'We'll re-write the ODM.!'

Fill the boom with sweating bodies
All with sick-bags pre-arranged,
'Ere she roars off, take the doors off.
Kick 'em out, it's all been changed.

On the flight deck, airborne lights check
Being done with greatest care.
Sixty paras dive like 'arras'.
Ninety miles from anywhere.

Now it's over, we're in clover,
No more freight or bods to move.
Britain conquers, let's get 'Honkers'
By the way, what did we prove?

Gerry and the the author also composed a poem, a parody on John Masefield's 'Cargoes', to try and compare the Beverley with two of its contemporary aircraft. The result is as follows:

Cargoes (airborne)
Fussy little Argosy flying from the Continent,
Whining back to Berkshire o'er the Germans and the Dutch,
Seats full of passengers,
Servicemen and families
And freight if it's not bulky and doesn't weigh too much.

VC-10 of 'Shiny Fleet' inbound from America,
To velvet whisper touch-down in Oxon country-side
With a cargo of VIPs,
Brass hats with their retinues,
Complete with curvy Quartermaid attending to their needs.

Dirty old Beverley flogging down to Aden,
Sand-encrusted fuselage and oil-streaked wings,
Freight bay full of vehicles,
Artillery and ammo,
Boom full of pongos all 'honking up their rings.'

Strips Prepared for Andovers - Squadron's Final Beverley SAR Sortie

July brought a requirement to lengthen some of the Gulf airstrips to make them suitable for Andovers, the successors-to-be of the Beverleys, and consequently the squadron was kept busy moving bulldozers and other earth-moving equipment around the various strips. Air Chief Marshal Sir David Lee, CBE, CB in his book *Flight from the Middle East* writes of this operation '...30 Squadron took on an unusual task in July. Some of the rough strips in central Oman were suitable only for Twin Pioneers by virtue of their length - or lack of it. Their value would be greatly enhanced if they could be made long enough for Beverleys to take off, which would involve extending most of them by several hundred feet. This was accomplished by flying in a Beverley, which was perfectly feasible, loaded with a bulldozer and a grader, off-loading them with their crews, and waiting until the strip had been lengthened sufficiently to enable the Beverley with its load to take off comfortably. This sounds a fairly hazardous operation in potentially hostile country but 30 Squadron found no difficulties and it was certainly a highly economical method of extending an isolated airstrip'. What other aircraft could have done that?

However, for Flight Lieutenant Blount and crew, these activities were interrupted when they were called on to perform 30 Squadron's final Beverley SAR mission in the Gulf after receiving a report that a dhow had sunk ninety miles north-east of Bahrain Island. Shortly after arrival at the estimated position, the survivors were sighted and flares were dropped to mark their position. The Beverley remained on station until relieved by a Shackleton, which in turn, remained in the area to home in surface rescue craft. A successful SAR mission, one of many undertaken by 30 Squadron during its tour in the Gulf, and although the Beverleys were totally unsuited for SAR work, the 30 Squadron crews had used them successfully with the utmost professionalism and airmanship.

Withdrawal from Aden

August 1967 brought the massive task of airlifting stores from Khormaksar to Muharraq and Sharjah due to the political decision to withdraw British forces from Aden. Flights were made direct from Khormaksar to Muharraq, overflying the vast inhospitable desert wastes of the Rub Al Khali and Saudi Arabia. Each aircraft carried a payload of about seven tonnes.

30 Squadron Disbands

Suddenly 30 Squadron's Beverley era came to an end. Although various rumours had been circulating regarding the future of the squadron, the decision to fly the Beverleys back to the UK and for the squadron to disband did come as something of a surprise. Thus at midnight on the 6th September 1967 the squadron was officially disbanded and Flying Officer Amin was given the privilege of taking the Squadron Standard to the RAF College at Cranwell where it was laid up.

The Squadron's Beverleys, which had done such yeoman service operating from Dishforth, Eastleigh and Muharraq, were unobtrusively ferried to the UK to await disposal. Sir David Lee, in *Flight from the Middle East* writes of the situation in Muharraq in January 1968, especially with regard to the withdrawal of the Beverleys: 'There was a continued need for a small number of medium range transport aircraft, particularly to lift vehicles and equipment beyond the capability of the Andover. In fact, the loss of the Beverley was keenly felt and those responsible for moving the Army's heavy weapons and vehicles began to realize just how valuable the 'old furniture van' had been to them'. After the Beverleys had left for the UK, the remaining personnel of 30 Squadron were dispersed, but many squadron members found themselves posted to Fairford where 30 Squadron was to re-equip with C-130K Hercules. In fact, when the squadron reformed at Fairford and once again the Squadron Standard was unfurled, 30 Squadron had entered its fifty-third year of service.

In the early '70s, the squadron moved to Lyneham, where at the time of writing, it is still stationed, acquitting itself as ever, with the highest degree of professionalism.

30 Squadron's Beverley Achievements

In the squadron's eleven-year Beverley era, nearly 150,000 passengers were carried together with 25,725 tonnes of freight, these figures not including paratroops and air-dropped supplies. The squadron flew about six million miles in a recorded total of 31,650 hours. Although 47 Squadron flew more hours than 30 Squadron, this is accounted for (a) by the UK-based Beverleys having to fly out from the UK to the overseas trouble spots where most Beverley work was done, and (b) by the fact that after 47 and 53 Squadrons amalgamated, 47 Squadron's complement of aircraft was about twice that of 30's.

30 Squadron carried a great deal more passengers than 47 Squadron; again, this is attributed to the large amount of trooping flights carried out locally in East Africa, South Arabia and the Gulf. In its Beverley era, which saw some of the most serious political disturbances ever to take place in the Middle East, 30 Squadron accomplished the many demanding tasks made on it with the panache and skill it had always demonstrated right from 1915 when those valiant efforts were made to supply the beleaguered garrison to Kut-el-Amara.

Chapter Four

84 Squadron

Brief History

No.84 Squadron was formed at Beaulieu in 1917 and saw First World War service in France. Disbanded in 1919, the squadron reformed in 1920 and moved to the Middle East. The unit spent eighteen years at Shaibah in Iraq, earning the nickname 'The Shaibah Squadron'.

In the Second World War, the squadron served in the Middle East and the Far East. Apart from a brief spell in Iraq in 1948, 84 Squadron remained in the Far East until disbanded in 1953. Shortly afterwards, the squadron reformed in the Canal Zone in Egypt with Valetta aircraft, thus commencing its life in the transport role. In 1957, another move took place, this time to Khormaksar in the then Colony of Aden.

After seven years at Khormaksar, mainly engaged in flying Army support missions to up-country airstrips in the struggle against Yemeni-inspired terrorists, the squadron moved to Sharjah to re-equip with Andovers. At the time of writing, the squadron is operating Wessex helicopters at Akrotiri, Cyprus.

A Beverley of 84 Squadron taxying to dispersal at Ataq. *W. Davidson*

Beverley Era Commences

The squadron's Beverley era started on 28th May 1958 when Flying Officers Herbert and Livermore and crews arrived from the UK in the first two Beverleys, which were immediately employed on the work for which they were so urgently required - the resupply of the garrisons in the Aden Protectorate where trouble with dissident tribesmen was now so rife. There had always been trouble with dissidents in Arabia: it seemed to be a way of life; in fact, it was said that during every hot season, the dissidents became more irritable, and tempers frayed by the torrid Arabian climate provoked the trigger-happy tribesmen to attack their neighbours and anyone else who happened to be in their territory. In the late '50s, terrorism was encouraged by Egypt's President Nasser, who after the Suez debacle, was so violently anti-British. This terrorism was also supported by the neighbouring country of Yemen, who for many years had laid territorial claims to Aden and the Protectorate.

Since Britain was still bound by treaty to protect the many tribes in the Aden hinterland, increasing terrorism on the part of the dissidents led to a build-up in the number of garrisons and outposts set up throughout the territory. Due to the almost total absence of roads, these outposts were maintained and supplied almost exclusively by air.

For nearly two years, the UK-based Beverley force had maintained a permanent detachment of at least two Beverleys at Aden. Their work in lifting supplies and equipment into the up-country airstrips had demonstrated beyond doubt how valuable the Beverley was for such work and resulted in the decision being made to re-equip 84 Squadron with Beverleys.

With the arrival of the first two aircraft which was closely followed by the arrival of four more, bringing the squadron up to operational strength, the detachment mounted by the UK Beverley force came to an end. The new 84 Squadron crews were nearly all drawn from the UK Beverley squadrons, so were well versed in operating in the Aden area and the Beverley Flight quickly worked up to operational readiness, mainly undertaking the up-country work, leaving the squadron's Valettas to do the RSM (Riyan, Salalah and Masirah) route station supply runs, other route work and transport of VIPs.

By November 1958, 84 Squadron's Beverleys had lifted nearly 500 tonnes of freight, 7 tonnes of mail and had carried

3,677 passengers, mostly on the short-haul, labour-intensive, up-country work. This work did not generate many flying hours since the aircraft spent a great deal of time on the ground being loaded and unloaded, and because of this, the number of up-country sorties per day seldom exceeded two. Nonetheless, the Beverley lifted a great deal more than its predecessor the Valetta, and its ability to airlift wheeled vehicles into the up-country airstrips was an almost unbelievable piece of good fortune to the commanders of the hard-pressed garrisons.

The airstrips most frequently visited in 84 Squadron's early days were Ataq, Beihan and Mukeiras, the latter being almost on the Yemen border, see *Map 2*. Ataq was quite a large airfield and the runway had, in the last two years, been improved tremendously by equipment and materials flown in by Beverley. Large garrisons were maintained at these three places and the resupply of these garrisons consititued the run-of-the-mill tasks for the Beverley Flight. A garrison was also maintained at Dhala, the high-altitude, marginal airstrip which demanded the highest degree of professional skill from a pilot, both to approach the strip from between a series of craggy mountain peaks, to making the landing on the strip which was located at the base of another mountain. Dhala was surrounded by mountains as were many other South Arabian airstrips, but Dhala seemed to come under fire from the dissidents more often than its neighbours, thus adding to its hazards.

This then, was how the first Beverleys and crews of 84 Squadron got down to business, mainly with up-country work but with the occasional route trip to the Persian Gulf or to East Africa. At the end of its first year of operations, 84's Beverley Flight had flown about 3,000 hours in about 1,600 sorties and had moved over 2,500 tonnes of freight, a good start considering the high rate of unserviceability caused, not only by the teething troubles of a new aeroplane operating in a harsh environment, but also by the servicing problems caused by the harsh climatic conditions.

The last of the Valettas left the squadron in 1959: 84 Squadron was now an all-Beverley unit.

Airlift for Hadrami Bedouin Legion
In the same month, the Squadron Commander, Squadron Leader Harry Guile and crew flew a platoon of the Hadrami Bedouin Legion from Riyan to Thamoud. The latter airstrip served a fort which was located on the edge of the Rub el Khali (The Empty Quarter), notorious for its vast, waterless expanses of featureless desert and for its arid climate. Up to the 1950s, few Europeans had penetrated far into The Empty Quarter, but modern motor vehicles, notably the ubiquitous Land Rover, now enabled this territory to be explored, particularly by oil prospectors.

Take-off from Dhala. To get maximum take-off run, aircraft used reverse thrust to 'back-up' right to the end of the airstrip. *British Aerospace*

The Hadrami Bedouin Legionaires were mainly recruited from the Hadramaut where the tribes were loyal to the British. This flight was noteworthy in that, in a mere one-hour trip, the legionaires had covered a distance which, hitherto, had taken them five days overland. This was a good demonstration of the value of the Beverley in South Arabia, where the absence of roads made communications so difficult.

The first three months of 1960 were almost exclusively occupied with up-country work, over 400 sorties being flown, carrying about 3,500 passengers. In April, Operation *Outpost*, mounted against dissident tribesmen in the Awdillah hills, airlifted a contingent of Aden Protectorate Levies (APLs) with their equipment, to Mayfah in two days.

Freight Jettisoned

May brought a hairy experience for Flight Lieutenant Bob Pitman and crew. On a flight to Eastleigh, an engine failed overhead Hargeisa in Somalia. Attempts to feather the propeller were unsuccessful and the aircraft began to lose height. Freight had to be jettisoned and 4½ tonnes were thrown overboard before height could be maintained.

Squadron Wins Lord Trophy - Stand-by at Eastleigh

The efficiency of the newly formed 84 Beverley Squadron was aptly demonstrated in June when Flight Lieutenant Mayall and crew represented the squadron in the Lord Trophy competition in the UK. Despite fierce competition from the UK-based Beverley force, the Trophy was won by 84 Squadron - a worthy achievement. In the same month, trouble in Kenya and Uganda led to six crews and four aircraft being detached to Eastleigh to stand by to fly troops to any trouble spots. This was the first of many detachments which the squadron had to undertake away from base and the lack of the Beverleys for up-country work was keenly felt by the Army. This particular Eastleigh detachment left only one crew and one aircraft at Khormaksar for the many up-country commitments.

Supply Drop

In September, Flight Lieutenant Charman and crew did a supply drop in the Nisab area, one of the squadron's first operational drops. Supply drops were rare in South Arabia as generally, the terrain was unsuitable: however, in the right conditions, when supply drops to the ground forces were feasible, they were carried out.

October 1960 brought a tragedy when XL151 crashed while on a night search for a small civil aircraft reported overdue. During the search, the Beverley flew into a high sand dune nineteen nautical miles north of Khormaksar airfield. The aircraft was destroyed and all aboard were killed. The wreckage was found next day by Squadron Leader Parry and crew flying XM107.

The first Beverley to show the ravages of South Arabia's corrosive climate was flown back to the UK in November. Corrosion was so bad on XM111 that the mainplanes had to be completely reskinned. Two crews, skippered by Flight Lieutenants Charman and Swales, did the ferry trip and no doubt, snatched a few days leave in the UK on its completion.

Operations Stunsail and Grout

The closing weeks of 1960 brought two stand-bys. The first, Operation *Stunsail*, was due to trouble brewing in the Persian Gulf and led to a detachment of two aircraft and crews being mounted at Bahrain. This was the first of a long series of detachments to the Persian Gulf that were to last until 1964. The second stand-by, Operation *Grout*, was mounted on 18th December, due to an attempted uprising in Ethiopia. In the event however, no air support was required and after a short period, the stand-by was called off.

Bahrain Detachment Kept Busy

During the Operation *Stunsail* stand-by at Bahrain, the squadron was usefully employed moving troops around the Gulf, presumably as a show of force. Exercise *Warden* involved a 60-hour task airlifting troops and equipment between Bahrain and Sharjah. A month later, Exercise *Placard* involved a massive air mobility scheme mounted at Sharjah lasting through the latter half of January to February. In March, 84 Squadron joined 30 Squadron in Exercise *Roulade*, a combined services exercise with Royal Marines from HMS *Bulwark* undertaking an amphibious landing.

Flying Officer Cripps and crew in XM107 moved a company of Coldstream Guards from Bahrain to Ibri and then took an SAS detachment from Ibri to Bahrain. This was ideal Beverley short-haul work and the movements of large amounts of men and equipment no doubt indicated to any subversive elements just how quickly and efficiently the Army could be moved to any trouble spots.

A new aircraft reached the squadron in February, XM109 having been collected from Brough by Wing Commander Pearson and crew, two engine failures being experienced during the delivery flight. Engine failures were becoming increasingly common and plagued 84 Squadron throughout its Beverley days. The incessant sand and dust together with necessity for the use of high rpm settings in the Arabian heat undoubtedly contributed to the squadron's high incidence of engine failures.

Medics to Kamaran

In March 1961, Flight Lieutenant Madden and crew in XM106 flew a medical team to Kamaran Island in the Red Sea, to the west of Hodeidah, one of Yemen's main seaports. This island was under British protection and a medical team visited Kamaran twice a year to conduct a surgery, an event much welcomed by the Islanders.

Three-engine Take-off from Ataq

In April, Flight Lieutenant Cripps, skippering XM109, had No.4 engine fail whilst descending into Ataq. It was impossible to repair the engine at Ataq so a decision was made to fly out on three engines. This was accomplished successfully but ten nautical miles from Khormaksar, a second engine failed. However, the aircraft was light and the approach and two-engine landing was without further problems.

It was not only Beverleys that had such troubles as Flight Lieutenant Shelton-Smith and crew found when they had to fly two engines to a Pembroke which had force landed at El Fasher, an airstrip in Sudan.

Detachments to Kenya

May saw Flight Lieutenants Madden and Charman and crews in XM106 and XM107 detached to Eastleigh to assist 30 Squadron in Exercise *Cheetah*. This involved moving troops of the 24th Independent Brigade Group to Nakuru, an airstrip some 100 miles north-east of Eastleigh. The following month, Flight Lieutenant Cripps and crew in XM107, while on a scheduled flight to Eastleigh, were diverted from their schedule to move troops and police from Nairobi to Zanzibar to deal with civil disturbances.

The Kenya detachments were nearly always welcomed by the 84 Squadron crews: the Kenyan countryside was much more attractive than that of South Arabia and the Gulf. In addition, Eastleigh's altitude of over 5,000 feet was extremely pleasant after the torrid heat of Aden. A further attraction was the active social life among the European community.

In June 1961, due to 84's stand-by in the Persian Gulf and the possiblility of detachments to Kenya to help out 30 Squadron with famine relief, flood relief and trooping operations, it was announced that Dakotas of Aden Airways would take over the resupply of the up-country strips. This caused groans of despair from the Army, since although the Dakota was a superb aeroplane, it just could not carry the bulk loads of which the Beverley made such light work. Heavy equipment required by No.5004 Airfield Construction Squadron at Beihan still had to be Bevved in, since no other aircraft could move such equipment. However, although the Dakotas did some excellent up-country resupply work, it was not long before the Beverleys were again called upon for this duty.

Operation Vantage

The uneasiness in the Persian Gulf came to a head in June, when the Sheikdom of Kuwait was threatened by Iraq. The whole of 84 Squadron was placed on a four-hour stand-by and on 29th June, the first aircraft, carrying a spare crew plus servicing personnel for No.8 Squadron (Hunter aircraft), left for Bahrain. A second Beverley, carrying 84 Squadron's ground equipment and servicing personnel followed. Operation *Vantage* had begun.

On 1st August, the squadron flew four lifts into Kuwait new airport which was only in a partially constructed condition. The main loads comprised support equipment and ground staff for No.8 Squadron; a Eureka beacon was also flown in to improve the almost non-existent landing aids. The next day, 30 Squadron's aircraft and crews arrived, and a continuous Beverley shuttle between Bahrain and Kuwait took place, flying troops, vehicles, armoured cars, artillery, rations and ammunition in addition to spares and equipment for the fighter aircraft now at Kuwait. Communications were still poor however, and on 21st June, Squadron Leader Parry and Flight Lieutenant Yates flew a Cossor mobile radar station into Rhaudahtan, an oil company airstrip to the north-west of Kuwait. This gave some radar assistance to ships of the Royal Navy.

Both 84 and 30 Squadrons spent all of July and August at Bahrain. After the initial rush to move a large part of the Strategic Reserve into Kuwait - a show of strength that had the desired effect on the Iraqis - both squadrons stood by awaiting further developments. But they were not idle: the force at Kuwait had to be supplied and the Beverley fleet made a big contribution to the resupply task and then participated in the withdrawal of the force at the end of the month.

Mid-air explosion

On 29th September, XL131, a 30 Squadron aircraft, flown on this occasion by an 84 Squadron crew, was on a routine flight airlifting equipment from Kuwait to Bahrain as part of the withdrawal operations. Flight Lieutenant Sneller was in command, other crew members were Master Navigator Ron Hansford, Master Engineer Don Glenn and Master Signaller Tom Hughes. The flight to Kuwait was uneventful; the load from Kuwait to Bahrain included Hunter rocket projectiles and detonators. Tom Hughes, the signaller, laconically recalls: 'The Hunter rocket heads were secured in groups of three, neatly and uniformly across the width of the freight bay, the detonators being stowed at the rear. Ten minutes after take-off, an explosion occurred in the freight bay and we immediately returned to Kuwait. Investigations revealed that a time bomb had been placed at the front of the freight bay near the 'bandstand', in front of the desert survival equipment.

'This was extremely fortunate; when the bomb went off, the blast was taken by the desert survival packs and was deflected sideways blowing a hole in the fuselage skin. Had the bomb been placed elsewhere, the story may well have had a different ending. Nevertheless, XL131 was too badly damaged to be of any further operational use and after temporary repairs, was ferried to the UK for repair by the manufacturers.'

Another Terrorist Time Bomb

The terrorists' next planting of a time bomb was more successful for them in that it destroyed an 84 Squadron Beverley, but by the most incredible good fortune, there were no casualties. On 6th October, XM110, skippered by Flight Lieutenant Charman, landed at Bahrain from Kuwait. The Army immediately set about off-loading the freight which consisted of ammunition, the servicing team did their after flight inspection and 'bedded' the aircraft down for the night. Shortly afterwards, an explosion occurred in the freight bay accompanied by fire. The prompt, efficient and brave actions by the Bahrain Fire Section saved the aircraft from complete destruction but their efforts were in vain. Damage within the freight bay was so severe that it was thought that had the aircraft been in flight, it would have broken up. XM110 was accordingly struck off charge after all useful spares had been removed, and the Army took over the hulk to use for synthetic training for paras.

XM110 damaged beyond repair by terrorist time bomb placed in freight bay. Note the scorching around crew entrance door. *T. Hughes*

The hulk of XM110 at Bahrain after being cannabalized for spares. *W. Binfield*

Always resourceful, the Army found a use for the hulk of XM110, using it as a synthetic trainer for paratroops. *C. Dales*

Opposite page: **Inspecting damage caused by terrorist time bomb which exploded during flight in XL131 after take-off from Kuwait in Operation *Vantage*, September 1961.** *T. Hughes*

Thus ended Operation *Vantage*, a costly operation but one which had demonstrated that Britain was still prepared to give assistance when requested by friendly Arab States. Who planted the time bombs? Iraqi agents who had infiltrated into Kuwait perhaps, or pro-Iraq Kuwaitis, or perhaps merely some of the many thousands of anti-British Arabs. Regardless of who planted the bombs, it was extremely fortunate that XM110's bomb did not explode during flight or indeed during unloading and servicing of the aircraft.

The Bahrain detachment, brought about mainly by Operation *Vantage* and events leading up to it, continued through the remaining months of 1961. Once the withdrawal from Kuwait had been accomplished, there was little for the squadron to do at Bahrain. There was plenty of work for the squadron in up-country operations from Aden, but due to the stand-by requirements at Bahrain, neither aircraft nor crews were available to undertake this work. This was a very frustrating situation: the crews knew how much the Army depended on the Beverley lifts into the up-country strips and would have gladly returned from Bahrain to undertake such work. However, operational requirements demanded a stand-by at Bahrain and this had to be implemented, regardless of its frustrating boredom caused by practically no flying. This situation was appreciated by the ground staff though, since *Vantage* had caused them an immense work-load and the subsequent slack period allowed them to catch up on the backlog of work.

Up-Country Work Resumed

In the new year, a detachment from 53 Squadron relieved 84 Squadron at Bahrain and the 84 Squadron detachment returned to base at Khormaksar. Up-country flying then resumed in earnest in an attempt to catch up on the massive backlog of outstanding commitments. The majority of lifts were into Mukeiras. A VIP trip relieved the monotony of up-country flying for Squadron Leader Parry and crew, when in XH122, they flew the Sultan of Socotra from Quisah on the Arabian mainland to his residence on the island of Socotra, see *Map 2*.

The Bahrain detachment featured again in the squadron's commitments in February 1962, when it was announced that 84 and 30 Squadrons would in future, cover the commitments both in East Africa and the Persian Gulf on a pooled basis. The detachment occupied 84 Squadron from February through to September 1962, a small element left at Khormaksar doing the up-country runs and the occasional route trips that came up. However, the Bahrain detachment did manage to get in quite a lot of Army support training, including supply dropping and paratrooping.

Aircraft Loses Dinghy Hatch - New CO

Flying Officer Palliser and crew in XM109 had an unnerving experience in September when the aircraft lost a dinghy hatch on take-off. The hatch struck the tail plane causing some damage but a safe landing was made. September was also highlighted by the arrival of Squadron Leader Ken Parfitt who took over the duties of Squadron Commander from Squadron Leader Parry. September also saw the 84 Squadron Bahrain detachment being relieved by a detachment from 30 Squadron. The up-country Army elements were delighted that the Beverleys had returned in force to Aden and immediately put in requests for massive airlifts of men and equipment, mainly to the garrisons at Ataq, Beihan and Mukeiras.

Now that up-country Aden was a Federation and not a Protectorate, the APLs (Aden Protectorate Levies) had become the Federal Regular Army and in October, a battalion of the FRA was airlifted into Beihan together with armoured vehicles and other equipment. The heavy workload of supplying and building up the up-country garrisons continued until the end of the year. One of the biggest tasks was flying large, complex loads into Mukeiras for setting up a radar station. Flying was so intense that essential training, especially Army support training, had to be curtailed.

Loading ramps being raised prior to closing the clamshell doors. Note the loading gantry in the freight bay roof: this was for use on airstrips which had no freight handling equipment such as fork-lift trucks. This picture was taken at Mukeiras. *T. Hughes*

The crew of XM109/U pitch camp for a night stop on Socotra. This island in the Indian Ocean off the Yemeni coast is now a Russian submarine base. *W. Binfield*

The 'hairiest' airstrip in South Arabia - Wadi Ayn. Due to its proximity to the Yemen border, the approach was very difficult. Like Dhala, the mountain at the end of the strip made overshooting an impossibility. *C. Ferguson*

'Hairy' Airstrip

In December, a new airstrip came into use when XM109, skippered by Flight Lieutenant Andruskeiwicz, made the first Beverley landing at Wadi Ayn. This airstrip became acknowledged as the 'hairiest' in South Arabia, due to it being almost completely surrounded by Yemeni territory and its difficult approach path which twisted between a series of dangerous mountain peaks. Dhala had previously been considered the hairiest airstrip, but this reputation was stolen by Wadi Ayn. Like Dhala, Wadi Ayn's strip terminated at the foot of a formidable mountain, thus making overshooting an impossiblity. Another airstrip was also used for the first time in December, when Flight Lieutenant Bower and crew in XM109 landed at Negub. Another highlight of December was Flight Lieutenant Lambert and crew being detached to Borneo for twelve days to assist 34 Squadron in operations concerned with the Brunei revolt. The crew flew 16 operational sorties, mainly supplying the Gurkhas and the Queen's Own Highlanders.

Back at Aden, Flight Lieutenant Palliser, a captain, who was flying co-pilot to Flight Lieutenant McTurk, displayed a brilliant piece of airmanship when, during a landing at Ataq, the nose wheel steering failed. By skilful use of reverse thrust, Flight Lieutenant Palliser kept the aircraft on the 'straight and narrow', thus avoiding the possibility of a serious accident due to the aircraft swinging off the narrow airstrip.

Map 9:
The Belvedere Ferry Route

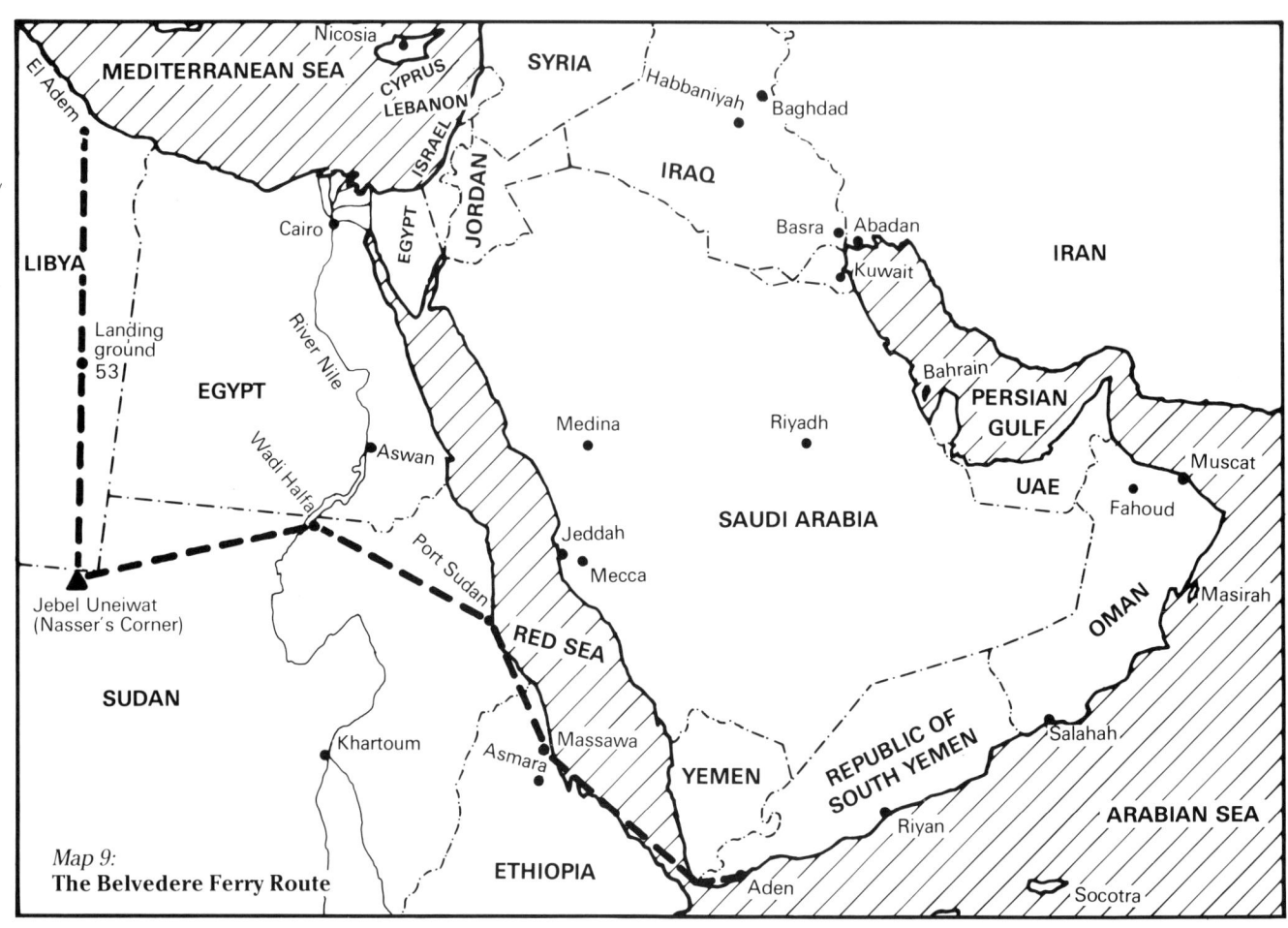

Ooh nasty! Master Engineer Bill Binfield surveys the result of an engine fire.
via 30 Squadron

Opposite page: **Fuel for the Belvederes taking part in Operation *Sandflight* being unloaded from Beverley XM107 at Landing Ground 53.** *W. Binfield*

More Engine Failures
January 1963 brought a spate of engine failures which cast doubts upon the reliability of the recently introduced Centaurus 175 engines. Seven engine failures occured at Khormaksar, two in the Persian Gulf and one at Riyan. The latter necessitated a three-engine ferry back to Khormaksar because the engine technicians were so hard-pressed changing engines at base, that neither men nor equipment were available to undertake engine changes elsewhere.

Up-country work had now assumed such importance that 84 Squadron was no longer allocated any scheduled route flights, the AFME (Air Force Middle East) schedules now being flown by 30 Squadron.

Exercise Sandflight
This was an important and interesting task undertaken to assist the ferrying of two 26 Squadron Belvedere helicopters from El Adem to Khormaksar. Commanded by Squadron Leader Parfitt and skippered by Flight Lieutenant Warren, the trip was made in XM107 to provide navigational assistance for the helicopters, and carry their ground staff, equipment and some fuel.

The first leg of the flight was from El Adem to LG (Landing Ground) 53, also known as Seizmic 3 by oil-men prospecting in the area, see *Map 9*. The Beverley landed ahead of the helicopters and then homed them in using RT. This was to be standard procedure in subsequent landings. After refuelling from drums carried in the Beverley, the Belvederes took off again, followed later by the Beverley, for Jebel Uneiwat. This 6,500 feet mountain is on the Libya/Sudan border and is a prominent navigational feature. After the Suez campaign, Egypt and the UK were not on the best of terms and for obvious reasons, British military aircraft were under strict orders to keep clear of Egyptian airspace. For flights from El Adem to Aden therefore, aircraft flew almost due south to Jebel Uneiwat at which point a turn was made to set course for Khartoum, Wadi Halfa or any other convenient en-route staging post. Jebel Uneiwat became well known as a turning point and due to its proximity to the Egyptian border, was dubbed 'Nasser's Corner' by Transport Command aircrew.

A Second World War airstrip still existed at Nasser's Corner and by special arrangement, Shell International had positioned fuel there in readiness for the Belvederes. The Beverley located the airstrip and then orbited until the helicopters had landed alongside their pile of fuel drums; the Beverley then landed. After servicing the three aircraft, the crews settled down to a desert night stop, first dining off compo rations washed down with some welcome cans of beer. Flight Lieutenant 'Bunny' Warren, the Beverley captain, provided great amusement by turning up for the meal dressed in full mess kit, reportedly to lay claim to being the first RAF officer to dress for dinner at Nasser's Corner. Apart from some airmen detailed to stand guard on the Belvederes, all hands eventually retired to the Beverley for the night.

The aircraft left for Port Sudan next morning, staging through Wadi Halfa. On the Wadi Halfa/Port Sudan leg, one of the Belvederes ran short of fuel and the whole

The crew that night-stopped at Nasser's Corner. Left to right: Flight Lieutenant Geach (navigator), Sergeant Carroll (AQM), Flight Lieutenant Warren (captain, wearing mess kit for the occasion), Flying Officer Gill (co-pilot), Flight Sergeant Rickard (signaller), Squadron Leader Parfitt (OC 84 Squadron), Master Engineer Binfield (engineer). *W. Binfield*

Preparing to take off from Nasser's Corner. *W. Binfield*

One of the Belvederes taking off from Nasser's Corner. *W. Binfield*

Opposite page: **Re-oiling the hard way at Massawa.** *W. Binfield*

detachment returned to Wadi Halfa where the Nile Hotel laid on sleeping accommodation on board a houseboat.

An 0800 hour take-off was made next morning for Port Sudan and after the usual refuelling stop, the aircraft took off for Massawa, flying along the Red Sea coastline. Things were a bit primitive at Massawa and the Beverley had to be re-oiled using a two gallon can and a length of rope. This must have taken considerable time since due to the Beverley's usual prodigious thirst for oil, at least fifty gallons must have been required.

The final leg of the ferry flight was intended to be a direct run from Massawa to Khormaksar but unexpected headwinds were encountered and the Belvederes had to land for fuel at Perim Island, an hour's flying time from Khormaksar. However, after a quick turn round, the helicopters took off and eventually reached Khormaksar in mid-afternoon.

The trip had covered a distance of 2,600 miles and was the longest overseas flight undertaken by RAF helicopters over some of the world's hottest and most inhospitable terrain. The Belvederes of 26 Squadron went on to give yeoman service in the Aden up-country troubles, especially in the Radfan campaign.

Help for Yemeni Refugees

March brought a great deal of up-country activity with elements of the Hadrami Bedouin Legion being flown to different locations in the Federation. A number of trips were also made to airlift 169 Yemeni royalist refugees from airstrips near the Yemen border to other airstrips in the Federation from where the refugees could disperse to safe abodes. Once again, the squadron mounted a detachment at Bahrain, but little was done there and the flying hours allocated to the detachment were not used. This caused more frustration for the planners who were being overwhelmed by requests for Aden up-country work.

This state of affairs continued into June with the up-country commitment continually on the increase. Men and supplies were lifted into the lesser known airstrips such as Mayfah, Zamakh and Lodar, the latter being used for the first time in two years. Wadi Ayn and Negub were also visited. But the bulk of the up-country work was in and out of Dhala, Ataq, Beihan and Mukeiras when Battalions of the Federal Army were changed over. A shuttle between Dhala and Beihan took eight sorties; twenty-four sorties were flown between Ataq and Mukeiras, the aircraft refuelling at Ataq from stocks of fuel pre-positioned there by Beverley.

Brevets for AQMs

On 17th May, Khormaksar's Station Commander, Group Captain A. C. Blythe, DFC, presented brevets to three of the squadron's air quartermasters: Flight Sergeant Weston, Sergeant O'Reilly and Sergeant Whelan. All the squadron were delighted that the AQMs, who worked so hard on the up-country trips, had now been awarded their much-deserved aircrew status, and were now able to enjoy the associated benefits.

Operation Alfred

On 11th June 1963, the squadron was called to readiness and ordered to move all available aircraft to Salisbury, Rhodesia (now Harare, Zimbabwe) from where they were to fly troops to Matsapa in Swaziland where a general strike had been declared. The workers were striking for a basic £1 per day per man regardless of job and the strike was proving so effective that the economy of Swaziland was threatened.

Four 84 Squadron Beverleys, XB266, XM106, XM109 and XH121 participated in the operation, crews being captained by Flight Lieutenants Bower, Gould, Smyth,

XM106 - one of 84 Squadron's original aircraft, later to be blown up by land mine.
W. Binfield

Flying Officer Colin Ferguson and Flight Lieutenant Bob Humphries have a round of golf at Stegi in Swaziland having landed XH121 on the fairway of the local golf course. *C. Ferguson*

Two 84 Squadron crewmen try their hands at driving a road roller which they had flown into an up-country airstrip. History does not recall the item which the roller has narrowly missed; it appears to be a Valetta or Hastings paratroop exit door.
J. Crews

Opposite page: **Beverley and Valetta at Lodar.** *B. Bevan*

Loading an Army truck at an Aden up-country airstrip. Note fort in background.
W. Binfield

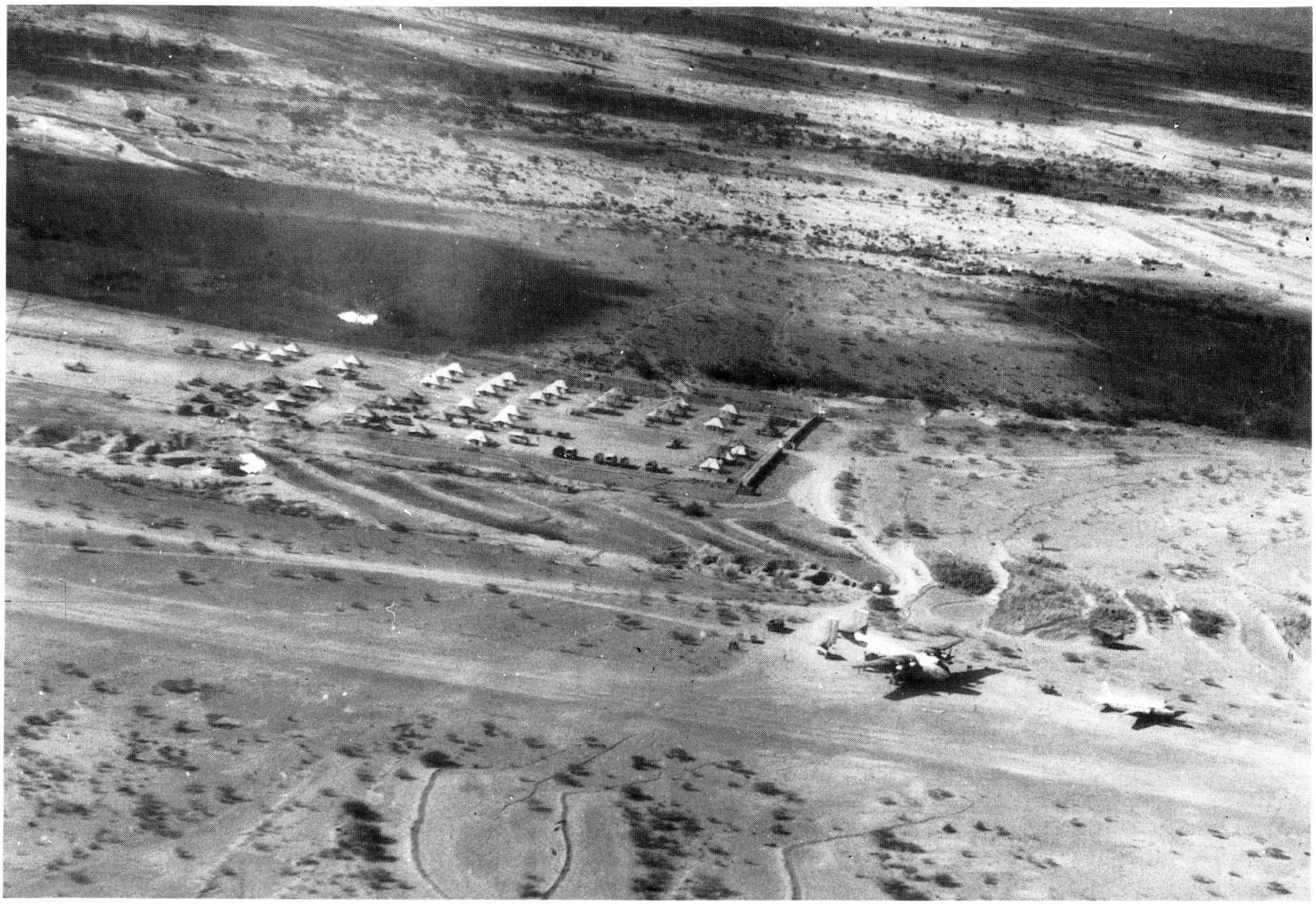

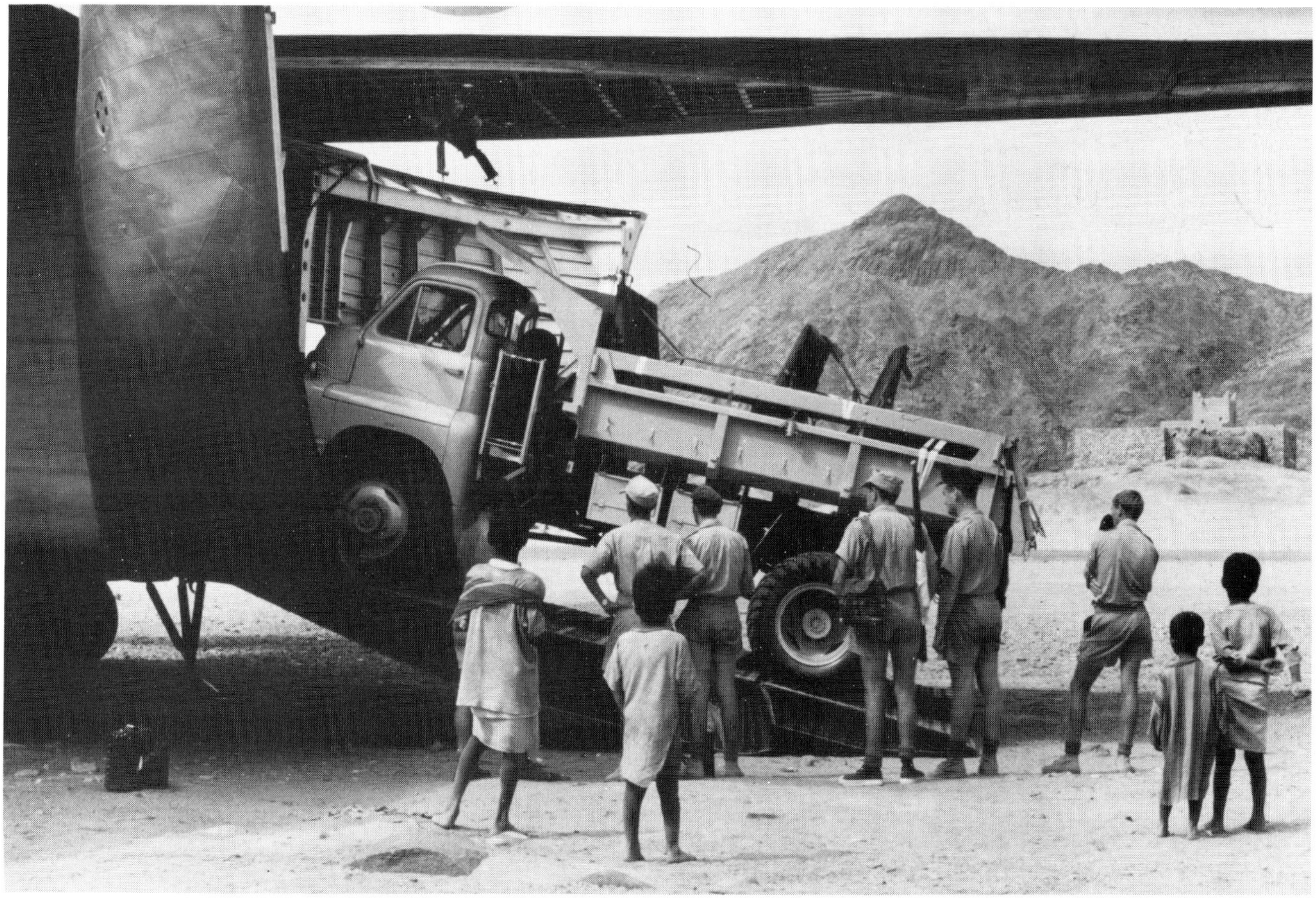

Andruskeiwicz, Lambert and Hayward. The detachment flew a battalion of Gordon Highlanders to the various trouble spots, the airlift being completed by 18th June. From then on, the force was supplied by air. The strike weakened and was called off and by 23rd June, the detachment was released and the aircraft made their way back to Khormaksar. This major task was a complete success and forty sorties were flown without any technical hold-ups.

A great deal of up-country work awaited the squadron on its return from Salisbury and intensive flying followed trying to complete the allotted tasks. However, another spate of engine failures occurred and this made severe demands on the ground staff who had worked so hard on the Salisbury detachment. The high failure rate of the new Centaurus 175 engines was again causing the technical staff concern since engines seemed to be failing at about 250 hours, less than half-way through the 600-hour life between overhauls.

Engine Failures Disrupt Operations

June, July and August 1963 brought more and more engine failures, thirteen unscheduled engine changes at Khormaksar being recorded for June and July. This setback caused the squadron to fall sadly short of its allotted task. The work done was mostly up-country, with Ataq, Beihan, Mukeiras, Lodar, and Thamoud being visited. The high engine failure rate was extremely worrying: other Beverley units, although far from satisfied with the reliability of the Centaurus, were not experiencing such a high engine failure rate as 84 Squadron. It was suggested therefore, that the 84 Squadron Beverleys were being 'flogged' much harder than the Beverleys of other units. This was fair comment: there was no more punishing work than constant operation into and out of the dust-laden South Arabian airstrips.

Operation Tusk

This was planned to bring administrative control to the hitherto unexplored area to the east of the Federation, on the edge of the Empty Quarter. The operation commenced in September 1963, when troops of the Hadrami Bedouin Legion were positioned at Thamoud by Flight Lieutenant Chris Gould and crew in XM109. Twenty sorties were flown in 29 hours. In October, more HBL troops were positioned at Al Ghayda and many resupply trips were flown to Thamoud. November saw elements of the HBL being flown into Murait, an airstrip only just within the limits of safety for a Beverley, and Sanau, another remote strip east of Thamoud. Supply drops were also made in the Thamoud area to elements of the HBL. These drops were one-ton containers and were the first one-ton containers to be dropped operationally in South Arabia. Operation *Tusk* highlighted the increase in terrorism in South Arabia, which although previously had been mainly confined to territory near the Yemen border, was now spreading eastwards. The crews flying on Operation *Tusk* found it very interesting despite the hostility which was said to be rife in some areas. Much of the terrain was inaccurately charted and navigation was often of the 'hit or miss' variety.

Detachments Continue

Despite the heavy demands for up-country work at Aden, the squadron was still manning two detachments, one at Bahrain and one at Eastleigh. Little work was done at Bahrain apart from some paratrooping and supply dropping mainly at Jebel Ali and Al Khatt. The Eastleigh detachment, mounted to give support to troops in the Northern Frontier District of Kenya engaged on anti-Shifta operations, flew supplies into the airstrips of Wajir, Garissa, Mandera and Tabora, see *Map 5*.

Operation Nutcracker

This was mounted in December 1963 and marked the beginnings of the Radfan campaign, the terrorism now relentlessly spreading southwards, from the Yemen border in the Dhala - Mukeiras area to the Radfan district, some 100 miles north of Aden. Fourteen sorties were flown in thirty hours to Dhala, Mukeiras and Lodar. One supply drop of SEAC packs was also made to troops participating in the operation. December was highlighted by the squadron moving over a million pounds (455

A platoon of Hadrami Bedouin Legionaires wait to board at Thamoud. *W. Binfield*

Opposite: **Navigator and signaller talk about fixes.** *J. Knight*

tonnes) of freight, plus over a tonne of mail. The million pound mark, comprising a combination of freight and mail, had been recorded before but this was the first recorded instance of a million pounds of freight, excluding mail, being airlifted. This was to become commonplace in future months.

Troops to East Africa

The New Year brought an urgent commitment for four aircraft to be despatched to Eastleigh, for flying troops to maintain law and order in disturbances which had broken out in East Africa. XM107, XB266, XM106 and XH121, skippered by Flight Lieutenants Gould, McTurk, Warren and Smyth, participated in the Eastleigh detachment which took place during the middle of January.

Back at Aden, Operation *Tusk* and *Nutcracker* continued into February with many flights into the Radfan and Thamoud areas. At Bahrain, now named Muharraq, the detachment was highlighted by an SAR flight in the Jebel Dhana coastal area searching for three persons in an open boat, overdue for three days. After searching for 90 minutes, the survivors were found near their beached craft and survival packs were dropped. A party of Trucial Oman Scouts, travelling overland, reached the wreck some thirty hours later and rescued the castaways.

Fighter Cover for Wadi Ayn

The approach into Wadi Ayn was so near the ill-defined Yemen border that a decision was made to position a forward controller at this airstrip in order to provide fighter cover for Beverleys. The equipment was positioned at Wadi Ayn in two sorties and thereafter, fighter cover was provided each time a Beverley used the airstrip.

In the Radfan, Flight Lieutenant Catcheside captaining XM109, made a night supply drop at Thumier, delivering medical supplies, rations and ammunition to an SAS patrol who had been isolated during a skirmish with the dissidents. The aircraft came under small arms fire and was hit a number of times, but damage was only superficial. In the east of the Federation, Operation *Tusk* continued, with more HBL movements to Murait, Al Ghayda and Thamoud. In the Gulf, two SAR flights were undertaken searching for survivors of a Caravelle airliner which had crashed in the Daharan area. More than a million pounds (455 tonnes) of freight were now consistently being moved each month together with as much as a tonne of mail. The Beverley was often the only postal link between the UK and the troops serving in the South Arabian Federation.

Radfan Troubles Intensify

At Aden, trouble in the Radfan was becoming so serious that it was imperative that an airstrip suitable for Beverleys be opened in that area. Flight Lieutenant Warren, captaining XM106, did a recce of Thumier on 19th May and three days later did another in XH121 with Flight Lieutenant Andruskeiwicz. Later in the month, dummy paratroops were dropped in the Radfan, presumably to note the reactions of the dissidents, and arms and ammunition were also dropped to friendly tribesmen to the north-east of the Radfan.

June brought twenty-one route trips which proved invaluable for crew members, especially navigators, to maintain route-flying experience. The trip of the month was when XM107, commanded by Squadron Leader Parfitt and captained by Flight Lieutenant Andruskeiwicz, toured South Africa with the AOC on board, visiting New Sarum, Pretoria, Labaski, Gaborone, Francistown, Matsapa, Blomfontein and Maseru.

June also saw the first landing at Thumier made by Flight Lieutenant Andruskeiwicz captaining XH121 with Group Captain Blyth (Khormaksar's Station Commander) on board. The opening of Thumier for Beverleys was a major feature of the Radfan campaign and heralded a massive airlift of men and equipment into the airstrip, with further reinforcements being taken into Dhala, Ataq, Mukeiras and Beihan.

Some awards were announced at the end of June, Flight Lieutenant A. H. Bower, late of the squadron, receiving the AFC, and Flight Lieutenant R. A. G. Catcheside receiving a Queen's Commendation for Valuable Service in the Air. AOC's commendations went to Master Engineer Bill Binfield, Warrant Officer Venables, Junior Technician Aitken and Senior Aircraftman Bills.

In spite of falling short of its planned commitment due to another spate of

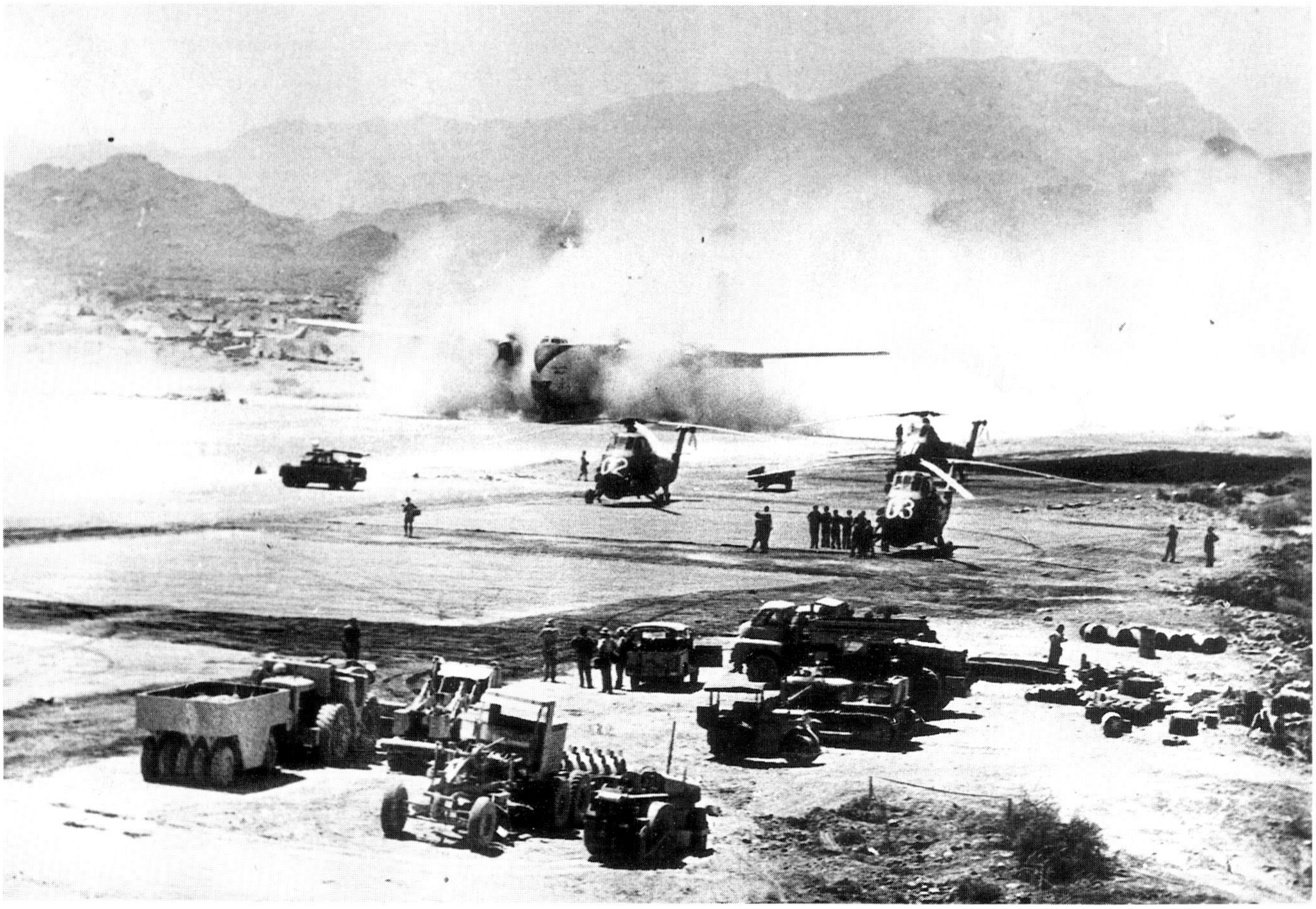

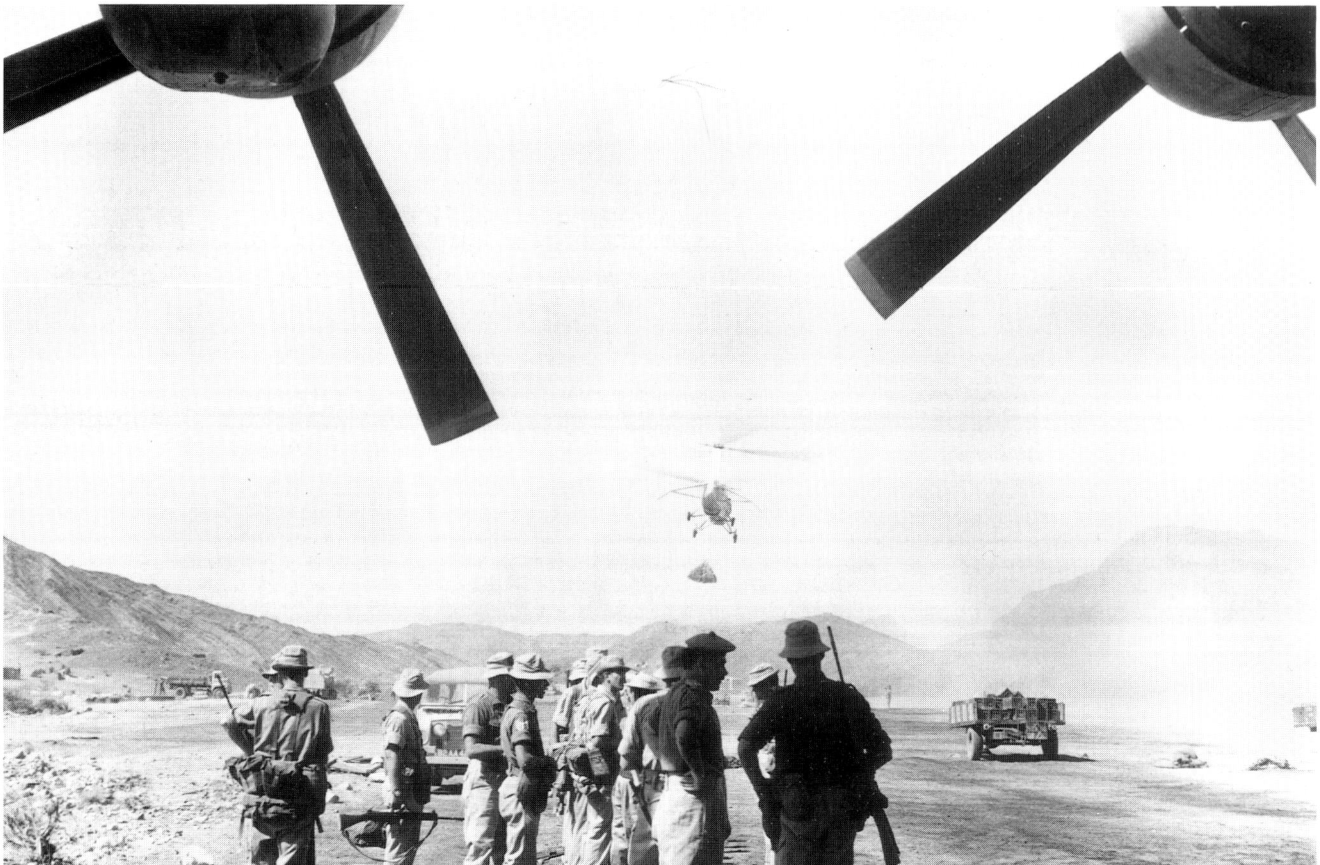

This page: **The first Beverley to land at Thumier, taxies past a 78 Sqn Twin Pioneer, outside Radforce HQ** *via 84 Sqn*

The 'Bevellydere'. Unusual view of a Belvedere helicopter parked in front of a Beverley. *via 84 Squadron*

XM108 taking off from Thumier. *W. Binfield*

Opposite page: **The first Beverley to land on Thumier's extended runway, XH121, using reverse thrust.** *via 84 Squadron*

A 26 Sqn Belvedere takes out a load brought into Thumier by Beverley. *W. Binfield*

engine failures, the squadron moved more than the usual million pounds of freight in June, together with 3,000 passengers and nine casevacs, injured in the Radfan fighting. In addition to troop movements, sixteen tonnes of supplies and equipment were flown into Thumier in seventeen sorties. In July, twenty-eight sorties were flown to Thumier and six supply drops were made to troops of 45 Commando on Jebel Wadina in which forty-nine one-ton containers were delivered. Jebel Wadina was a difficult DZ, the small mountain plateau being 5,500 feet high. Dropping was difficult due to the unpredictable winds which blew around the steep sides of the plateau. Nevertheless, the drops were successful.

August brought a large airlift of men and supplies into Ahwar, near the coast, and a new airstrip, Mukmuq, was opened up, Flight Lieutenant Warren making the first landing there. In addition to the detachments mounted at Muharraq and Eastleigh, XM111, XB266 and XM107, skippered by Flight Lieutenants Lambert, Rankin and Warren respectively, were detached to Matsapa. But in spite of all the commitments away from base, ninety-nine sorties into the Federation were recorded for September. The Matsapa detachment finished in October, but one aircraft remained at Eastleigh to maintain the detachment strength there at two aircraft and crews. The Shifta were still giving trouble in the Northern Frontier District of Kenya and numerous sorties were flown into Wajir, Garrissa, Moyale and Mandera to resupply the garrisons of the Kenyan Army. The squadron was so heavily committed at this time that training flights had to be curtailed. This presented difficulties as there were a number of new arrivals on the squadron who needed various training exercises and also needed to be checked into the many marginal airstrips. The year ended with Flight Lieutenant Livermore and crew being detached to the Congo in XH121, staging through Eastleigh, Entebbe and Stanleyville, then doing a shuttle between Stanleyville and Leopoldville, flying out refugees.

Squadron Catches up on Training

In January 1965, the serious shortfall in training resulted in no specific tasks being given to the squadron so that essential training could be completed and new arrivals could be checked into the marginal airstrips. However, the Beverleys did not let the Army down; ten resupply trips were flown to Thumier and Operation *Stab*, involving troop movements between Lodar, Beihan and Mukeiras was completed. The Muharraq detachment was now finished since 30 Squadron was in permanent residence there, but since 30 Squadron had left Kenya, the loss of the 'old furniture vans' was keenly felt by the Kenyan government and requests by the Kenyans for air support was met by a permanent detachment from 84 Squadron. This two-aircraft detachment, although popular with the crews, naturally depleted the squadron's resources for coping with the Aden up-country work.

SAR on Mount Kenya - Aerial Funeral Service

February was marked by an SAR sortie, flown from Eastleigh by Flight Lieutenant R. W. J. Wright and crew in XB266, looking for three British Army mountaineers reported missing on Mount Kenya. The Beverley search was unsuccessful but a Kenyan Police Air Wing light aircraft found the bodies on the Darwin Glacier at 14,000 feet. A ground party subsequently located the bodies and buried them in a temporary grave pending a decision on how the bodies were to be brought down. It was eventually decided that it was not practicable to bring the bodies down and thus it was decreed that the bodies were to be re-buried where they were. An ex-RAF chaplain was found to be living in retirement in Nairobi, and he agreed to conduct the funeral service, but due to his advancing years, could not possibly undertake the climb to the burial site.

It was then decided that the chaplain would conduct the funeral service from a Beverley overhead the site where the climbers were to be re-interred. Flying Officer Hamish Raynham skippered XB266 on the burial service flight and his engineer, Gordon Barlow, described the event: 'We were to rendevous at 1100 hours with the burial party who had set up a radio link. Timing was important because at noon the cloud build-up at the summit of Mount Kenya becomes dangerous due to turbulence and poor visibility. However, after a long climb to 19,000 feet with everybody on oxygen of course, we ran in dead on time at 1100. The view of the glacier was breathtaking, absolutely incredible. By the time we had completed our fourth run over the burial site, the padre had finished conducting the funeral service and we then cleared the area, thankfully, as conditions were rapidly worsening and the turbulence was becoming dangerous. We were glad to have made the trip and to have played a part in giving three British soldiers a Christian burial!' The Beverley did many unusual jobs; providing an airborne platform for a funeral service added another such task to the Beverley's impressive list of achievements.

February 1965 saw XM106, one of the Squadron's original aircraft, being ferried home for overhaul, captained by Flight Lieutenant Lambert and Flying Officer Ferguson and crews, the route being by way of Jeddah, El Adem and Luqa, overflying Egypt now being permitted due to improving British/Egyptian diplomatic relations. The same crews brought XL149, XM106's replacement, back to Khormaksar.

There was a great deal of up-country activity again, both in February and March, many sorties being flown into Thumier, Dhala, Beihan, Mukeiras and Ataq. Raudah, a new strip, was used for the first time. In Kenya, the detachment also got down to some hard flying. This was a welcome change, since hitherto, the Eastleigh stand-bys had in fact, consisted of just 'standing by' and not doing much flying. In addition to nine resupply trips to the Northern Frontier District airstrips, a trip was made to Entebbe in support of an Andover of the Queen's Flight, and in XM111, Flight Lieutenant Rankin and crew did a photographic survey of the Eastleigh district.

In March, a detachment concerned with policing elections in Bechuanaland was carried out by Flying Officer Colin Ferguson and crew in XM107, visiting Salisbury, Matsapa, Waterkloof and Maseru, most of the sorties being flown from Matsapa. A 30 Squadron aircraft and crew also participated in this task.

April brought a requirement for another aircraft and two crews to be detached to Eastleigh. This depleted 84's resources so badly that two crews from 30 Squadron were attached to 84 to assist in up-country operations. However, the 30 Squadron crews were not permitted to operate from some of the marginal airstrips until checked out on them. This caused a temporary set-back but the crews were soon checked out and once cleared to operate into and out of the marginal strips, gave invaluable assistance in meeting the up-country requirements. This assistance enabled the squadron to log 212 hours operational flying. The 30 Squadron crews were no new boys to operating and out of short airstrips, but some of the South Arabian strips such as Wadi Ayn, due to their proximity to the Yemen border, required very precise flight paths, and in the interests of safety, it was best for a new crew to be checked in and out of such airstrips. The airstrip at Perim Island, in the Red Sea close to the Yemen border, was now visited frequently, moving in men and supplies presumably due to threats of attack by the dissidents from the Yemen mainland.

All personnel were delighted to learn that Flight Lieutenant Andruskeiwicz DFC, had been awarded the AFC for outstanding service in the Radfan operations. He was the first pilot to land a Beverley at Thumier, which was now known as Habilayne.

Intensive up-country work prevailed right through April and May of 1965, 169 air landing sorties being flown in May at an average of three sorties per day, each sortie being of about fifty-two minutes duration. This was an excellent effort considering

An air-to-air of 84 Squadron's XM106 later blown up by land mine at Habilayne.
W. Binfield

the high rate of engine faults which occurred so often in up-country work. Throughout this period, there were only four aircraft on the flight line, and it was seldom that more than two of these were serviceable at any given time. The other aircraft, of course, were all away on detachment. This led to a shortfall in the completion of training exercises.

Another detachment to Swaziland took place in June, with Squadron Leader Barnden, the Squadron Commander, skippering XH121 to withdraw the First Battalion The Lancashire Regiment from Matsapa. In July, XB266, XM103 and XH121 skippered by Flying Officer Ferguson and Flight Lieutenants Corbin and Kemp respectively, revisited Matsapa to undertake a changeover of the troops garrisoned there.

More Activity in Thamoud Area

In August, one aircraft and two crews spent four days at Riyan flying reinforcements and supplies to the HBL at Sanau, Al Ghaydah, Murait and Thamoud. These garrisons and the surrounding district were again being troubled by terrorists. The high demand for up-country work continued and as a result, two crews from 30 Squadron, captained by Flight Lieutenants Jenkins and Clark and one crew from 47 Squadron, captained by Flight Lieutenant P. F. H. Walker, were attached to 84 Squadron. These crews were soon checked into the up-country strips being used with the result that some 84 Squadron crews were able to carry out route flights.

The Kenya detachment was now reduced to one aircraft and two crews. There was plenty of work: in addition to flying resupply sorties to the Northern Frontier District airstrips, fourteen paratrooping sorties were flown on a joint British/Kenyan Army exercise. The heavy work-load was still affecting training. Captains were naturally given priority and managed to complete sufficient training hours for them to retain their categories, but co-pilots, keen for training to help them prepare for future captaincy, missed out severely.

Lame Aircraft at Hostile Airstrips

Terrorism was now so rife up-country that any aircraft on the ground at any of the airstrips was a prime target for the dissidents. Night-stopping was quite out of the question since terrorist attacks with mortars were quite common at night and the most incompetent bombardier could scarcely miss a parked Beverley. On four occasions, aircraft became unserviceable on up-country turn-rounds. At Dhala, Flight Lieutenants Livermore and Corbin were both faced with the possibility of having to night-stop and run the risk of their aircraft being attacked. To avoid night-stopping, Flight Lieutenant Livermore flew out with a partially repaired engine and a fuel leak; Flight Lieutenant Corbin, who had starter motor trouble, did a successful windmill start - quite an achievement at Dhala - and thus was able to depart. The problem of aircraft being benighted at up-country strips was now regarded as being extremely serious and various methods of evolving some kind of 'rescue cum protection' were considered.

Once again, a 30 Squadron crew skippered by Squadron Leader R. P. J. King and a 47 Squadron crew skippered by Flight Lieutenant J. R. Nicholls were detached to 84 to help out with the up-country work which in October, reached an all-time high. Flying hours for route and up-country work totalled 290 and just under one and a half million pounds (682 tonnes) of freight were moved, along with 2,673 passengers and 4,650 troops. The allotted task was exceeded by 81 hours. Flight Lieutenant Robinson and crew from 47 Squadron also helped out during October. This splendid achievement had been made possible by the help of crews loaned from the other Beverley squadrons, also by the loan of a 47 Squadron aircraft. Up-country trips now seemed to be mainly confined to Dhala, Habilayne, Beihan, Ataq, Mukeiras, Perim, Lodar and Negub, most sorties being flown to Dhala and Habilayne. This clearly indicated the intensity of the terrorism near to Aden. A highlight of the month was a drop of cement in eight one-ton containers on Jebel Radfan, made by Flight Lieutenant W. W. Howell and crew in XM106.

CSE Show for Federal Army

November brought a most unusual commitment in that the Arab equivalent of a CSE (Combined Services Entertainment) show was flown to Mukeiras, Dhala, Ataq and Beihan for entertainment of the Federal Army. Somehow, time and capacity was spared for three flights to be made between Salalah and Midway (a small strip inland from Salalah) for the Mekon Oil Company. Flight Lieutenant Ferguson captained the flight and reported the suitability of Midway as a possible diversion airstrip for Salalah. Colin Ferguson had recently been promoted from Flying Officer and the squadron diary noted that 'now he was a Flight Lieutenant, he was spared the embarrassment of being mistaken for co-pilot.

All aircraft bar one were now camouflaged and after many discussions, a standard scheme for squadron markings was agreed. The first aircraft to be adorned with the new markings was XM106, carrying the squadron's black scorpion on either side of the nose, a playing card symbol on each fin, code letter in grey on each side of the freight bay below the flight deck windows and spinners finished in yellow. The camouflage finish was said to blend in well with the Arabian sands.

Operation Brickbat

December 1965 was marked by Rhodesia's Unilateral Declaration of Independence and its attendant diplomatic shocks. The squadron was again called to readiness and in Operation *Brickbat*, airlifted part of an Airfield Control Unit to Lusaka, and then moved heavy equipment into Zambia.

Eastleigh Detachment Finishes

The Beverley detachment at the now Royal Kenyan Air Force Base Eastleigh finished in December when the Royal Kenyan Air Force acquired its fourth DH Caribou and assumed full responsibility for Kenya's air support tasks. However, the Beverley detachment finished in style with a major paratrooping exercise at Nanyuki, and with a number of low level cross country flights. The latter were sponsored by the Kenyan Ministry of Agriculture and flew around Lake Victoria to give students of Masumo Agricultural College a bird's-eye view of land conservation problems. The cessation of the Kenya detachment brought all the squadron back to base at Khormaksar for the first time in six or seven years and the flight line at Khormaksar certainly looked crowded with 84's full complement of six Beverleys parked there.

Co-pilot Colin Ferguson 'props up' a Beverley fin. *via 84 Squadron*

An 84 Sqn crew up country. L to R Flt Lt Colin Ferguson, next two unknown, Fg Off Mike Westwood. *C. Ferguson*

Revetments constructed from water-filled drums for protection of aircraft from mortar shells. *S. Hitchen*

Trouble in Aden
This was now rife, many RAF personnel were murdered in Aden by terrorists when off duty and several terrorist outrages were committed. Mortars were occasionally fired on to Khormaksar airfield and to protect the aircraft, protective pens of water-filled oil drums were constructed. There was no shortage of oil drums or sea water so this was a most expedient protective measure. The drums were only stacked two high as the ballistics experts stated that mortar bomb shrapnel always travelled close to the ground.

Fuel Strike
The new year started with an immense commitment of up-country tasks but 84 was well able to cope now that the whole squadron was at base. Dhala received 27 loads, ten shuttles were flown between Dhala and Habilayne, eight sorties were flown to Ataq and six to Mukeiras. In addition, Sanau, Thamoud, Midway, Lodar and Mayfah were visited, making a total of 120 up-country sorties. These included thirteen sorties flown to Thamoud and Sanau in support of the HBL. In addition to troops, fuel was carried plus large numbers of goats and dried fish. One sortie to Beihan was to deliver a combine harvester presented by Her Majesty's Government to the Sharif of Beihan. It seemed that Britain still had some friends in South Arabia.

Operations were hampered by a strike at Aden which depleted stocks of aviation fuel, but permission was obtained from the authorities at Djibouti to fly the Beverleys there for refuelling. This unaccustomed high usage of Djibouti's fuel stocks caused this source of supply to dry up for a few days until stocks were replenished. The fuel shortage put a stop to all training flights.

Flights to Kamaran
Back at Aden, the terrorism seemed to be moving inexorably southwards and 66 sorties were flown to Dhala and Habilayne. The terrorism had also spread to Kamaran, the Red Sea island off Hodeida, and two sorties were flown to Perim Island in a massive build-up of the garrison there. Little did the authorities know that within six months, the garrison would have to be evacuated and Perim abandoned to the dissidents. The latter were no longer hill tribesmen with itchy trigger fingers; they were a well armed guerilla organization supported by FLOSY (Front for the Liberation of South Yemen) which had rapidly dominated the Aden political scene and was now demanding the withdrawal of British forces.

Aircraft to Hong Kong
Two months previously, RAF Maintenance Command in the UK announced that it could no longer accept Beverleys for major overhaul. Arrangements were therefore made for HAECO (The Hong Kong Aircraft Engineering Company) to overhaul 84 Squadron's Beverleys together with the Beverleys of 30 and 34 Squadrons. XH121, which had been awaiting overhaul for almost two months, was then flown to Kai Tak by Flight Lieutenant Ware and crew, staging through Masirah, Bombay, Calcutta, Changi and Saigon.

May brought the beginnings of frequent up-country air-dropping sorties, Flight Lieutenant Warden captaining XM103, dropping ten one-ton containers loaded with cement into Beihan and later, the same crew flying two sorties to Ataq, dropping fuel in one-ton containers. In addition to the air-drops, over 160 up-country sorties were flown in June and July, some to evacuate the Perim Island garrison, and an 18-sortie shuttle between Wadi Ayn and Beihan, reportedly to withdraw troops from Wadi Ayn's vulnerable position so near the Yemen border.

Aircraft Impounded in Congo
A near-international incident occurred on 9th July when XM106, en route for Matsapa, was impounded by the Congolese Army while staging through Lubumbashi. The ill-disciplined Congolese soldiers broke open cargo containers, desert survival packs and emergency water containers showing total disregard for the invaluable lifesaving equipment.

After intervention by the British Consul, the aircraft and crew were released some five hours later, to take off in disgust, for Ndola before proceeding to Matsapa. The object of this trip was to support the Royal Irish Fusiliers in attempts to stabilize civil unrest in Basutoland. Things returned to normal a few days later and on 12th July, the detachment returned to Khormaksar.

Between 22nd and 26th July, XL149, with two crews aboard captained by Flight Lieutenants Ferguson and West carried out a major redeployment of the HBL, operating between Riyan and Thamoud, Muirait and Al Ghayda. The crews were well entertained by the Legion and at the end of the operation, the HBL Commander Colonel Gray, presented each crew member with an HBL head-dress. Tragically, the Colonel was murdered a few days later.

More supply drops were now taking place, fourteen one-ton containers being dropped at Beihan and eight at Ataq. This seemed a most expedient way to deliver non-bulky supplies, the aircraft being spared the wear and tear of landing and take-off and long turn-round time whilst unloading.

August 1966 saw many more up-country lifts to Dhala and Habilayne and ten sorties were flown in a shuttle between Wadi Ayn and Beihan. Dissident activity in the Riyan area resulted in four airlifts of men and materials. At the end of the month, Operation *Aloe* was mounted to withdraw a Javelin fighter squadron from Zambia. A detachment of four Beverleys, com-

Bev's-eye view of married quarters at Khormaksar. W. Binfield

Airport terminal building at Beihan. via 84 Squadron

84 Squadron Beverley parked outside Beihan's terminal building. J. Sevier

Opposite page: **SAS 'Pink Panther' vehicle, so named because of its pink paint scheme, used to protect Riyan during final withdrawal of British Forces.** S. Hitchen

manded by the Squadron Commander, Squadron Leader Barnden, flew to Lusaka staging through Mombasa in order to take on maximum fuel for the long Mombasa - Lusaka leg.

Flag Waving at Riyan

September brought more terrorist activity in the Mukalla area and this prompted an exercise to mount a show of force which was hoped would discourage the dissidents. In two Beverley lifts, 108 troops together with rations, ammunition, barbed wire and other infantry support equipment, were airlifted into Riyan under an escort of Hunters. HMS *Kildatan* also showed the flag by standing to off Mukalla.

Another Matsapa detachment was mounted, XL149 and XM103, skippered by Flight Lieutenant Ferguson and Flying Officer Craig, flying to Matsapa via Mombasa. The detachment provided air mobility for the First Battalion The Royal Irish Fusiliers during the Independence celebrations in neighbouring Bechuanaland and Basutoland. During the detachment, Flight Lieutenant Ferguson and crew flew an emergency casevac sortie to take an airman, seriously injured after a fall from the sixth floor of a tall building, to Pretoria for hospitalization. On 14th October, the same crew flew two sorties from Matsapa to Lourenco Marques taking troops of the Irish Fusiliers to catch a charter aircraft to the UK. This was the only known occasion for a Beverley to visit Lourenco Marques.

October also brought a new CO. Squadron Leader Stan Hitchen arrived fresh from a VC-10 flight in the middle of a party for Squadron Leader and Mrs Barnden.

There were comparatively few up-country sorties in the closing months of 1966, only thirty-eight in November and forty-three in December. This was a possible indication that the authorities realized that the South Arabian campaign was a lost cause and were running down their garrisons before abandoning them to the FLOSY elements. The territory was extremely hostile as Flight Lieutenant Ware found on 19th December after he and his crew had landed at Dhala in XH121. The Army Commander informed him that the aircraft had been fired on by machine gun during final approach and advised against further aircraft movements in or out of the airstrip until the terrorists had been removed. A second Beverley en-route for Dhala was accordingly turned back and XH121 stayed put until the Army had dispersed the terrorists. Fortunately, the aircraft was undamaged.

Squadron's Fiftieth Birthday

This was celebrated on 23rd February 1967 and marked nearly forty-seven years of continuous overseas service, all of which had been spent in the Middle East except for six years in the Far East during and immediately after the Second World War, and another three years in the Far East in the 1950s. No wonder the squadron's badge included a Scorpion.

At the anniversary celebrations, a display of silver and other trophies included a ceremonial sword and a specially bound copy of the memoirs of Lord Douglas of Kirtleside, a former commander of the squadron. The sword and memoirs had recently been presented at an 'Old Scorpions' dinner in London.

The opening months of 1967 were again quiet as regards up-country work, sorties to the airstrips only averaging about thirty per month. The sorties were dangerous though, with increasing risk of aircraft coming under ground fire, as Flying Officer Craig and crew in XL149 found when their aircraft collected bullet holes just after take-off from Dhala, injuring one soldier. The squadron was doing more route trips now; presumably because of the decreasing up-country commitments, and flew the Riyan, Salalah and Masirah supply schedules.

A record was claimed in February when XM103 was flown for a one-ton container drop to Francistown in Botswana, the entire 4,500 miles trip being flown in the slow, 'doors off' configuration.

Operation Snaffle

By March, terrorism had spread to Socotra and the dissidents were said to be plotting to overthrow the Sultan and Council. Operation *Snaffle*, involving four Beverleys, two from 30 Squadron and two from 84, was mounted at Riyan and flew a large contingent of the HBL from Al Ghayda to Socotra where they successfully dealt with the rebels.

Up-country work was still slack in April, a mere thirty-one sorties being flown, nine of these being Dhala-Habilayne shuttle trips. Zamakh, a new airstrip, was visited and found to be suitable for Beverleys and in the following month, a large-scale famine relief airlift, comprising forty sorties, was carried out delivering the supplies to Zamakh.

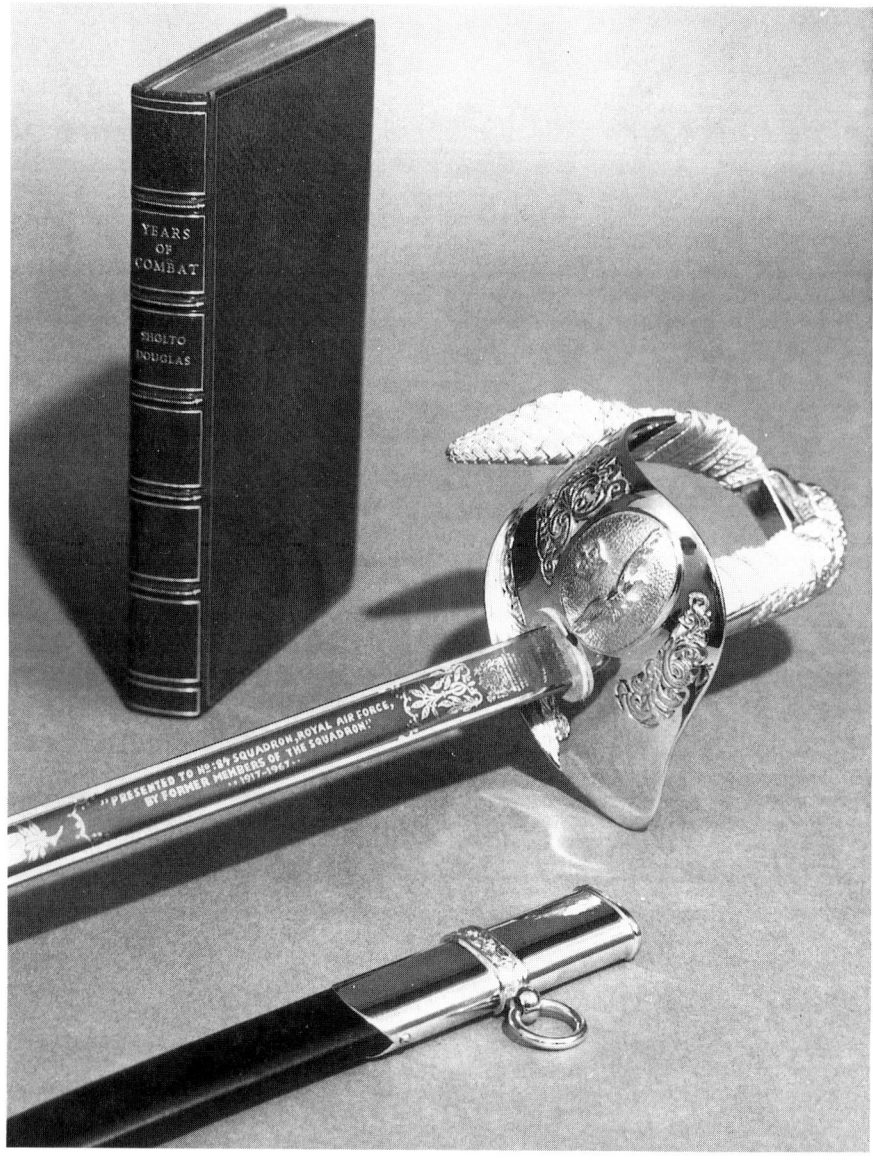

Co-Pilot becomes Captain

May 1967 was highlighted by Flying Officer Mike Westwood, one of the squadron's co-pilots, becoming an 'instant captain'. Mike was an outstanding pilot and was awarded his captaincy after intensive on-the-spot examinations, both on the ground and in the air, by the Transport Command Examining Staff. Most co-pilots had to attend a lengthy conversion course before becoming captains, but Mike Westwood's superb airmanship enabled him to short-circuit the system.

Beverley becomes Fuel Tanker

An intense fuel shortage at Aden occurred in June, both in Avgas fuel for the piston-engined aircraft and in Avtur fuel for the jets. The Beverley rose to this occasion and XH121 was modified to carry 2,500 gallons of Avtur in four of its eight fuel tanks, and commenced a shuttle to Djibouti where maximum loads of Avtur and Avgas were uplifted and flown back to Khormaksar, the Avtur to be discharged into Avtur fuel trucks. Many a keen airman spotted the anomaly of an Avtur refuelling truck positioned at an aircraft which used Avgas and reported this to higher authority. Full marks for flight safety awareness.

Final Kenya Detachment

Shifta terrorism disrupting comunications together with severe flooding caused a famine situation in Northern Kenya in June and the Kenyan Government requested assistance. A detachment consisting of two aircraft and crews commanded by Squadron Leader Hitchen was despatched to Nairobi to fly in and drop supplies to the Northern Frontier District airstrips, sorties which had been everyday occurences in previous years on the Kenya detachments. With the Beverley's tremendous capacity for airlifting supplies, the famine relief work was soon completed and the detchment returned to base, the final Beverley flight from Kenya.

Top: **84 Squadron crew members of the last Beverley to be detached to Kenya to assist the Kenyan Government, drink a toast before departure for Aden. Left to right: Sergeant Dunne, AQM; Sergeant McMillan, AQM; Flight Sergeant Barlow, engineer; Sergeant Eyre, signaller; Master Air Quartermaster O'Hare.** *G. Barlow*

Ceremonial sword and specially bound copy of his memoirs presented to 84 Squadron by Marshal of the Royal Air Force Lord Douglas of Kirtleside, a former 84 Squadron commander, on the occasion of the Squadron's Golden Jubilee. *via 84 Squadron*

Opposite: **XM106 blown up by land mine while taxying at Habilayne.** *RAF Museum*

This photograph from 84 Squadron's album typifies the sardonic humour of Beverley aircrew. *via 84 Squadron*

Land Mine Claims Beverley

On 21st June, XM106, captained by Flight Lieutenant Manley, taxied over a land mine buried by the terrorists on the airstrip at Habilayne. The port undercarriage was blown off and the wing collapsed to the ground, causing irreparable damage. After salvaging as much as possible from the wreck, it was dragged off the airstrip and abandoned to the Arabs. Squadron personnel were sorry to see XM106 come to such an untimely end, she was one of the squadron's original aircraft and apart from a short spell back in the UK for overhaul, had spent her entire career with 84 Squadron. However, as later events caused the remainder of 84's Beverleys to fall victim to the scrap-man, it was perhaps appropriate that XM106's days ended during active service.

Last Beverley to Kamaran - Squadron gets Dakota and Andover

On July, Flight Lieutenant Craig and crew took the GOC on a visit to Kamaran Island in XH121 and flew out the remaining British personnel on the island. Flight Lieutenant Craig was reported to have been the last Beverley captain to sign Kamaran's visitor's book. The island was occupied by the Yemenis on the following day.

A Dakota, very 'clapped out' according to pilots who flew it, was acquired by the squadron in June. It was used for up-country work and made a useful contribution to the squadron's work-load, although due to its age and condition, the ground staff had great difficulty in keeping it airworthy.

The squadron also acquired an Andover, a foretaste of the aircraft that would succeed the Beverley, and this was used for VIP duties. Crews were impressed by the Andover's performance but as one crewman remarked: 'It hasn't got the Beverley's character'.

Fuel Lift Ends - Preparations for Pull-out

The Djibouti fuel lift continued until 19th July when stocks at Djibouti became almost exhausted. More fuel was then flown from Assab, an airfield along the coast from Djibouti. A large number of sorties were then flown to Assab to collect food, aircraft spares and a great deal of other stores which had been held up by the Ethiopian customs. On one of these sorties, Flight Lieutenant Coutts landed XB284 at Khormaksar in a 20 knot crosswind. His cargo included 130,000 eggs which were all said to have survived the landing.

Although July was a busy month for up-country work, there were indications that the garrisons were being run down. Squadron records lists mail carried for June and July as a mere 171 and 242 kilos respectively. A year before, twenty times that amount was being carried, so it seems that there were considerably less British troops up-country. However, in August the squadron flew 399 hours, with seventeen up-country sorties and fifteen shuttles. Three of the squadron's Beverleys completed the British withdrawal from Riyan on 2nd September, and Riyan was left to be taken over by the new regime of South Arabia. In August, training flights from Khormaksar were suspended due to the danger from small arms fire from the ground.

Squadron Moves to Sharjah

Later in September, the Squadron Standard, silver and other trophies were taken from Khormaksar to Sharjah. This was to be 84 Squadron's new base after re-equipping with Andovers. Meanwhile, back at Khormaksar, preparations were in hand to fly the Beverleys back to the UK for disposal. A suitable route was sought, as due to the Arab/Israeli six-day war, overflying Egypt did not seem to be practicable. An itinerary following the so-called CENTO route was then negotiated with the authorities in all the countries concerned; this route was by way of Sharjah, Teheran, Diyarbakir in Turkey, Nicosia, Luqa, Nice and Lyneham. The VMC (Visual Meteorological Conditions) safety height for Turkey was about 16,000 feet and because of this unprecedented height for both Beverleys and Beverley crews, all crew members had to have dentistry to ensure that their fillings were sound. Many crew members wondered whether the tired old Beverleys could in fact, make the required safety height.

Before the Beverleys left Aden, they put in a very hard month's work, flying a total of 309 hours, involving trips to the Persian Gulf, the Riyan withdrawal, a shuttle to airlift fuel from Salalah to Al Ghaydah and the final batch of up-country sorties. The up-country situation was now extremely hostile and unstable and because of this, fighter cover was provided for most sorties.

Beverleys Leave Aden

Suddenly, the Beverley's Aden days were over and the first three aircraft departed for the UK by way of the CENTO route via Iran and Turkey.

A few days later, on 29th October, the last three Beverleys performed a formation fly-past in company with the Dakota. By this time, the route to the UK was changed and by courtesy of President Nasser, the Beverleys were permitted to overfly Egypt. The last three Beverleys were XM111, XM103 and XL130, skippered by Flight Lieutenants Barton and Coutts and Squadron Leader Hitchen respectively. All aircraft were loaded to full capacity, mainly with private 'loot'. Squadron Leader Hitchen recalled: 'I had a few cases of liquers on board; I didn't see why I should leave them behind for FLOSY - sooner let the UK customs have them.'

Before leaving Khormaksar, XM111 and XM103 were decorated with various bits of humorous graffiti with special reference to the 'flower power' of the 'swinging '60s', and the squadron code letter U of XM103 was suffixed to give a UK and/or BUST slogan. Ranks and names of crew members were also stencilled on each aircraft near the crew entrance door.

Eventful Flights to UK

The aircraft left Khormaksar at 15-minute intervals on 6th November. Squadron Leader Hitchen's Beverley, XL130, being the last to leave. Flight Lieutenant Coutts and crew in XM103 were first off; they flew into a violent hailstorm over the Red Sea which shattered the astrodome, the eyebrow windows above the windscreen and made sizeable holes in the nose. Undeterred, they continued to El Adem where temporary repairs were carried out mainly by a carpenter. The remaining legs to the UK were uneventful.

XM111 skippered by Flight Lieutenant Barton suffered a double engine failure over the Red Sea and was forced to divert to Jeddah. Squadron Leader Hitchen also diverted to Jeddah to give what assistance he could, but the Saudis, very much anti-British at the time, ordered him off again at gun point. XM111 needed a replacement engine; the crew were able to repair the other unserviceable engine and then had to wait delivery of the new engine which arrived from the Gulf by Argosy.

After being forced to take off from Jeddah, Squadron Leader Stan Hitchen and crew set course for Ras Banas, a promontory on the Egyptian coast of the Red Sea.

84 Squadron's last Beverley flypast accompanied by the Squadron's Dakota.

She made the UK without busting only to fall victim to the scrap man. XM103 at Bicester awaiting disposal, late 1967.
both via 84 Squadron

Map 10:
The UK and/or Bust Route

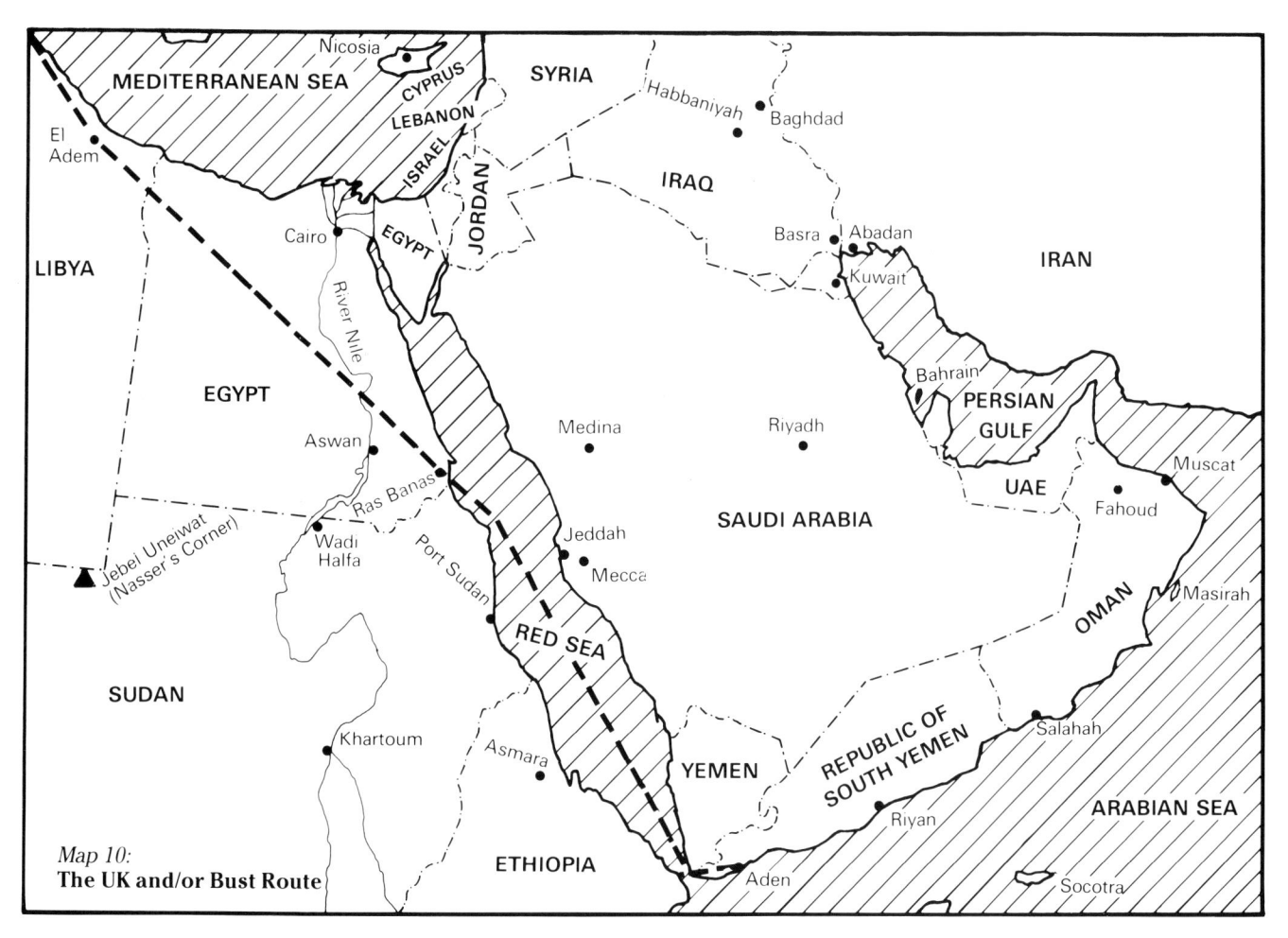

When approaching the Egyptian coast, Flight Sergeant Hankes the engineer, reported two MiGs formating to starboard; they then pulled away. Shortly afterwards, one MiG came in from the starboard side and fired a salvo of rockets across the Beverley's bows. The other MiG then came in from the port side and completely bracketed the Beverley with cannon tracer. Some urgent radio transmissions to Cairo naturally followed which resulted in Cairo asking 'what are your intentions?' After being informed in no uncertain terms of the Beverley's intentions, which of course, had been clearly stated on the flight plan, Cairo called off the MiGs who departed, much to the relief of the Beverley's occupants. It appears that the fighters were from a new Egyptian Air Force base at Ras Banas and that the attack was the result of over-enthusiasm on the part of the MiG pilots. The Beverley's radio transmissions had been intercepted by an Argosy in the Persian Gulf and London was informed of this near-international incident. As a result, Squadron Leader Hitchen, as soon as he had landed at El Adem after the long and eventful flight, was escorted by service policemen to the Operations Room, where he underwent an intense, high-level debriefing.

Next day, the flight was resumed and XL130 was in due course, delivered to Bicester for disposal. Thus ended the last Beverley flight from Aden, a flight marked by the hostile actions of a few trigger-happy pilots of the Egyptian Air Force.

84 Squadron's Achievements with the Beverley

In nine and a half years of operating the Beverley, 84 Squadron logged about 27,000 flying hours, moved 42,675 tonnes of freight and carried 122,876 passengers. The hours flown are comparatively small; this is to be expected in view of the tremendous amount of short-haul work done. However, the tonnage of freight moved and the number of passengers carried is almost double the equivalent figures recorded for 47 Squadron, which operated more Beverleys than 84 over a longer period.

The tonnage of freight moved however, is relatively unimportant. What is important is the bulky items of freight moved: vehicles and artillery; building materials and sectional buildings; radar equipment; agricultural machinery; oil drilling equipment; earthmoving machinery; and many other large items which could never have been moved into the remote up-country outposts of South Arabia except by air and almost exclusively by Beverley. Such was the Beverley's contribution to the operations in South Arabia and the Gulf, and to this day, there must be many Arabs who still remember the Beverley as the aeroplane which made their lives more tolerable by bringing them essential foodstuffs and medical supplies in times of need.

It is perhaps appropriate to end 84 Squadron's Beverley history with an extract from a letter written from the British Embassy in Khartoum, by diplomat Mr Hugh Leach who wrote: 'I was in South Arabia for some years as a Political Officer and on many occasions, our stores were airlifted in by Beverley. I once asked a pilot what it was like to fly an aircraft of that size and shape and I shall never forget his reply: "It's like driving a large warehouse from the upstairs lavatory window." The Beverley was certainly a wonderful aircraft.'

Humourous graffiti specially applied for XM111's last trip - from Aden to the UK for eventual scrapping. *via 84 Squadron*

Chapter Five

The Far East Beverley Force

The 48 Squadron Beverley Flight

It is not generally known that before 34 Squadron received its Beverleys in October 1960, that for the previous eighteen months, a flight of four Beverleys had been operated by 48 Squadron from Changi. 48 Squadron was the Far East Air Force's first transport squadron, having been engaged on transport duties in the Far East since 1945 when Dakotas were received in India. The squadron later moved to Singapore where the Dakotas were exchanged for Valettas in the early '50s. In August 1957, the squadron re-equipped with Hastings at Changi, and when the decision was made to deploy Beverleys to the Far East, it seemed appropriate that 48 Squadron, as the resident transport unit, should operate them. The first Beverley, skippered by Flight Lieutenant J. W. Adams, arrived on 11th March, and on 18th March, did a proving flight around Malaya, then went on to Borneo and Bangkok, the crews thus gaining experience of operating in their new terrain.

Flying Officer John Nimmo and crew arrived in XB266 on 13th May followed by Flight Lieutenants Grobler and Salmond in XB260 a month later. The first three Beverleys all arrived on schedule after quiet, trouble-free trips. However, the fourth Bev to arrive, XH112, captained by Flight Lieutenant K. C. Smale, arrived on 16th June after a five-day delay due to unserviceability in Calcutta.

The complement of Beverleys now complete, the Beverley flight got down to flying the various routes around the Far East. The Army also started Beverley familiarization with air portability training, Captain G. Murray leading an Air Despatch Team from 55 Company RASC. One of the first long route trips was in XB260 captained by Flight Lieutenant Adams to the USAF base at Tachikawa near Tokyo. A number of liaison officers from HQ FEAF went along and Wing Commander Stevenson, the FEAF flight safety officer, deplored the Beverley's lack of an autopilot. But despite the Wing Commander's comment, it was to be a long time before autopilots were installed in the Beverleys of the Far East Air Force.

The first trip to Gan, the RAF staging post nearing completion in the Maldive Islands, to the south-west of Ceylon, was made by Flight Lieutenant Grobler and crew in XM112. A number of shuttles were flown in August, September and October to take Auster aircraft from Singapore to Hong Kong. Paratroop training also commenced in September, drops being made at Sembawang on Singapore Island. September was highlighted by the first Beverley flight to Australia, made in XM104 captained by Flight Lieutenant Adams and Flying Officer Nimmo. The object of this flight was for a Beverley to participate in the Queensland Centenary celebrations and the route was by way of Djakarta, Bali and Darwin. Flying and para-dropping displays were given at various Royal Australian Air Force bases.

Excitement in New Zealand

New Zealand was visited in October by XM104, skippered by Flight Lieutenant Grobler, the aircraft staging through Djakarta, Bali, Darwin, Amberley, Whenuapai, Ohakea, Wellington and Rotorua, see *Map 11*. Group Captain Griffiths, ex-Station Commander of RAF Abingdon, and one of the first RAF pilots to fly the Beverley, now 'flying a desk' at the Air Ministry, met XM104 in New Zealand and undertook liaison duties, arranging flying displays and other activities associated with the Beverley's visit which was primarily for celebrations concerned with the opening of Rongatai Airport at Wellington. The Group Captain recalled:

'In the week prior to the opening of Rongatai, the visiting aircraft were asked to fly round the islands to show themselves off to local populace. There were complaints that the aircraft flew too high; to UK pilots who were used to perpetual complaints regarding aircraft noise, it seemed most unnatural to fly at low altitude over built-up areas. Nevertheless, that is what the New Zealanders wanted and on 23rd October, I was approached by the Publicity Officer at Ohakea, the base at which we were stationed. He asked us to fly over Ohura and Rotorua, as residents of these places had expressed disappointment due to other visiting aircraft having flown too high. We therefore set off in XM104 for Ohura which was deep down in a valley and really, only an aircraft such as an Auster should have been sent there. However, we managed to put on a flying display without colliding with the neighbouring mountains and then set course for Rotorua where, to our amazement, we found the airfield swarming with hordes of children. Apparently, the local radio had announced that the Beverley was visiting Rotorua, and the schools had closed down for the day. We hadn't really intended to land as the airfield was a little small: 1,000 yards uphill, one-way landings only, coming in over high trees and taking off downhill towards the trees. However, it was a perfect "Beverley airfield" and we had no trouble whatsoever except for controlling the crowds. As soon as we had stopped engines, opened the doors and lowered the ramps, we were immediately invaded by masses of people. So great was their enthusiasm that we had to clear the ship, close the doors and ask the police to try and keep control. At one time we had about thirty or forty children on each sponson and others doing acrobatics from the under-fuselage radio aerials. When 5 o'clock came, half the town turned up in their cars, thus adding to the congestion on the airfield. It was only with the greatest difficulty that we managed to get clear enough space for take-off.

'The opening of Rongatai Airport was not without incident as one of our Vulcans knocked off its port wheels on landing and a Royal New Zealand Air Force Sunderland tore its bottom during a low-level fly-past. The Beverley showed its versatility by flying off to collect crash equipment to raise the Vulcan; within ten minutes of landing and unloading, the Beverley then took off again with parachutists from No.1 Parachute Training School to give a sky-diving perfomance which thrilled the crowd immensely.'

Beverleys for Crop Dusting?

Group Captain Griffiths carried out an interesting and impressive demonstration when flying from Ohura to Rotorua. He takes up the story:

'We were at about 4,000 feet flying north-east from Ohura; I was flying the aircraft as first pilot at the time and so took full responsibility for subsequent events. It was fairly mountainous country and we were flying quietly along in good visibility when, way ahead of us in a deep valley, we suddenly saw a plume of white. A couple of minutes later the plume reappeared and this time we could see an aircraft crop-dusting so I thought we'd drop down and take a look at the operation. We circled

The Rotorua Post

Price: **Fourpence**   ROTORUA, N.Z., FRIDAY, OCTOBER 23, 1959   **PERIODS OF RAIN**

FOR ROTORUA A DAY OF AIR THRILLS

The usual heralds of important events, children, hundreds of them, swarmed on to the Rotorua airfield yesterday afternoon to give a terrific welcome to the R.A.F. Blackburn Beverley transport aircraft, which paid a surprise visit at 4 p.m. and stayed for two hours.

Within minutes of the huge aircraft coming to rest, the children were sitting and climbing on anything which could be climbed and sat upon, while equally large hordes of them clambered around the vast rear doors as they opened. The crew and passengers had no time at all to breathe before autograph books, scraps of paper, school books and anything handy were thrust forward for autographs.

It was the children's moment and for a while it looked as if the aircraft was to be taken by storm. But with quiet efficiency and exemplary courtesy, the crew restored order among the exited crowds.

THE FINAL THRILL

The children had reason to be excited. The Beverley, unheralded, came to add a real thrill to a day of aircraft.

During the afternoon, three high-speed American jets, two Voodoos and a Destroyer, screamed over the town at almost the speed of sound, and 15 minutes or so later a beautifully graceful Avro Vulcan delta-wing bomber of the R.A.F. circled lazily over Rotorua, its terrific power harnessed to a subdued rumble.

Then at 4 o'clock the Blackburn arrived, circled slowly a couple of times and then, before the large crowd already waiting, dropped in and shortly pulled to a stop. At the moment of its wheels touching the ground, the Beverley became the largest aircraft to ever land at Rotorua.

EVERYTHING OUTSIZE

And large it is—everything is outsize. The huge fixed undercarriage, the four Bristol Centarus engines, the vast slab-sided body and the tail fins which are 38 feet 8 inches from the ground at their tips. With a wing span of 162 feet, the aircraft is 99 feet 6 inches long, while the tail plane is 43 feet 2 inches in span. This is a greater length than the wing span of some fighter aircraft.

The only thing small about the Beverley is its landing distance. With its reversible pitch airscrews the aircraft, with full load, 20,000 lb, giving a total weight of 143,000 lb, can be brought to a halt within 310 yards. And this was demonstrated yesterday.

CARRIES 96 SOLDIERS

The Beverley is a heavy duty military transport as well as a freighter. It is equipped to carry 96 troops for normal landings or 70 paratroopers ready for dropping. The men can be carried in either the 40ft x 10ft x 10ft freight compartment, or in the 44 feet long tail boom, or both. From there, the paratroopers drop through a deck hatch.

Carrying a crew of six, the Beverley has a range of 3690 miles with a small load. This distance is three times that to Sydney!

Aboard the aircraft as a passenger was Group Captain E. A. Griffiths, who is deputy-Director of Air Transport in the Air Ministry.

BASED ON CHANGI

Group Captain Griffiths said he had just come along for the ride and it was a change because he "flies a Mahogany Bomber" in London, and because his brother-in-law lives in Rotorua. The latter was one of the first persons he met on the airfield.

Flight Lieutenant J. Grobler is captain of the aircraft, which is attached to a Beverley Flight at the R.A.F. air base at Changi, near Singapore. Members of the flight are in the course of a two and a-half year tour of duty in the Far East.

During the time the aircraft was on the ground most of the crew were able to take a quick look at Whaka and at last one officer was able to set his mind at rest.

"Is it all right to smoke, the geesers won't catch fire, will they?"

IT'S A LONG WAY DOWN—This picture was taken from the astro-hatch in the top of the Blackburn Beverley on the Rotorua airfield yesterday, and indicates how the huge aircraft overshadowed everything, even the hangars. Two Cessnas are visible under the engines of the Beverley.

A CAPTAIN IN HIS HALL—The captain of the Beverley, Flight-Lieutenant J. Grobler, R.A.F., middle, at the top of the loading ramp.

---

well downwind and then began the approach. We saw the crop-duster fly back, land and taxi to the fill-up/take-off point where in a matter of seconds, a lorry refilled the crop-duster which immediately took off again. The ground party had driven the lorry well to one side and they were still watching the crop-duster climbing away when they noticed the Beverley. Although I say so myself, it was a beautiful approach and we did a touch and go landing, rumbling our wheels for about 100 yards. The expressions on the faces of the crop-dusting ground crew just had to be seen to believed and I'm sure that XM104 was the first ever four-engined aircraft to touch down in that field. We then continued on our way to Rotorua.

'What a versatile aircraft was the Beverley: she could easily have operated from that field and it did cross my mind that the Beverley could have been used for crop-dusting vast areas such as forests. She would undoubtedly have proved a superb fire-fighting aircraft for dropping water on forest fires just as the Canadians do today with their Catalinas.'

SEAC Drop in Borneo

In November, severe flooding in the Kota Belud are of North Borneo, see *Map 12,* caused British troops to be cut off from their base and run short of rations and other essential supplies. Flying Officer John Nimmo and crew in XM104 relieved the situation by dropping the necessary

Cutting from *The Rotorua Post* for 23rd October 1959 describing the Beverley's visit to the local airfield.

Opposite: From the *Sarawak Tribune* describing the 'cat drop'.

stores in SEAC packs. This was the first ever SEAC drop in the Far East and is believed to have been the first operational SEAC drop made by the Beverley.

November also saw trips to Vientiane in Laos and a major air portability exercise, code-named *Flyaway,* involved the movement of 1,350 troops, their equipment, fifty Land Rovers and trailers, and a large fire tender, from Changi to Kuantan.

Cats by Parachute

March brought the 'cat drop' in which about twenty five cats were parachuted into Bario, an outpost in the Kelabit highlands of Sarawak. Bario was suffering from a severe plague of rats due to the cat population having died out and according to an article published in the New Straits Times in November 1980: 'Operation *Cat Drop*, organized by the World Health Organization, was found necessary because the rat population suddenly exploded. The population explosion resulted from the strange deaths of hundreds of cats. Many died because the insecticide DDT (which is banned in the US but still in use in Malaysia) for the anti-malarial programme had accumulated in the fatty tissues of the poor pussies.'

The drop was made in XM104 captained by Flying Officer John Nimmo, the cats being securely contained in wicker panniers which ensured their safe arrival at their destination. The Army Despatch team was commanded by Captain G. Murray. Other supplies dropped at Bario included a vibratory roller, a quantity of seeds for crops, and four cartons of stout for a convalescent tribal headman, the total load weighing in at just over three tonnes. A Mr McSporran sent the following message from Bario: 'Many thanks to RAF and all responsible for air drop, also to cat donors and cat basket makers. All cats safe and sound and much appreciated.' The Beverley had scored again. A newspaper cutting describing the drop is reproduced below.

The cat drop marked the end of the 48 Squadron Beverley Flight's first year in the Far East, a very successful year in which most of the Far East, and places beyond, had been covered by the four Beverleys of the Far East Air Force.

More Supplies Dropped in Borneo

April and May 1960 were highlighted by Army support work in Borneo, and in a fourteen-sortie shuttle flown between Changi and Jesselton, 14 tonnes of freight including 114 vehicles, plus 563 passengers were carried. More supplies were also dropped to Army units at Kota Belud. In the next two months, Army support was concentrated in Malaya with paratrooping and air portability exercises.

Two Tries And The Beverley Made It
Air-Drop Over Bario

Mission Accomplished In An Hour

The Sarawak Tribune

TUESDAY, MARCH 15, 1960 ★ 10 CENTS

By Lim Nai Teck
Kuching, Monday

MORE THAN 7,000 lbs of cargo, ranging from a 800-lb vibrating roller for air-strip construction to vegetable seeds for planting, and from cartons of stout for the chieftain's recuperation to more than 20 cats to wage war against mice and rats, were successfully air-dropped into Bario in the Kelabit highlands in the Fourth Division yesterday, in the biggest single airlift operation carried out by a Beverley aircraft of the Royal Air Force over Sarawak territory in post war years.

'Lucky Mascot'

With press and radio representatives on board and the Operations Officer of the Civil Aviation Department, Mr. John Seal who was in charge of the operations, there also went Liang Labang of the Sarawak Museum to whom this trip was not at all new.

It will be recalled that Liang participated in a similar operation last year when he guided a RAF plane in a mercy flight over Bario to airdrop a medical team and medical supplies in a bid—and a very happy and successful one—to save a patient who is Liang's sister.

Liang, who has from that occasion, been regarded more or less as a 'lucky mascot' accompanied the party on this occasion to assist in the location of the air-drop region.

The aircraft, piloted by Flight Officer John Nimmo, left Jesselton at 9 a.m. on Saturday for the air-drop operations. Even before the destination was sighted there was already a gathering mass of thick clouds, and the formation seemed almost un-ending; so thick was it that it appeared to be unpenetrable.

Visibility Poor

This kept the Beverley flying at a height of approximately 10,000 feet and after a short while it was evident that the mission could not be accomplished that day but had to be postponed.

Once a decision was made the aircraft made for home ground and this time it flew, instead of Jesselton, to Brunei, arriving there at 11.45 a.m.

Here members of the mission stayed overnight and early the next day—Sunday—the plane left Brunei and at 8.40 a.m. Bario was sighted. Weather condition was now favourable, and the aircraft began to circle over the target area, gradually descending from an altitude of 10,000 feet to a bare 400 feet.

The course which it was taking followed the mountain range and looking down the binoculars the airstrip could be seen very distinctly.

First Drop

By this time members of the crew had their safety belts on around their waist, standing at the verge of the store' of the aircraft—tense and attentive—watching the signal board.

Nothing, however was showing, and one could sense an atmosphere of restlessness among those who were in charge of the actual dropping operation. Even so, this did not in any way decrease one bit their attentiveness.

As the plane continued its circling at a minimum height above the ground one could perceive on one side, the wing of the plane rising slightly above the mountain slope while on the other the tip pointing skywards.

The first drop was at last made after much manoevring —this was at 9.15 a.m. From then on, Captain Murray and his men of the 55th Company Air Despatch Unit (stationed at Singapore) who were responsible for the packing, harnessing of parachutes and the drop itself, worked unceasingly for about an hour, offloading the total of eighteen crates.

The mission successfully completed, the Beverley turned in the direction of Kuching and touched down at Kuching Airport at 1 p.m.

Bario Says 'Thank You'

Today the following messages was received by Mr. John Seal, Operations Officer of the Civil Aviation Department, from Mr. M. M. McSporran at Bario:

"Many thanks to Royal Air Force and yourself and all others responsible for air drop arrangements. Also to cat donors and cat basket-makers. All cats safe and much appreciated. Very accurate dropping but unfortunately parachute dropping wheels* failed to open. All other stores received safely including heavy roller."

*Motor cycle wheels fitted with axles required' for earth carrying.

Map 11: The Far East

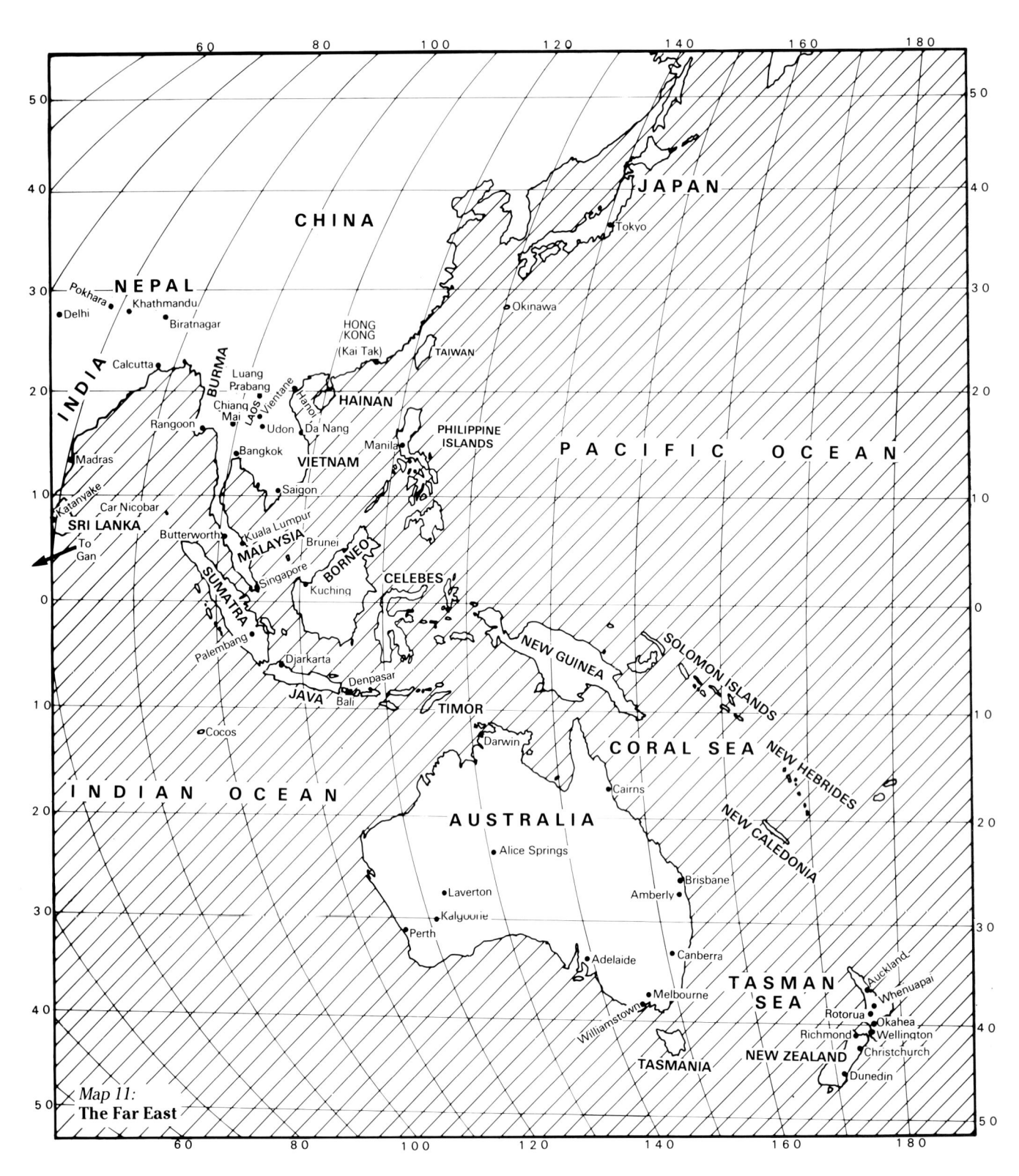

August brought the end of the State of Emergency in Malaya and XB262 participated in a fly-past which formed part of the celebrations. News was also received in August that the Beverley Flight was to be given squadron status and would shortly reform as No.34 Squadron at Seletar.

Preparations were put in hand to secure accommodation at Seletar for the new unit and during September, equipment was flown from Changi to Seletar in readiness for the redeployment.

Thus 48 Squadron's brief period of operating the Beverley came to an end - a period during which the Beverley had proved its worth in the Far East to the extent that the powers-that-were decided that the Far East Air Force should have an independent Beverley squadron.

No.34 Squadron - Brief History

Formed at Castle Bromwich in 1916, the squadron served in France during the First World War, disbanding in 1919. In 1935 the squadron was reformed and spent the war years in the Far East before disbanding again in 1947. In 1954 the squadron reformed again with Meteor aircraft, later changing to Hunters prior to yet another disbandment in 1958.

From Fighters to Transports

On 1st October 1960, 34 Squadron reformed again at Seletar in Singapore, taking over the four Beverleys and six crews which hitherto had operated as a flight of 48 Squadron at Changi. Historically, the squadron had spent a large part of its career in the Far East, so it was appropriate that this unit should be brought back into service again in this theatre. But for the first time in its career, 34 Squadron was now a transport unit.

The new aircrew of 34 were all experienced Beverley operators, drawn mainly from the UK-based Beverley force and of course, after their spell with 48 Squadron were reasonably familiar with flying conditions in the Far East. Most of the ground technicians were also Beverley experienced, a necessary attribute for a unit operating the Beverleys which had always had the infuriating habit of developing difficult and hard-to-diagnose snags.

The event of 34 Squadron being back in business was marked by a fly-past and the unit soon got down to work with two routes to Kai Tak airport at Hong Kong, Flying Officer John Nimmo and Flight Lieutenant George Moralee skippering XB260 and XM104 respectively. Squadron Leader J. W. Adams, OC Squadron, and crew also took XH112 to Korea. In the transport support role, the squadron's first heavy drop was made at Changi.

However, conditions were poor, the flight line accommodation was inadequate and in November, an SIB (Special Investigations Branch) probe into attempted sabotage lowered the morale of the ground crew. In December, Flight Lieutenants Moralee and Grobler and crews took medical supplies and equipment to Bangkok, Korat and Vientiane, making four shuttle trips between Korat and Vientiane. Rioting and civil unrest prevailed in the latter city necessitating quick turn-rounds to prevent becoming involved. Russian, French and Dutch ambassadors were carried on these flights.

Back at Seletar, the Army was finding plenty of support work for the squadron with Exercises *Achilles, Razor Keen* and *Nacelle*. The mind boggles at the fertile brains that conjured up the names of such

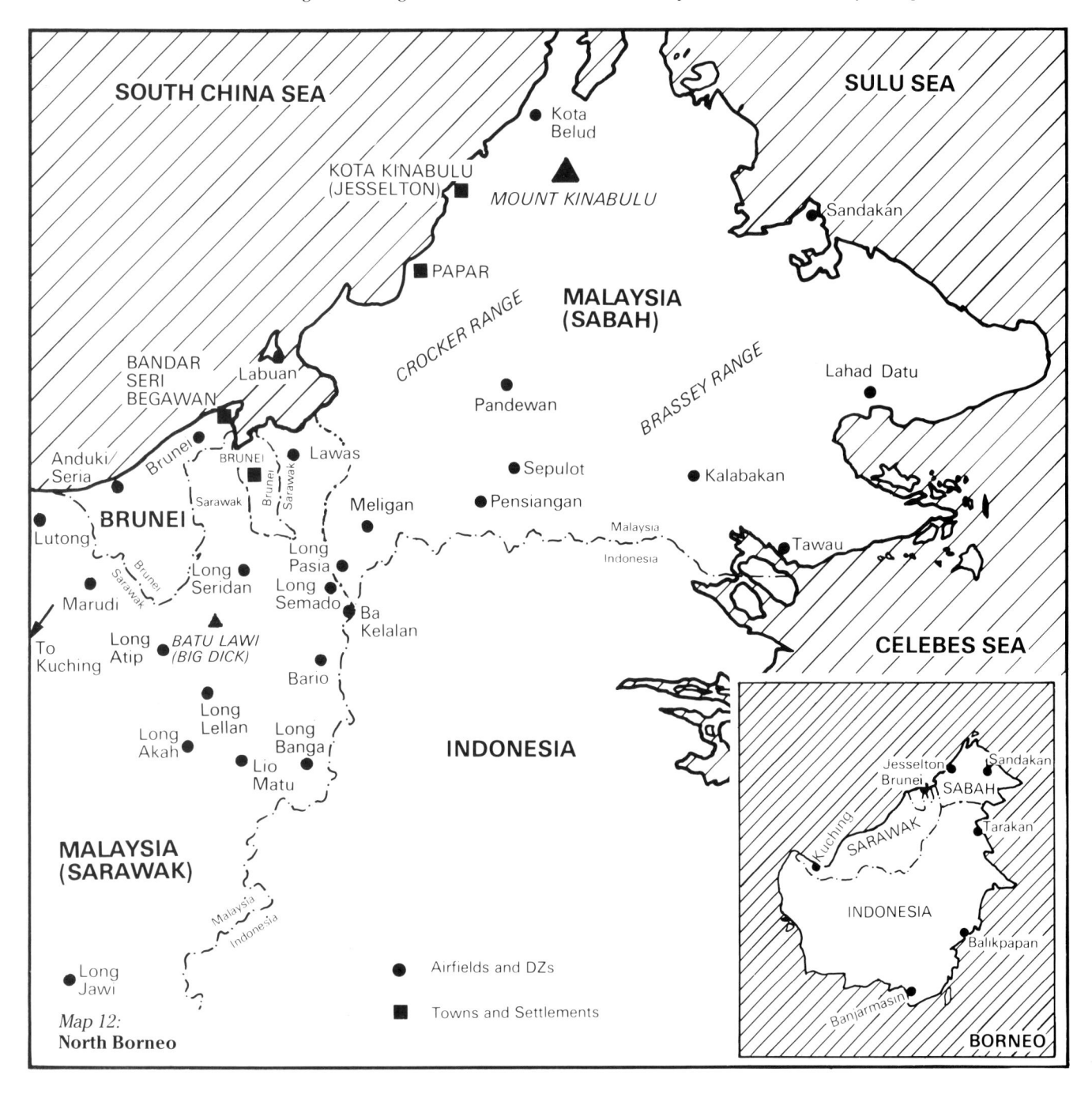

Map 12:
North Borneo

One-ton containers being despatched from a 34 Squadron Beverley. S. Corton

Opposite: **Flight line at Seletar.** A. Fairbairn

exercises and operations! Exercise *Nacelle* involved moving Gurkha troops from Kuala Lumpur to Malacca. The year ended with 613 flying hours logged - a good figure for the three months' work put in by the newly formed unit.

The new year (1961) saw the arrival of the squadron's fifth aircraft. Three routes to Kai Tak were flown to familiarize crews with the long sea crossings. Two flights were also made to Butterworth carrying ground staff and equipment for 60 Squadron.

In February 1961, a one-ton container was dropped, the first of many thousands subsequently to be dropped in the Far East. Due to the State of Emergency which had recently prevailed in Malaya, crews were detached to Fraser's Hill for ground defence training courses, and jungle survival courses were also started, the latter being an essential for all aircrew operating over equatorial rain forest.

The ground staff's morale had improved by now; they all seemed to have developed a feeling of belonging to their new squadron, and their high morale was reflected in their hard work and enthusiasm, so much so that Air Vice Marshal C. D. Candy, Senior Air Staff Officer, Far East Air Force, complimented them in a personal speech. The squadron was suffering a very high engine failure rate at this time but the efficiency of the ground crew was such that despite these problems, the squadron still managed to fulfil its tasks.

March was highlighted by a mass SEAC pack drop, 42 packs carrying 4½ tonnes of supplies being dropped in a distance of 320 yards. The packs were despatched by men of 55 Air Despatch Company, RASC. These men and their colleagues were to perform an integral part of 34 Squadron's history in the coming years. April saw a Borneo flight to drop a Ferguson tractor and Land Rover at Sepulot. This was the first large load to be dropped by the squadron, the tractor being gently lowered on the DZ by two enormous parachutes, each of sixty six feet diameter. Prior to air-dropping at Sepulot, supplies to this outpost were taken from the coast on pack-horses, the trip taking at least eight days. It is unlikely that a dismantled tractor could have been transported by such means.

May, June and July 1961 were spent on intensive Army support work, Exercise *Brown Boots* for example, involving the uplift of twelve Land Rovers and trailers and 131 troops from Singapore to Malacca. Supply dropping enabled the squadron to put in plenty of practice with the CARP (Calculated Air Release Point) dropping technique which had been used so successfully by other Beverley units.

June was highlighted by the evacuation from Jessclton, now named Kota Kinabulu, of fifty-one malaria patients to Seletar for transfer to the British Military Hospital in Singapore. June also saw Flying Officer John Nimmo posted back to the UK much to the regret of his colleagues. John was one of the first Beverley pilots in FEAF and had captained the celebrated 'cat drop' flight at Bario in Borneo, described earlier in this chapter. By July 1961, the squadron had worked up to an aircraft utilization rate on a par with that of the UK Beverley force, a commendable effort in view of the demanding flying and servicing conditions so often experienced in the tropics. Routes had by now been flown to Labuan; Clark Field USAF base, and Manila in the Philippines; Hong Kong; Okinawa; and Saigon.

New Buildings for Squadron

The squadron's first 'year of the Beverley' was marked by the erection of new squadron offices and other administrative buildings. This was particularly welcomed by the ground staff, whose offices and crew room accommodation could only be described as primitive. So ended 34's first year with the Beverley, a year in which over 1,600 hours were logged, more than 3,500 passengers carried, and 437 tonnes of freight had been uplifted, about 100 tonnes of this being airdropped. This tonnage was almost equivalent to a million pounds (455 tonnes).

Squadron's First SAR Mission

The beginning of the squadron's second year with the Beverley was marked by an intensive search for a missing Canberra of 75 Squadron. The search lasted six days and involved three Beverleys, putting in twenty five hours search time. Other Beverleys were used to support the Twin Pioneers of 209 Squadron at Malacca, by flying in fully loaded fuel tankers and observers, returning these to their bases at the termination of the search, which regrettably, was unsuccessful. October 1961 was a busy month for Army support work, 450 troops and 46 vehicles being carried, together with a mixed bag of 81 tonnes of supplies air-landed and dropped.

Squadron covers the Far East

In contrast to the large amount of Army support work carried out in October, November brought a great many route trips, giving crews much valuable experience in operating to and from the extremities of the Far East theatre. Eleven trips totalling 137 flying hours took the squadron to Gan in the Maldive Islands, Vientiane, Manila, Kai Tak, Saigon and closer to base, Brunei. Another SAR operation involved flights from Seletar, Butterworth and Alor Star in connection with a missing Auster. The squadron further assisted in this search by moving, for participation in the search, all 209 Squadron's personnel and equipment to and from Alor Star.

Building of the new offices was completed and squadron personnel moved in, bringing aircrew and ground staff into much closer contact with each other. This move gave the ground staff an even greater sense of belonging to their unit and was instrumental in further raising morale and promoting tremendous enthusiasm, which in turn, greatly improved the servicing efficiency.

December 1961 brought more wideranging route trips, two to Gan via Car Nicobar Island and Katunayake in Ceylon, and three to Kai Tak via Tourane and Saigon.

Flood Relief for South Vietnam

During the above-mentioned flights to Kai Tak, emergency supplies were delivered to Saigon, these being donated by New Zealand under an aid programme known as the Colombo Plan. Later in the month, three 34 Squadron Beverleys, accompanied by three Bristol Freighters of the Royal New Zealand Air Force, took flood relief supplies to Saigon. This mercy mission provoked a storm of political abuse from Hanoi in North Vietnam, this country being at war with South Vietnam. The year finished with an airlift of full fuel tankers to Malacca for 209 Squadron's Pioneers. This airlift was due to a fuel shortage prevailing in that part of Malaya.

First Free-fall Parachute Descent in Far East

In January 1962, the Far East's first recorded free-fall parachute descent was made by Parachute Jump Instructor Flight Sergeant Teasdale. He jumped from 9,000 feet and steered himself perfectly on to a DZ at Sembawang. The new year was also marked by Squadron Leader M. G. Bennet taking over command of the squadron from Squadron Leader Adams, the squadron's commander since its reforming in October 1960. Squadron Leader Adams was awarded the MBE in the New Year Honours List.

Canberras to Okinawa

Together with route trips to Gan, Kai Tak and Jesselton, March saw 34 Squadron participating in Exercise *Joss Stick* by taking the ground staff and equipment for No. 45 Squadron's Canberras into Kadena, Okinawa. Back in the Singapore-Borneo area, a Beverley escorted a Single Pioneer to Kuching for DZ marking duties concerned with dropping a D4 bulldozer at Belaga, a DZ near Kuching. In the event, the bulldozer turned out to be a D6, some 909 kilos heavier and much larger than a D4. Flying Officer Arthur Hyland and crew in XM104 dropped the 'dozer' at Belaga, but a malfunction caused the load to disconnect prematurely from its parachutes and 'crunch in' becoming totally wrecked in the process. The 'dozer' was required to make an airstrip suitable for civil aircraft from Malaya to fly in rubber plants which would die if not planted within thirty six hours of being lifted. History doesn't record how this problem was solved.

Operation Bibber

In May 1962, the squadron was placed on stand-by for the commencement of the activation phase of this operation. Part of Operation *Bibber* involved flights to Chiang Mai in North Thailand. During the stop-over at this airfield, a local Thai was arrested while attempting to steal rations from a parked Beverley. The thief was dressed in jungle green apart from his civilian slacks which aroused suspicion. Apparently the man was an escapee from the local mental hospital and during his time on the run, had acquired almost a complete RAF uniform. Operation *Bibber* continued into June moving men and equipment of No.20 Squadron (Hunter aircraft) at Tengah to Chiang Mai, the Beverley crews 'slipping' at Bangkok. Eight sorties were flown.

Nairobi Visited

New ground was again covered in June 1962 when a special flight was made to Eastleigh, Nairobi. Two crews were carried, the aircraft commander being Flight Lieutenant Eddie Davies. On the return flight, a Single Pioneer aircraft was picked up at Khormaksar for delivery to Seletar. This trip brought about the reunion of many old colleagues at 30 Squadron and 84 Squadron, based at Eastleigh and Khormaksar respectively, where a good deal of professional and non-professional chat took place. In Thailand, Operation *Bibber*, reportedly mounted to stop the infiltration of communist terrorists southwards into Malaya, continued into July, with further trips to Chiang Mai taking in supplies and equipment. Back at base, aircraft departed for Gan, Labuan, Kuching and Clark Field. DZ reconnaissance flights were also made from Kuantan in Malaya in readiness for Exercise *Grass Cushion*, shortly to be mounted.

Japan Visited

Exercise *Joss Stick* accounted for most of August's route flying time, XM104 captained by the Squadron Commander and with the OC Flying Wing aboard, visiting Tachikawa USAF base, near Tokyo. The flight carried twenty passengers, mainly VIPs, representing all aspects of transport flying in the Far East. The trip went by way of Clark Field and Naha in Okinawa to Tachikawa and returned via Kai Tak. For the VIPs visiting Japan, XM104 was specially fitted out for luxurious (by Beverley standards) seating in the boom, a dining area was laid out in the freight bay, together with a number of casevac stretchers rigged for those who wished to travel in a horizontal position.

Exercise Grass Cushion

This exercise got underway in August and September and involved forty-four sorties in the supply-dropping role, delivering 100 one-ton containers, eight medium stressed platforms and eleven Boscombe platforms to Kuantan. The Boscombe platform had only just entered service having been developed and tested thoroughly at the A & AEE Boscombe Down. This was the first recorded use of the Boscombe platform in FEAF. For details of one-ton containers, heavy-drop platforms and other supply-dropping equipment, refer to *Chapter 7*.

Emergency on Indo-Chinese Border

In November, China adopted a threatening attitude towards India and massed troops on the international boundary north-west of Calcutta. In response to a request for assistance from the Indian government, a detachment, with the Squadron Commander in charge, flew supplies to Calcutta via Car Nicobar. To supplement this detachment, aircraft engaged on Operation *Bibber* were recalled and dispatched to Calcutta, where the 34 Squadron detachment flew Indian troops into the forward areas near the Chinese border. Refugees were carried out on the return flights.

The Brunei Revolt

On 8th December 1962, an armed revolt occurred in the British-protected Sultanate of Brunei. This revolt led to the Indonesian Confrontation and events leading up to it are described in *Chapter 2*. At 08.00 on the morning of 8th December, the squadron was called to immediate readiness for Operation *Ale*, this code name being subsequently changed to Operation *Borneo Territories*. Crews were issued with side arms and briefed for an assault landing on Brunei airfield, and at 14.00, XM112 captained by the Squadron Commander, took off with ninety four troops of the 1/2 Gurkhas plus four servicing crew. The assault landing was executed as per plan, the troops deplaned in battle order and XM112 departed for Labuan to await further orders.

The next Beverley, XM120 skippered by Flight Lieutenant Joe Harvey, after a delay due to heavy rain, landed at Brunei at 16.35 with three Land Rovers and trailers together with thirty-five more troops of the 1/2 Gurkhas. Five more servicing crew were also carried. The first load of Gurkhas had secured the airfield and now wished to deploy further afield, hence the need for vehicles. After delivering its load, XM120 took off for Jesselton to collect another three Land Rovers and trailers plus twelve more Gurkhas. In the meantime, Flying Officer Arthur Hyland and crew in XB262 were on their way to Brunei with more vehicles, ammunition and other supplies including rations. XB262 landed in a violent rainstorm with cloud base down to 100 feet and visibility less than 300 yards.

To provide back-up to the aircrews now operating in Borneo, a spare crew was flown to Labuan by Britannia. The last Beverley to land at Brunei on 8th December took in fourteen tonnes of freight and a further thirty-two troops, returning to Labuan with eight stretcher cases, nineteen walking wounded and seventy-nine civilian evacuees. A successful day resulting in the securing of Brunei airfield and most of the surrounding district. No other contemporary aircraft but the Beverley could have airlifted such large quantities of men, vehicles and materials. Despite severe problems caused by the Beverley's notoriously unreliable radio compass system, which was the only navaid available, all navigators found their way around Northern Borneo regardless of poor visibility caused by heavy rainstorms in the Brunei-Labuan area. Next day, twenty sorties were flown to Brunei, reinforcing and resupplying the Gurkhas already entrenched there.

Assault on Anduki/Seria

The highlight of 9th December was the air-landing assault on the airstrip at Anduki/Seria, subsequently referred to, for brevity, as Anduki. This airstrip, located on the coast south-west of Brunei, was known to be in rebel hands. Accordingly, XM112 flown by Flight Lieutenat G.M. Fenn and crew, proceeded from Brunei at thirty feet en route for Anduki with a Shell representative, who had accurate knowledge of the terrain, on board. The aircraft made a straight-in, tactical short-field landing, deplaned its ninety troops and took off again in the same direction, touch-down to take-off being timed at 108 seconds. Complete surprise was attained for the landing, but the rebels had recovered by the time XM112 took off and the aircraft came under fire from the control tower sustaining superficial damage to the rear fuselage. Despite fears concerning the surface of the airstrip which was known to be very wet, the landing and take-off were both uneventful, another demonstration of the Beverley's superb ability to operate in conditions unsuitable for any other contemporary aircraft of its size.

Anduki airstrip was soon recaptured and on 10th December, received six Beverley lifts bringing in a total of 235 troops, ten Land Rovers and trailers, plus fourteen tonnes of ammunition, rations and other freight. XB262 left Anduki for Brunei carrying prisoners for interrogation, this aircraft, operated by Flight Lieutenant Tarran and crew, having been recalled to Seletar from its detachment in Calcutta where it had been used to airlift Indian troops and equipment into the border areas threatened by the Chinese. From Seletar, XB262 brought into Brunei two Auster aircraft, thirty-eight passengers and 455 kilos of freight before proceeding to Anduki.

Reinforcements for Ground Staff

By 11th December, the squadron, now operating from Labuan, had its full complement of six aircrews, five aircraft and their ground servicing crews. The original servicing party of nine who had arrived at Labuan on 8th December had worked unceasingly ever since their arrival with little or no rest and due to their magnificent efforts, no sortie had been delayed due to unserviceability or excessively long turn-round times - a tribute to their resourcefulness and high morale. For once, the Beverleys had 'played ball' too, and had not developed any snags that could not be tolerated. XB260, the aircraft that brought in the remainder of 34's servicing personnel, also carried two further aircrews, one from 30 Squadron at Eastleigh, the other from 84 Squadron at Khormaksar.

Aircrew quarters at Labuan; they were not always so luxurious as these. *S. Corton*

Opposite: **Hen and chick. Beverley XB289 and Pembroke WV752 at Labuan, 1964.** *S. Corton*

More Men and Equipment for Anduki and Brunei

Between 11th and 16th December, thirty sorties were flown to Brunei and thirteen to Anduki, airlifting 728 personnel, 51 vehicles and 172 tonnes of freight into Brunei, and 239 personnel, 17 vehicles and 48¼ tonnes of freight into Anduki. Due to the lack of mechanical handling equipment, e.g. fork-lift trucks, particularly at Anduki, most of the freight had to be manhandled from the aircraft, the flight crews frequently assisting. The weather was good throughout this resupply period, a welcome change from the adverse conditions during the opening days of the operation.

Money, Money, Money

On Saturday, 14th December, Flight Lieutenant Joe Harvey and crew flew XB262 from Labuan to Jesselton, the purpose of this trip being to collect three million Malay dollars and guards from the Hong Kong and Shanghai Bank in Jesselton. Again, history omits to record what this money was for: it has been suggested that it was to meet escalating petroleum bills occasioned by the Beverley's prodigious thirst for fuel and oil.

Army Lengthens its Supply Lines

With the Sultanate of Brunei now secured from the rebels, many of whom had moved off into the interior, the Army deployed into Sarawak and Sabah in hot pursuit. The so-called 'North Borneo Liberation Army' had shown little enthusiasm for fighting the world-famous Gurkhas, and due to the former's reluctance to fight, casualties on both sides were low. However, Indonesians were carrying out terrorist raids on outposts in Sarawak and Sabah near the Indonesian border, and the army commenced patrolling these areas in order to counter this menace.

On the night of 15th December, two Beverleys took four Land Rovers and ten trailers, with assorted loads of freight into Kuching, flying through turbulent cumulonimbus clouds which produced violent thunderstorms. In spite of the appalling weather and the lack of navaids, the crews managed to find Kuching without too many problems.

Air Drops Commence

By 16th December, the Army was so widely deployed, often in difficult terrain, that resupply via the airfields of Brunei and Anduki was becoming increasingly difficult. It therefore became necessary to commence supply-dropping, the first air drop in the campaign being made by XM104 captained by the Squadron Commander, at a DZ near Anduki. A total of seven tonnes was dropped in harness packs in sixteen runs. After the drop, XM104 went on to land at Anduki to deliver a further 410 kilos of supplies.

Redeployment to Tawau

With the situation in Brunei and northeast Sarawak much more stable, the Army turned its attention to the Tawau area in East Sabah. Accordingly, on 17th December, a shuttle was commenced, aircraft leaving Labuan and delivering loads to Brunei, then flying empty to Anduki from where troops were airlifted to Tawau. This was carried out in the small hours of 17th December so that the troops could be positioned at Tawau by dawn. Good weather prevailed for this shuttle which was fortunate as the route from Anduki to Tawau is over very mountainous terrain, which even today is inaccurately charted. With the Beverleys' radio compasses still giving their usual unsatisfactory performance, it was highly desirable to have visual contact with the ground.

MEAF Crews Return

By 18th December, the squadron's workload was such that the presence of the two crews from the Middle East Air Force could no longer be justified and reluctantly they made their respective ways back to their units. The 84 Squadron crew, skippered by Flight Lieutenant Lambert, started the first leg of their journey by taking XM104 to Seletar for major servicing. The 30 Squadron crew returned to Seletar by Hastings en route for Khormaksar, after participating in the redeployment phase described next.

More Redeployment

The Army, having reappraised the general situation, now decided on another redeployment phase and accordingly on 20th and 21st December, three Beverleys were used to move troops to Kuching, Tawau and Jesselton. After the redeployment trips, the work-load seemed to be diminishing and it was therefore decided to return two aircraft and three crews to Seletar. Flight Lieutenant Stan Hitchen and crew took XH120 to Seletar on 22nd December: next day, two more crews returned to Seletar on board XB262, skippered by Flight Lieutenant Joe Harvey.

Busy Christmas Eve

December 24th brought the second air supply task when Flight Lieutenant Fenn and crew in XH112 dropped Christmas fare at a number of DZs, not completing the task until after dark. The sortie then continued to Anduki to air-land supplies before returning to Labuan. All the drops were successful and much appreciated by the Army who sent congratulatory signals. Flight Lieutenant Tarran and crew took XB262 to Butterworth to collect two Sycamore helicopters, but due to loading problems, could not take off again until Christmas

Day. After arriving at Seletar, this crew then stood down. Later on Christmas Day, XH122 captained by Flight Lieutenant Fenn, took 25 passengers plus 7½ tonnes of freight from Labuan to Seletar via Tengah.

With the exception of Flight Lieutenant Eddie Davies and crew with XB262 in Labuan, all the squadron's aircraft and crews were now back at Seletar to enjoy a well-earned rest for Christmas Day and Boxing Day.

Back to Business

Operations recommenced on 27th December with two aircraft, XB260 and XH122 returning to Labuan, XB260 with Flight Lieutenant Tarran in command, delivering the two Sycamores. XH122, operated by Flight Lieutenant Joe Harvey and crew, flew up to Butterworth to pick up a third helicopter for Labuan. The next two days were marked by a number of so-called 'courier' flights into Anduki and Brunei, delivering 4¾ tonnes of freight to Anduki and 51 passengers, one dog and 1½ tonnes of freight to Brunei.

The highlight of 28th December was a supply drop at Lawas and on other DZs near Tawau, delivering a total of 5½ tonnes. All packs fell safely on their DZs and the Army signalled their thanks. Next day was marked by completely unexpected inactivity and the opportunity was taken to get in two hours of continuation training - something of a change from the urgent operational sorties so frequently flown during the month. The last day of December saw XH122 and XB262, skippered by Flight Lieutenant Joe Harvey and the Squadron Commander respectively, being despatched at short notice to Brunei, for further redeployment of troops. In the event, the well-worn cry of 'It's all been changed' caused both aircraft and crews to spend New Year's Eve at Brunei.

Impressive Statistics

December 1962 must have been one of the most illustrious months of 34 Squadron's service. In first 24 days of Operation *Borneo Territories*, 147 sorties occupying 162 hours were flown by day, together with 99 sorties in 91 hours flown by night. Passengers carried, including one dog, totalled 4,075; 864 tonnes of freight including aircraft and vehicles were air-landed and 15 tonnes were dropped. Casevacs carried comprised ten stretcher cases, 22 walking wounded and nine corpses.

Tractor to Long Seridan

January 1963 was highlighted by the Squadron Commander and crew in XM104 dropping a D4 tractor weighing in at seven tonnes at Long Seridan. A bulldozer blade for the tractor was successfully dropped later. The weather became increasingly difficult later in the month, heavy rains causing severe flooding in northern Sarawak. The adverse weather naturally hampered air-dropping operations for the security forces and for a while, it became imperative to drop relief supplies for the flood victims. The drops were made using SEAC packs and harness packs on numerous DZs.

A route training flight to Kai Tak in XB260 skippered by the Squadron Commander made a change from the now familiar Army support work in Borneo, the aircraft staging through Da Nang in South Vietnam. A welcome navaid was provided by the United States Air Force in the form of an early warning radar system which could be used as a fixer service, using the call-sign *Stargazer*. This proved invaluable in view of the Beverley's notoriously unreliable radio compass system.

Army support work in Borneo continued with air-landing sorties and many supply drops on a variety of jungle DZs, crews attaining a remarkable degree of accuracy despite adverse weather and difficult, often uncharted terrain. Flight Lieutenant Stan Hitchen and crew landed XH120 late one night at Kuching to be greeted by eight armoured cars with guns trained on them right from touch-down to dispersal. Apparently, there had been warnings of unidentified aircraft in the area, and the Army boys were taking no chances, not even with a Beverley.

The crews found flying in Borneo most interesting and in adverse weather conditions, sometimes almost terrifying. The jungle-covered mountains assumed their own rugged grandeur and the view of Mount Kinabulu, when clear of cloud, was said to be exhilarating. Due to the build-ups of heat cloud around noon, wherever possible, supply drops were undertaken in the morning, not only to take advantage of the better visibility, but also to avoid the severe turbulence associated with such cloud formations. Drops could not be made until the stratus clouds in the valleys, where most DZs were located, had been burnt off by the sun. Timing of drops therefore was most critical.

By the end of February 1963, the tempo of flying had slackened somewhat, enabling squadron personnel to catch up on leave, aircrews being allocated a weeks leave after returning from detachment in Labuan. XB264, which had been delivered from the UK earlier in the month, had now been flown by quite a few crews. All were impressed by the new twin radio compass installation which was a tremendous improvement on the old, unreliable single compass system. This aircraft also had an autopilot, the only aircraft on the squadron so equipped. And, to the delight of the pilots, it worked. At long last, instead of replying 'Still at the factory' to the 'Autopilot' challenge on the landing and pre-dropping check list, pilots could now respond with satisfaction. 'Disengaged.'

More Route Trips

Further route trips were flown in March, the Squadron Commander taking XB264 to Katmandu via Calcutta. His return payload included a corpse. Two trips were also made to Kadena in Okinawa carrying personnel and equipment of 45 Squadron (Canberras) from Tengah. XB264 was used for one of the Kadena trips and the twin radio compasses again proved to be an invaluable navaid.

Mount Kinabulu from 12,000 feet. *S. Corton*

Opposite: **Pensiangan - smallest and remotest DZ of the Borneo campaign. Note how the load (arrowed) has been precisely put down, safely away from buildings, on the only available piece of flat ground.** *S. Corton*

On Operation *Borneo Territories*, the main task was airlifting passengers and freight to the airfields of Labuan, Brunei, Tawau, Jesselton, Kuching and Sandakan. Air-drops were also made to isolated military units in the Territories, one-ton containers being dropped at Long Semado, Long Seridan and other DZs which were mere grid references on the map. In the Malay Peninsula, a one-ton container drop was made at Fort Kapong, near the Thai border, to supply 66 Squadron with fuel. This unit's Belvedere helicopters had been in action against border terrorists.

April was a busy month, with 10,600 miles flown in 75 hours on routes to Okinawa, Kai Tak and Gan. In Borneo, in addition to the work done by the detachment at Labuan, the Seletar-based Beverleys did a large amount of Army supply sorties to Kuching, airlanding personnel, vehicles and equipment. These sorties were occasioned by terrorist incursions in to the Kuching area of Sarawak. Over twenty-two tonnes of supplies were dropped into the Borneo jungle DZs including a medium stressed platform carrying a 'wobbly wheel' roller dropped at Long Seridan. The roller was required for levelling the airstrip which was considered to be somewhat 'marginal' for the light aircraft that used it.

Hairy DZ

In May, Flight Lieutenant Eddie Davies and crew flew two sorties in XB264 to Pensiangan, an extremely difficult DZ near the Indonesian border in South Sabah. As the photograph shows, Pensiangan, like most Borneo DZs, is in mountainous terrain and the DZ itself is almost an island, being bounded on three sides by a river. Apart from the navigational difficulties in finding this remote DZ, dropping was extremely difficult. However, seven tonnes of stores, mainly defensive barbed wire, were dropped in twenty-one runs on the first sortie; 3¾ tonnes were dropped in eleven runs on the second. An interesting feature of this drop was that the SEAC packs were too bulky to be despatched from the paratroop doors: the aircraft was therefore rigged and flown in the 'doors off' configuration and the packs were despatched over the freight bay sill. After the second sortie to Pensiangan, the aircraft continued to Long Pasia, where a further drop was made.

Exercise Dhanarajata

This was a major SEATO (South East Asia Treaty Organization) exercise and was mounted at Korat in Northern Thailand, signatory countries of the Treaty taking part. Three 34 Squadron Beverleys and crews participated, moving troops and their equipment to various Thai airfields including Don Muang, Chiang Mai, Roiet Koke Khatien, Yan Heedam, Lomsak, Ubon and Lampang. Korat was a very dusty airfield but as was proved so many times in the Middle East, the Beverley's engine air intake system minimized this problem. The three-week exercise concluded with the three Beverleys doing a formation fly-past over Bangkok. Whilst in Thailand, navigation had been greatly helped by the USAF's radar network which now covered the entire country.

Exercise *Dhanarajata* started in May and continued through June into the early part of July. It was a massive deployment of men and equipment, the Beverleys carrying 18 vehicles, 902 passengers and 344 tonnes of freight. A total of 130 sorties were flown in 269 flying hours, covering over 10,600 miles.

Stone Crusher for Tawau

In June, the Borneo operations were mainly confined to air-landing sorties carrying troops and their equipment, a Single Pioneer aircraft, an SAS storm boat and a 10½ tonne stone crusher to the RAF Airfield Construction Squadron at Tawau. Other air-landing sorties visited the now familiar Borneo airfields and supplies were dropped at Pensiangan and Long Pasia.

The end of June brought some awards for meritorious service, the British Empire Medal going to Chief Technician P. G. Dunworth. Squadron Leader Bennet, the CO, and Flight Lieutenant G. M. Fenn received Queen's Commendations for Valuable Service in the Air, and Flight Lieutenant Joe Harvey, Corporal Technician D. Baker, and Corporal T. H. Khoo were mentioned in despatches.

'Don't Shoot: I'm a Beverley'

June 1963 brought a somewhat hair-raising experience to Flight Lieutenant Stan Hitchen and crew when returning from a drop to SAS troops who had infiltrated across the Indonesian border. Such drops were occasionally made in support of the secret operations of the SAS and supplies were dropped at a mere grid reference on the map, the only DZ marking often being one or more coloured balloons. The flight to and from the DZ was made at low level to keep under the Indonesian's radar screen, and returning from one such drop, after crossing the border into Sarawak, a message from the RAF ground-based fighter controller was intercepted. The controller was informing a Javelin fighter that a target was 'dead ahead, range five miles.' This naturally aroused some interest on the Beverley flight deck; more interest was aroused when the controller announced: 'Target dead ahead, range two miles: arm your missiles.' At this time, one of the Beverley crew reported sighting an aircraft about two miles astern and identified it, as it closed, as a Javelin. Some rather urgent radio transmissions followed, resulting in the Javelin being diverted elsewhere, much to the relief of the Beverley crew. Nonetheless, it was comforting to know that some form of fighter back-up was available should the Indonesian Air Force choose to infiltrate Malaysian airspace in search of RAF aircraft.

Beverley pilots often wondered what to do should they be jumped by an Indonesian MiG. Since it was known from intelligence reports that the MiGs were armed with cannon only and not any form of homing missile, it was agreed by most Beverley pilots that the best course of action would be to dive into the nearest valley and then orbit until the MiG ran short of fuel and was forced to depart. No MiG could perform the incredibly tight turns, at low speed, in confined spaces that the Beverley could and thus it would be virtually impossible, in such circumstances, to get a Beverley in its sights. However, intelligence had intimated that the Indonesians employed an American mercenary who

Unloading a stone crusher. *W. Binfield*

SAS DZ in Borneo, location unknown. *S. Corton*

flew a Mustang. This mercenary was promptly nicknamed 'Hank the Yank' and commanded some healthy respect from the Beverley fleet, since he was far more likely to shoot down a Beverley than an Indonesian MiG.

One-ton Container Drops
These were now becoming standard for the Borneo operations, largely replacing the harness packs and SEAC packs. Although it was possible to drop one-ton containers automatically in sticks, due to the small size of most DZs, the containers were usually despatched manually, one at a time. No.10 Air Despatch Company were the unsung heroes of the Borneo air drops; these soldiers prepared and rigged the containers, loaded them into the aircraft, then flew with the aircraft and despatched the containers. They always felt that 'it was all worthwhile' when, looking out from the rear of the open freight bay, secured by their safety harnesses, they saw their loads land precisely on the DZ which indeed, they almost invariably did, thanks to the aircrews' proficiency.

In July and August, XM104 and XH112 were delivered to Kai Tak for modifications, which included fitting the new twin radio compasses, by HAECO, the Hong Kong Aircraft Engineering Company, a major civilian aircraft engineering concern which had been commissioned to undertake major overhauls and repair work on the Beverleys of the Far East Air Force.

Borneo Situation Worsens
In late August and early September, there was a considerable increase in terrorist attacks along the 970 mile Indonesian border into Sarawak and Sabah. This was said to be due to the Indonesians' displeasure at the declaration of the Federation of Malaysia, which took place on 16th September 1963. Next day, Malaysia broke off diplomatic relations with Indonesia. Malaysia now included Sarawak and Sabah, but Brunei opted out of the Federation due to disagreements over oil revenues. These border incidents brought an increased work-load to the Labuan detachment and many more air-landing and air-supply sorties were undertaken. DZs visited included Long Akah, Long Lellan, Bario, Ba Kelalan, Long Semado, Pandewan, Long Pasia, Lio Matu and Pensiangan. (The name prefaced by the word 'Long' indicates the presence of a native long-house). Large quantities of fuel in drums were delivered, some by the free drop technique, others in one-ton containers. Some DZs were very remote, unnamed and uncharted, being mere grid references on the map, but thanks to excellent marking by the Army and by superb navigation by the Beverley navigators, DZs were invariably found.

The increased activity in Borneo continued for the remaining months of 1963 averaging over sixty sorties per month - a first - class achievement for what was mainly a one-aircraft detachment. The December statistics recorded a total of 67 sorties flown in 131 hours, 45 of these being air-landings and 22 being supply drops. A total of 1,091 passengers was carried together with 23 tonnes of freight, while 203 tonnes of supplies were air-dropped on all the charted DZs near the Indonesian border. On 16th December, the British Forces in Borneo and elsewhere, were saddened by the news of the Indonesians shooting down an unarmed Auster near the southernmost border of Sarawak. An Army chaplain flying as passenger in the aircraft was killed.

Incident in Tawau
The new year started with a rebel attack on a Malaysian outpost at Kalabakan, near Tawau, severe casualties being inflicted on the defenders. A Red Alert was declared and the Labuan detachment Beverley took off immediately to move reinforcements to Tawau. Two more Beverleys from Seletar followed shortly afterwards to join the detachment. A period of intense flying then followed, culminating in a record 154 sorties being flown to move over 2,000 troops, mainly Ghurkas, and 121 tonnes of equipment into the Tawau area. Supply drops to the border outposts continued, plus resupply sorties to the troops deployed from Tawau. All told, 137 tonnes were air-dropped.

New Zealand Revisited
A route trip to New Zealand highlighted February 1964, Squadron Leader Bennett and crew taking XM104 to RNZAF Ohakea via Butterworth, Cocos Island, Pearce, Richmond and Edinburgh RAAF bases. The Butterworth-Cocos leg was flown to avoid overflying Sumatra which was now 'out' due to the Indonesian Confrontation. At Ohakea, the Beverley participated in an air display and dropped two medium stressed platforms, each carrying a Land Rover and trailer. After an enjoyable stay, the return trip was made by way of Rotorua, RNZAF Whenuapai, Richmond and Pearce RAAF bases, Kalgoorie and Cocos.

Another hard month's flying was undertaken in Borneo, 13 vehicles and two light aircraft comprising part of the 442 tonnes of freight air-landed. In the air-supply role, 500 harness packs were dropped together with 269 one-ton containers, giving a total air-dropped weight of just under 300 tonnes. Again, all the Borneo airfields and most of the charted DZs were visited plus many uncharted DZs.

Free Building Materials
The increasing tonnage of supplies being dropped made a useful source of DIY materials for the Borneo natives, since it was impossible to recover most of the empty fuel drums and one-ton containers. Many buildings were constructed from these materials and at one airstrip, the natives had the unexpected windfall of a damaged Twin Pioneer which was beyond repair and consequently abandoned. The missionaries immediately converted the fuselage into a school room.

A welcome addition to the squadron arrived in February in the form of Beverley XB291, flown out from the UK by Flight Lieutenant Galyer and crew. This brought the Beverley strength up to eight and in view of the increasing demands for Beverleys to participate in Operation *Borneo Territories*, the arrival of XB291 was most timely. However, March brought a slight let-up in the requirements for work in Borneo. This perhaps, was just as well as Exercise *Air Boon Choo*, another major SEATO exercise, again mounted in Thailand, accounted for 133 flying hours, in which 173 tonnes of freight were moved. Yet another Beverley arrived from the UK on 28th March, this time XB289, skippered by Flight Lieutenant Hugh Crawley. The squadron's aircraft strength was now nine.

Thanks to good weather, good aircraft serviceability and improved efficiency brought about by experience, the 'million pounds' barrier of freight moved was broken in March, the total tonnage of supplies moved being 513. April, May and June saw renewed demands made on the squadron but with increased crew and aircraft strength, 34 was able to meet these demands more effectively.

Labuan Detachment Reduced
July and August saw a reduction in the Labuan detachment when a system was instituted which required one aircraft and crew to man the detachment for nineteen days at a time. Changeovers overlapped for three days thus giving extra capacity to catch up on any backlogs of work. This reduction in the detachment was by no means due to any let-up in activity since increased 'productivity' was now enabling the detachment to move a million pounds (455 tonnes) of freight consistently per month; in fact, during August, over half a million pounds of freight were air-landed, with half a million pounds air-dropped. A million pounds of freight moved was the magic target of many an Air Movements Section.

At this time, the squadron strength was eleven crews, an increase much appreciated by the old hands who had flown so hard during the early days of the Indonesian Confrontation. But the intense demands made on the Beverleys in Operation *Borneo Terroritories* were taking their toll in an increasing number of engine failures, due almost certainly, to the punishing conditions under which they were oper-

Sqn Ldr Dalston, OC 34 Squdron, third from left with crew at Katmandu. *S. Corton*

Take-off from Katmandu as seen from the astrodome of the Beverley. *S. Corton*

ated. The engine failure rate had always been high: this had long been a problem with the Beverley and in FEAF, the increasing rate of engine failure was attributed largely to the necessity of having to operate the engines at high rpm, especially when dropping. Despite the high engine failure rate, the Beverley nearly always had sufficient reserves of power to continue a sortie with an engine out, and still have a good chance of reaching an airfield should yet another engine fail. One blessing of flying in the dropping role - jettisoning cargo was no problem.

Flight Lieutenant Stan Hitchen and crew had another disconcerting experience on a one-ton container drop when, on applying power to go round again after the first dropping run, all the engine fire warning lights came on. They went out shortly afterwards and since all engines seemed to be performing normally and there were no visual signs of fire, the fire warning system was assumed to be faulty. The same thing happened on subsequent runs and the crew accepted these apparently spurious fire warnings as some obscure electrical malfunction. On landing back at Labuan, when reverse pitch was selected for the landing run, the fire warning lights came on again, but went out when reverse pitch was cancelled. Investigations showed that in fact, the fire warnings had been real fires, caused by loose induction pipe joints on all four engines. The leaking joints allowed, in certain circumstances, the inflammable fuel/air mixture which should have gone into the engines' cylinders, to escape around the engines and become ignited by the hot exhaust gases. Damage was superficial, being mainly restricted to scorching of the engine cowlings. The crew considered themselves extremely lucky to have returned to base safely, blissfully unaware that at any time, a catastrophic fire could have broken out in any one or more of the four engines. Had this happened, the chances of surviving a forced landing in the mountainous jungle terrain of Borneo were extremely remote.

Indonesians Land in Johore

On 17th August, an Indonesian patrol landed in Johore in the south of the Malay Peninsula, and although the invaders were quickly mopped up by the security forces, the landings had demonstrated the Indonesians' determination to harass and terrorize Malaysia. On 4th September, a curfew was imposed in Singapore and all crews were brought to readiness including those on leave. From 7th - 14th September, many sorties were flown to Alor Star and Kuantan, moving men and equipment to reactivate these airfields and to move RAAF Sabre squadron personnel and equipment from Tengah and Butterworth. During this period, 228 passengers, 17 vehicles and 170 tonnes of freight were moved. Defensive measures were taken at Seletar in the form of preparing trenches and aircraft dispersals in case of air attack. Anti-aircraft defences were also prepared.

State of Emergency Declared

On 3rd September 1964, due to the Indonesian threat, a State of Emergency was declared throughout Malaysia. This brought massive movements of troops and war materials to all parts of the Federation including Alor Star, Kuantan, Butterworth, Kuching, Labuan and Tawau. A large number of these movements stemmed from the redeployment of 500 men of the Rhine Army, who were flown to Singapore from their bases in Europe.

In Borneo, all the well-known DZs in Sabah and East Sarawak were regularly visited but there was a significant reduction in the number of harness packs dropped. This was due to an Argosy joining the detachment at Labuan and taking over most of the harness pack dropping commitment. At this time, news was received of a new, cheaper one-ton container weighing much less than the model currently being used and therefore able to carry a bigger payload. This cheaper container was much welcomed by the accountant planners, since the older one-ton containers, costing about £50 each and dropped into the jungle at a rate of over 300 per month, most of them never to be recovered, were imposing a severe financial burden on the British taxpayer.

More Awards for Borneo Service

News arrived in late November that Flight Lieutenant Stan Hitchen, who had by now finished his tour and returned to the UK, had been awarded the Queen's Commendation for Valuable Services in the Air - a much deserved award to a first-class pilot who was later to command 84 Squadron during that unit's last turbulent days in Aden. Master Engineer F. Watson was also awarded a Certificate of Good Service by the Air Command FEAF.

A Katmandu trip marked the last month of 1964. En route, the aircraft, XB262, captained by Squadron Leader Dalston, the new Squadron Commander, and with Seletar's Station Commander Group Captain Freer on board, went unserviceable at Bangkok. This was much to the delight of the crew who used their enforced leisure time to visit the fleshpots and other interesting places of that exotic city. When XB262 finally arrived at Katmandu, the British Embassy again extended superb hospitality to the crew, who were privileged to meet Sir John Hunt of Everest fame.

'Million Pound Barrier' again Broken

This time the figure was not simply for freight moved: it was for freight air-dropped. This magnificent achievement marked the end of December and brought a warm congratulatory message from the Air Commander FEAF. Nearly 500 tonnes, mainly one-ton containers, make a lot of weight to be loaded and rigged, manhandled in to aircraft and pushed out again in a succession of runs over many DZs. Full marks to the Army Despatchers who made this achievement possible.

Relief Supplies to Da Nang

To start 1965, Flight Lieutenant Dornan and crew took XB260 to Kai Tak via Da Nang, delivering seven tonnes of relief supplies for victims of flooding in the Saigon area. Despite the continuing requirement for two aircraft to be detached to Labuan, nine other route trips were flown almost to the extremities of the Far East, taking in Japan, Car Nicobar, Gan, Butterworth and Kuching.

In Borneo, the 'million pound barrier' of supplies dropped was again broken, 554 one-ton containers and 149 harness packs being delivered to all the now familiar DZs plus a few ad hoc ones.

Towards the end of January, very poor weather conditions hampered operations, this type of weather prevailing throughout most of February. Apart from the usual heavy rain and thunderstorms, low clouds and poor visibility made map-reading extremely difficult and dropping sometimes impossible with the result that only 150 one-ton containers and 20 harness packs were dropped, a disappointing anti-climax when compared with the massive tonnage dropped in January. However, two new DZs, Sepulot and Pa Main were opened up and a large amount of supplies delivered to them.

Prince Philip Visits Labuan Detachment

March brought the reduction of the Borneo detachment to one aircraft and crew, supplemented occasionally by a second Seletar-based aircraft and crew. March also saw HRH The Duke of Edinburgh visit the Labuan detachment. Prince Philip was intrigued to hear about Batu Lawi, the obelisk-shaped rocky outcrop which had become a familiar landmark for so many

After take-off from Katmandu. *S. Corton*

Batu Lawi (Big Dick) - prominent Borneo landmark. *S. Corton*

navigators, and was highly amused at 34 Squadron's name for it - 'Big Dick' - because of its phallic shape. When offered a trip in a Beverley to see Big Dick, HRH laughingly declined, reportedly saying 'Not bloody likely!' The Malay translation of Batu Lawi is somewhat less crude than the squadron's nickname, the rough translation being: 'Tail feather of a stone bird.'

Air landings were made at a new airstrip, Kota Belud, in the north-east of Sabah, one hour's flying from Tawau. On one Labuan trip, Flight Lieutenant Flemington and crew in XH116, were forced to return to base with a severe fuel leak - a troublesome and potentially dangerous problem.

Supplies delivered to the Borneo DZs for March, April, May and June only averaged around 200 tonnes per month, but this apparent shortfall of air-dropped supplies was partially compensated for by about 90 tonnes being air-landed each month.

One of the more interesting air drops was made by Flight Lieutenant R. P. Galyer and crew, in XH116 when delivering a Ferguson tractor by means of a medium stressed platform, on Long Banga DZ; next day the same aircraft and crew dropped a D4 bulldozer, reportedly for preparing an airstrip suitable for Twin Pioneers and single engined light aircraft. Poor weather conditions again hampered dropping, the detachment only managing to deliver 268 one-ton containers, two medium stressed platforms and sixteen harness packs. Meligan, another new DZ, was used for the first time as troops became established in the south-west of Sabah.

Rogue Aircraft to Hong Kong

XM104, the first Beverley to be delivered to the Far East, had in 1965 developed into something of a rogue, and due to persistent unserviceability, had only flown for some six weeks out of the past six months. With some relief, this aeroplane was despatched to Kai Tak for major overhaul by HAECO, but due to Typhoon *Freda* raging somewhere north of the Philippines, the trip was delayed until *Freda* had subsided. XM112, the replacement for XM104, was pronounced serviceable after seven air tests and took off for Seletar on 28th July. After being airborne for two and a half hours, a fire on the flight deck occasioned a hasty return to Kai Tak. The aircraft, with a tired and jittery crew, finally landed at Seletar on 31st July after two more in-flight fires. One of the crew is reported to have remarked: 'Quite a hot trip!'

Preparations for Squadron Standard Presentation

These were feverishly put in hand in July when it was announced that 34 Squadron would be presented with its Standard on 1st October by Air Marshal Sir Peter Wykeham, KCB, DSO, DFC, AFC, Air Officer Commanding FEAF, on behalf of Her Majesty The Queen. July ended with Wing Commander D. J. Green taking command of the squadron which due to its increased size, was now deemed to warrant a Wing Commander as commanding officer.

New Local DZ

August was highlighted by the squadron acquiring a suitable DZ near to base: the new DZ was named Kanga Kahang. The squadron had long been without a suitable DZ for its increasing role in supply-dropping and the acquisition of this DZ permitted a best-ever month for support training, in which one medium stressed platform, 12 one-ton containers, two heavy stressed platforms, and 112 paratroops were dropped.

Trouble in Pakistan

September saw the squadron called to readiness with three aircraft standing by to undertake the evacuation of British subjects from East Pakistan where rioting and other forms of civil unrest had broken out. This came as something of a blow to the squadron since many preparations had been made for the forthcoming presentation of the Squadron Standard. In the event however, things worked out well as in the middle of the month, a detachment from the UK-based Britannia fleet took over the stand-by.

In Borneo, the detachment consisted of two Beverleys and crews but on the 28th, one Beverley was replaced by a 215 Squadron Argosy. The remaining crew was replaced by the Seletar Wing crew, known as 'The Trappers' because of their duties of examining and route-checking aircrew. The Trappers gallantly took over the detachment's duties to enable the 34 boys to get back to base for the Standard presentation. A very busy month in Borneo - the million pound barrier was again broken on 24th September with 508 tonnes dropped. In addition, 106 tonnes of freight were air-landed and 1,406 passengers were carried.

Back at Seletar, much use was again made of the new DZ at Kanga Kahang, with considerable free-fall parachuting being undertaken in addition to dropping one-ton containers and stressed platforms. New crews were now able to become fully proficient at supply dropping before trying their hands at some of the notoriously difficult Borneo DZs.

Members of 34 Squadron pose in front of XB289 at around 1965. *via W. Stark*

Squadron Receives Standard

On 1st October, the Squadron Standard was presented on behalf of Her Majesty the Queen by Air Marshal Sir Peter Wykeham. The ceremony, which due to bad weather had to be held in a hangar, was attended by many distinguished guests including: Mr J. V. Robb, CMG, British Government Representative; Air Vice Marshal W. Foxley-Norris, DSO, OBE, AOC HQ 224 Group; Air Vice Marshal H. G. Leonard-Williams, CBE, AOA HQ FEAF; 34 Squadron's first commanding officer, Air Commodore Sir Adrian Chamier, CB, CMG, DSO, OBE; and 34's first commanding officer of its Beverley era, Squadron Leader J. W. Adams.

After the ceremonial parade, the squadron personnel dispersed to participate in a monumental party, rightly so, since a Standard presentation only occurs once in a squadron's lifetime and is invariably presented to mark the meritorious service of a unit.

Another Million Pounds Dropped

Imbued with further enthusiasm after the Standard presentation, the squadron resumed the Labuan detachment with two aircraft and crews participating and went on to break the million pound barrier once more, dropping 481 tonnes and air-landing 9 tonnes. In addition, the squadron flew more hours than ever before in its Beverley era - a total of 436 - a superb achievement in this month of 34 Squadron receiving its Standard.

November brought the first heavy drop into Long Pasia in the extreme south-west corner of Sabah when a D4 tractor was dropped with complete success. This drop was followed by the delivery of an earth-moving blade weighing in at 3.8 tonnes. A further sortie dropped a 'Green's' vibratory roller: this weighed 5.7 tonnes and was the first operational drop of this type of roller. The delivery of this equipment enabled yet another rough airstrip to be improved to give greater safety to its users. The tonnage of this heavyweight equipment dropped sped the squadron on to break the 'million pound barrier' once again, this time with 552 tonnes dropped and 120 tonnes air-landed.

For interest's sake, total tonnage uplifted in November both in Borneo and elsewhere in the Far East was 728 tonnes. Breaking the 'million pounds dropped in Borneo' was now commonplace, this target being exceeded for every successive month right up to the end of the Confrontation and the subsequent pull-out of the British forces from Borneo. The squadron, the Army despatch teams and the Beverley had certainly made child's play of dropping vast quantities of supplies, and undoubtedly this could not have been achieved by any other contemporary aircraft.

Harness Packs Free-dropped in Jungle

An interesting experiment was carried out in November when on a local support training flight, harness packs were successfully free-dropped from 150-200 feet into the Johore jungle. The jungle canopy retarded the descent of the packs thus permitting a safe delivery despite a few hang-ups in the trees. Since this drop was not carried out on any recognized DZ, tethered balloons controlled by the ground party indicated the dropping position.

Rogue Aircraft Comes Home

December saw Flight Lieutenant C. R. Dornan and crew bring XM104 back to base after major overhaul by HAECO, XB262 being delivered for its overhaul. XM104 was air-tested and flown back to base with some trepidation in view of its previous bad record of unserviceability. However, 104 behaved perfectly and it certainly seemed as though the HAECO engineers had chased the gremlins from this aircraft, the first to be delivered to 34 Squadron.

Squadron's Fortieth Birthday

This was celebrated on 7th January 1966, the occasion being marked by the squadron marching past Seletar's Station Headquarters where AVM Foxley-Norris took the salute. During the march-past, four Beverleys thundered overhead in perfect formation, the result of much hard practice, the leader being Flight Lieutenant B. G. Nicholls in XB283. The other aircraft were XB264 (Flight Lieutenant P. D. Mitchell), XB289 (Flight Lieutenant Hugh Crawley) and XM112 (Flight Lieutenant Lou Wilcox). After the parade, all personnel retired to the Malcolm Club where the Air Vice Marshal toasted the squadron's past and sadly, as events were to show, its short-lived future. Since the squadron clearly had its hand in at formation flying, a Beverley flypast was organized for the visit to Changi, of HRH The Duke of Gloucester. Sadly, weather conditions precluded the fly-past taking place.

In Borneo, the Labuan detachment was visited by the Rt.Hon. Edward Heath MP as part of his Far East tour. A large contingent of press and cameramen was flown to Labuan to cover this visit. Work in Borneo proceeded normally, all commitments being fulfilled. An Australia trip in January relieved the monotony of flying in Borneo, and Flight Lieutenant Crawley and crew took XM112 to RAAF Laverton near Melbourne via Butterworth, Cocos Island and RAAF Pearce near Perth. There was also a route trip to Kai Tak via Labuan. Due to the intensity of the Vietnam war, staging through Vietnamese airfields, now extremely busy with American military traffic, was discouraged.

January was also marked by extraordinary aircraft unserviceablility including engine changes, hydraulic failures and oil leaks. Both the aircraft of the Labuan detachment were grounded for a short period when a defect on one of them indicated the possibility of asymmetric flap - a lethal situation. But the fault was soon rectified and in spite of all the technical problems, the squadron managed to fulfil all its tasks and to log 469 hours in the process.

Vietnam Detachment

The highlight of February 1966 was a week's detachment to Saigon with XB264 skippered by Wing Commander D. J. Green and Flight Lieutenant Landsell. The object of the detachment was to take relief supplies, donated by the International Red Cross, Oxfam and various other charities, to a number of airfields including: Pleiku, Kontum, Qui Nhon, Dalat Ban Methout and Da Nang. The trip was highly successful and deep gratitude was expressed by the recipients of the goods. An interesting and surely a one-off feature of the detachment was the carriage of mail for Uncle Sam in a slow, noisy, oily Beverley, the mail being a United States Forces consignment which XB264 flew from Da Nang for onward transmission to America.

Airstrip Recces in the New Territories

In March, the Squadron Commander with Squadron Leader A. J. Hannah and crew took XM112 to Kai Tak. Whilst there, recces were flown of the Sek Kong area in the New Territories of Hong Kong to investigate any potential landing grounds suitable for Beverleys. The squadron received its eleventh aircraft in March, when XL150, skippered by Flight Lieutenant R. M. Williams, arrived from the UK via Luqa, Akrotiri, Bahrain, Bombay, Madras and Butterworth. This aeroplane evoked a series of 'Yuks' from squadron personnel due to its camouflage paint scheme, the RAF's latest livery now that Transport Command regrettably no longer existed and was known as Air Support Command. Gone forever for the tactical transports was the familiar white-topped fuselage, separated by the blue zig-zag cheat line from the remainder of the fuselage finished in silver. Somehow the camouflage seemed bizarre and out of place in the lush green terrain of Malaysia: it looked much more appropriate in the sands of Arabia and the Persian Gulf.

Visit by Chief of the Air Staff

The squadron was honoured in March by a visit from Air Chief Marshal Sir Charles Elworthy, KCB, CBE, DSO, MVO, DFC, AFC, MA, Chief of the Air Staff. Sir Charles took refreshments in the squadron crew room and showed keen interest in the unit's activities, especially the Borneo operations which were still proceeding at their usual hectic pace. Later in the month. Air Marshal Sir Christopher Hartley, KCB, CBE, DFC, AFC, BA, Deputy Chief of the Air

Staff, also visited the squadron. The Air Marshal was just in time to be informed of the squadron's best-ever month for flying hours, which by the end of the month, stood at 522.

New CO -
Rumours of Beverley Run Down

April and May were uneventful but busy, one of the largest commitments being a five-trip shuttle between Clark Field in the Philippines and Kai Tak, flown by Flight Lieutenant M. G. Lodge and crew in XB260. Wing Commander D. J. Green handed over command of the squadron to Wing Commander H. W. Guile. Harry Guile was no newcomer to Beverleys having commanded 47 Squadron at Abingdon and 84 Squadron at Khormaksar. The changeover of Commanding Officers brought rumours of a possible run-down of the Beverley force due to the MoD's decision to acquire C-130 Hercules from the United States.

Meanwhile, the Borneo detachment remained at two aircraft and crews and although there was more than enough for the detachment to do, rumours were circulating that Confrontation might be at an end. All squadron personnel were delighted to hear that SAC E. Hamlin had been awarded an AOC's Commendation for outstanding service in Borneo. This cheerful, hard-working young airman typified the flight line lads who kept the Beverleys flying with such enthusiasm despite their indifferent living and working conditions.

AFM for Exhausted Engineer

In June, Flight Sergeant Clive 'Groppo' Philips was awarded a well-earned Air Force Medal for keeping a sick engine (with a severe oil leak) going by almost continuous operation of the overload oil transfer pump in the 'dog kennel'. This incident happened on a trip to Kuching during which one engine was shut down due to malfunction. When a second engine showed signs of oil starvation, Clive was quick to diagnose the fault and take the strenuous remedial action required. It was said that due to the aircraft's weight together with high ambient temperature and humidity, it was unlikely that Kuching could have been reached on two engines.

Flight Sergeant Alan Dunbar also received a Queen's Commendation for Valuable Service in the Air during Operation *Borneo Territories*. It was refreshing to know that the sheer hard work and dedication of both aircrew and ground staff was being suitably rewarded.

Confrontation Ends

In July, more rumours began to circulate about the possiblity of the Indonesian Confrontation ending. These did not, however, diminish the squadron's task and 620 tonnes were airlifted during the month to most of the Army bases and outposts in Malaysian Borneo, 525 tonnes being air-dropped. The rumours came true in August with the official ending of Confrontation, an agreement between Malaysian and Indonesian politicians being reached on 11th August in Djakarta. The ending of Confrontation brought about feverish activity in North Borneo to commence the tremendous task of withdrawing the British troops, this activity placing such demands on the two Labuan-based Beverleys that the monthly flying task was exceeded by thirty-three hours. Bario and Sepulot seemed to attract the most attention in terms of requirements for air-dropped stores, whilst Long Semado, Long Pasia, Long Banga, Pensiangan and Kota Belud also made heavy demands.

Beverley Rides out Typhoon

September brought many route trips due to the now declining requirements for support work in Borneo. One of these route trips was to Japan and during the stop-over at Tachikawa, a typhoon struck the Japanese islands. Back at Seletar, the Squadron Commander was worried about the safety of one of his aircraft but in the event, the Beverley rode out the typhoon without any bother, proving the the cumbersome picketing gear, so often carried but seldom used, worked superbly well when used as per the instructions in the Ground Handling Notes. A great deal of flying was done in Thailand and Laos which again had suffered severe flooding, Bangkok, Ubon and Nong Khai being visited many times for delivering flood relief supplies.

As stated earlier, the run-down in Borneo was now taking effect. Two aircraft remained on detachment at Labuan but only one was rigged in the dropping configuration, the other was in the PCF (passenger cum freight) role for moving out the troops. Many of the old familiar DZs were now closed, never again to be visited by Beverleys; those that were still open were soon to be supplied by Caribou aircraft of the Royal Malaysian Air Force. For the first month in 1966, the squadron failed to achieve the magic 'million pounds dropped' target, dropping only a mere 947,168 pounds (431 tonnes) in Borneo. This was hardly surprising since only one aircraft was in the dropping role and the requirements for air drops were naturally now diminishing.

Labuan Detachment Ends

'Murphy's Law' prevailed in October in as much that as soon as 34 Squadron had its highest-ever complement of aircraft, aircrew and ground technicians, the Labuan detachment, the squadron's biggest-ever commitment, ended. The detachment went out in a blaze of glory however, by doing numerous trips in Sabah in connection with the pull-out of the British forces. In addition, twenty-four dropping sorties were flown, the last on 22nd October. The detachment at Labuan then ended, and the Royal Malaysian Air Force with their Caribou aircraft (called 'Cari-boo-boos' somewhat disrespectfully by the Beverley boys) were left to undertake whatever tasks in Borneo that the future was to bring. One thing was certain: no other contemporary aircraft could have done the magnificent job that the Beverley had done in Borneo during the three year, ten month Indonesian Confrontation. The 'old furniture vans' had moved about 18,000 tonnes of freight, 13,600 tonnes of which were air-dropped. In imperial units, these figures are even more impressive: almost forty million pounds of freight carried with thirty million pounds dropped. Operations in South Arabia and the Persian Gulf had demonstrated the Beverley's usefulness in air-landing vast quantities of materials on short, virtually unprepared airstrips. But prior to the Borneo campaign, very little supply-dropping had been done 'in anger'. However, the Beverley's performance in the supply-dropping role during Operation *Borneo Territories*, dispelled any doubts about the Bev's capability in this role.

Many lessons were learnt during the Borneo campaign, not only by the planners, but also by the aircrew, ground staff and the Army Despatch Teams. How sad that within a short while after its splendid performance in Borneo, the Beverley was to be withdrawn from service. Nevertheless, the lessons learnt in Borneo could still be used to good effect by those concerned with operating the Beverley's successor.

Families 'Jolly'

Not many people can lay claim to have taken their wives along on a 'business trip' to Nepal, but this is precisely what happened on a Katmandu trip in November, when crew members' wives accompanied them as indulgence passengers. The 'outing' was a great success but was spoilt by the irksome and frustrating delays caused by the bureaucratic Indian customs authorities at Calcutta.

Now that the Borneo detachment was finished, transport support exercises became very fashionable one such exercise sporting the exotic code-name of *Winged Haggis*. History does not reveal it but a Scottish Army unit must surely have been involved. December brought the announcement of a DFC for Flight Lieutenant Hugh Crawley for service in Borneo. AOC's Commendations were also received by Junior Technician D. T. Davies and Corporal W. L. McIntosh for their efforts in Operation *Borneo Territories*.

Beverleys Invade Bangkok

March 1967 brought a one-off sight at Bangkok International Airport in the form

The Instrument panel showing instrument readings for a 'normal' engine configuration. J. Knight

of eight serviceable Beverleys lined up on the apron, dwarfing the Caravelles and Boeing 707s of the commercial airlines. This unique occasion happened on Exercise *Fina*, the object of which was not revealed during researches for this narrative. However, eight Beverleys, and serviceable ones too, at a Far Eastern civil airport, must surely be a record.

Squadron's Future in Doubt

Many wild rumours concerning the future of the squadron had been circulating since January 1967. It was known that the Beverley fleet was being run down; it was also known that the next generation of RAF tactical transport aircraft was to be the C-130K Hercules on which crews were already being trained in the USA. It was hardly surprising therefore that a spate of rumours did the rounds, and these rumours prompted the Squadron Commander to address the aircrew in the crew room, announcing disbandment of 34 Squadron on 31st December, dependent on 48 Squadron re-equipping at Changi with Hercules at that time. He also announced that a gradual run-down of 34 Squadron would commence in September.

Dysentry Strikes at Katmandu

In April 1967, all but one of the crew of a Beverley visiting Katmandu were laid low with dysentry. Flight Lieutenant Wheldon, a South African, managed to avoid this troublesome malady and is said to have capitalized on his good fortune by monopolizing all the female company whilst his colleagues were languishing in the local hospital.

May brought two route trips to Kai Tak despite riots in the colony caused by Communist China's so-called Cultural Revolution. Due to reinforcements having been brought into Hong Kong because of the political situation, the messes were somewhat overcrowded. Later in the month, a route training flight to Japan had to be cancelled due to the trouble in Hong Kong where the Red Guards were becoming increasingly militant.

Bureaucratic Frustration in Nepal

In June, Flight Lieutenant D. Maslin and crew took XB264 to Katmandu. They started the trip in XH122 but this aircraft 'retired' at Butterworth with an engine failure and a replacement engine was flown up from Seletar. At Katmandu, a load was taken on board for Pokhara, but on start-up the engineer spotted an engine gulping, i.e. oil pumping out of the breather pipe, a fault almost unheard of since the early days of the Beverley. Two days afterwards, the fault having been rectified, the crew started engines once again and requested clearance to taxi out ready for take-off as per the flight plan. Half an hour later, they were still awaiting clearance, but then came the crunch with Katmandu Tower stating: 'Regret your diplomatic clearance for this flight is refused.' The disgusted crew shut down the engines again and logged another inexplicable frustration so often provoked by the Nepalese and Indian authorities.

Can't Get Away From It!

June also saw Flying Officer G. O. Fairford, the last of the Borneo campaign co-pilots, leave Singapore for England in his private car, a Renault 4L, his planned itinerary being by way of India, Pakistan, Turkey and Western Europe. Unfortunately, a few hours after setting out on his journey, his vehicle was involved in an accident with an Army truck. The damage to his car, however, was not serious and a roadside panel-beating job soon had the Renault roadworthy again. Flying Officer Fairford was unimpressed when he heard that the truck was on its way to recover a load from a Beverley drop at Kanga Kahang, 34 Squadron's training DZ. It seemed that 34 Squadron was reluctant to sever its relations with this officer.

In the same month, Flight Lieutenants J. W. Turner and J. B. McCarthy skippered

XB291 on a Thailand trip, and during this trip landed at Luang Prabang in Laos. This airstrip was located in a deep valley behind a mountain which was constantly covered in cloud, and it was said that even the AQM thought the airstrip was a 'bit difficult to find'. However, the strip was found successfully and a safe landing and subsequent take-off were made.

More News of Squadron Run-down
In late July 1967, it was announced that December was scheduled for the cessation of Beverley operations and that postings for squadron members would be announced by the end of July. This announcement caused an air of great expectancy to permeate the squadron and also an air of finality: personnel now knew what was going to happen, unless of course that well-worn cry of 'It's all been changed' was to be heard. This possibility was considered to be most unlikely.

In August, four trips to Kai Tak were scheduled, the purpose of which was to take in supplies for the garrison which had been substantially increased in size due to the unrest in the colony.

Three aircraft made Kai Tak but typhoons in the area of the Philippines caused the fourth aircraft to turn back. A seven-day task was carried out in Vietnam by Squadron Leader Nigel Bacon and crew in XL150, delivering relief supplies donated by the Red Cross and other charitable organizations. An engine change was carried out at Loc Ninh; this was done in haste as the Viet Cong were active in that area and could have attacked at any time.

Unusual Configuration
September was highlighted by the squadron's last Australia trip flown by Flight Lieutenant McCarthy and crew in XM112. On the return flight, during the Cocos to Seletar leg, No.3 engine had to be shut down due to surging caused by a faulty pantograph control linkage. The three good engines were then set at 2,400 rpm, the recommended setting for three-engined flight under the prevailing conditions. After a while, No.4 engine showed its disapproval of running at high revolutions by indicating excessive cylinder head temperature: this was brought under control by reducing rpm to 2,100. No.1 engine then began misbehaving with fluctuating torque pressure: this problem was alleviated by reducing rpm to 2,200. The instrument panel then looked most odd to say the least; the pointers on the engine synchroscope, an instrument which showed, by means of miniature rotating propellers, whether the engines were synchronized or not and indicated which engines needed to be sychronized, were all madly gyrating in protest at the three engines all set at different rpm. Flight Lieutenant McCarthy was so impressed by this visual disapproval of unorthodox engine settings that he photograped the instrument panel and framed the best picture. Had he had a tape recorder aboard, he could have recorded the clamourous cacophony caused by this unusual engine configuration. The vibration was also said to be 'far worse than usual.'

Now that Operation *Borneo Territories* was ended, the squadron enjoyed a great deal of route flying which came as a welcome change from the seemingly endless succession of supply-dropping sorties undertaken during the Borneo campaign. To avoid repetition, no attempt is made here to describe these route trips, but one trip to Indonesia in October is noteworthy in that it was a welcome indication of normal relations being resumed between Indonesia and Malaysia.

The run-down of the squadron was highlighted at this time by only five serviceable Beverleys standing on the flight line, the remainder had faults which were not considered worth the expense of repairing. Accordingly, these aircraft were being cannibalized for spares and the flight line was beginning to look like a 'knackers yard.'

December brought the final trip for 34 Squadron to Katmandu. The original purpose of this trip was to go to Kabul in Afghanistan to collect a 1935 Hawker Hind. However, at the last moment 'it was all changed' by those in high authority and the task was carried out by one of the recently acquired C-130 Hercules, the Beverley's successor. On the return flight from Katmandu, the aircraft suffered an engine failure and was delayed at Butterworth to await an engine change. Eager to be home for Christmas, the crew hitched a ride to Seletar on an RNZAF Bristol Freighter. One crew member said, on de-planing at Seletar: 'Who said the Beverley was noisy?'

A tragedy struck the squadron on 15th December when XL150, the only camouflaged aircraft on strength, crashed into the hills of Johore in poor weather, killing the entire crew. The crew had been practising for the Bennet Trophy competition. The sadness of this crash was heightened by it being the squadron's first serious accident since operating Beverleys, and by the fact that the crash occurred within sixteen days of the squadron's official disbandment.

Squadron Disbands
34 Squadron seems to have gone out in a bigger blaze of glory than all the other Beverley squadrons. A disbandment parade was planned for 5th January 1968 and Air Marshal Sir Richard Hughes, CBE, BA, BSc, FRAeS, kindly accepted the duty of reviewing officer. The squadron's longest serving captain, Flight Lieutenant C. H. Lansdell, was chosen to command the final Beverley flypast and on a rehearsal for the parade, as the squadron marched off, and as Wing Commander Harry Guile gave the order 'Eyes right', XM104 roared overhead the saluting base. How fitting that this aircraft should be XM104, FEAF's first Beverley, and now, on this occasion, the last. Master Navigator John Lennard took credit for the impeccable timing, but declined to 'guarantee a repeat'. In the event however, the parade

XM116 being scrapped at Seletar, 1968. *E. Davies*

Opposite: **34 Squadron's Beverleys: the beginning of the end, Seletar 1968.** *E. Davies*

was rained off but a contigency plan went into operation whereby the flypast was still performed, but after landing and taxying to dispersal, the clamshell doors opened, the ramps descended and out strode the Seletar pipe band, marching in the rain to the skirl of the pipes, a sight and sound that must have aroused the emotions of the dourest and most cynical of Scots.

The crew of 34 Squadron's final flight consisted of:

Captain .... Flt Lt C. H. Lansdell
Co-pilot .... Fg Off Weldon
Navigator .... M Nav John Lennard
Signaller .... Sgt Cooper
Engineers .... M Eng 'Gillie' Potter and Flt Sgt Honey (was XM104 so tired that she needed nursing by two engineers?)
AQM .... Sgt Chane

After watching a demonstration by the pipers, the squadron personnel and invited guests moved into a marquee for liquid refreshments, and Air Marshal Hughes made a farewell speech to which Wing Commander Guile replied. On 15th January, an auction was held of trophies acquired by the squadron to help defray the costs of the many social functions always held at such a sad time in a squadron's history. Arrangements were made for the Squadron Standard to be laid up on 24th March 1968 during Matins at St.Clement Danes church, and for the Squadron Operational Record Book to be forwarded to the Air Historical Branch.

Demise of the Far East Beverley Fleet
Despite interest being shown by the Singapore Government and various local entrepreneurs, no bids were made to buy the Beverleys for commercial use. They were sold for scrap, together with all stocks of spares, and the 34 Squadron flight line became a scene of desolation whilst the scrap men ruthlessly cut up the once immaculate Beverleys into easily handled chunks. But the Beverley lived on for a while after the fleet was scrapped, the freight compartment floor panels reportedly being used for flooring in the buses of the Singapore Traction Company.

Thus ended 34 Squadron's illustrious Beverley era. It is sad to think that with the continuing cutbacks in men and equipment in the Royal Air Force, it seems most unlikely that this squadron will ever be resurrected.

34 Squadron's Beverley Achievements
In their 7¼ years of service, 34 Squadron's Beverleys moved approximately 24,500 tonnes of freight, over 75 per cent of this being uplifted during Confrontation. Passengers carried totalled 79,776 and total hours flown amounted to 26,064. It is interesting to note that 34 Squadron carried almost as much freight in 7¼ years of Beverley operations as the Abingdon Wing and 30 Squadron each carried during their 11-year Beverley eras. Most of 34 Squadron's freight was air-dropped during Confrontation and it was this magnificent acheivement for which 34 Squadron's Beverleys will always be remembered. Undoubtedly, the Beverley played a major role during the Borneo campaign and no other aircraft could have delivered such a massive tonnage of supplies to the security forces in the jungle, demonstrating the Beverley's incredible capabilities in the supply-dropping role. Ironically, the Borneo campaign offered the one and only chance for the Beverley to show her mettle at supply dropping

242 OCU's Beverleys at Idris during a night-flying training detachment. *C. Pearson*

Master Signaller John Parsons instructing a student. *C. Pearson*

Chapter Six

242 Operational Conversion Unit

This unit was formed in April 1951 at Dishforth, Yorkshire, and combined what had previously been Nos. 240 and 241 Operational Conversion Units, the former having been based at North Luffenham in Rutland, and the latter at Dishforth. The unit started with a Valetta Flight, phased out shortly afterwards and a Hastings Flight, to be supplemented in 1957 by the Beverley Flight. In the days before flight simulators, a course consisted of about a month in the ground school, followed usually by a somewhat longer period on the 'Flights', doing the incessant circuits and landings, instrument flying, instrument approaches, etc. The course terminated in a route training flight, invariably to somewhere in the Mediterranean area.

There is little to be written about an Operational Conversion Unit, since its duties were so humdrum and mundane. The instructors, however, must be praised for their patience and dedication. Pilots, of course, were Qualified Flying Instructors who had passed the RAF Central Flying School's Qualified Flying Instructor course. All ground school instructors were also fully qualified in instructional techniques, having passed the RAF School of Education's Instructor Course and each instructor was checked for competence about once a year, a 'trapper' from the Instructional Training School sitting in at the back of the class - very off-putting. All ground school instructors also had to fly as often as they could, not only to keep in flying practice, but also to maintain their Transport Command categories. In addition, they manufactured training aids, obtaining the necessary parts by devious means and not always by going through the proper channels. In those days, the now ubiquitous overhead projector, which is used in just about every educational establishment in the country, had just become available and the ground school instructors had to make their own slides and develop techniques for using this new training aid.

In addition, the ground school instructors had to become typists (of the two-finger variety) and duplicating machine operators in order to generate course notes and examination papers. It can be seen therefore that a position of ground school instructor was by no means a 'skive' and these men must be complimented on their dedication to what was sometimes a rather boring duty.

The flight instructors were also busy men, hand picked for the job and holders of at least a Transport Command B category. Each instructor normally had one student and during the time he had his student under his wing, he made his student put into practice all the theory he had learnt at ground school. Sending a new crew solo was always quite eventful. After one or two circuits and landings to ensure that the student crew were not having an 'off day', the staff pilot and engineer climbed out of the aircraft, and watched, usually with great satisfaction, their charges complete their first solo take-off, circuit and landing.

'Abbo Engineers'

Hitherto, flight engineers had been, to use the then current expression, 're-treads', i.e. engineers converting on to Beverleys from some other type of aircraft, or resuming flying duties after a ground tour. With the increasing number of transport aircraft with highly complex systems coming into service, the role of the flight engineer began to assume great importance and more engineers were required than ever before. This led to training *ab initio* engineers called, rather disrespectfully, 'abbos'. These men were all volunteers of course, from skilled aircraft servicing trades but with no flying experience. They attended a course at St.Athan, and later at Newton, which taught them the basic elements of their new trade and then did another course usually at Topcliffe in Yorkshire where they flew performing the duties of safety pilot, e.g. keeping a lookout, in Varsity and other aircraft. This gave them valuable flying experience and some idea of crew discipline and general airmanship. On conversion to a type of aircraft on 242 OCU, the 'abbos', in addition to being thoroughly trained on type, were generally polished up in airmanship and invariably became first class flight engineers, lacking the experience of their seniors of course, but rapidly acquiring experience as their flying careers progressed.

Beverley Rears up

The technical staff of 242 OCU were the first to discover, that with all engines removed, the Beverley tipped backwards on to the base of its fins, taking on the appearance of a praying mantis. From then on, the anti-tip strut, a device which was secured to the underside of the rear of the freight bay, and did precisely what its name suggested, was always fitted when removing engines. Ballast was also placed in the nose for good measure.

Brakes-on Landing

The Dunlop Maxaret anti-skid system, as fitted to the wheel brakes of the Beverley, only worked if the wheels were rotating and then became locked, as when skidding. The brakes were then automatically released and the cycle could be repeated. However, if the aircraft landed with its wheel brakes on, the Maxaret system did not operate and all eight main wheels suffered spectacular and expensive tyre bursts. The pre-landing check list called for 'parking brake off' and 'feet off brake pedals' but occasionally, a student pilot, usually a relatively inexperienced young co-pilot, became so engrossed in making a good approach, that his toes crept on to the brake pedals, resulting in a landing of the type previously described. This caused the QFI some annoyance since officially, he was the aircraft captain and would later be required to make the appropriate report. On one such disastrous occasion, the QFI sent the recalcitrant co-pilot to open the crew entrance door while he and the engineer shut down the engines and completed the after-landing checks. The co-pilot, not being familiar with the procedure for opening the entrance door, inadvertently pulled the door jettison lever, causing the door to fall off on to the head of an unfortunate fireman who had turned out with the fire crew to deal with a potential fire. All was well, however, the fireman was wearing his hard fireman's helmet and suffered no more than a severe headache.

Market Days

Dishforth's location, on the edge of the Yorkshire moors, put the RAF base within easy distance of Boroughbridge, Ripon, Thirsk and other such market towns. In inclement weather, staff and student crews on the flying phase of the course hung around the crew rooms, the students learning what they could from their instructors by discussions. If the weather had not improved by at least mid-afternoon, the flights were stood down. This was known as 'declaring a market day' since in the Dishforth area, on any given day of the week, excluding Saturdays and Sundays, there was a market. This meant the pubs were open all day. A declaration of a market day inevitably saw the student aircrew (and some staff) roaring off in their cars to the town where a market was being held. Some hard drinking naturally followed and it is a blessing that there were no breathalysers in the fifties and that there was much less traffic on the roads than there is today.

OCU Moves South

In December 1961, the OCU moved from Dishforth to Thorney Island, reportedly to relieve the congested airspace in the Dishforth area. This seemed to be a jump from the frying pan into the fire since the Thorney Island area had numerous chunks of airspace reserved by the Royal Navy for ground to air, ground to sea, sea to air and air to air firing. These areas had to be avoided for obvious reasons, adding to the pressures on the student navigators and pilots. Among the residents of the Thorney Island area, there were many prominent people, such as retired Admirals, Generals and the like. These people objected strongly to the night flying and its attendant noise which was such an essential part of the flying course and many irate letters appeared in the local press. To be Orderly Officer when night flying was taking place was not pleasant duty, dealing with incessant telephone calls from residents complaining about the noise.

Beverley Engine in Back Garden

Matters came to a head in May 1962, when XL132 suffered an uncontrollable engine fire. The engine, with an overspeeding propeller, wrenched itself from its mountings and fell on to someone's property in the village of Bosham. This aroused such a public outcry that night flying training at Thorney Island was virtually forbidden from then on and a system was implemented whereby the night flying was done overseas, usually at Idris, El Adem or Luqa. The flights to and from the night flying venues gave route flying experience and were often classed as route training flights.

Letter from Irate Arab

After one night flying detachment at Idris, a letter is said to have appeared in the local press purporting to come from an Arab dignitary in the Idris area. The writer complained of the noise he had had to endure from the night flying Beverleys and stated that the inmates of his harem were being unduly disturbed, the milk yield from his goat herd was seriously depleted, and that some of his pregnant camels had aborted. He concluded his letter by asking the OCU to take their infernal machines somewhere else for their wretched night flying exercises.

This letter was taken quite seriously by the OCU's commanding officer until the story leaked out that the letter had been sent by one of the personnel of the squadron - every squadron has at least one wag.

Waves from Bikini-clad Beauties

One glorious summer's morning saw the take-off for a 'mutual continuation' flying detail. Mutual continuation training was for two experienced pilots who took turns at being captain and co-pilot. Engines were deliberately cut to give all crew members propeller feathering and engine shut-down practice and other emergencies were also simulated.

On this occasion, the first take-off of the day with a full fuel load, the aircraft was pretty heavy. At V1, decision speed, the first pilot decided to cut No.3 engine by feathering the propeller using the pitch control lever. The engineer reported this as a power failure and the second pilot, who preferred to feather propellers and shut down engines himself, instead of delegating these duties to the engineer, punched No.4 engine's feathering button, despite the engineer's anguished cry of 'wrong engine'. The aircraft now had two propellers feathered.

Now a Beverley, lightly laden, could cruise comfortably on two engines, but with a heavy load, a climb to a safe altitude was impossible, so the aircraft lurched into the air in a very uncertain manner and remained, supported by ground cushion effect, at the dangerously low altitude of fifty feet. Whilst the second pilot struggled to keep the aircraft airborne, the first pilot and engineer set about restarting the two dead engines. A turn at that altitude and low airspeed was out of the question and the aircraft pursued a path directly over the beach at Hayling Island.

This enormous aircraft, flying so low, attracted many a wave from bikini-clad females sunbathing on the sands. No doubt they would be topless nowadays. However, the Beverley crew were far too preoccupied to wave back. Little did those bathing belles know how that crew were sweating. But all was well, with the two dead engines restarted, the aircraft climbed safely away, turned out over the Solent and made its way back to Thorney Island to resume its two-hour detail of circuits and bumps.

Unit Gets New Badge

Whilst at Thorney Island, 242 OCU's stock of unit badges, which were worn by all flying staff on their flying overalls, ran out. A new supplier was sought and after a number of firms had quoted for supplying a new stock of badges, the job was given to a firm whose terms seemed particularly favourable. In due course, the new badges arrived and were distrubuted amongst those who needed them.

One sharp-eyed squadron member, however, noticed the wording around the edges of the badge. Instead of reading '242 Operational Conversion Unit', it read '242 Operational Conversational Unit'. The badges were used up however, and the error was seldom noticed.

OCU Beverley Flight Disbands

After training nearly 200 Beverley crews, in March 1967, the Beverley Flight disbanded and prepared for setting up facilities for training crews on the C-130 Hercules, which was shortly to come into service. The Flight's four Beverleys were either flown to join 47 Squadron at Abingdon, or flown to the Maintenance Units at Bicester or Shawbury for disposal.

The staff, many of which had trained on the Hercules in the United States, naturally looked forward to training crews on this exciting new aircraft. However, it was with some regret that they saw the Beverleys go.

The Beverley's ungainly and antiquated appearance, its appallingly low speed, together with its exasperating habits of developing obscure faults, somehow gave it a unique character that endeared the Beverley to all who flew in or worked on this grand old aeroplane.

At the time of writing, 242 OCU is based at Lyneham training crews on the C-130K Hercules. Flight simulators are now used; these were almost unheard of when 242 OCU was first formed in the '50s.

Chapter Seven

The Army and the Beverley

Throughout the Beverley's service career, the Army featured prominently in nearly all aspects of Beverley operations, particularly in air portability and aerial delivery of supplies. Air portability was a relatively simple matter and the Army acted on the premise that 'if it will go into a Beverley then the Beverley can carry it', and indeed this was invariably so, the Beverley carrying, at one time or another, almost every conceivable piece of Army equipment that was capable of being crammed into its cavernous freight compartment.

The Beverley acted as a troop carrier too; in times of emergency such as the Oman uprising in 1957; the Syrian threat to Jordan in 1959; the Iraqi threat to Kuwait in 1961; various other 'brush-fire' outbreaks of trouble in Cyprus and the Middle East; and the assault landings and massive troop movements undertaken in Borneo during the Indonesian Confrontation.

The Beverley was never a comfortable aircraft to travel in: it was slow, noisy, vibrated dreadfully, the heating and air conditioning was inefficient and erratic, so much so that one either 'froze or fried'. But the Army never seems happier than when roughing it and the troops who flew in Beverleys certainly roughed it and always appeared to enjoy doing so. Their humour was typified by a piece of graffiti chalked on the side of a truck participating in some air portability exercise in the 1960s; the slogan read: 'Time to spare, fly Bev Air.'

Major W. R. Davidson recalled one of his 'air experiences' as he delightfully calls them: 'While serving in Aden, I flew as a passenger in a Beverley with two other officers from a strip north of Ataq. We were placed right at the end of the boom "to give some leverage at take-off." The clamshell doors were off the aircraft and by the time we got as far as the Aden Protectorate Levy camp at Mukeiras, two of us had climbed down into the hold to look at the countryside from over the sill. The pilot decided to give Mukeiras something to talk about and dived down, beat up the camp and then pulled up steeply completely unaware that two soldiers were hanging on, literally for dear life, a few feet below him.'

It was always dangerous to swan around a Beverley freight bay when in the doors-off configuration; sudden turbulence, evasive action by the pilot to avoid another aircraft, or any unusual motion could cause the unwary passenger to lose his footing and plummet to earth through the enormous aperture which was so useful for loading and discharging bulky items of freight. A safety net was usually fitted when flying in the doors-off configuration on a non-dropping sortie, but operational necessity often precluded the fitting of such nets.

Major Davidson recalls another two incidents which occurred during his service in Borneo: 'In early January 1963, I was detached from Brunei when the trouble flared up at Kalabakan and I got a lift on the first Bev from Labuan to Tawau, carrying 85 troops of the 1/10 Gurkhas plus two tonnes of stores. Five aircraft loads of Gurkhas and eleven tonnes of stores were subsequently landed at Tawau and moved to Kalabakan where the Malaysian troops had been attacked by the Indonesians, losing nine dead and seventeen wounded.

'Within a very short time, the laterite runway at Tawau, which only handled the occasional Borneo Airways DC-3 in normal circumstances, started to break up and from then on, keeping the runway in some sort of order was a major headache. I took a road roller from the PWD (Public Works Department) and hired a gang of labourers for the task: these were eventually replaced by prisoners from the local jail and they were kept hard at it maintaining the runway in usable condition.

'Another thing I recall was the changeover of the RAF Regiment detachment who were tasked with looking after the many aircraft using Tawau. The detachment seemed to change every few days and there was no question of the men changing over and leaving the equipment stores and vehicles behind. Everything was packed and shoved into a Bev which had previously flown in the replacement unit. We Army types thought this was a dreadful waste of useful aircraft payload.

'We had defence stores delivered by Beverleys into Sandkan and another place along the coast called Semporna. The Bevs free-dropped sand bags, pickets, barbed wire, etc. - by shunting along at a low level - then a quick pull up and crash! Load delivered in a bloody spectacular manner.'

Bakalalan. Note DZ markings. *S. Corton*

Opposite: **This was the fate likely to befall anyone wandering around the freight bay when flying in the 'doors off' configuration.** *A. Dilke-Wing*

The Major was right: a free drop of heavy stores from a Beverley was a most spectacular sight, but most stores were delivered in a much more sophisticated manner and the Army was very closely involved in the organization, planning, preparation and despatch of air dropped stores.

Equipment and stores could be air-dropped in numerous ways and indeed, many Beverley dropping procedures are probably still being used with the Hercules. some methods of dropping supplies are described in the following paragraphs:

SEAC Pack: This was a rectangular container made from stout canvas reinforced with webbing and with four loops for ease of handling at the sides. A so-called percussion head filled with a material such as straw was built into the bottom of the container to absorb the shock of landing. Maximum all-up dropping weight was 84 kilos.

Airborne Pannier: This was of wicker construction and comprised one basket slightly smaller than, and fitting inside another. Originally developed for side-loading aircraft such as the Hastings, the panniers were uneconomical in use as only about sixty per cent of its all-up weight was payload. However, panniers were extremely useful for dropping medical stores and small items such as vehicle spares.

Harness Pack: The harness pack consisted of a half inch base-board on which the load was placed then secured by a universal harness. Harness packs gave considerable flexibility to the Air Despatch Units, enabling them to rig and air-drop practically any equipment that had been cleared for dropping and was within the weight limitations; they were also more economical than the wicker panniers. Originally, the all-up weight was 318 kilos but this was increased to 1,136 kilos after a stronger universal harness had been developed.

SEAC packs, panniers and harness packs were all delivered by parachute, each parachute being opened by means of a static line secured to a suitable strongpoint inside the aircraft. The supplies were despatched from the Beverley through the port and starboard parachute exit doors located in the clamshell doors or alternatively, in the doors-off configuration, the supplies could be despatched directly from the freight bay sill.

Free Drop Sack: Also described in Chapter 2 and sometimes known as the Derby sack, this comprised an inner jute sack measuring 33 x 33 inches fitted inside an outer jute sack measuring about 36 x 36 inches. Should the inner sack burst on contact with the ground, the outer sack invariably restrained the contents. Loads of 91 kilos could be dropped by this method, either from the freight bay sill with clamshell doors off, or through the para-doors with doors on. Dropping height was fifty feet and naturally, the DZ needed a good unobstructed approach and exit flight path. Derby sacks were used extensively for flood and famine relief in East Africa and Malaysia, being eminently suitable for dropping maize, rice, flour and other such foodstuffs.

Larger items of equipment such as rolls of barbed wire which were unlikely to sustain any appreciable damage on impact with the ground, could also be free-dropped from fifty feet from the freight bay sill. However, large items of relatively complex equipment such as vehicles and guns, were dropped by much more complex and highly technical means. Before describing these however, mention must be made of the one-ton container that eventually became the life-line of the security forces operating in the Borneo jungle during the Indonesian Confrontation.

One-ton Container: Known officially as the Container Aerial Delivery One Ton, this device was by far the best means of delivering fairly large quantities of bulk supplies. The container was made from stout canvas reinforced with nylon webbing straps, a suspension web assembly being used to suspend the container from its parachute system. Landing shock absorption when required, was taken by layers of corrugated cardboard. Payload, as the name suggests, was nominally one tonne, but could vary between about 500 and 1,200 kilos. The container cost £50 in the early '60s but the operational use, in Borneo, of thousands of containers never to be recovered, prompted the development of a cheaper utility version. The Beverley could drop single containers or containers in sticks of up to sixteen, either manually, with despatchers simply pushing the containers out of the aircraft along a roller conveyor system or automatically by means of extractor parachutes. Many thousands of one-ton containers were dropped in Borneo and during the Borneo campaign, the speed and efficiency with which one-ton containers were prepared, loaded, flown to the DZs and then despatched, enabled as many as 300 containers per month to be dropped. This was

This page: **Running up to a Borneo DZ.** *S. Corton*

Is it on the DZ? Army despatchers of 55 Air Despatch Unit watch their load descending. *S. Corton*

A one-ton container on its way. *S. Corton*

Opposite page: **XM109 of 84 Squadron dropping harness packs.** *RAF Museum*

'Load gone'. A one-ton container being dropped on a Borneo DZ. *S. Corton*

made possible not only by the Beverley and its aircrews who dropped them on near impossible DZs, but also by the Army Despatch Teams who worked incredibly long hours, in difficult conditions, preparing the loads. The efforts of these men enabled the Beverley to drop the massive tonnage of supplies which highlighted its participation in the Borneo campaign.

Wheeled vehicles or large loads, too bulky for dropping in a one-ton container, were dropped in a much more sophisticated manner. In essence, the principle of aerial delivery of a large, heavy piece of equipment was to mount it on some form of platform to which was secured a parachute harness and parachutes. A device, usually a system of air bags, for absorbing the landing shock was fitted on the underside of the platform. The freight compartment floor of the Beverley was fitted with roller conveyor tracking plus a side guidance system to enable the platform to roll smoothly out of the aircraft when required, the aircraft of course, being rigged in the doors off configuration. Release of the platform from the device which anchored it securely within the aircraft was accomplished by a small extractor parachute, fitted to the freight bay sill and released by the supply aimer, normally the navigator. After safe extraction of the platform from the aircraft, an automatic device transferred the pull of the extractor parachute to the bags of the main parachutes which were pulled off, allowing the main parachutes to deploy and lower the platform to the ground. These platforms were known as stressed platforms and came roughly in four sizes and types as follows:

Stressed Supply Platform: Also known as the Boscombe Platform, this was used for delivery of bulk supplies but due to its complexity was less economical to use than the one-ton container. Nevertheless, it had a useful maximum payload of just over four tonnes and a stick of four Boscombe Platforms could be dropped from the Beverley. There is little evidence of this platform having been used operationally to any great extent.

Medium Stressed Platform: This was by far the most popular and most extensively used stressed platform for dropping from the Beverley since it was capable of carrying an astonishing assortment of artillery, engineer and infantry equipment. A list of items suitable for dropping by Medium Stressed Platform (MSP) reads like an inventory of the quartermaster's store: artillery loads included a missile vehicle complete with two missiles; a missile resupply vehicle complete with the nine missiles; a Land Rover and 105 mm gun plus five rounds; an Austin truck and mounted Wombat gun; two 105 mm guns plus 18 rounds; an Austin truck and 4½ inch mortar plus 52 rounds; and various infantry support weapon loads. The list of engineer loads was even more formidable: a variety of earthmoving and resurfacing equipment ranging from a Green's vibratory roller and a Wobbly Wheel roller, to a dumper vehicle and a load of wheelbarrows. An impressive list of general vehicles and trailers carrying generating sets, compressors and other equipment was also cleared for dropping by MSP. An interesting load consisted of : 'Six Boats, Stream Crossing Mark 4 with Crated Engines' – the Army seemed to have thought of everything.

Two MSPs could be dropped from the Beverley either singly or as a stick of two. MSPs were used world wide by the Beverley Force but more in training than in anger. Nonetheless, a substantial number were dropped in East Africa and in Borneo, mainly to deliver earthmoving equipment for improving the surfaces of various airstrips. The useful payload of the MSP Mark 1 was almost 5 tonnes: the Mark 2 MSP delivered a payload of 5½ tonnes, all-up weights being 6.4 tones for the Mark 1 and 7¼ tonnes for the Mark 2. For delivering the Malkara Hornet Missile Vehicle, a special clearance increased the permissible all-up weight of the Mark 2 to just over 8 tonnes.

Heavy Stressed Platform: The HSP was mainly used for dropping extra-large and heavy vehicles such as large bulldozers and graders which were beyond the capacity of the MSP. The HSP was one and a half times the length of the MSP, measuring 24 feet and carried a maximum payload of 9½ tonnes, all-up weight being 13 tonnes. Although a significant number of loads were cleared for delivery by HSP, only a small number were dropped operationally. However, much useful dropping experience was acquired in the art of dropping heavy loads by this platform.

Light Stressed Platform: Developed late in the Beverley's career, reportedly for carrying a variety of Land Rovers, the LSP does not appear to have been used to any extent operationally and the Beverley retired from service before dropping procedures for the LSP were finalized. The LSP is mentioned here for completeness only.

This page: **Heavy stressed platform carrying a grader leaving the aircraft.** *via JATE Brize Norton*

Medium stressed platform and load immediately after extraction.
British Aerospace

Opposite page: **Medium stressed platform leaving aircraft - the extractor parachute can be seen on the left of the load.** *J. Ward*

Main parachutes of heavy stressed platform almost fully deployed.
via JATE Brize Norton

Heavy drop using the ULLA technique.
via JATE Brize Norton

Heavy stressed platform about to land. via JATE Brize Norton

The RAF Parachute Display Team, later to become The Falcons, board XB269 at Abingdon in May 1964. Crown Copyright

Paras emplaning using special emplaning ladder. C. Dales

Most stressed platforms and one-ton containers were dropped from about 1,000 feet above ground level. The MSP and HSP were often dropped from 1,200 feet to give adequate time for deployment of the main parachutes.

An interesting technique which to the author's knowledge was never used operationally, was the ULLA technique. ULLA is an acronym for Ultra Low Level Airdropping and involved the aircraft trailing an arrestor gear type of hook which released the extractor parachute. The aircraft flew just above the ground and the hook engaged a cable strung from a goal post structure. Engagement of the hook released the extractor parachute which deployed, extracting the platform carrying the load from the aircraft, the platform being equipped with skids and shock-absorbing devices which ensured a safe arrival on the DZ. ULLA could obviously only be used on very flat terrain which had a perfect approach and exit flight path to and from the DZ. The surface of the DZ also had to be perfect; free from trees, rocks and without any undulations in the ground. For this reason ULLA was of little use in the Borneo jungles or on the rocky, mountainous terrain of South Arabia. Nevertheless, the ULLA technique was pioneered with the Beverley and is believed to be in use with today's Hercules Force.

THE ARMY AND THE BEVERLEY

Parachuting

This was one of the Beverley's important roles, but one in which the Beverley did not win any great acclaim, due to the fact that very little operational parachuting was done from it. However, many thousands of paras made their first jump from the Beverley which was used extensively for training recruits to the Parachute Regiment and also for keeping the trained paras in practice. Seventy parachutists were carried, 40 in the freight bay and 30 in the boom, the freight bay occupants exiting through the para-doors in the clamshell doors and the boom occupants through the hatch in the boom floor. When rigged for parachuting, tubular strop guards were fitted to the clamshell doors to prevent damage caused by the straps which flailed about in the slipstream. The strops were of course, eventually pulled back into the aircraft by the despatchers after all the parachutists had jumped. The strop guards were sometimes called 'elephants ears'.

The Beverley scored a number of 'firsts' in parachuting: the free-fall technique, developed by instructors from the RAF's No.1 Parachute Training School, was done almost exclusively from the Beverley; the RAF Parachute Display Team, later to become the world-famous 'Falcons', certainly cut their teeth on the Beverley; and the first recorded free-fall descent in the Far East, was also made from a Beverley. The men of the Parachute Regiment held the Beverley in very high esteem, appreciating its stability as a jumping platform and the roominess of the freight bay and boom which made for easy checking of their equipment during preparations for a jump.

During researches for this book, the author spoke to and corresponded with many paras and ex-paras, none of whom had a bad word to say about the Beverley except some ribald remarks about it 'being a bit slow'.

Major R.Till Retd., writing from his home in Australia, made an interesting and quite understandable comment: 'One memory of jumping from the Bev was that when jumping at night from the freight bay, it was always possible to see the flashing red anti-collision light underneath the fuselage, reflected on the landing wheels. Very off-putting sometimes!'

Ex-para A. Langford writes: 'I did many jumps from the Bev and prior to that from the Hastings. My opinion of the Bev was that it was terrific, especially jumping from the boom which must be the easiest jump possible.'

Perhaps the greatest tribute, not only to the Beverleys, but also to the aircrews (and indirectly to the ground crews) and the parachute packers comes from ex-para P. Hignett who writes: 'When the Beverley first came into service, I was a member of The Parachute Regiment and clearly remember doing conversion training. It was entirely new to us as up to that time we only had experience of the Hastings. After ground training we made several drops from the freight bay by way of the port or starboard para-doors and everybody immediately took to the Beverley considering it to be safer than the Hastings from which anything but a perfect exit meant a rough ride through the slipstream.

'The aperture drop from the boom was very popular due to the lack of slipstream. We were first introduced to the aperture on ground training by means of a mock-up and then progressed to a static balloon which had been adapted for aperture exit. Up to that time, we had been used to exiting from a door, looking straight ahead. Looking down through a "hole in the floor" from 800 feet caused a few stomach butterflies but we soon got used to the idea and looked forward to our first aircraft descent via the aperture.

'The hardest part of jumping from a Beverley tail boom was getting aboard. Unless a special emplaning ladder for the boom was available, we emplaned via the crew entrance ladder into the freight bay, and then up another ladder into the boom, all this wearing a parachute plus a reserve. On going to action stations, the AQM opened the door and on the "green" out we went. It was just like going down a slide with an almost gentle opening of the canopy.

'One problem came to light: some paras were not getting into the centre of the aperture with the result that the parachute pack caught on the edge of the aperture, tipping the parachutist into a dive. To correct this we did more ground training on the mock-up. On making further drops from the aircraft, it was found that some paras were making too much effort and were hitting the far side of the aperture with their helmets - a good way to get a severe headache. This was known as "ringing the bell."

'I made quite a number of descents from Bevs, some accompanying heavy drops. I also made a few flights in the Bev to and from the Middle East but found her a bit slow. I well remember at Amman airport in Jordan in 1958, seeing USAF aircrew watching in amazement as a Beverley landed and neatly reversed up to a party of

Para awaiting deployment of his 'chute after jumping from the tail boom. *J. Knight*

Opposite page: **Para exiting from the tail boom aperture.** *J. Knight*

Stick of paras en route for DZ in the Jebel Ali (near Sharjah) area. *J. Knight*

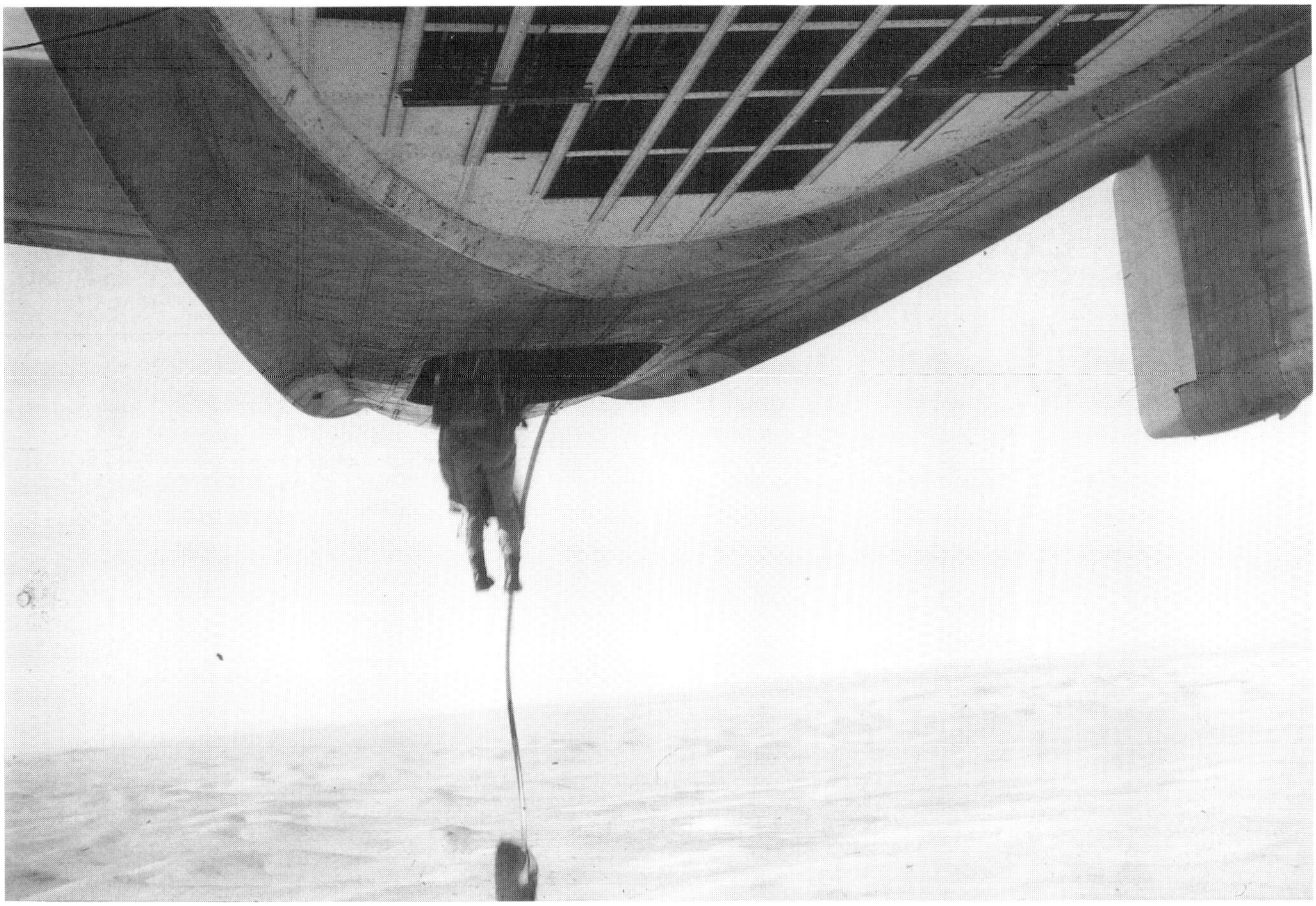

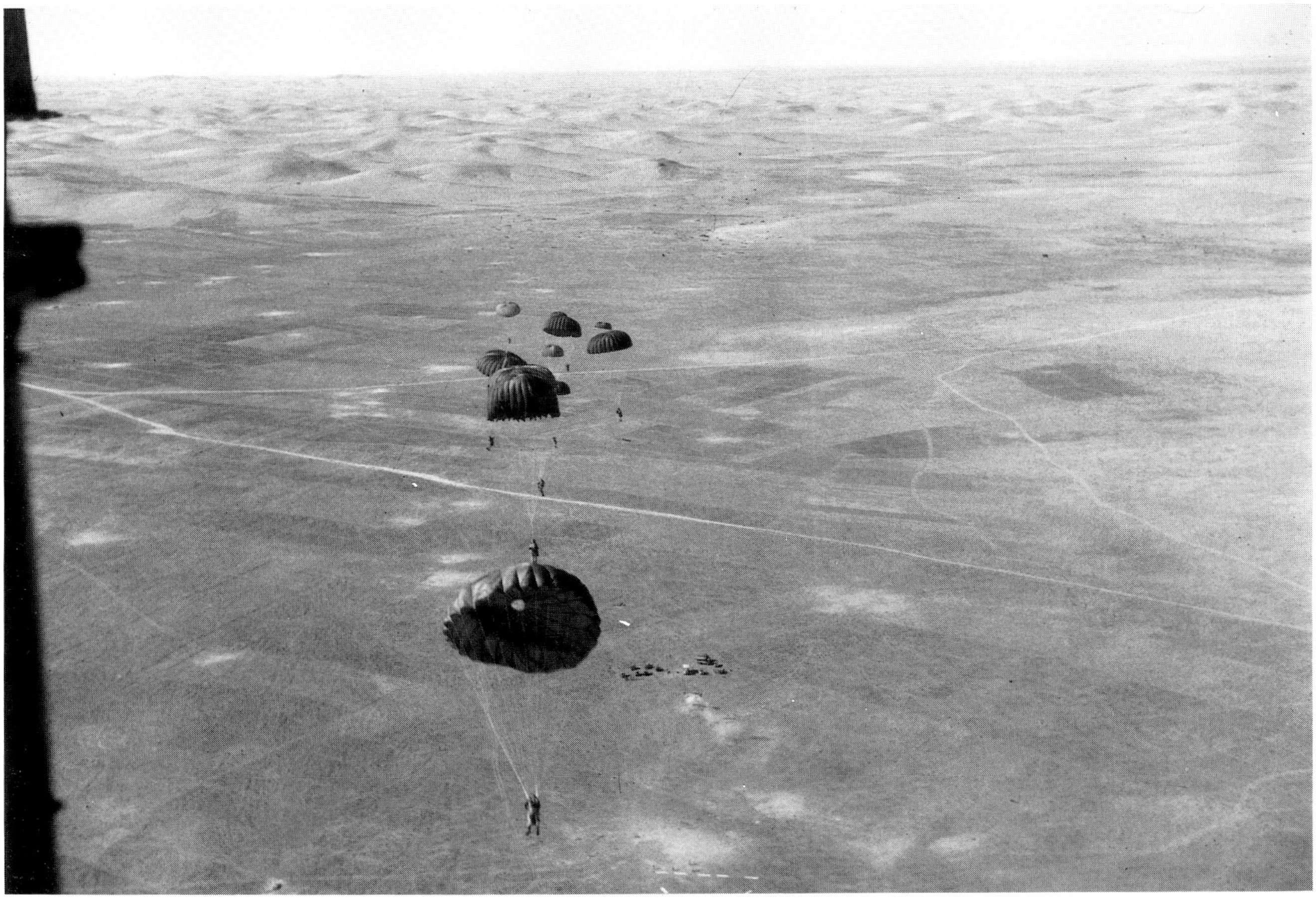

Paras seated in the freight bay. Staff Sgt Dales, contributor of this photograph, is third from left. *C. Dales*

Paras jumping from the freight bay of XB261. *Airborne Forces Museum*

troops waiting to unload it.

We were all very sorry to see the Bev disappear: I have jumped from a number of other aircraft including Hastings, Argosy, Hercules, Twin Pioneer and the French Noratlas, but remember the Bev with most affection. We always appreciated the way in which the pilots would do their best to keep the aircraft steady on the approach to the jump: it was very rare to be deposited in the wrong place.

'In parachuting there are unfortunately fatalities, but at no time did I ever hear blame levelled at aircrew or packer when a para "whistled in". It was always regarded as bad luck or a moment's carelessness on the part of the victim.'

'It was also highly appreciated when the captain of the aircraft and the despatcher attended the funeral of the victim who had made his final jump. The RAF sometimes appeared to be a little shocked at the paras' strange sense of humour when jokes were cracked to the effect that the dead para should have asked for another parachute when he found that the one he had drawn was not working.'

What better praise could be given to the Beverley, its aircrew or the parachute packers?

Chapter Eight

The Brough 'Planemakers' and Royal Air Force Ground Staff

The Brough Planemakers

In the late '40s the Blackburn Aircraft Company at Brough, East Yorkshire (now North Humberside) were beginning to look around for new contracts. Production of the Firebrand had ceased in 1945 and up to 1950, the Brough works was subcontracted to build Fairey Barracudas and Percival Prentice aircraft. Prototypes of two anti-submarine aircraft were built in 1949 and 1950 for the Ministry of Supply, but no orders were placed. The company certainly tried hard to win a place among the post-war civil aircraft manufacturers and produced design studies for many civil transport aircraft, one of the most ambitious studies being for the Clydesman. This was a six-engined flying boat, similar in appearance to the Sunderland

'The Brough Planemakers' - a carefully composed photograph around 1957.
British Aerospace

which Blackburns had built under subcontract at their Clydeside works during the war. Other proposals for civil transports ranged from a five-seater executive to Rapide and Dakota replacements. None of these proposals was accepted.

At the end of 1948, Blackburns merged with General Aircraft Ltd. and the subsequent removal of the GAL60 Universal Freighter from Feltham to Brough for re-erection and flight testing brought some much-needed work to the company.

The successful flight trials of the Universal Freighter Mark 1 led to the development of the Mark 2 and the Ministry of Supply's order for 47 Beverleys, providing work not only for the Brough factory but also for Blackburn's other factories at Bradford and Dumbarton. The Beverley in fact provided the company with over ten years' work, building the aircraft, providing spares and modification kits, and doing major overhauls, repairs and modifications.

Although Blackburns had produced a number of seaplanes and flying boats between the wars, the company became firmly established as a manufacturer of Naval aircraft, the Skua, Roc, Firebrand, and latterly the Buccaneer being well-known examples of Blackburn aircraft used by the Fleet Air Arm. But in spite of many design studies and proposals for civil airliners and military transports, Blackburns were never successful in landing a contract for a transport aircraft until the Beverley contract was secured. Then, in an impressive demonstration of overcoming the enormous production difficulties of building such a massive aeroplane, the RAF's 47 Beverleys were delivered precisely on schedule.

The Beverley contract brought much-needed work to the company which, in fact, had to expand in order to fulfil contractual obligations, and Beverley components were made at the firm's Bradford and Dumbarton plants. Although somewhat

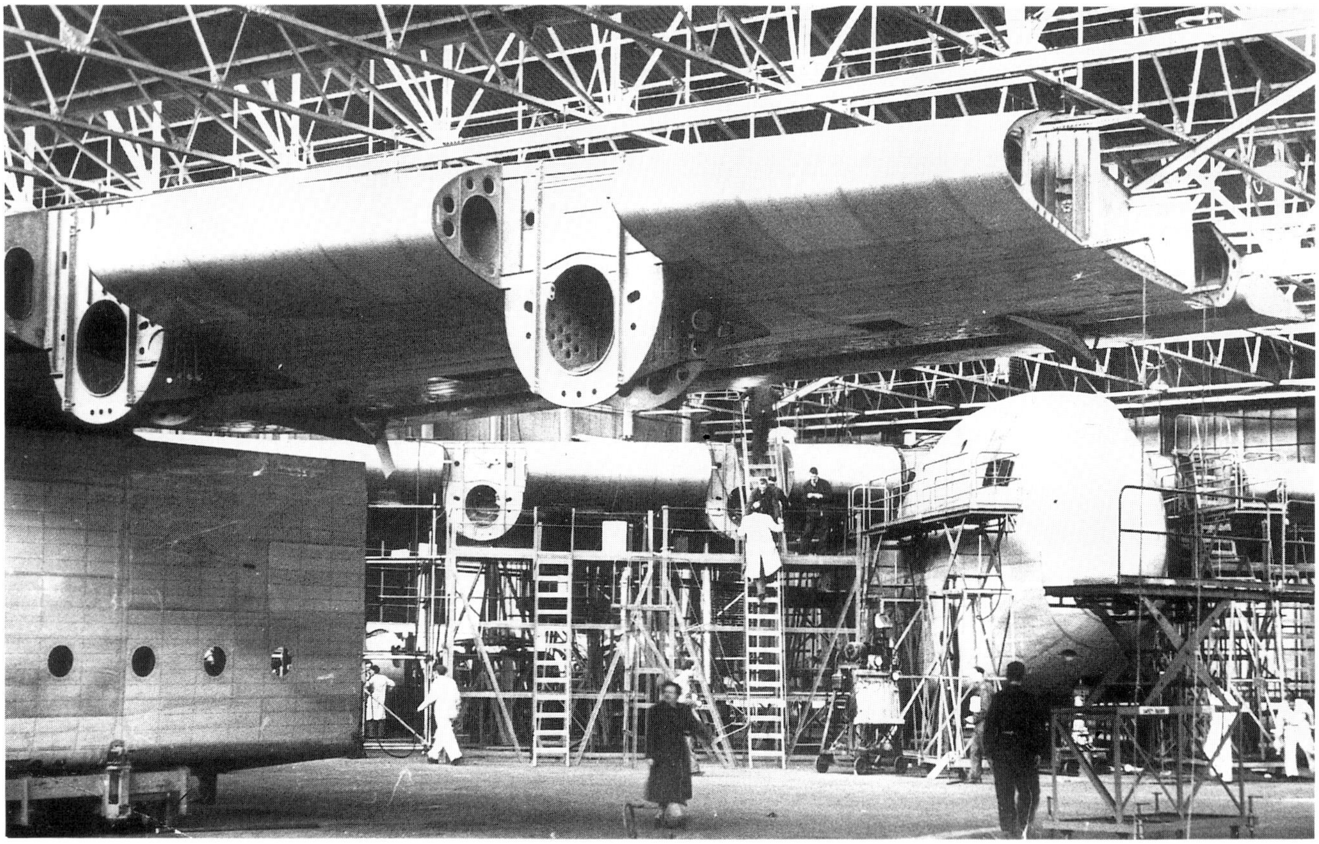

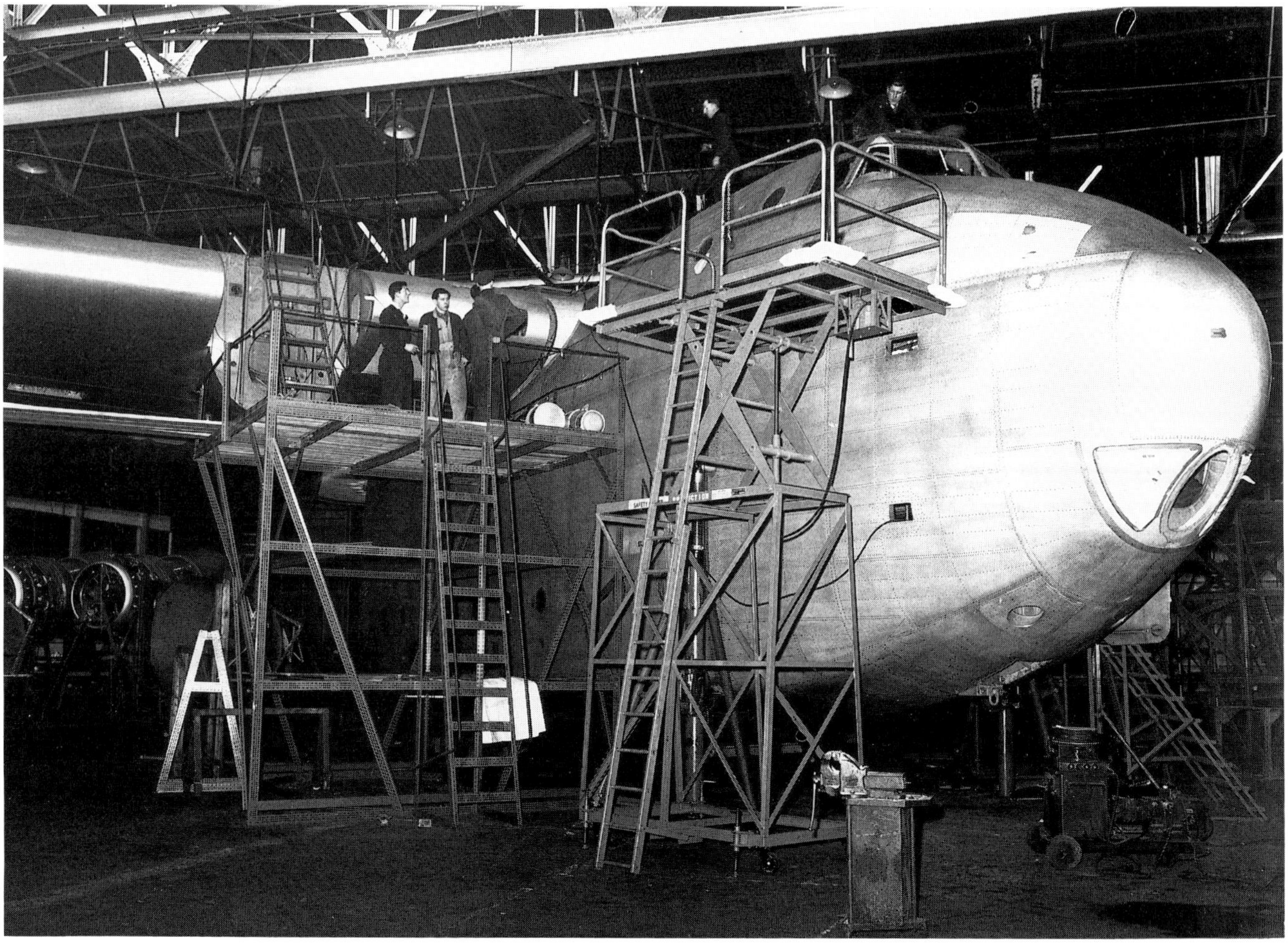

daunted by the sheer size of the Beverley, the Brough work-force soon got used to 'working at altitude' from complicated arrays of scaffolding. Lack of headroom in the main assembly hangar was a problem but this was solved by positioning the aircraft in a tail-down attitude for final erection.

Access to the Centaurus engines of the Beverley was difficult right from the beginning and remained so throughout the Beverley's career. At Brough, this difficulty really became evident when the flight line became congested and it was not always possible to position a faulty engine over a smooth and level piece of concrete hardstanding. The access equipment then had to be manhandled, usually with considerable cursing, over ground which was frequently very soft and muddy. Once outside the erection hangar at Brough, an aircraft invariably stayed outside until delivered to the RAF: thus all work on that aircraft during the flight testing schedule, had to be done out in the open, often under extremely poor conditions. Brough airfield, on the banks of the Humber, can be very cold, wet and bleak in the depths of winter. However, the employees seemed to take it all in their stride and one never heard of any industrial disputes concerning the severe working conditions.

The late Mr Bill Brattan, ex-Blackburn employee, wrote of the Beverley with obvious affection:

'The Bev was my "baby"; I spent fifteen years working on this ugly but beautiful, yet immensely practical monster - the Queen of the Skies. I followed this baby right through production, flight testing, experimental work and five years on service liaison with 47 Squadron at Abingdon. In my forty years in the aircraft industry, and of all the types of aircraft that I have worked on, the Bev made the deepest and longest-lasting impression. I was really saddened when the Bevs were superseded by the C-130 Hercules.

'My first flight in a Bev was a never-to-be forgotten experience. In the early days, a flight was arranged to Westland Aircraft at Yeovil, the object being to undertake loading trials of a Westland helicopter. I went

This picture shows the 'Safety Raiser' access equipment used at Brough. BAe

A group of Brough planemakers after preparing a Beverley for flight test. Left to right: Gerry Dodsworth, Albert Honold, Jimmy Rudd, Bill Brattan, Tom Craft, unknown, Roy Bond, unknown.
Yorkshire Post

Opposite: **Beverley production line in Blackburn's North Sea Erection Hall.**
Hull Daily Mail

Beverley being assembled at Brough. BAe

Bill Brattan, Blackburn engineer, surveys the repair job on bomb-damaged XL131. This aircraft was patched up with plywood and fabric for the flight from the Persian gulf to the UK. *W. Brattan*

The Beverley that never got off the drawing board - model of the projected Blackburn B107A military freighter as shown at the 1958 SBAC show. *British Aerospace*

along as 'flying spanner' and on take-off from Brough we had a double engine failure. Tim Wood (Blackburn's chief test pilot) was in command and he radioed Brough tower that we were returning for an emergency landing. Now this occurred just about a week after Bristol Aircraft's chief test pilot Bill Pegg had crash-landed the No.2 production Britannia on the mud flats in the Severn estuary. This was flashing through my mind as we came in low over the Humber: it was low tide and those mud flats looked uncomfortably close. However, we made it safely to the airfield.

'My time at Abingdon was very enjoyable. Whilst there, I was privileged to see a formation of twelve Bevs and to hear 48 Centaurus engines throbbing away over the Berkshire countryside - a sight and sound never again to be experienced.

'One Sunday morning when working in the hangar, I had the crazy notion to ride a bicycle along the wing of a Bev and did so - I don't know if anyone else had ever done that.'

Bill's cycle ride could well be a one-off; however, many aircrew rode bicycles around Beverley freight bays during flight just for a laugh, and one AQM was known to have sampled the delights of riding a motor cycle around the freight bay during flight. Yes, the wings and cargo compartment of the Beverley were large enough to permit such activities.

Bill Brattan recalled the last Beverley flight made by Blackburn's then chief test pilot: 'I recall the time when Tim Wood flew the Bev for the last time prior to his retirement. He took a party of reporters for a joy-ride and to their amazement, and discomfort, this grandfather pilot, the oldest in the business, put that aircraft through some incredible manouevres, a fitting way to end a great flying career.'

The team that repaired XL131 which was damaged in flight by a terrorist time bomb during the Kuwait crisis in 1961 included Bill Brattan. The aircraft had been roughly patched up, mainly with plywood and fabric and dope for the flight to the UK for a permanent repair. Bill took up the story: 'The repair was done at Dishforth and took three to four months together with a scheduled inspection and modifications. For the repair, most of the parts were unobtainable and consequently had to be manufactured on site but we eventually managed to get it all put back together again. On measuring up, we found that the contour of the aircraft's nose was about 1½ inches out of true, but this did not seem in any way to be detrimental to flight and as far as I know, XL131 ended her days in that condition. The airtest was completed without a single fault being reported and we took this as a great compliment.'

Mr Len Brattan, Bill's brother, also writes of the Beverley with particular reference to its rugged construction:

'As a fitter, I worked on all 47 production aircraft. The Bev was built like a tank as was proved when a student RAF pilot thought he was nearer the ground than he really was, and dropped the aircraft from about twenty feet. Severe damage was suspected and the aircraft was gingerly flown to Brough for checks to be made. We stripped the undercarriage and wings and subjected the whole structure to a complete flaw detection test. No structural damage whatsoever was found, the only parts scrapped were some wing skinning and the wing-to-fuselage fillets.' The Beverley was subsequently to prove its ruggedness in operating from some of the roughest airstrips anywhere in the world, often in the harshest of climatic conditions.

When Beverley work at Brough ceased, the workers, their attentions now turned to building and overhauling Buccaneer aircraft, like Mr Bill Brattan, were saddened. The success of the Beverley had prompted Blackburns to undertake design studies for the B-107 and B-107A. The B-107, projected in 1956, incorporated the Beverley wings and tail unit, and a massive freight compartment capable of carrying much more equipment than that of the Beverley. Seating was for 108 troops; alternatively, 75 paras or 92 stretcher cases could be accommodated. The B-107 was to be powered by four Rolls-Royce Tyne turboprops. The principal attractions of this projected design were its STOL capability together with its long range and high cruising speed, the latter two attributes, of course, being features that the Beverley so desperately lacked.

The B-107A was proposed in 1959 and was similar to the B-107 but incorporated front loading doors in addition to the rear cargo doors which could be opened in flight for supply dropping. The Ministry of Defence however, showed no interest in these second-generation Beverleys, preferring instead to buy the well-proven Lockheed Hercules as the Beverley's successor. And so, for the Beverley planemakers, their 'baby' passed into history. But such was the Beverley's character, typfied by its immense size and the leisurely but businesslike way in which it thundered over the East Yorkshire towns and villages, that it will always be remembered by the people of North Humberside. These memories will be enhanced by the preservation of XB259 (the first Beverley to roll off the Brough production line) in the Museum of Army Transport at Beverley.

The RAF Ground Crews

The Beverley, by virtue of its tremendous size, demanded physical fitness and stamina from the men who worked on it. Seventeen steps had to be climbed to reach the flight deck from the ground, and a similar number of steps also had to be negotiated to get into the tail boom from the ground. To reach an engine, about twenty steps had to be climbed depending upon the type of access equipment used. In isolation, the act of climbing this comparatively small number of steps does not seem to demand much physical stamina, but in practice, a technician investigating say an engine fault, seldom had the correct tools with him when he first climbed up to an engine, having first laboriously positioned the necessary access equipment. Indeed, he seldom knew what tools or spare parts he needed until he opened the engine cowlings to see what was amiss. Thus, often an airman had to make frequent trips up and down ladders to get tools, spares, to ask advice or to get a superior to check his work. The access equipment also had to be repositioned sometimes, for example, to reach another part of an engine, an activity that required further muscle power. A well-known cry of a Beverley technician was that: 'By the time you've got yourself up to the job, you're too bloody clapped to do it!'

The access equipment used by the RAF tradesmen included the 'Giraffe' hydraulic platform. This was mounted on a wheeled base and could be raised or lowered by means of a handpump situated at the base of the structure. This curious piece of design meant that every time the unfortunate airman working on the platform required it to be raised or lowered, unless he had an accomplice, he had to descend the ladder, adjust the position of the platform and then ascend the ladder again, often to find that the position was still not correct. The 'Safety Raiser' type of access equipment used by Blackburns had the handpump situated on or near the platform, thus making life somewhat easier for those who used this type of equipment.

But in the early days of the Beverley, before the Giraffe ladders became freely available, the 'Merryweather' access ladder was used. This was produced by a well-known manufacturer of fire-fighting appliances. The operating mechanism for this equipment, like that of the Giraffe ladder, was at the base: worse still it was purely mechanical in operation and was actuated by a hand crank which required considerabie energy to turn.

For all-around access to an engine, the RAF used the 'Basix' type of working platform. This was fabricated from material similar to Dexion slotted angle-iron and provided an excellent platform from which to work, having adequate room for tool boxes, bins of consumables such as cleaning rags, and other equipment. In the

Using the 'Basix' engine access equipment for an engine change. *J. Knight*

early days of the Beverley at Abingdon, before equipment was available to put a Beverley into a hangar, a 'dock' constructed of Basix was erected, all four engines of an aircraft being surrounded by these excellent working platforms. The whole structure was roofed over to give the technicians some protection from the elements. A Beverley was carefully towed into and out of the dock, the nosewheels being guided along a timber track to ensure that the aircraft was correctly positioned. When the sidetracking equipment for hangaring the Beverleys came into service, the dock fell into disuse and was dismantled. However, it served a very useful purpose in the interim period before the sidetracking equipment was delivered.

Although the Giraffe and Basix engine stands were first-class pieces of equipment, they were virtually useless in soft ground or on sand, the latter of course, being typical of nearly all the airstrips in the Middle East. This was due to the small-diameter solid wheels which became bogged in any type of soft or sandy ground. For work on sandy surfaces, the 'Zip-Up' collapsible staging was vastly superior. This lightweight equipment could be lifted into position when soft ground made wheeling it an impossibility: another unique feature of Zip-Up was that it could be dismantled and stowed flat, and since it occupied very little space and was light enough not to impose any undue payload limitations, it could be carried in the aircraft. This was a boon for aircraft operating 'off-route' into airfields not equipped with access equipment for large aircraft. A Beverley with an engine fault at such an airfield always posed a problem for those who had to rectify the fault and much resourcefulness was employed in order to get up to the engine. The standard ploy was to 'borrow' a truck or indeed anything high enough and flat enough to place the inter-deck freight bay-to-boom ladder on to get the necessary height to reach the engine. Technicians frequently 'lived dangerously' using precarious makeshift extension ladders and painful tumbles were sometimes taken. However, when the Zip-Up staging became freely available, most aircraft carried a set stowed in one of the clamshell doors.

Not all problems of servicing were concerned with gaining access to lofty parts of the Beverley. A lot of work had to be done in the wing crawlways and engine accessory bays, and due to the many obstructions such as wing leading edge ribs, considerable agility was required to move about in these claustrophobic places. In the tropics, the crawlways and accessory bays became unbearably hot and cases of heat exhaustion were often reported; in fact, one airman lost his life in Aden as a result of heat exhaustion from working in a crawlway. Another job constituting a health hazard, especially in the tropics, was working inside a fuel tank, a task which was necessary when changing a tank. In spite of draining the tank and thoroughly venting it, dangerous concentrations of fuel vapour remained, and any airman working inside a fuel tank was obliged to come up for air frequently. Nowadays, with a more positive attitude to health and safety, breathing apparatus is no doubt essential for such jobs, but in the early days of the Beverley, no-one seemed to think of such innovations.

The airframe of the Beverley gave little trouble and since this was the first RAF transport aircraft to have power-assisted flying controls, many people doubted the reliability of such new-fangled devices. Although the Universal Mark 1 had a manual reversion system, this was deleted on the Beverley, giving rise to much suspicion among pilots and technicians. However, practically no trouble was experienced with the power-assisted flying control system and the two independent hydraulic systems, driven from pumps fitted to the port and starboard engines respectively, always gave sufficient power for the controls, even with two engines out.

Undoubtedly, the engines gave the biggest headaches. The Bristol Centaurus, considered to be the ultimate in sleeve valve engine design, had been used with success, in a number of civil and military aircraft. Such success however, was not achieved with the Beverley installation and even when most of the bugs had been chased out of the Centaurus as fitted to the Beverley, the life between overhauls was only a mere 600 hours and even then, premature engine changes were all too common.

However, it must be remembered that the Beverley's engines were subjected to the harshest treatment possible. Although the Beverley was by no means underpowered, high engine rpm had to be used during cruising in order to maintain the recommended airspeed and this imposed severe wear and tear. In addition, the use of reverse thrust for landing, despite an excellent air intake filtration system, did cause the ingestion of a certain amount of sand and dust, especially in the Middle East, which obviously caused premature internal wear of the engines. It was also thought that the large, heavy, steel propeller which caused so much vibration, also imposed a severe strain on the Beverley Centaurus.

Much trouble was caused when the Beverley first came into service, with oil cooler blockages. These were caused by carbon particles and sludge accumulating in the oil cooler and restricting the flow of oil through the cooler resulting in uncontrollable overheating. Some trouble was also caused by engines 'gulping' but this was far less frequent than the oil cooler blockage problems. Since all the UK-based Beverley squadrons started operating their aircraft at roughly the same time, the engines of these aircraft all became heavily contaminated with sludge at about the same time, causing the oil coolers to become blocked. Consequently, just about the whole Beverley fleet went down with oil cooler unserviceability during a given period and for a few fraught weeks, Beverleys were landing at just about every airfield between the UK and Aden, with their captains frantically signalling for new oil coolers to enable them to get airborne again. Replacement coolers and technicians to fit them were flown out as fast as resources would permit, to clear this accumulation of grounded Beverleys. The trouble was said to be caused by the RAF not using the oil which the engine manfacturers had recommended. This was Aeroshell 100U oil but the Air Ministry had been reluctant to use this oil since just about every other piston engine in the RAF used 'straight' Aeroshell 100 oil and the Ministry wished to standardize on that particular oil.

In the event, the Beverley was cleared for using 100U oil and although additional filters were eventually fitted to stop oil cooler sludging, most experts agreed that the Aeroshell 100U oil, with its sludge-dispersant properties, cured the oil cooler sludging problem.

The Beverley Centaurus engines also suffered from mixture problems caused by deposits of carbon on the sleeve and cylinder ports restricting the amount of air that could be drawn into the cylinders, thus causing a rich mixture. Richness did not adversely affect performance in temperate climates, but had serious effects when operating in the tropics. The trouble could be cured by an adjustment to the fuel

Resourceful (and dangerous)! Master Engineer Bill Binfield uses the freight bay-to-boom ladder and a Hadrami Bedouin Legion truck to get to a troublsome engine at a Hadramaut airstrip. *W. Binfield*

Single Pioneer aircraft and motor bike aboard a 34 Squadron Beverley. Note the Zip-up access staging, neatly stowed in the port clamshell door. *S. Corton*

Opposite page: **Engine change the hard way. On remote airstrips, there was never a crane available and a wing-mounted gantry with block and tackle had to be used. This had to be manhandled on to the mainplane - no job for weaklings. This photograph shows the gantry being used together with Zip-up engine access staging.** *J. Knight*

injector; this needed the attentions of an experienced and skilled tradesman and caused a great deal of work for the hard-pressed engine fitters. Other troublesome faults included frequent failure of exhaust pipes due to vibration, and failure of the dynafocal engine mountings. These two faults were extremely difficult to rectify, the parts concerned being very inaccessible and requiring a multitude of special tools designed to reach the many awkwardly situated nuts and bolts.

Faults with the propeller reverse pitch electrical circuit were also very common. Again, these were frequently caused by vibration and ingestion of abrasive matter and were frequently located in the propeller itself which necessitated a propeller change - more work for the long-suffering engine fitters.

The combustion heaters, which provided hot air for anti-icing and space heating, gave a lot of trouble initially, but as the technicians became more experienced with their complexities, the heaters seemed to give less and less trouble. At first, both aircrew and ground technicians were highly suspicious of the combustion heaters which burnt fuel from the aircraft's tanks, the fuel, for the heaters fitted in the fuselage, actually being piped into the aircraft interior. Suspicions regarding the fire hazards of the heaters however, turned out to be quite unfounded and the heaters eventually became very reliable and trouble-free.

Soon after the Beverley came into service, side-tracking equipment for hangaring the aeroplane became available. Since the wing span of the Beverley was substantially greater than the width of the doorway of the standard hangar, the side-tracking gear enabled the aircraft to be hangared sideways. Lack of headroom presented a further problem but this was overcome by raising the nose in order to lower the fins to enable them to pass under the lowest parts of the hangar roof trusses. The aircraft was towed into position so that each set of main wheels mounted a low-slung wheeled platform, the wheels of which were disposed at 180° to those of the air-

Starboard wing crawlway looking inboard from No.3 (starboard inner) engine accessory bay. There was just sufficient room to sit or kneel. *Author*

Accessory bay of No.3 engine showing accessory gearbox. This drove a generator, an alternator and a hydraulic pump. As in the crawlways, there was only just enough room to sit or kneel. *Author*

Roll-out after servicing. side-tracking skates. *R. Honeybone*

Removing a Beverley from the side-tracking skates. *R. Honeybone*

103
ROYAL AIR FORCE
TRANSPORT COMMAND
V

ROYAL AIR FORCE
TRANSPORT COMMAND
V

craft. A trolley was then positioned under the nose and an electric motor (with a hand-operated back-up gear) drove the elevating mechanism. With the aircraft now positioned in a nose-up attitude and with the main wheels on the side-tracking 'skates', it was possible to tow it sideways into a hangar. Once inside the hangar, the aircraft was positioned so that the fins were under the highest parts of the roof trusses. The nose could then be lowered to the ground. Hangaring such a large aeroplane was a complicated procedure which demanded precision team-work from all those involved in the operation. Cliff Lowe, ex-MT driver who drove refuelling tankers and the tractors that towed the Beverleys, writes: 'At Abingdon, there was quite a slope from the perimeter track into "E" hangar and when towing the Beverley down that slope, you suddenly remembered that you were hooked on to a hell of a big "trailer".

Ray Honeybone, ex-chief technician engine fitter, writes of an interesting experience concerned with a Beverley which had force-landed at Kinloss in Scotland with severe vibration and overheating on one of its engines.

'We collected tools and a few spares and loaded them together with a Giraffe ladder on to another aircraft and took off from our base at Dishforth. On arrival at Kinloss we found the flight engineer dismantling the injection carburetter but a quick look around the outside of the engine revealed an ominous brown burnt patch on the cowling. The injector was hastily reassembled and attention was diverted to the part of the engine under the scorched cowling to reveal a sparking plug which had been blown out of its cylinder. The failure seemed to have been caused by the plug vibrating loose causing burning gases from the cylinder to escape with a "torching" effect, thus burning the adjacent area. After a while, the heat and vibration had destroyed the threads in the plug hole, thus allowing the plug to blow out.

'There was nothing we could do to rectify the fault on the spot, as clearly a new junk-head (cylinder head) was required, so after consulting the "book", the captain announced that we would do a three-engine take-off and return to base. We loaded up all our gear, climbed aboard, and after an uneventful take-off, we two ground crew settled down in the boom for a kip during the forty minutes or so flight to Dishforth. We were awakened by the navigator, almost it seemed, as soon as we had dozed off and we both thought what a quick trip that had been. However, the navigator soon enlightened us with the knowledge that another engine had been shut down due to overheating and vibration, and that we were diverting to Dyce airport at Aberdeen. All this occurred in the early days of the Beverley and I don't think that a great deal of two-engined flying had been done, and as we were flying over some rather rocky, inhospitable looking hills at that time, our trepidation of two-engined flight in a Beverley was not exactly dispelled. But we were soon descending into Dyce where Wing Commander Rixon made a perfect landing much to everyone's relief.

'After we had landed, a look at the second failed engine revealed - yes, you've guessed it - another brown scorch mark on the cowling caused by another plug blowing out. Again, there was little we could do apart from signalling base requesting the necessary spares. We spent the night in the aircraft and discovered that one of the fittings for the paratroop seats seemed to have been specially designed for opening beer and Coke bottles.

'The spares turned up next morning and we soon fixed the two engines and returned to base when we learnt of other similar failures. Investigations revealed that the master gauge, by means of which the special break-back torque spanners for the sparking plugs were set, was faulty. Strangely enough, this problem also occurred at other Beverley units. As a result of this spate of "plug-blowing", torque spanners and particularly the master gauges were checked more frequently and a set procedure established for tightening sparking plugs. The procedure was that a sparking plug was screwed into the cylinder head until the sealing washer just seated, then the plug was slackened and retightened to the correct torque. There was nothing new about this: before torque spanners were introduced, spark plugs were fitted to Bristol engines in precisely the same manner - screwing in the plug until finger-tight, slackening half a turn and then retightening.'

This was one of the many problems encountered by the hard-pressed engine technicians. However, this was a problem in which good old-fashioned engineering know-how provided the solution.

Al Ussher recalled his days when he worked as an airframe fitter doing major overhauls on Beverleys. He writes:

'I helped to complete the last major servicing of a Beverley to be undertaken at Dishforth. This was prior to the majors being carried out at St Athan. As far as I remember, most of my time was spent replacing the windows in the boom and refitting the interior trim.

'At St. Athan, I was on a mainplane reskinning team for some time. Another job I recall was changing elevators, a task which demanded some ingenuity. A tall Giraffe servicing platform with an extension eyelet was employed, the elevator being lowered and raised by a rope which passed through the eyelet and was controlled by half a dozen or so people positioned down the steps of the Giraffe holding the rope. It was a bit unnerving, despite wearing a safety harness, trying to align the hinge bearings as the elevator swung into position.'

This was a good example of how the ground staff coped with 'altitude' problems when servicing the Beverley, and again illustrates how fit and agile these technicians had to be. There was no place for weaklings in a Beverley servicing team.

Ground staff of 84 Squadron having a party. Note the empty beer cans stacked to form an '84'. *S. Hitchen*

Chapter Nine

The Bristol Centaurus Engine

It is surprising that in the many books written about aeroplanes, such small coverage is given to the engines that powered them and made them famous. Although a lot of technical jargon about pistons, crankshafts and connecting rods does little to improve the readability of a book, it is nevertheless felt that the engines that powered an aeroplane about which a book has been written, deserves some space, albeit small. This is particularly so of the Bristol Centaurus engine, the last in a long line of famous radial sleeve valve aero engines manufactured by the Bristol Aeroplane Company. The Late Walter R. Royce of Rolls-Royce Bristol, formerly of the Engine Division of the Bristol Aeroplane Company, and ex-Bristol representative who served with Beverley units both in the UK and overseas, kindly contributed the following brief history of Bristol sleeve valve engines, with particular reference to the Centaurus. He writes:

'The single sleeve valve, with reciprocating and rotary motion, was invented independently by Peter Burt of the Argyll Company, and a Canadian, James McCollum. A motorcycle embodying this feature was built by Messrs Barr and Stroud in the 1920s. Following development work on single-cylinder sleeve valve engines, Bristols built a nine-cylinder radial engine incorporating the sleeve valve principle. This was known as the Perseus and had a swept volume of 26.8 litres. The Perseus was first run in 1932 and was flown in a Bristol Bulldog at the 1934 Hendon Air Pageant. In 1937, it became the world's first sleeve valve aero-engine to enter service when it was installed in a Vickers Vildebeest.

'A Perseus 12 powered the Blackburn Skua which in September 1939 became the first aircraft to shoot down an enemy, a Dornier, in the Second World War. The Perseus was also fitted to the Blackburn Roc and Botha; the latter unfortunately, was somewhat underpowered. The Aquila, another nine-cylinder radial sleeve valve engine, with a capacity of 15.6 litres, was also developed, and flew in the Vickers Venom at the 1936 SBAC show. This smaller engine however, never went into production.

'A fourteen-cylinder, two-row radial sleeve valve engine, with a capacity of 38.7 litres, was then developed, making its first run in 1936. This engine became known as the Hercules and many Second World War bombers and post-war multi-engined civil and military aircraft were powered by this famous engine. The Hercules is still running in surviving specimens of the French Noratlas and the Bristol Freighter. In the latter aircraft, the Hercules had an approved life of 3,000 hours between overhauls.

'A smaller version of the Hercules, the Taurus, was a fourteen-cylinder, two-row radial with a shorter stroke, giving a capacity of 25.4 litres. This engine powered the Second World War Fairey Albacore and Bristol Beaufort.

'The forerunner of the eighteen-cylinder, two-row, 53.6 litre Centaurus, as fitted to the Beverley, first ran in 1938. The Air Ministry showed little interest in this engine, as at this time, radial engines were not looked upon favourably for use in fighters. However, the success of the German FW 190 was subsequently to change this outlook. Nevertheless, early in the Second World War, the twenty-four cylinder, in-line "X" configuration Vulture, made by Rolls-Royce, was regarded as a most likely source of power for future fighters. With a capactiy of 42.48 litres, and a potential power output of 3,000 horse power, the Vulture was first installed experimentally in a Hawker Tornado.

'The Vulture suffered a number of serious failures in the twin-engined Manchester bomber, and although the problems could probably have been overcome, the Vulture and "X" configuration concept were discontinued and the Lancaster, developed from the Manchester and powered by four Merlins, came into service. As a result of the Vulture's demise, the Centaurus was installed in the Tornado, resulting in further development leading to the installation of the Centaurus 5 in the Hawker Tempest 2. Subsequently, later marks of the Centaurus were fitted to the Blackburn

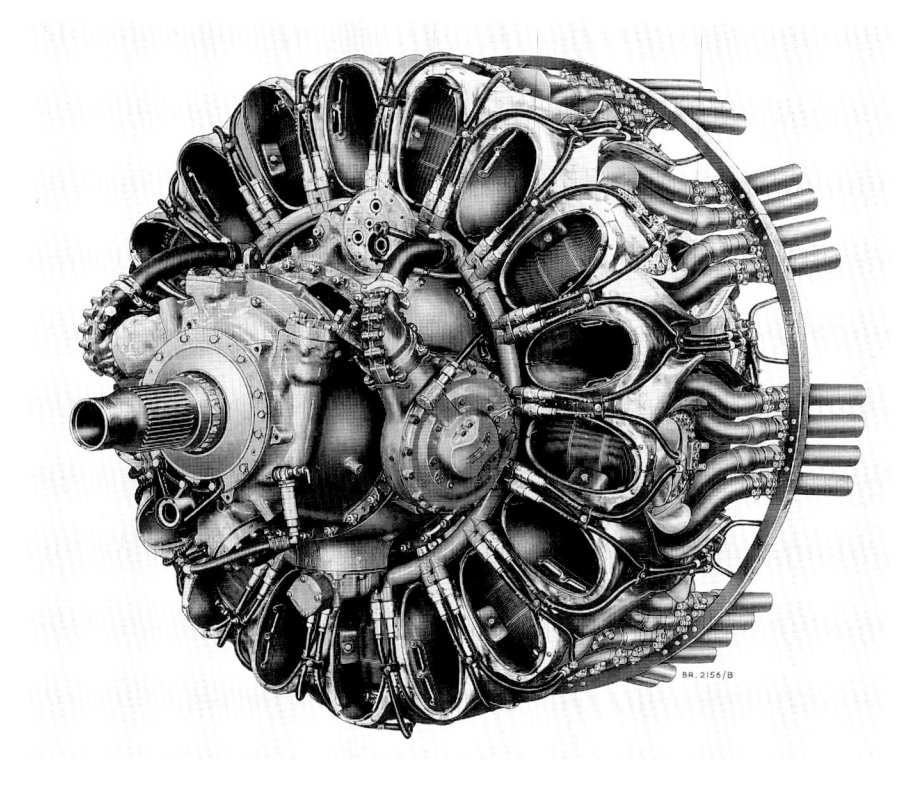

Centaurus 175 engine (uncowled) with single exhaust pipes - a big improvement on the earlier troublesome 'Y' exhaust pipes. *Rolls-Royce Aero Division*

Firebrand, the Hawker Sea Fury and the Bristol Brigand. In the Bristol Brabazon, eight Centaurus 20 engines were coupled in pairs to drive the four propellers of that massive aeroplane. The Airspeed Ambassador, used by British European Airways and called the Elizabethan by BEA, was powered by the Centaurus 661 which proved extremely reliable, being granted a life of 3,000 hours between overhauls, prior to a similar life being granted to the Hercules.

'Although the Centaurus 173, and later the 175, as fitted to the Beverley, were almost identical to the 661 as fitted to the Ambassador, its reliability was relatively poor. Possible explanations include the high cruising power settings necessary, the heavy steel-bladed propeller, and the ingress of abrasive foreign matter due to the use of reverse pitch for braking.

'In November 1956, four Centaurus 373 direct fuel injection engines were installed in a Beverley for trials. These engines would have powered the Universal Freighter, the Beverley's civil counterpart, but since the Universal failed to attract any customers, the Centaurus 373 engine was discontinued. A pity, since this engine showed great potential.

'In March 1964, the Centaurus 173 engines were modified and became known as the Centaurus 175 series. One important modification cured the problem of power loss caused by mixture becoming richer with advancing engine age. This modification increased the area of the sleeve ports by ten per cent to minimize loss of power due to excessive carbon build-up on the sides of the ports. At the same time, the injection carburettor was modified so that a fuel control mechanism, which previously tended to enrichen the mixture as it became worn, had the reverse effect. The reduction in air drawn into the cylinders due to carbon build-up on the sleeve ports, was balanced by the reduction in fuel caused by wear of the injector mechanism, thus avoiding loss of power due to rich mixture and any necessity to adjust the mixture settings during service.

'Other modifications improved the reliability of the crankshaft main bearings, replaced the troublesome "Y" exhaust pipes with much simpler single exhaust stubs, and introduced redesigned rubber bushes for the dynafocal mountings of the engine. These gave a great deal of trouble, and changing dynafocal mounting bushes was probably the most unpopular job amongst the engine technicians.'

Walter Royce was right: the dislike of changing dynafocal mounting bushes was due to the intense inaccessibility of the parts, the time-consuming nature of the job, and the fact that lifting gear had to be used for almost the entire duration of the job. When cranes were required for the many engine changes and propeller changes always being carried out on a Beverley unit, the need for long-term use of lifting tackle placed severe demands on the resources of the technical staff. It is interesting to recall that an engine with defective dynafocal mounting bushes could often be spotted with the naked eye, since the engine seemed to be sagging downwards, as indeed it invariably was. This could be confirmed by measurements and by sighting the defective engine against its (hopefully) unaffected neighbour. This apparent change in the thrust line did not seem to affect the flying characteristics of the aircraft, thus demonstrating how forgiving the Beverley could be when called upon to tolerate potentially serious defects.

It has often been said that the Centaurus 173 and 175 engines were rather unsuccessful members of the Centaurus family. Had these engines been fitted to a less demanding aircraft than the Beverley, especially a civil airliner whose engines spent most of their time at low rpm cruising power, it is certain that they would have enjoyed a far greater degree of success. The Beverley imposed the severest possible work-load on its engines, the short-haul work done so much on the rough up-country airstrips of South Arabia being perhaps the most punishing. On this type of work, in severe heat and humidity, maximum continuous cruising power at 2,400 rpm from departure airfield to destination was often necessary, with a full-power, reverse thrust landing creating a dust storm so dense that visibility was seriously impaired, being an essential feature of arrival. This sort of punishment, considered together with the humid and corrosive atmosphere in which the Beverley operated, was undoubtedly a contributory factor to the doubtful reliability of the Centaurus 173 and 175 engines.

The Bristol Belvedere twin-rotor helicopter which did yeoman service in Aden and in Borneo, also suffered poor engine reliability, especially in Aden, the dust-laden atmosphere and the tremendous demands made upon the engines being blamed for their shortcomings.

It seems a pity that the Centaurus 173 and 175 engines, the last of a long line of Bristol sleeve valve piston engines, did not acquit themselves better in the Beverley. But it must be remembered that just as no other aircraft but the Beverley could do the jobs that the Beverley was called upon to do, then no other engines but the Centaurus could have powered the Beverley, allowing it to accomplish its many near-impossible tasks. Viewed in that light, the Centaurus 173 and 175 do not appear to have done so badly; perhaps it is just as well that these engines were available to enable the Beverley to become one of the RAF's most unforgettable transport aeroplanes.

Two Centaurus 175s in full song. *J. Knight*

Chapter Ten

Where did all the Beverleys go?

For most of them, the short answer is 'into the melting pot'. However, three examples were preserved until recently, though the future of only one of these seems secure at the time of publication.

XH124 is at the RAF Museum at Hendon where gallant efforts were made to combat the ravages of corrosion. All instrumentation and other delicate equipment was removed and preserved in the Museum's stores. But the airframe had to stand outside and despite careful sealing of hatches, windows and other known places of water penetration, some water still gets in and adds to the problems of corrosion and general deterioration. XH124 has been visible not only to Museum visitors, but also a landmark for travellers on the M1 and the nearby railway. Sadly, at the end of 1989 came the news that the Museum Director had reluctantly decided that in its deteriorating state it was no longer a good advertisement for the Museum, that the funds required for its restoration and/or removal were sorely needed for other projects, and that it was therefore being offered for disposal by tender.

Further north, on Humberside, the Beverley fleet is represented by XB259. The first production Beverley ever to fly, XB259 has the distinction of also being the last Beverley ever to take to the air. After almost twenty years service with RAE Farnborough, XB259 was acquired by Court Line in late 1973, reportedly to be used for transporting spare engines for TriStar airliners. It is doubtful if XB259 was ever used for this purpose since Court Line went into liquidation shortly after acquiring the Beverley. XB259 was then bought by North Country Breweries Ltd., who entrusted the aircraft to the care of Hull Aero Club, based at Paull Airfield near Thorngumbald, Hull quite near Brough where the Beverleys were built.

David Carsberg, Editor of the *Hull Daily Mail*, described XB259's final landing, the last landing ever to be made by a Beverley: 'The Beverley touched down at Paull at approximately 1730 hours on Saturday 30th March 1974. After one low approach and overshoot, the crew brought her in for a perfect landing and with the aid of reverse thrust, the Beverley was halted in less than half the available distance of 750 yards. To the surprise of Hull Aero Club members, very little damage was done to the grass runway, the drainage of which is notoriously poor in the winter months. Thus, for the very last time, as on countless occasions in the past, was the Beverley's superb short-field perfomance demonstrated. The crew privileged to make the last Beverley flight consisted of: Squadron Leader Peter Sedgwick, captain; Flight Lieutenant Brian Peaty, co-pilot; Master Engineer John Oakes, engineer.'

XB259 remained in Hull Aero Club's care for the next seven years and the Club is to be complimented on keeping the aircraft in such good condition. On at least one occasion, they even managed to get the engines running. However, disaster struck in 1981 when the Club had to quit Paull airfield due to its lease having expired, leaving XB259 parked forlornly on its hardstanding. Although the land owner was patient, he did request that the Beverley be moved at the earliest opportunity, and the North Country Breweries, faced with the problem of moving the massive aircraft from the site, along narrow country roads, put XB259 up for sale by tender. A bid made by a Captain T. Robb of Gateshead, for an undisclosed sum, was accepted and XB259 changed hands, regrettably as it turned out since it transpired that the new owner intended to scrap the aeroplane.

Attempts were made by various bodies to save XB259 from the scrap man: a number of preservation societies were contacted, even the Imperial War Museum, but nothing came of these enquiries. At last, local night club owner Mr Francis Daly, who reportedly used to fly in Beverleys in the '60s, became involved. Mr Daly was well known locally for saving the Humber paddle steamer *Lincoln Castle* from the breaker's yard and restoring the ancient vessel for use as a floating restaurant. An article in the *Hull Daily Mail* on 22nd April quoted Mr Daly as saying: 'A team of businessmen are intending to break her (XB259) up. They were on their way to do just that, armed with the necessary tools, when I invited them to think again. They immediately said: "Put your money where your mouth is." So I gave them a number of thousands of pounds.'

Thus, by the public-spirited generosity of Mr Daly, who could not bear to see the Beverley scrapped, XB259 was saved from the scrap man. But the landowner still wanted the aircraft moved from its site and the new owner desperately sought a solution to this problem. *The Hull Daily Mail* reported Mr Daly as saying: 'Moving her could be a problem but she could even be literally wrapped in a plastic bag and floated up the river (Humber) to a new location somewhere else in the county.' However Mr Daly could not even find a new site or even a new use for the Beverley, having decided that it was too small for use as a restaurant or club. So XB259 languished on at Paull until in mid-1982, the Museum of Army Transport accepted Mr Daly's offer of the aircraft. With characteristic Army thoroughness, a team of

XH124 outside the RAF Museum.
W. J. Bushell

The final indignity. Victims of the scrapman's blowtorch. *E. Davies*

Forlorn-looking line of Beverleys awaiting disposal at Bicester. *A. Fairbairn*

Opposite **XB261 at the Southend Historic Aircraft Museum. It spent its entire service career at the A&AEE Boscombe Down.** *Southend Historic Aircraft Museum*

Nose Section of XL149 which finished its career as a static display at RAF Finningley before being broken up. The nose section is now in Newark Aircraft Museum. *P. Nops*

volunteers, assisted by the Army, British Aerospace and a number of local companies, dismantled XB259 at Paull and moved it by road to the Museum of Army Transport at Beverley, where it has been refurbished and re-erected. It has withstood the elements remarkably well and after a repaint to full aircraft standard, should last indefinitely. At the time of writing, the interior is being fitted out as an exhibition of airborne Army supply equipment. The curator of the Museum, Lieutenant Colonel Teddy Penn, and Mr Rodney Melling, retired Blackburn production engineer, are to be complimented on the workmanlike manner in which the operation has been carried out. How appropriate that the 'first and last' Beverley should be preserved for posterity in the town from which its name had been taken.

The third of the 'survivors' had a more chequered career as a museum exhibit. XB261, the third production Beverley was handed over to the A & AEE Boscombe Down by the manufacturers in March 1955 and remained with A & AEE until 1971, when it was acquired by the Southend Historic Aircraft Museum. Along with most of the Museum's aircraft, it was parked in the open and after many years of exposure to the elements, corrosion and general deterioration was very much in evidence by the time of the Museum's closure on Sunday 27th March 1983. An article in *Aeroplane Monthly* for that month noted 'It has proved impossible for the Museum's limited workforce to maintain aircraft when permanently parked outside.' The collection was put up for sale by auction on 10th May, but XB261 failed to find a buyer willing to take on the prodigious task of moving and then maintaining such a large aircraft, and the Beverley lingered at the Museum site whilst the other aircraft were slowly dispersed to their new owners.

Eventually a good samaritan came forward and the aircraft remained on the same site, which became 'Roller City'. However, corrosion had become so extensive that there was little alternative but to scrap the aircraft, in April 1989. Even so, the cockpit section has gone to the Imperial War Museum at Duxford.

One further 'chunk' of Beverley, the nose section of XL149 is at the Newark Air Museum. On its retirement it was found a home at RAF Finningley on static display, but after a few years was broken up. Newark Air Museum acquired the nose section which contains the flight deck and it was preserved inside. Sadly however, due to vandalism, the exhibit has been relegated to an 'adventure piece' for children.

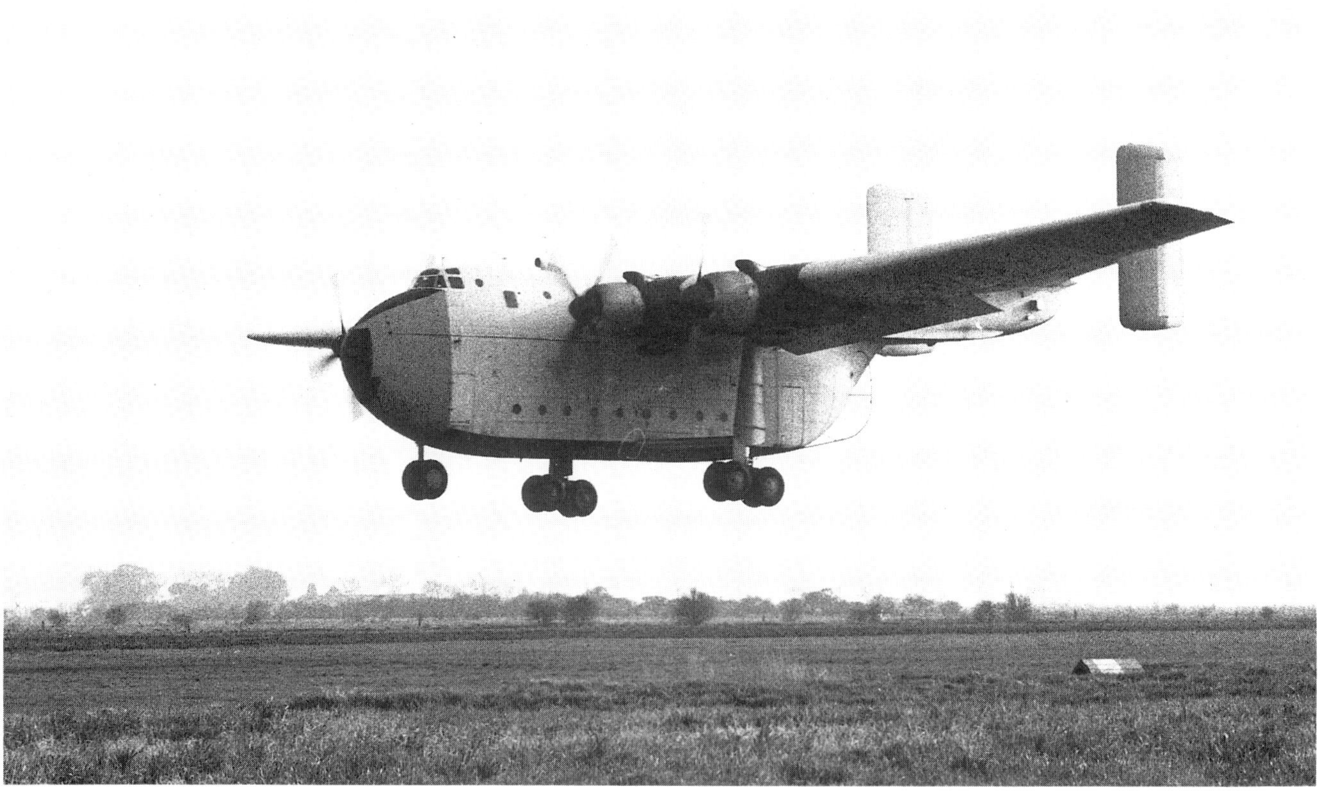

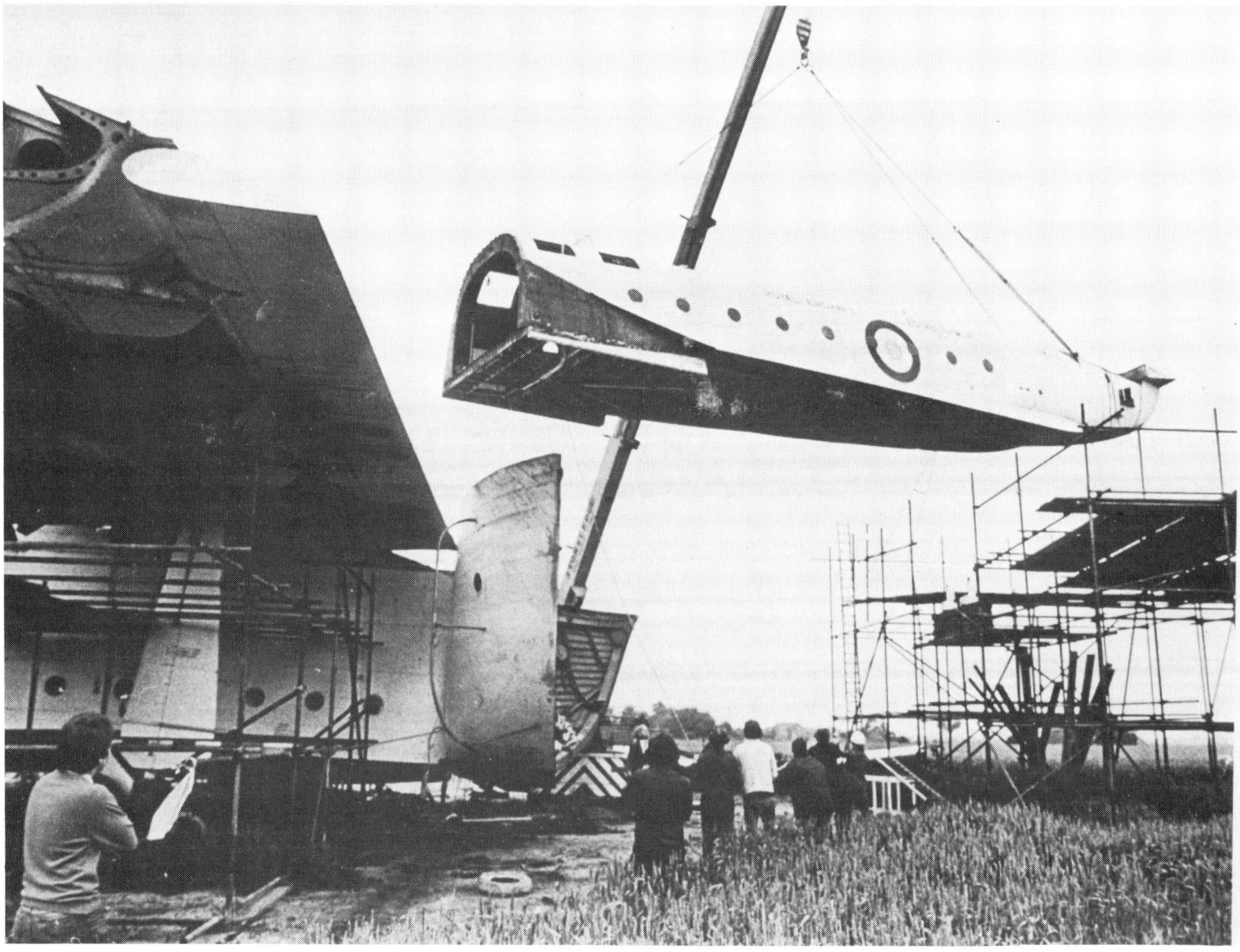

Members of 129 Field Squadron, Royal Engineers, laying track-way at the former Paull airfield in readiness for XB259's removal to the Museum of Army Transport.

XB259 awaiting re-erection outside the Museum of Army Transport at Beverley.

Restored to former glory (almost), XB259 at the Museum of Army Transport - February 1986.

Opposite: The first and the last. XB259 was the first Beverley off the production line and appropriately, was the last Beverley in service. XB259 is seen here making its last landing at Paull airfield, Hull on 30 March 1974.

Lifting the tail boom of XB259 at Paull.
All Hull Daily Mail

Historical details of the 47 Beverleys built, together with details of the two Universal Freighters follow: in the text, the following abbreviations are used: c/n — constructor's number; Aw/cn — awaiting collection; NEA — non-effective aircraft: SOC — struck off charge.

The GAL60 Universal Freighter Mark I

Built by General Aircraft Ltd. at Feltham in 1948/1949. After General Aircraft merged with Blackburns, the GAL60 was dismantled, transported to Brough and re-erected there, being allocated Constructor's No. 1000. Flew as WF320 on 20th June 1950, registered as G-AMUX, granted C of A in April 1953. After reverting to WF320, the aircraft was used extensively during Beverley development trials, particularly for supply dropping. Reduced to produce at Brough in 1958.

The GAL65/B-100 Universal Freighter Mark II

Constructor's No. (c/n) 1001, built at Brough during 1952/1953, registered as WZ889 and first flew on 14 June 1953. Registered G-AMVW, then reverted to WZ889 and used during Beverley development trials. Took part in SBAC shows at Farnborough in 1953 and 1954. Modified to full Beverley standard c.1955. Reduced to produce at Brough in 1958 after being unsuccessfully offered for sale.

Blackburn and General Aircraft Co.Ltd. B-101 Beverley C Mk.1
(47 built)

Contract No. 8631 for Serials XB259 to XB269 and XB283 to XB291.

XB259 c/n 1002, the first and the last production Beverley to fly. First flew 29.1.55, retained by Blackburns for trials. Allocated civil registration G-AOAI. Carried out handling trials including RATOG tests with Napier Scarab rockets. Delivered to RAE Farnborough as XB259 and remained with RAE until early 1970s when acquired by Court Line. Acquired by North Country Breweries Ltd. when Court Line collapsed and cared for by Hull Aero Club at Paull Airfield. Sold for scrap but bought back from merchant by local entrepreneur Mr Francis Daly. Acquired by the Museum of Army Transport in 1982 and placed on exhibition in the Museum at Beverley.

XB260 c/n 1003, first flew 30.3.55. Aw/cn 13.6.55. Retained by Blackburns for manufacturer's trials. C of A issued 22.9.55 and civil registration G-AOEK allocated. Flew on Fahoud oil drilling equipment airlift in Oman. Delivered to A & AEE Boscombe Down for tropical trials at Idris 1956 followed by winterization trials at Edmonton later. To Brough 27.9.57 for mods and delivered to 27 MU 21.7.58. To 53 Squadron on 14.8.58 coded 'O' but returned to 27 MU on 12.11.58. To Brough for mods on 2.1.59, returning to 27 MU on 12.3.59, then to 48 Squadron Beverley Flight on 20.4.59 coded 'U'. Transferred to 34 Squadron on 1.10.60, later re-coded '260'. Transferred to 389 MU Seletar 1.1.68, SOC on 14.2.68 and scrapped.

XB261 c/n 1004, first flew 5.7.55. Aw/cn 20.7.55. To A & AEE Boscombe Down for trials and acceptance tests (sold to MoA 20.3.59) and became A & AEE's permanent Beverley. Trials included paratrooping and most forms of supply dropping including trials in ultra low-level airdropping (ULLA). Acquired by Southend Historic Aircraft Museum in 1971. Broken up 4.89.

XB262 c/n 1005, first flew 8.7.55. Aw/cn 20.7.55. To A & AEE for acceptance tests, then to Idris on 5.8.55 for tropical trials. Winterization trials at Edmonton 12.56 to 8.57. Appeared at SBAC show in 1957. To Brough on 23.10.57 for fitting to production standard, then to 27 MU on 11.8.58. Back to Brough for further mods 12.3.59, returning to 27 MU on 8.4.59. To 48 Squadron Beverley Flight on 5.6.59 coded 'W'. Transferred to 34 Squadron on 1.10.60 still coded 'W', later re-coded '262'. SOC at Seletar 23.10.67 and scrapped.

XB263 c/n 1006, first flew 26.8.55. Aw/cn 6.12.55. Appeared at SBAC show in 1955, then delivered to RAF Handling Squadron 19.12.55 for trials. Returned to Brough 24.3.56. To A & AEE 30.4.56 for navigational equipment and radio trials. Returned to Brough for mods 3.10.56, then back to A & AEE 15.3.57. To 47 Squadron 27.9.57 coded 'K'. Back to Brough for further mods 7.3.59 returning Abingdon 1.5.59. Birdstrike at Abingdon 21.11.60 and repaired on site by 71 MU, returning to service 28.11.60. Transferred to 30 Squadron 7.11.61 still coded 'K'. To Hawarden for mods 31.1.63, then to 47 Squadron 21.6.63 becoming 'A'. To 27 MU 18.1.67 and SOC 30.1.67. Sold for scrap to BKL Alloys 5.9.67.

XB259, the first and last production Beverley to fly. Opposite: XB261, A&AEE's permanent Beverley. both W.J. Bushill

XB264 c/n 1007, first flew 7.11.55. Aw/cn 19.2.56. To 47 Squadron 19.3.56 coded 'C'. To Brough for mods 1.2.59 returning Abingdon 17.3.59. To Brough again 21.7.60, returning Abingdon 1.11.60. To Hawarden for mods 5.1.62, returning Abingdon 2.5.62. Transferred to 34 Squadron 20.2.63, becoming '264'. SOC at Seletar 1.10.67 and scrapped.

XB265 c/n 1008, first flew 26.2.56. Aw/cn 12.3.56. Delivered to 47 Squadron 12.3.56 and coded 'A', the first Beverley to enter squadron service. To Brough for mods 12.5.59 returning Abingdon 4.8.59. Back to Brough for Cat 3 repairs 5.6.61, returning Abingdon 29.6.61. To Hawarden for mods 21.1.63. Transferred to 242 OCU 17.5.63 coded 'W'. Cat 5 for main spar cracks 10.10.66. Re-Cat 4 for flight to 27 MU 3.11.66. Re-Cat 5 8.2.67 and sold for scrap 6.6.67.

XB266 c/n 1009, first flew 23.11.55. Aw/cn 23.1.56. To A & AEE 23.1.56, tropical trials at Idris 6.56 to 7.56. To Brough for modification to production standard 25.2.59 returning A & AEE 17.9.59. To 84 Squadron 4.2.60 coded 'X', returning 27 MU 8.7.60, then to Abingdon Wing becoming 'E'. Returned to 84 Squadron 4.11.61 and re-coded 'V'. Overhauled and camouflaged at 32 MU 19.10.65 to 14.1.66 and delivered to 30 Squadron 1.2.66 coded 'E'. Transferred to 84 Squadron 21.2.67, returning 27 MU 3.5.67. Declared NEA 4.5.67 and sold for scrap to BKL Alloys 27.11.67.

XB267 c/n 1010, first flew 30.12.55. Aw/cn 14.3.56. To 47 Squadron 14.3.56 coded 'B', then to 53 Squadron still coded 'B'. To Brough for mods 9.8.61 returning Abingdon 27.2.62. Remained with 47 Squadron after 53 disbanded. Repaired for Cat 3 damage Abingdon 3.64 to 4.64. To 27 MU 15.11.67 and declared NEA. Sold for scrap to BKL Alloys 25.9.69.

XB268 c/n 1011, first flew 14.3.56. Aw/cn 23.3.56. To 47 Squadron 23.3.56 coded 'D'. To Brough for repair of Cat 4 damage 17.2.59 returning Abingdon 16.7.59. To Hawarden for mods 27.9.62 returning Abingdon 5.3.63. Crashed at El Adem 13.4.63. SOC 17.4.63.

XB269 c/n 1012, first flew 22.3.56. Aw/cn 28.3.56. To 47 Squadron 3.4.56 coded 'F'. To Brough for mods 22.2.60 returning Abingdon 14.6.60. To Hawarden for mods 20.3.62 returning Abingdon 22.6.62. Remained with 47 Squadron at Abingdon when 53 Squadron disbanded on 28.6.63. Loaned to MoA 1.5.64 returning 47 Squadron 28.8.64. To Air Transport Development Unit Abingdon 1.11.67. To 27 MU 6.12.67. Declared NEA 7.12.67. Sold for scrap 25.9.69.

XB283 c/n 1013, first flew 17.4.56. Aw/cn 27.4.56. To 47 Squadron 30.4.56 coded 'G'. Slightly damaged in flying accident 3.12.58 whilst on loan to 84 Squadron. Re-Cat 4 31.12.58 and sent to 131 MU Khormaksar 23.2.59. Returned to UK 2.3.59, then to Brough for repair 13.3.59. To Abingdon Wing 11.1.60. To Hawarden for mods 20.8.63. To 34 Squadron 17.1.64 coded '283'. To 389 MU Seletar 1.1.68, SOC 14.2.68.

XB284 c/n 1014, first flew 7.5.56. Aw/cn 22.5.56. To 47 Squadron 22.5.56 coded 'H'. To Brough for mods 23.7.59, then on loan to A & AEE 16.11.59 for radio compass trials, returning Abingdon 15.2.60. To Brough 22.4.60, back to Abingdon 9.5.60, returning Brough 15.9.61 on loan to MoA. Returned Abingdon 17.11.61. To A & AEE for trials on extractor parachute hang-ups following accident to XB289. To Hawarden 5.3.63 for mods returning 47 Squadron, still coded 'H' 9.7.63. Transferred to 84 Squadron 1.7.67 returning 27 MU 18.9.67. Declared NEA 18.9.67. Sold for scrap to Bushells Ltd. 7.1.69.

XB285 c/n 1015, first flew 25.5.56. Aw/cn 6.6.56. To 47 Squadron 6.6.56 coded 'J'. To Brough for mods 1.5.59 returning Abingdon 16.9.59. To Hawarden for mods 16.11.62. To A & AEE 3.4.63 returning Abingdon 17.10.63 re-coded 'C'. To A & AEE 11.9.64 for VOR and Elliot VHF mods, returning Abingdon 2.7.65 still coded 'C'. To 71 MU 19.10.67, declared NEA 12.11.67. Sold for scrap 8.1.69.

XB286 c/n 1016, first flew 13.6.56. Aw/cn 25.6.56. To 47 Squadron 25.6.56, then to 53 Squadron 2.7.56 coded 'S'. Cat 3 accident 24.1.61 due to loss of hatch in flight, repaired at Abingdon by 71 MU returning to service 3.3.61. To Hawarden for mods 31.1.62 returning Abingdon 25.5.62. Remained with 47 Squadron when 53 Squadron disbanded. Transferred to 242 OCU 17.1.64 still coded 'S' but re-coded 'Z' 11.6.64. Transferred to 47 Squadron 17.2.67 when OCU flight disbanded, still coded 'Z'. To 27 MU 14.11.67, declared NEA same date. Sold for scrap to BKL Alloys 25.9.69.

XB287 c/n 1017, first flew 4.7.56. Aw/cn 19.7.56. To 53 Squadron 24.7.56 coded 'T'. To Brough for mods 16.2.59 returning Abingdon 2.4.59. To Hawarden for mods 10.5.62, returning Abingdon 27.8.62. Remained with 47 Squadron when 53 Squadron disbanded. Loaned to MoA 23.8.65, returning Abingdon 9.9.65. Loaned to 84 Squadron 7.10.66, returning UK 6.11.66. To 27 MU 10.11.67, declared NEA same date. Sold for scrap to BKL Alloys 27.9.69.

XB288 c/n 1018, first flew 3.8.56. Aw/cn 31.7.56. To 53 Squadron 6.8.56 coded 'U'. To Brough for mods 1.9.60, returning Abingdon 15.12.60. To Hawarden for mods 25.5.62, returning Abingdon 24.9.62. Remained with 47 Squadron when 53 Squadron disbanded. To 71 MU 19.10.67, declared NEA 12.11.67. Sold for scrap 8.1.69. Hulk still in the yard of Fred Ford at Worminghall, Bucks, 1988.

XB289 c/n 1019, first flew 21.8.56. Aw/cn 18.9.56. Appeared at SBAC show 1956. To 53 Squadron 20.9.56 coded 'V'. To Brough for mods 2.10.60, returning Abingdon 29.3.61. Cat 3 flying accident 26.3.62 when dropping one-ton containers, one container damaged rear fuselage. Repaired on-site at Abingdon by 71 MU. Remained with 47 Squadron when 53 Squadron disbanded. To Brough for mods 5.11.63 returning Abingdon 11.3.64. To 34 Squadron 4.4.64 coded '289'. To 389 MU 1.1.68, SOC 14.2.68 and scrapped at Seletar.

XB290 c/n 1020, first flew 7.9.56. Aw/cn 27.9.56. To 53 Squadron 2.10.56 coded 'W'. To 103 MU 23.7.58 following minor ground accident, returning Abingdon 1.8.58. Transferred to 242 OCU 14.6.62 still coded 'W'. To Hawarden for mods 14.5.63 then to 47 Squadron 1.10.63 and re-coded 'X'. Formation flypast with XB269 over Upavon en route to 27 MU on 6.12.67. Declared NEA 7.12.67, sold for scrap to BKL Alloys 25.3.70.

XB291 c/n 1021, first flew 3.10.56. Aw/cn 18.10.56. To 53 Squadron 25.10.56 coded 'X'. To Brough for mods 14.6.60 returning Abingdon 26.7.60. To Hawarden for mods 30.9.63, then transferred to 34 Squadron 18.2.64 coded '291'. To 389 MU 1.1.68. SOC 14.2.68 and scrapped at Seletar.

Contract No. 11153 for Serials XH116 to XH124

XH116 c/n 1022, first flew 24.10.56. Aw/cn 6.11.56. To 53 Squadron 8.11.56 coded 'Y'. To Brough for mods 10.5.60, returning Abingdon 23.5.60. To Hawarden for mods 15.6.63, then transferred to 34 Squadron 3.12.63 coded '116'. Cat 3 taxying accident 29.10.65. Returned to service after repairs 15.12.65. SOC at Seletar 1.10.67 and scrapped.

XH117 c/n 1023, first flew 7.11.56. Aw/cn 21.11.56. To 53 Squadron coded 'Z' 23.11.56. Crashed at Drayton, near Abingdon 5.3.57, SOC same date.

XH118 c/n 1024, first flew 3.12.56. Aw/cn 19.12.56. To 30 Squadron 4.4.57 coded 'A'. Crashed at Beihan, South Arabia 4.2.58, SOC 18.2.58.

XH119 c/n 1025, first flew 3.1.57. Aw/cn 16.1.57. To 27 MU 17.1.57, then to 30 Squadron 5.4.57 coded 'B'. Cat 3 after engine fire at Azaibah, Muscat 2.2.59, repaired by 131MU returning to service 25.2.59. To Hawarden for mods 17.7.62, then to Abingdon 7.11.62. To Eastleigh to rejoin 30 Squadron 16.11.62 still coded 'B'. To 32 MU 4.1.66 for refurbishing, returning 30 Squadron, still coded 'B' 6.6.66. To 27 MU 23.3.67. Declared NEA 29.3.67 and sold for scrap to BKL Alloys 3.1.68.

XH120 c/n 1026, first flew 18.1.57. Aw/cn 30.1.57. To 27 MU 6.2.57, then to 30 Squadron coded 'C' 7.5.57. Returned 27 MU 13.4.60 and transferred to 34 Squadron 10.12.60 coded 'X'. Returned UK 20.2.63 and to Hawarden for mods 28.3.63. To 30 Squadron 19.8.63 re-coded 'H'. To Hong Kong for refurbishing by Hong Kong Aircraft Engineering Company 28.1.67. Transferred to 84 Squadron 26.6.67. To 27 MU 18.9.67, declared NEA same date. Sold for scrap to Bushells Ltd. 7.1.69.

XH121 c/n 1027, first flew 21.2.57. Aw/cn 8.3.57. To 53 Squadron coded 'Z'. To Brough for mods 7.8.59 returning Abingdon 16.2.60 and again to Brough for mods, returning Abingdon 8.7.60. To Hawarden for mods 25.7.62, returning Abingdon 7.12.62. Transferred to 84 Squadron 18.12.62 still coded 'Z'. To Hong Kong for refurbishing by Hong Kong Aircraft Engineering Company 25.5.66, returning 84 Squadron 9.10.66. To 27 MU 18.9.67, declared NEA same date. Sold for scrap to Bushells Ltd. 7.1.69.

XH122 c/n 1028, first flew 13.3.57. Aw/cn 21.3.57. To 30 Squadron 27.3.57 coded 'D'. To Brough for mods 16.4.59, returning 30 Squadron 30.6.59. Cat 3 26.10.59 at Dijon for minor damage, repaired on site by 71 MU, returning 30 Squadron 5.2.60. To Hawarden for mods 6.9.62, returning 30 Squadron 8.2.63 still coded 'D'. To Hong Kong for refurbishing and camouflaging by Hong Kong Aircraft Engineering Company 15.9.66, rejoining 30 Squadron 21.1.67. Transferred 84 Squadron 27.7.67. To 27 MU via Abingdon 6.10.67 and declared NEA same date. Retained at Bicester for Army Air Portability training, as Ground Instructional Airframe No.8045M. Scrapped in 1971. Recognisable parts still lying in scrapyard near Bicester in 1986.

XH123 c/n 1029, first flew 21.3.57. Aw/cn 24.4.57. To 27 MU 25.4.57, then to 30 Squadron 6.6.57 coded 'F'. Loaned to 84 Squadron 21.5.59, returning 30 Squadron 31.7.59. To Hawarden for mods 12.7.63, returning 30 Squadron 25.11.63 re-coded 'C'. Cat 3 6.2.64 after birdstrike, returned to service 20.5.64. Transferred to 47 Squadron 3.5.66 and re-coded 'N'. To 71 MU 6.10.67 and declared NEA same date. Sold for scrap 8.3.68.

XH124 c/n 1030, first flew 1.4.57. Aw/cn 30.4.57. To 27 MU 1.5.57, then to 30 Squadron 2.7.57 coded 'G'. Loaned to 84 Squadron 21.5.59, returning 30 Squadron 31.7.59 still coded 'G'. To 60 MU 12.3.62 for wing re-skinning, returning 30 Squadron 12.9.62. To 32 MU for refurbishing and camouflaging 14.12.64. To 242 OCU 12.3.65, transferred to 47 Squadron 2.3.67 when OCU flight disbanded. To 27 MU 4.4.67. Displayed at Abingdon for Royal Review of RAF 6.68. To Hendon 19.6.68 for display at RAF Museum as Ground Instructional Airframe No. 8025M.

Contract No. 12264 for Serials XL130 to XL132 and XL148 to XL152.

XL130 c/n 1031, first flew 27.4.57. Aw/cn 22.5.57. To 27 MU 30.5.57, then to 30 Squadron 22.7.57 coded 'H'. To 60 MU 13.2.58, returning 30 Squadron 18.2.58. Transferred to 242 OCU 26.7.60 still coded 'H'. To 60 MU for refurbishing 7.4.64, returning 242 OCU 30.5.64 and re-coded 'Y'. To Abingdon 2.67 when OCU flight disbanded, then to 30 Squadron 9.3.67, still coded 'Y'. Transferred to 84 Squadron 15.7.67. To 71 MU 9.11.67, declared NEA 18.11.67. Sold for scrap to BKL Alloys 29.8.69.

XL131 c/n 1032, first flew 23.5.57. Aw/cn 13.6.57. To 27 MU 19.6.57, then to 30 Squadron 9.8.57 coded 'J', later re-coded 'C'. To Brough for mods 12.3.59, returning 30 Squadron 17.4.59. Damaged in flight 22.9.61 by time bomb planted at Kuwait, flown back to UK for repair by Blackburns, returning 30 Squadron 13.7.62. To Hawarden for mods 6.12.63, then to 47 Squadron 1.5.64 and re-coded 'L'. To 71 MU 19.10.67, declared NEA 22.10.67. Sold for scrap to BKL Alloys 29.8.69.

XL132 c/n 1033, first flew 11.5.57. Aw/cn 28.6.57. To 27 MU 2.7.57, then to 242 OCU 27.8.57 coded 'Z'. Crashed into Chichester harbour 17.5.62 after uncontrollable fire in No.3 engine which fell out. SOC 18.5.62.

XL148 c/n 1034, first flew 8.7.57. Aw/cn 24.7.57. To 27 MU 26.7.57, then to 242 OCU 25.9.57 coded 'Y'. To 60 MU for refurbishing returning 242 OCU 7.10.64 and re-coded 'U'. To 30 Squadron 10.3.67 still coded 'U'. To 27 MU 18.9.67 and declared NEA same date. Sold for scrap to BKL Alloys 25.3.70.

XL149 c/n 1035, first flew 15.7.57. Aw/cn 6.8.57. To 27 MU 9.8.57, then to 242 OCU 1.11.57 coded 'X'. To 32 MU 28.10.64 for refurbishing and camouflaging. To 84 Squadron 8.2.65 coded 'X' then to 30 Squadron 14.8.67 still coded 'X'. To 27 MU 18.9.67 and declared NEA same date. To Finningley 6.11.67 for static display as Ground Instructional Airframe No. 7988M. Broken up in 1977, nose section including flight deck acquired by Newark Air Museum and exhibited there.

XB269 in heavy drop role, rear doors removed on finals. *A. Fairbairn*

Opposite: **XM104, 34 Squadron's rogue aircraft, pictured here at Katmandu.** *J. Parsons*

XL150 c/n 1036, first flew 2.8.57. Aw/cn 17.9.57. To A & AEE 17.9.57 for UHF trials, then to Brough for mods 1.9.59, returning to A & AEE 31.3.60 for heavy dropping trials. To 27 MU 24.1.61, delivered to 84 Squadron 7.2.61, returning 27 MU 17.8.61. To 47 Squadron 16.1.62 coded 'K'. To 32 MU 2.12.65 for refurbishing and camouflaging. To 34 Squadron 25.3.66. Crashed in Johore 90 miles north of Seletar 15.12.67. SOC 21.12.67.

XL151 c/n 1037, first flew 11.9.57. Aw/cn 29.9.57. Loaned to A & AEE 2.10.57. To 27 MU 10.12.57, then to 47 Squadron 20.1.58 coded 'R' later coded 'L'. To Brough 9.4.59 for mods returning Abingdon 12.5.59. Heavy landing damage 29.6.59, to Brough for repairs 23.7.59. To 27 MU 11.2.60, returning 47 Squadron 26.2.60 still coded 'L'. To 27 MU 5.3.60, then to 84 Squadron 19.8.60 still coded 'L'. Crashed into high ground north of Aden during night search for missing light aircraft 10.10.60. SOC 11.10.60.

XL152 c/n 1038, first flew 27.9.57. Aw/cn 23.10.57. To 27 MU 25.10.57, delivered 30 Squadron 12.2.58 coded 'A'. To 60 MU 8.11.64 for refurbishing, returning 30 Squadron 8.12.64 and re-coded 'J'. To 27 MU 8.9.67, declared NEA 11.9.67. Sold for scrap to BKL Alloys 25.3.70.

Contract No. 13088 for Serials XM103 to XM112

XM103 c/n 1039, first flew 23.10.57. Aw/cn 6.11.57. To 27 MU 8.11.57 then delivered 242 OCU 22.5.58. To 103 MU 24.7.58 for repair to damage caused in ground accident, returning 242 OCU 3.11.58. Transferred 30 Squadron 11.11.58 coded 'K'. To Brough for mods 20.1.59, returning 30 Squadron 11.3.59. To 242 OCU 6.4.59 coded 'V'. Battery exploded in flight 24.5.61 causing Cat 3 damage. Repaired on site by Blackburns, returning 242 OCU 8.9.61. To 32 MU 8.3.65 for refurbishing and camouflaging. Delivered 84 Squadron 23.5.65 coded 'J'. To 71 MU 15.11.67, declared NEA 18.11.67. Sold for scrap to BKL Alloys 29.8.69.

XM104 c/n 1040, first flew 8.11.57. Aw/cn 28.11.57. To 27 MU 29.11.57, then delivered 30 Squadron 23.7.58. To Brough for mods 3.12.58, then to 27 MU 14.1.59. Delivered to 48 Squadron Beverley Flight 13.2.59, transferring to 34 Squadron 1.10.60 coded 'P', later re-coded '104' after refurbishing at Hong Kong by Hong Kong Aircraft Engineering Company. To 389 MU 1.1.68, SOC 14.2.68 and scrapped at Seletar.

XM105 c/n 1041, first flew 29.11.57. Aw/cn 19.12.57. To 27 MU 19.12.57 then delivered 53 Squadron 23.7.58 coded 'E'. To Brough for mods 7.11.58, returning 53 Squadron 19.12.58 and re-coded 'P'. Remained at Abingdon with 47 Squadron when 53 Squadron disbanded in 1963. To 60 MU for refurbishing 1.3.64, then to 30 Squadron 6.8.64 coded 'A'. To 27 MU 12.9.67, declared NEA same date. Sold for scrap to BKL Alloys 25.9.69.

XM106 c/n 1042, first flew 20.12.57. Aw/cn 8.1.58. To 27 MU 13.1.58 then to Brough for mods 3.3.58, returning 27 MU 18.4.58. Delivered 84 Squadron 5.6.58 coded 'R'. To 27 MU 28.4.60 returning 84 Squadron 18.7.60 and re-coded 'X'. To 32 MU 25.1.65 for refurbishing and camouflaging, returning 84 Squadron 16.4.65 and re-coded 'S'. Blown up by land mine planted on airstrip at Habilayne in Radfan while taxying 21.6.67. SOC 31.10.67.

XM107 c/n 1043, first flew 3.1.58. Aw/cn 29.1.58. To 27 MU 3.2.58 returning to Brough for mods 4.3.58. Back to 27 MU 24.5.58, then delivered 84 Squadron 6.6.58 coded 'S'. To Brough for mods 25.1.60 returning 84 Squadron 23.5.60 still coded 'S'. To 32 MU 10.4.65 for refurbishing and camouflaging returning 84 Squadron 16.7.65 and re-coded 'P'. Declared Cat 5 (flyable) due to wing skin damage and delivered to 27 MU 29.3.67. Declared NEA same date and sold for scrap to J.Bailey 1.11.67.

XM108 c/n 1044, first flew 5.2.58. Aw/cn 26.2.58. To 27 MU 11.4.58 then delivered 84 Squadron 28.5.58 and coded 'T'. Returned 27 MU 21.10.59, then back to 84 Squadron 14.12.59. Repaired for damage sustained in engine fire 10.9.63. Returned to service 2.12.63. To 32 MU for refurbishing and camouflaging 20.7.65, returning to 84 Squadron 14.10.65 still coded 'T'. To 30 Squadron 20.7.67, then to 27 MU 8.9.67 and declared NEA 11.9.67. Sold for scrap to BKL Alloys 23.3.70.

XM109 c/n 1045, first flew 26.2.58. Aw/cn 31.3.58. To 27 MU 11.4.58, then delivered 84 Squadron 28.5.58 and coded 'U'. To 27 MU 12.5.59 returning 84 Squadron 9.7.59 still coded 'U'. To Brough for mods 8.9.60 returning 84 Squadron 23.2.61. To 32 MU 31.5.65 for refurbishing and camouflaging. Back to 84 Squadron 29.8.65 re-coded 'R'. Cat 3 damage (birdstrike) 21.11.66 at Aden. Repaired and returned to service 26.1.67. To 30 Squadron 17.1.67, then to 27 MU 18.9.67 and declared NEA same date. Sold for scrap to BKL Alloys 25.3.70.

XM110 c/n 1046, first flew 19.3.58. Aw/cn 18.4.58. To 27 MU 2.5.58, then to Brough for mods 10.7.58. Returned 27 MU 14.7.58. Delivered 84 Squadron 16.7.58 coded 'V'. Loaned to Abingdon Wing 23.7.68, returning 84 Squadron 5.1.59. To 27 MU 23.10.59, returning 84 Squadron 5.1.60 still coded 'V'. Damaged beyond repair by time bomb concealed in freight bay while parked at Bahrain 6.10.61. SOC 31.10.61 and cannibalized for spares. Hulk used by Army for synthetic paratroop training until late '60s.

XM111 c/n 1047, first flew 19.4.58. Aw/cn 25.4.58. To 27 MU 13.5.58, delivered 84 Squadron 15.7.58. Loaned to Abingdon Wing 23.7.58, returning 84 Squadron 9.9.58 coded 'W'. To Brough for re-skinning 15.11.60. Loaned to MoA 5.6.61, then to 27 MU 22.6.61 returning 84 Squadron 28.7.61 still coded 'W'. To 32 MU 7.9.65 for refurbishing and camouflaging. Transferred to 47 Squadron 24.11.65 and re-coded 'D'. To 30 Squadron 4.1.67, then transferred to 84 Squadron 21.7.67 still coded 'D'. To 71 MU 13.11.67, declared NEA 18.11.67. Sold for scrap to BKL Alloys 29.8.69.

XM112 c/n 1048, first flew 15.5.58. Aw/cn 22.5.58. To 27 MU 28.5.58, then delivered 30 Squadron 31.7.58 returning 27 MU 11.11.58. To Brough for mods 13.1.59 returning 27 MU 6.4.59. To 48 Squadron Beverley Flight 21.5.59, then to 34 Squadron 1.10.60 coded 'V' later re-coded '112'. To 389 MU 1.1.68, SOC 14.2.68 and scrapped at Seletar

Appendix One

Beverley C. Mk.1 General Specification

Leading particulars
Length .... 99 ft 5 in
Height .... 38 ft 9 in
Track .... 33 ft 5 in
Wing span .... 162 ft
Wing area .... 2,916 ft^2
Basic weight .... 37,318 kg (82,100 lb)
Maximum all-up weight:
  (normal) .... 61,363 kg (135,000 lb)
  (emergency) .... 64,545 kg (142,000 lb)
Maximum speed ..... 238 mph at 5,700 ft
Rec cruise speed .... 173 mph at 12,500 ft
Rate of climb -
  (initial from sea level) ...... 760 ft/min
Service ceiling .... 16,000 ft
Take-off distance to 50 ft .... 447 yd
Landing distance from 50 ft .... 303 yd
Range with 454 kg (1,000 lb)
  payload .... 3,690 statute miles
Range with 20,000 kg (44,000 lb)
  payload .... 200 statute miles
Fuel consumption -
  take-off and climb ...... c.1,000 galls/hr
  cruising .... c.400 galls/hr

Power plants
Four Bristol Centaurus 173 or 175, 18 cylinder, two row, radial, air-cooled, sleeve valve piston engines each delivering 2850 horse power at maximum power, using water methanol injection.
Bore .... 146.05 mm (5.75 in)
Stroke .... 177.8 mm (7 in)
Swept volume ...... 53.6 litres (3,270 in^3)
Weight .... 1,545 kg (3,400 lb)

Performance details

BHP	RPM	Boost (Hg)	Altitude (ft)
Maximum take-off power -			
2,850	2,800	56	sea level
Maximum continous power -			
2,370	2,500	49	5,000
Maximum weak mixture power -			
1,720	2,400	38	11,500

Air Conditioning
Space heating and ventilation were provided by three separate systems, one for the flight deck, one for the freight bay, and one for the tail boom, each system incorporating a Lucas combustion heater which burnt Avgas from the aircraft's fuel system. Heat ouputs were as follows:
Flight deck heater .... 50,000 Btu/hr
Freight bay heater .... 400,000 Btu/hr
Tail boom heater .... 250,000 Btu/hr

Ground operation of the flight deck and tail boom heaters was accomplished by electrically driven fans supplying the necessary airflow. The freight bay heater operated from ram air during flight only.

Anti-icing
Thermal anti-icing of wing, tailplane and fin leading edges was accomplished by ducted hot air supplied by five 400,000 Btu/hr Lucas combustion heaters, three mounted in the wings and two, for the tail surfaces, in the rear of the boom. One of the wing heaters was a back-up system whose full output could be diverted to either wing in the event of the heater for that wing failing.

The engines were fitted with oil-heated throttles and the air intake shutter mechanism of each engine delivered warm air when required. Propellers and pitot heads were de-iced electrically and alcohol spray systems served the windscreens.

Electrical
This was a 24 volts d.c. system served by four 6 kW generators, one driven by each engine. A smaller generator, driven by the Airborne Auxiliary Power Plant (AAPP), more commonly referred to as the Auxiliary Power Unit (APU), supplied electrical power for ground servicing and engine starting. Two inverters supplied a.c. for flight instruments and autopilots: power for propellor de-icing was supplied by two 15 kVA alternators, one driven by each inboard engine.

Fuel and Oil
Approximately 6,000 gallons of Avgas were carried in eight flexible, self-sealing bag-type tanks, four tanks in each wing. Each outboard pair of tanks were interconnected and functioned as a single tank. The tanks on each wing fed into a collector manifold from where the engines were supplied, the collector manifolds in each wing being linked by a cross-feed pipe.

The aircraft could be pressure refuelled at 300 gallons/min, the connector points being located in the fuselage underneath each sponson. The tanks were also equipped with conventional fuel caps for gravity refuelling. Fuel contents gauges were calibrated in mass units (pounds x 1,000) - this was an innovation since the fuel gauges of most other aircraft of the era were calibrated in gallons.

Each engine had a ten gallon water methanol tank, water methanol being used to obtain maximum take-off power.

Lubricating oil for each engine was carried in a twenty-nine gallon tank mounted in the accessory bay. Due to the heavy oil requirements of the Centaurus engines, overload tanks were fitted in the 'dog kennel' a compartment between the spars in the wing centre section. Each overload tank contained fifty-two gallons and a transfer system and hand pump enabled each engine to be replenished during flight. A hand pump was installed in preference to an electrically driven pump on the principle that while an electrical device was prone to failure, there was always bound to be some muscle power available on the aircraft to operate the hand pump.

Hydraulic
Two completely independent hydraulic systems were provided, the port system being powered by pumps driven from the port engines and the starboard system by pumps driven from the starboard engines. An accumulator was installed in each system which operated at 2,500 lbf/in^2. Both systems powered the duplex Fairey hydroboosters for the flying controls, whilst the starboard system also powered the nose wheel steering system and the wheel brakes, the latter operating at a reduced pressure of 1,500 lbf/in^2. Feed-back devices in the flying control hydrobooster assemblies gave 'feel', feed-back ratios being: rudder 1:5, elevator 1:10 and aileron 1:14.

Carrying Capacity
Trooping - 94 fully equipped troops, 58 in the freight bay, 36 in the boom.
Parachuting - 70 troops, 40 in the freight bay, 30 in the boom.
Ambulance (casevac) role - 48 stretchers in the freight bay, 34 sitting cases plus two attendants in the boom.
Typical freight loads - two complete Sycamore helicopters; a Bloodhound missile; a Hunter fighter (with wings removed); various Army vehicles such as Ferret scout cars, 25-pounder guns and trailers; personnel carriers.

Appendix Two

Colour Schemes and Squadron Markings

Colour Schemes

All Beverleys were initially delivered to the RAF finished in the standard RAF Transport Command livery. This was a white and silver combination, the white being on the topside of the fuselage. Soon after the aircraft entered service, a blue cheat line was added (to some aircraft) to separate the two colours; this was sometimes zig-zagged on the nose section. A matt black finish was applied to the upper surface of the nose as anti-glare protection for the flight crew.

XB260 and XB262 were painted with red dayglo marks for winterization trials in Canada in the winter of 1956. During the 1960s, some, mainly UK-based aircraft, were also painted with red dayglo noses and bands around the tail boom, but this paint scheme was discontinued shortly afterwards. XB259, which spent its career with the RAE Farnborough, was finished in white with red markings and XB261, which spent most of its career with the A & AEE Boscombe Down, also had red marks.

1964 brought the camouflage paint scheme, initially it is believed, for aircraft of the Middle East Air Force. Camouflaging was almost always applied after the aircraft had been refurbished at 32 MU, St Athan. The finish consisted of a matt dark earth, light stone and black combination, with the flight deck roof in white.

Squadron Markings

When 47 Squadron and 53 Squadron first formed at Abingdon, 47 Squadron aircraft were decorated with green fin diamonds overpainted with '47' in white. 53 Squadron aircraft carrried yellow fin diamonds with '53' in black. When 30 Squadron equipped with Beverleys, similar fin markings were used, the colour being red overpainted with '30' in white. 242 OCU used a combination red and yellow fin diamond with no number: some OCU aircraft carried the serial number (numerals only) on the fins. Aircraft of the above units were all marked with their individual code letters on each side of the nose aft of the crew entrance door.

After RAF Abingdon had been granted the freedom of the borough of Abingdon, the Abingdon Wing Beverleys were adorned with the Abingdon coat of arms on either side of the nose forward of the crew entrance door. When 53 Squadron disbanded, fin diamonds were replaced by the 47 Squadron badge motif, a Nile crane. All UK-based Beverleys carried the Royal Air Force Transport Command insignia on each upper side of the tail boom. Some aircraft also carried this insignia on each side of the nose in a position forward of the crew entrance door. In the late '60s when the medium range tactical units became part of Air Support Command, the Royal Air Force Transport Command insignia was amended to read Royal Air Force Air Support Command.

At Khormaksar, the 84 Squadron Beverleys were decorated on the fins with any one of the four suits of playing cards, e.g. a club or a spade. The aircraft of both 84 and 30 Squadrons carried the Royal Air Force Middle East insignia on the tail booms and sometimes on the noses. Squadron code letters were also painted on the noses and 84's aircraft carried the scorpion motif, also on the noses.

In the Far East, 34 Squadron used fin diamonds overpainted with the squadron number in white, the numerals of an aircraft's serial number later being painted, in black, on either side of the nose. This number was subsequently added to the fins below the diamonds.

When 34 Squadron first formed, its aircraft were coded by letters painted on the nose, but this was changed to code numbers, each number being the numerals of an aircraft's serial number. 34's aircraft all carried the Royal Air Force Far East insignia both on the tail boom and on the nose.

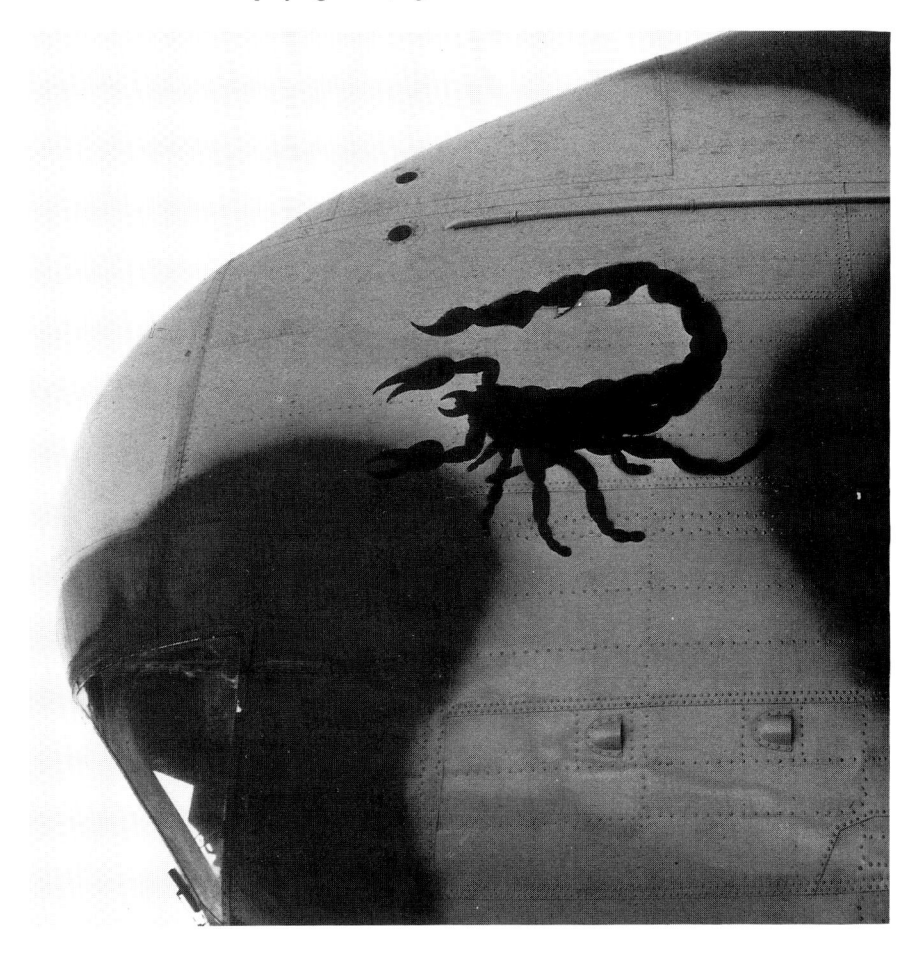

Close-up of 84 Squadron's scorpion insignia. *K.Wilson*

List of Abbreviations

A & AEE	Aircraft and Armament Experimental Establishment
AFME	Air Force Middle East
ALM	Air Loadmaster
AOA	Air Officer Administration
AOC	Air Officer Commanding
APL	Aden Protectorate Levy
AQM	Air Quartermaster
AVM	Air Vice Marshal
BFAP	British Forces Arabian Peninsula
BOAC	British Overseas Airways Corporation (now British Airways)
CARP	Calculated Air Release Point
Ch Tech	Chief Technician
Cpl Tech	Corporal Technician
C in C	Commander in Chief
CRDF	Cathode Ray Direction Finding
CSE	Combined Services Entertainment
DC	District Commissioner
DZ	Dropping Zone
FEAF	Far East Air Force
Fg Off	Flying Officer
FLOSY	Front for the Liberation of South Yemen
Flt Lt	Flight Lieutenant
Flt Sgt	Flight Sergeant
FRA	Federal Republican Army
GOC	General Officer Commanding
HAECO	Hong Kong Aircraft Engineering Company
HQ	Headquarters
HSP	Heavy Stressed Platform
JATE	Joint Air Transport Establishment
KAR	King's African Rifles
LOX	Liquid Oxygen
MAQM	Master Air Quartermaster
MEAF	Middle East Air Force
M Eng	Master Engineer
M Nav	Master Navigator
M Sig	Master Signaller
MSP	Medium Stressed Platform
MT	Motor Transport
MU	Maintenance Unit
OCU	Operational Conversion Unit
QTR	Quick Turn Round
RAE	Royal Aircraft Establishment
RATOG	Rocket Assisted Take-off Gear
RNAS	Royal Naval Air Service
RSM	Riyan, Salalah and Masirah - route supply stations scheduled flights for Arabian Peninsula
SAC	Senior Aircraftman
SAR	Search and Rescue
SARAH	Search and Rescue Aircraft Homing (Beacon)
SAS	Special Air Service
SASO	Senior Air Staff Officer
SBAC	Society of British Aircraft Constructors
SEAC	South East Asia Command
Sqn	Squadron
Sqn Ldr	Squadron leader
STOL	Short Take-off and Landing
RT	Radio Telephone
Wg Cdr	Wing Commander

Flown from Brunei to Labuan in Royal Brunei Malay Regiment Bell 212 AMDB106. 23 November 1972.
Pilot: Captain F G A Ray   Flight time: 15 minutes

Flown from Labuan to Singapore (Tengah) in 511 Squadron Britannia CCI XM490. 23 November 1972
Captain: Flt Lt D Collins RAF   Flight time: 2 hours 45 minutes

Flown from Singapore (Tengah) to UK (RAF Brize Norton) in 10 Squadron VC10 XR806. 29-30 November 1972
Stage: Tengah-Gan   Gan-Dubai   Dubai-Akrotiri   Akrotiri-Brize Norton
Captain: Sqn Ldr M J Cawsey RAF   Sqn Ldr N J H Tabberer RAF   Sqn Ldr C S Baldwin RAF
Flight time: 3 hours 53 minutes   4 hours 5 minutes   3 hours 48 minutes   4 hours 40 minutes

Postal Courier: Brunei-RAF Museum, Flt Lt M G Ralph RAF

R.A.F. Museum
Aerodrome Road
Hendon NW9 5LL

Index

A&AEE 14, 105, 147, 150, 151, 153, 155
Abingdon 17, 18, 23, 26, 27, 29, 30, 34, 37, 41, 45, 52, 99, 116, 122, 135, 136, 138, 142, 150-153, 155
Abingdon Wing 23, 30, 36, 38, 41, 45, 46, 51, 119, 150, 151
Adams Flt Lt 24-26, 99
Adams 'Piano' - see Adams Flt Lt
Adams Sqn Ldr 105, 115
Aden 20-22, 27, 29, 34, 37, 38, 41, 46, 47, 51-53, 55, 56, 61, 64-71, 73, 76-85, 88-91, 94, 96, 98, 112, 123, 138, 139, 144, 153
Aden Protectorate 20, 21, 53, 56, 58, 71, 73, 76, 123

Aero engines:
  Aquila 143
  Avon 15
  Centaurus 8, 9, 12, 15, 41, 46, 79, 84, 135, 136, 138, 143, 144, 154
  Hercules 9, 10, 143
  Mercury 9
  Merlin 9, 143
  Perseus 143
  Taurus 143
  Tyne 137
  Vulture 143
AFME 68, 69, 79
Airborne pannier - see Supply dropping equipment

Aircraft types
  Albacore 143
  Alouette 59
  Ambassador 143
  Andover 68, 70, 71, 95, 96
  Argosy 43, 65, 67, 69, 70, 96, 98, 112, 114, 130, 132,
  Auster 15, 99, 104, 106, 111
  Barracuda 133
  Beaufort 143
  Beaver 58, 59
  Belfast 44, 45
  Belvedere 45, 79, 81, 109, 144
  Blackburn B-107/B-107A 137
  Blenheim 17, 45
  Boeing 707 56, 116
  Botha 143
  Brabazon 12, 144
  Brigand 144
  Bristol Freighter 105, 118, 143
  Britannia 55, 56, 58, 67, 106, 114, 136
  Buccanneer 47, 133
  Bulldog 143

Canberra 38, 56, 59, 104, 105, 108
Caravelle 63, 85, 116
Caribou 90, 116
Catalina 100
Cessna 63, 69
Clydesman 133
Comet 30, 34
Concorde 50
C-130 58
C-130K - see Hercules
Dakota 8, 12, 17, 51, 73, 95, 96, 99, 133
DC-3 123
DH9A 51
Dornier 143
Elizabethan 144
Firebrand 133
FW 190 143
GAL60 Universal Freighter Mk.1 9, 10, 12, 133, 150
GAL65 Universal Freighter Mk.2 12-14, 150
Gordon 17
Halifax 8, 17
Hamilcar 9, 10
Hastings 8, 15-17, 24, 30, 32, 43, 47, 56, 99, 107, 121, 124, 130, 132
Hercules 44, 47, 50, 69, 70, 116-118, 122, 124, 128, 132, 135, 136
Hind 118
Hotspur 9
Hudson 34
Hunter 38, 56, 64, 68, 69, 74, 91, 93, 102, 105, 154
Javelin 91, 110
Lancaster 8, 143
Liberator 17
Manchester 143
Meteor 10, 55, 102
MiG 6, 29, 98, 110, 111
Monospar 9
Mustang 111
Noratlas 132, 143
Pembroke 56, 73
Prentice 133
Provost 60
Rapide 133
Roc 133, 143
Sabre 112
Sea Fury 143
Shackleton 30, 56, 61, 67, 70
Single Pioneer 33, 36, 105, 109
Skua 133, 143
Skyraider 32
Spitfire 50
Stirling 8
Sunderland 99, 133
Sycamore 108, 154

Tempest 143
Tornado 143
TriStar 145
Twin Pioneer 33, 34, 56, 59, 60, 63, 64, 104, 105, 111, 113, 132
Valetta 8, 16, 20, 21, 27, 51, 71, 72, 99, 121
Valiant 55
Varsity 121
VC-10 34, 70, 93
Venom 143
Vildebeest 143
Vincent 17
Vulcan 99
Wellesley 17
Wessex 45, 71
Whirlwind 46
York 8, 18
Air Despatch Units 8, 40, 52, 57, 99, 104, 124, 126
Air dropping - see Supply dropping
Air supply - see Supply dropping
Aitken Jun Tech 85
Aked Flt Lt 59
Albacore - see Aircraft types
Alden Flt Lt 27
Al Ghayda 69, 84, 85, 89, 91, 96
Alouette - see Aircraft types
Ambassador - see Aircraft types
Amin Fg Off 70
Andover - see Aircraft types
Anduki Seria 106-108
Andruskeiwicz Flt Lt 37, 77, 84, 85, 88
Aquila - see Aero engines
Arabia 8, 13, 21, 22, 29, 46, 47, 66, 73, 84, 91, 96, 98, 128, 144, 152
Argosy - see Aircraft types
Ataq 20, 72, 73, 77, 81, 84, 85, 88-91, 123
Atcherley Air Marshal Sir Richard 23
Auster - see Aircraft types
Avon - see Aero engines
Bacon Sqn Ldr 118
Bahrain 22, 26-29, 38, 41, 46, 53, 56-60, 63-70, 73, 74, 76, 81, 84, 115, 153
Baker Flt Lt 24
Baker Cpl Tech 110
Bangkok 99, 103, 105, 109, 113, 116
Bario 101, 104, 111, 116
Barlow Gordon 88
Barnden Sqn Ldr 89, 93
Barr Wg Cdr 45
Barracuda - see Aircraft types
Barton Flt Lt 96

Beaufort - see Aircraft types
Beaver - see Aircraft types
Beihan 32, 51, 72, 73, 76, 81, 84, 85, 88-91, 152
Belfast - see Aircraft types
Bell Flt Lt 51
Bentham Flt Lt 69
Belvedere - see Aircraft types
Bennet Sqn Ldr 105, 110, 111
Bills SAC 85
Binfield Ch Tech 18
Binfield Master Eng 85
Blackburn Aircraft Co/ Blackburn & General Aircraft Co 7, 12-14, 16, 24, 25, 63, 133, 135, 136, 150-153
Blackburn B-107, B-107A - see Aircraft types
Blenheim - see Aircraft types
Blythe Grp Capt 81, 85
Blount Flt Lt 66, 68, 70
Boeing 707 - see Aircraft types
Borneo 45, 77, 99-101, 104-109, 111-119, 123, 125-128, 144
Boscombe platform - see Supply dropping equipment
Botha - see Aircraft types
Boulnois Sqn Ldr 15
Bower Flt Lt 77, 81, 85
Brabazon - see Aircraft types
Brade DG 12
Bradford Flt Sgt 18
Brattan Bill 135-137
Brattan Len 137
Brigand - see Aircraft types
Bristol Freighter - see Aircraft types
Britannia - see Aircraft types
Brough 7, 12, 13, 15, 47, 73, 133, 135-137, 145, 150-153
Brown Flt Lt 56
Brunei 45, 77, 104, 106-109, 123
Buccaneer - see Aircraft types
Bulldog - see Aircraft types
Butler Flt Lt 59
Butterworth 26, 68, 104, 107, 108, 111-113, 115, 117, 118
Burt Peter 143
Calcutta 68, 91, 99, 106, 108, 116
Calvert Flt Lt 56
Canberra - see Aircraft types
Candy Air Vice-Marshal 104
Caravelle - see Aircraft types
CARP drop sight: invention of 36
use of in Borneo 104

The Beverley appeared on postage stamps. Reproduction of first day cover, November, 1972. *A. Theobald*

Caribou - see Aircraft types
Carsberg David 145
Casualty evacuation - see Casevac flights
Casevac flights 10, 33, 34, 56, 64, 65, 68, 88, 93, 108, 154
Catcheside Flt Lt 85
Catalina - see Aircraft types
Centaurus - see Aero engines
Cessna - see Aircraft types
Chamier Air Commodore Sir Adrian 115
Chane Sgt 119
Charman Flt Lt 73, 74
Changi 26, 68, 91, 99-103, 115, 116
Clark Field 104, 105, 116
Clark Flt Lt 65, 89
Clarke Flt Lt 26, 27, 66
Clinch Flt Lt 44, 64-66
Clydesman - see Aircraft types
Comet - see Aircraft types
Concorde - see Aircraft types
Cooper Sgt 119
Corbin Flt Lt 89
Coutts Flt Lt 96
Craig Fg Off 93
Craig Flt Lt 95
Crawley Flt Lt 36, 111, 115, 116
Cripps Flt Lt 73
Crocombe F F 9
Cropper Wg Cdr 45
Cyprus 17, 18, 29, 30, 33, 46, 51, 55, 71, 123
C-130 - see Aircraft types
Dakota - see Aircraft types
Dalston Sqn Ldr 113
Daly Francis 145, 150
Dar es Salaam 54, 56, 61, 62
Davidson Major 123, 124
Davies Flt Lt 105, 108, 109
Davies Jun Tech 116
DC-3 - see Aircraft types
Derby sack - see Supply dropping equipment
Dhala 20, 21, 72, 77, 81, 84, 85, 88-93
DH9A - see Aircraft types
Dishforth 22, 27, 51, 70, 121, 122, 137, 142
Dornan Flt Lt 113, 115
Dornier - see Aircraft types
Dorricott Flt Lt 54-57
Douglas Fg Off 52
Drew Flt Lt 69
Dudley Flt Lt 26
Dunbar Flt Sgt 116
Dunworth Ch Tech 110
Dye Flt Lt 51
Dyson Fg Off 66, 67
Dyson Flt Lt 68
Eastleigh 36-38, 51, 53-61, 64. 65, 70, 73, 84, 85, 88, 90, 105, 106
El Adem 6, 24, 29, 33, 37, 38, 45-47, 54, 65, 79, 88, 96, 98, 122, 151

Elizabeth HM The Queen 30, 114, 115
Elizabethan - see Aircraft types
Ellis Fg Off 65, 68
Elworthy Air Chief Marshal Sir Charles 115
Entebbe 29, 36, 55-58, 61, 88
Embakasi 38, 54-57
Evans Sqn Ldr 58, 59
Exercises (major ones only listed):
  Bar Frost - NATO exercise in Norway 32, 52
  Flat Earth - construction of 'instant' airfield by air drop 37, 45
  Holdfast - airborne assault exercise on Kiel Canal 36
  Sandflight - shepherding Belvedere helicopters on ferry flight from El Adem to Khormaksar 79
  Starlight - airborne assault exercise in Libya 6, 33, 34, 54
Fairford Fg Off 117
Famine relief flights 37, 56, 73, 94, 125
Far East 9, 17, 26, 27, 45, 47, 51, 71, 93, 99-105, 113, 115, 119, 130, 155
Far East Air Force/FEAF 6, 68, 99, 101, 102, 104, 105, 111-115
Federation of South Arabia 46, 81, 84, 85, 88
Fenn Flt Lt 106-108, 110
Ferguson Fg Off 88, 89
Ferguson Flt Lt 90, 93
Field Flt Lt 58
Firebrand - see Aircraft types
Flemington Flt Lt 113
Flood relief flights:
  Kenya 38, 41, 57, 73
  Tanganyika 57
  Vietnam 105, 113, 116
  Sarawak 108, 125
Foxley-Norris Air Vice-Marshal 115
Free drop sack - see Supply dropping equipment
Freer Grp Capt 113
FW 190 - see Aircraft types
GAL60 Universal Freighter Mk.1 – see Aircraft types
GAL65 Universal Freighter Mk.2 - see Aircraft types
Gale Fg Off 63
Galyer Flt Lt 45, 111, 113
Gan 26, 69, 99, 104, 105, 109, 113
Garforth Flt Lt 51, 52
Garissa 40, 60, 61, 63, 84
General Aircraft Co 9, 12, 13, 133, 150
Giraffe hydraulic servicing platform 17, 137, 138, 142
Glenn Master Eng 74
Gloucester HRH Duke of 115
Goodhew Flt Lt 22
Gordon - see Aircraft types
Gordon Major 60
Gould Flt Lt 81, 84, 85
Gray Colonel 91
Green Wg Cdr 114-116

Griffiths Grp Capt 16, 18, 20, 23
Grobler Flt Lt 99, 103
Groups:
  38 6, 33, 34, 57
  224 115
Guille Sqn Ldr 72
Guile Wg Cdr 116, 118, 119
Gurkhas 77, 104, 106, 107, 111, 123
Habbaniyah 26, 29
Habilayne (see also Thumier) 88, 89, 91, 93, 95, 153
Hadrami Bedouin Legion/HBL 69, 72, 73, 81, 84, 85, 91, 93
Hong Kong Aircraft Engineering Company/HAECO 68, 91, 111, 114, 115, 152, 153
Halifax - see Aircraft types
Hall Flt Lt 47
Hamilcar - see Aircraft types
Hamlin SAC 116
Hanks Flt Sgt 98
Hannah Sqn Ldr 115
Hansford Master Nav 74
Harness pack - see Supply dropping equipment
Harrington General 34
Harrison Sqn Ldr 61, 62, 64-66
Hartley Air Marshal Sir Christopher 115
Harvey Flt Lt 106-108, 110
Hastings - see Aircraft types
Hatt Gerry 7, 69
Hawarden 150-152
Hayward Flt Lt 84
Heath Rt Hon MP 115
Heavy drop platform - see Supply dropping equipment
Heavy stressed platform - see Supply dropping equipment
Hendon - see RAF Museum
Herbert Fg Off 71
Herbert Flt Lt 36
Hercules - see Aircraft types and Aero engines
Hignett P 130
Hind - see Aircraft types
Hitchen Flt Lt 107, 108, 110, 112
Hitchen Sqn Ldr 93, 94, 96, 98
Holloway Flt Lt 56, 58
Honey Flt Sgt 119
Honeybone Ray 142
Hong Kong 68, 91, 99, 103, 107, 115, 117, 152, 153
Horrocks Fg Off 53
Hotspur - see Aircraft types
Howell Flt Lt 'Tammy' 55
Howell Flt Lt W W 89
Hudson - see Aircraft types
Huggett Flt Lt 26
Hughes Air Marshal Sir Richard 118, 119
Hughes Master Sig 74
Humphrey Flt Lt 61, 64, 66
Hunt Sir John 113
Hunter - see Aircraft types

Hussein King of Jordan 30
Hyland Fg Off 105, 106
Ibri 21, 22, 53, 73
Idris 14, 27, 29, 34, 46, 122, 150
Idris King of Libya 29
Indonesian Confrontation 45, 47, 106, 111, 116, 123, 125
Iraq 30, 56, 58, 74, 76
Javelin - see Aircraft types
Jebel Ali 59, 64, 65, 84
Jenkins Fg Off 67, 68
Jenkins Flt Lt 89
Jesselton (Kota Kinabulu) 101, 104-109
Johnson Air Vice-Marshal 65
Kai Tak 91, 103-105, 108, 109, 111, 113-115, 117
Kamaran 73, 91, 95
Kano 26, 27, 29, 34, 36
Karachi 26, 38, 55, 56, 63, 69
Katmandu 108, 112, 113, 116-118
Katunayake 26, 104
Keegan Mike 50
Kemp Flt Lt 89
Kenya 37, 38, 40, 41, 52, 53, 55-65, 73, 84, 88-90, 94
Khartoum 17, 24, 29, 38, 73, 79, 98
Khormaksar 21, 22, 27, 29, 34, 38, 46, 47, 51-53, 55, 56, 58, 64-71, 73, 76, 79, 81, 84, 85, 88, 90, 91, 94, 96, 105-107, 116, 155
Khoo Cpl 110
King Sqn Ldr 66-69, 89
King's African Rifles 55-57, 59, 60
Kirtleside Lord Douglas 93
Kota Belud 100, 101, 113, 116
Kuantan 100, 105, 112
Kuching 105, 107-109, 112, 113
Kufra 45-47
Kuwait 37, 38, 56-58, 67-69, 74, 76, 123, 137, 152
Labuan 45, 104-109, 111-113, 115, 116, 123
Lambert Flt Lt 77, 84, 88, 107
Lancaster Flt Lt 66
Lancaster - see Aircraft types
Langford A 130
Lansdell Flt Lt 115, 118, 119
Leach Hugh 98
Lee Air Chief Marshal Sir David 70
Lennard Master Nav 118, 119
Leonard-Williams Air Vice-Marshal 115
Leopoldville 26, 34, 88
Letton Flt Lt 63
Lewis Flt Lt 34, 36
Liberator - see Aircraft types
Light stressed platform - see Supply dropping equipment
Livermore Fg Off 71
Livermore Flt Lt 88, 89
Lodar 81, 84, 88, 89, 91
Lodge Flt Lt 116
Long Pasia 109, 111, 115, 116
Lord Trophy 26, 46, 50, 52, 73

Lowe Cliff 142
Luce Sir William 66
Luqa 24, 26, 46, 88, 96, 115, 122
Madden Flt Lt 73
Maintenance Units
  27 150-153
  32 150-153, 155
  60 152, 153
  71 150-153
  103 151, 153
  131 151, 152
  389 150, 151, 153
Malacca 104, 105
Malaya/Malaysia 26, 99, 101, 104, 105, 111, 112, 115, 118, 125
Mandera 59-61, 84, 88
Manchester - see Aircraft types
Manley Flt Lt 95
Maslin Flt Lt 117
Masirah 22, 29, 53, 55, 65, 66, 69, 71, 91, 93
Matsapa 60, 85, 88, 89, 91, 93
Mayall Flt Lt 73
McCarthy Flt Lt 117, 118
McCleod Flt Lt 51
McCleod Rt Hon MP 54
McCollum James 143
McDonald Air Commodore 34, 61
McIntosh Cpl 116
McTurk Flt Lt 77, 85
McSporran Mr 101
Medium stressed platform -
see Supply dropping equipment
Melling Rodney 147
MEAF 24, 27, 33, 34, 53, 107
Mercury - see Aero engines
Merlin - see Aero engines
Meteor - see Aircraft types
Middle East 17, 32, 34, 38, 50, 51, 56, 64, 65, 70, 71, 93, 109, 123, 130, 138, 155
MiG - see Aircraft types
Mitchell Flt Lt 115
Mombasa 41, 56, 57, 59, 61
Monospar - see Aircraft types
Moralee Flt Lt 103
Mountbatten Lord Louis 34, 55
MU - see Maintenance Units
Muharraq 46, 63-67, 69, 70, 85, 88
Mukeiras 58, 72, 76, 81, 84, 85, 88-91, 123
Mulligan Flt Lt 68, 69
Murait 84, 85, 89, 91
Murray Capt 99, 101
Museums
  RAF 145, 152
  Army Transport 137, 145, 147
  Newark Aircraft 147, 152
  Southend Historic Aircraft 145, 147
Mustang - see Aircraft types
Nairobi 24, 36, 38, 41, 51, 53, 54, 56-58, 64, 73, 88, 94, 105
Nasser President of Egypt 71, 96
Newark Aircraft Museum -
see Museums

New Zealand 99, 105, 111
Nicholls Flt Lt 89, 115
Nicosia 26, 33, 46, 51, 96
Nimmo Fg Off 22, 99-101, 103, 104
Noratlas - see Aircraft types
North East Province (of Kenya) -
see North/Northern Frontier District
North/Northern Frontier District 56, 58-65, 84, 88, 94
Nyere President of Tanganyika 61
Oakes Master Eng 145
OCU - see Operational Conversion Units
ODM/Operating Data Manual 16, 20, 70
Ogilvie Flt Lt 20
Okinawa 104, 105, 108, 109
Oman 13, 23, 53, 60, 70, 123
One-ton container -
see Supply dropping equipment
Operational Conversion Units
  240 121
  241 121
  242 41, 46, 121, 122, 147, 150-153, 155
Operations (major ones only listed)
  Alfred - movement of troops concerned with strike in Swaziland 60, 81
  Borneo Territories - operations in Indonesian Confrontation 106, 108, 109, 111, 116, 118
  Brickbat - flights concerned with Rhodesia's Unilateral Declaration of Independence 90
  Cat Drop - delivery of cats by parachute in Borneo 101
  Dark Bottle - probing sorties in East German air corridors in defiance of Russians 41
  Desert Blenheim - recovery of bodies from World War Two Blenheims in Libyan desert 45
  Nutcracker - start of Radfan Campaign 84, 85
  Hazland - troop movements due to coup in Abu Dhabi 68
  Hogmany - airlift of helicopters, vehicles, troops and freight to Cyprus 46
  Oliver - famine relief for Northern Kenya 37, 56
  Private Eye - policing elections in Nigeria and Cameroons 36
  Snaffle - airlift of Hadrami Bedouin Legion to Socotra to quell trouble 69, 93
  Tantrum - stand-by concerned with threat to Kuwait from Iraq 58-60
  Tusk - airlift of Hadrami Bedouin Legion to airfields in Eastern Aden Protectorate 84, 85
  Vantage - airlift of Strategic Reserve to Kuwait in reply to Iraqi threat 37, 38, 56, 58, 74
O'Reilly Sgt 81
Osman Ahmed 29
Owen Fg Off 20
Palliser Fg Off 76, 77
Parachute Regiment 57, 59, 60, 64-66, 130

Parachuting/paratrooping 10, 14, 18, 19, 26, 32, 33, 36, 37, 43, 47, 50-52, 57-60, 63-65, 76, 85, 89, 90, 99, 101, 105, 114, 130, 132, 150, 154
Parfitt Sqn Ldr 76, 79, 85
Parry Sqn Ldr 73, 74, 76
Pearson Wg Cdr 73
Peaty Flt Lt 145
Pegg Bill 136
Pembroke - see Aircraft types
Penn Lt Col 145
Pensiangan 109, 111, 116
Perim 81, 89, 91
Perseus - see Aero engines
Persian Gulf 13, 38, 47, 56, 57, 59, 60, 63, 72-76, 79, 96, 98, 115, 116
Philip HRH Duke of Edinburgh 16, 113
Philips Flt Lt 68
Philips Flt Sgt 116
Pitman Flt Lt 73
Platform - see Supply dropping equipment
Potter Master Eng 119
Prentice - see Aircraft types
Pretoria 24, 25, 85, 93
Protectorate -
see Aden Protectorate
Provost - see Aircraft types
Radfan 46, 66, 81, 84-89, 153
RAF Regiment:
  in Brunei 45;
  at Tawau 123
RAF Museum - see Museums
Rankin Flt Lt 88
Rapide - see Aircraft types
Raynham Fg Off 88
Reeder Sqn Ldr 33
Refugee evacuations:
  from Congo 34, 36, 55, 88;
  from Yemen 81
Richards Flt Lt 32
Rixon Wg Cdr 142
Riyan 53, 65, 69, 71, 72, 79, 89-93, 96
Robb Air Chief Marshal Sir James 66
Robb Capt 145
Robb Mr 115
Robinson Flt Lt 89
Roc - see Aircraft types
Rotorua 99, 100, 111
Royce Walter 143, 144
Sabah 45, 107, 109, 111, 113, 115, 116
Sabre - see Aircraft types
Saigon 68, 91, 104, 105, 113, 115
Salalah 46, 53, 65, 66, 69, 71, 90, 93, 96
Salisbury (Harare) 24, 26, 81, 84, 88
Salmond Flt Lt 99
Sanau 58, 84, 89, 91
Sanders Wg Cdr 36, 38
Sarawak 45, 101, 107-111
SAR Operations 63, 66-70, 85, 88, 104

Scorey Flt Lt 55
Sea Fury - see Aircraft types
SEAC pack -
see Supply dropping equipment
Secker Cpl 8
Sedgewick Sqn Ldr 145
Seletar 45, 102-109, 111-119, 150, 151, 153
Selway Flt Lt 58, 60, 63
Shackleton - see Aircraft types
Sharjah 21, 23, 53, 56-58, 64-71, 73, 96
Shelton-Smith Flt Lt 73
Shifta 59-61, 63, 84, 88, 94
Sierwald Fg Off 67, 69
Singapore 26, 45, 99, 103-105, 112, 117, 119
Single Pioneer - see Aircraft types
Skua - see Aircraft types
Skyraider - see Aircraft types
Sleaman Sqn Ldr 20
Slessor Marshal of the Royal Air Force Sir John 38
Smale Flt Lt 99
Smyth Flt Lt 64, 81, 85
Sneller Flt Lt 74
Socotra 69, 76, 93
South Arabian Federation -
see Federation of South Arabia
Southend Historic Aircraft Museum
- see Museums
Spitfire - see Aircraft types
Sproates Wg Cdr 33
Squadrons
  8 74
  20 250
  21 59, 60, 63
  24 52
  26 79, 81
  30 22, 27, 30, 31, 36, 38, 51-53, 55-70, 73-76, 79, 88, 89, 91-93, 105-107, 119, 150-153, 155
  34 45, 47, 77, 91, 99, 102-109, 111, 114-119, 150, 151, 153, 155
  37 61
  45 105, 108
  47 13, 17, 22, 23, 26-30, 33, 34, 36, 38, 41, 45, 46, 50, 52, 70, 89, 98, 116, 121, 135, 150-153, 155
  48 99, 101-103, 117, 150, 153
  53 17, 22, 23, 27, 30, 34, 36-38, 41, 44-46, 52, 70, 76, 150-153, 155
  60 104
  66 109
  73 59
  75 104
  84 20, 22, 27, 38, 46, 47, 52, 56, 58, 59, 61-65, 68, 69, 71-76, 79, 84, 88-93, 95, 96, 98, 105-107, 112, 116, 147, 150-153, 155
  105 65
  152 59
  208 56, 58, 61, 64, 69
  209 104
  215 33, 114
  230 47
5004 Airfield Construction 73, 109

Stalker Flt Lt 57
Statham Flt Lt 63-65
Stevenson Wg Cdr 99
St Athan 67, 121, 142, 155
Stirling - see Aircraft types
Stockwell Grp Capt 65
Strangeway Sqn Ldr 38, 41
Strategic Reserve 8, 38, 56, 74, 145
Stressed supply platform - see Supply dropping equipment
Sunderland - see Aircraft types
Supply drops 10, 13, 14, 18, 26, 30, 36, 43, 45, 52, 56-61, 63-67, 73, 76, 84, 85, 88, 91, 94, 101, 103-105, 107-119, 123, 124, 150, 153
Supply dropping equipment
  Airborne pannier 124
  Boscombe platform 105, 126
  Free-drop sack 124
  Derby sack 40, 57, 124, 125
  Harness pack 107, 111-113, 115, 124
  Heavy stressed platform 114, 127
  Light stressed platform 127
  Medium stressed platform 47, 105, 109, 111, 113, 114, 126
  One-ton container 84, 88, 89, 91, 93, 104, 105, 109, 111-114, 124-128, 151
  SEAC pack 84, 100, 104, 108, 109, 111, 124
Stressed supply platform - see Boscombe platform

Suez 18, 29, 71, 79
Swales Flt Lt 51, 73
Swaziland 58, 60, 81, 89
Sycamore - see Aircraft types
Tachikawa 99, 105, 116
Tanganyika (Tanzania) 54-57, 61
Tarran Flt Lt 106-108
Tawau 107-109, 111-113, 123
Taurus - see Aero engines
Taylor Sqn Ldr 26
Teasdale Flt Sgt 105
Tempest - see Aircraft types
Tengah 105, 107, 112
Thamoud 72, 84, 85, 89, 91
Thorney Island 41, 46, 58, 122
Thumier (see also Habilayne) 85, 88
Till Major 130
Tmimi 33, 34
Tornado - see Aircraft types
Transport Command 8, 13, 15, 16, 21, 29, 32, 44, 56, 79, 94, 115, 121, 155
TriStar - see Aircraft types
Tropical Trials 14, 23, 150
Trucial Oman Scouts 32, 59, 60, 66, 68, 85
Trucial Oman Coast 29, 65
Turner Flt Lt 117
Twin Pioneer - see Aircraft types

Tyne - see Aero engines
Uganda 55, 56, 58, 61, 73
ULLA drop technique 128, 150
Ussher Alan 142
Valetta - see Aircraft types
Valiant - see Aircraft types
Varsity - see Aircraft types
VC-10 - see Aircraft types
Venables WO 85
Venom - see Aircraft types
Vildebeest - see Aircraft types
Vincent - see Aircraft types
Von Haven Major USAF 45
Vulcan - see Aircraft types
Vulture - see Aero Engines
Wadi Ayn 77, 81, 85, 88, 91
Wajir 55-57, 60-63, 65, 84, 88
Walker Flt Lt 69, 89
Ward John 36, 44, 66
Warden Flt Lt 91
Ware Flt Lt 91, 93
Warren Flt Lt 79, 85, 88
Watson Master Eng 112
Waugh Sqn Ldr 54
Webb Fg Off 67
Webster Flt Lt 18, 20, 26
Weir Air Vice-Marshal 34
Weir Flt Lt 36

Weldon Fg Off 119
Wellesley - see Aircraft types
Wessex - see Aircraft types
West Fg Off 59
West Flt Lt 91
Weston Flt Sgt 81
Westwood Fg Off 94
Whelan Sgt 81
Wheldon Flt Lt 117
Whirlwind - see Aircraft types
Wilcox Flt Lt 117
Wildenrath 17, 41, 51
Williams Flt Lt 115
Wing Flt Lt 30
Winterization trials 15, 150, 155
Wood H 'Tim' 12, 136
Wright Bob 45
Wright Fg Off D G M 53, 56, 57
Wright Flt Lt R W J 88
Wykeham Air Marshal Sir Peter 6, 114, 115
Wykeham Air Vice-Marshal 34
Yates Flt Lt 73
Yemen 20, 21, 65, 71-73, 81, 84, 85, 88, 91
York - see Aircraft types
Zanzibar 56, 59, 61, 73
Zip-Up access equipment 22, 138

Bibliography

But not in Anger - The RAF in the Transport Role
Roderick Grant
Ian Allan, London.

Flight from the Middle East
Air Chief Marshal Sir David Lee
HMSO.

Fighting Gliders of World War 2
James E. Mrazek
Robert Hale Ltd, London.

British Air Arms
Edited by B. Billington
and P. H. Butler
Merseyside Aviation Society Ltd.

Blackburn Aircraft since 1909
A. J. Jackson
Putnam and Company, London.

The Undeclared War
Harold James and Denis Shiel-Smith
Leo Cooper Ltd.

Squadron Histories, RFC, RNAS, and RAF Since 1912
Peter Lewis
Putnam and Company London.

The Squadrons of the Royal Air Force
James A. Halley
Air-Britain (Historians) Ltd, Tonbridge.

Blackburn Beverley C Mk.1
Chris Hobson
Alan W. Hall (Publications) Ltd.

The Beverley Association

A Beverley Association has been formed for those who were involved with the Beverley or those who are interested in it.
For details please contact -

Mr B. R. Holt
46 Aller Brake Road
NEWTON ABBOT,
Devon
TQ12 4NL